UNDERSTANDING
COVENANTS
AND
Communities

UNDERSTANDING
COVENANTS
AND
Communities

JEWS AND LATTER-DAY SAINTS IN DIALOGUE

EDITED BY

MARK S. DIAMOND
ANDREW C. REED

RSC
BYU

RJP
CCAR
Press

Published by the Religious Studies Center, Brigham Young University, Provo, Utah, in cooperation with the Central Conference of American Rabbis, New York, New York.

Visit us at rsc.byu.edu and ccarpress.org. A discussion guide is available at covenants.ccarpress.org.

Printed in the United States of America by Sheridan Books, Inc.

Cover and interior design by Carmen Durland Cole
ISBN 978-1-9443-9496-7

Library of Congress Cataloging-in-Publication Data

Names: Diamond, Mark S., 1954- editor. | Reed, Andrew C., 1979- editor.
Title: Understanding covenants and communities : Jews and Latter-day Saints in dialogue / edited by Mark S. Diamond and Andrew C. Reed.
Description: Provo, Utah : Religious Studies Center, Brigham Young University ; New York City, New York : Central Conference of American Rabbis, [2020] | Includes index. | Summary: "A group of scholars began convening the Jewish-Latter-day Saint Academic Dialogue Project semiannually in 2016. Seeking to strengthen the bonds between the dialogue partners and their respective institutions and faith communities, the participants presented these academic papers during the first five conferences of this groundbreaking interfaith project"-- Provided by publisher.
Identifiers: LCCN 2020006044 | ISBN 9781944394967 (paperback)
Subjects: LCSH: Church of Jesus Christ of Latter-day Saints--Relations--Judaism. | Judaism--Relations--Church of Jesus Christ of Latter-day Saints.
Classification: LCC BX8643.J84 U53 2020 | DDC 261.2/6--dc23
LC record available at https://lccn.loc.gov/2020006044

FOR MY WIFE LOIS

AND OUR CHILDREN AND CHILDREN-IN-LAW—
ADINA, ARIELLA AND JASON, JEREMY AND SARA,
AND OUR GRANDSON MATTHEW

"Only love gives us the taste of eternity." (Jewish proverb)

—MARK DIAMOND

FOR MY WIFE KAYLYN

AND OUR CHILDREN—
RILEY, BENTLEY, KELSIE, BRADLEY, JOSIE, AND WRIGLEY

With hope that we will "find peace in this world, and eternal life
in the world to come." (Doctrine and Covenants 59:23)

—ANDREW REED

CONTENTS

ACKNOWLEDGMENTS

This book and the project from which it emerged owe their existence to many individuals and institutions. We welcome the opportunity to thank them here for their contributions and support. The participants in the Jewish and Latter-day Saint Academic Dialogue deserve our sincere appreciation, especially the esteemed colleagues whose essays appear in this volume: Tamar Frankiel, Joshua Garroway, Kristine Garroway, Shon Hopkin, Holli Levitsky, Jared Ludlow, Quin Monson, Brent Top, Thomas Wayment, and Steven Windmueller. We also extend our thanks to those individuals whose efforts are not included in this book but were nonetheless part of our dialogue sessions. Barbara Morgan Gardner (BYU), Elder Richard Holzapfel (BYU), Jacob Rennaker (Widtsoe Foundation, University of Southern California), Robert Hurteau (LMU), Wendy Top, Lois Diamond, Michelle Windmueller, Jennifer Hopkin (who worked miracles as our logistics coordinator in Jerusalem), Janiece Johnson (BYU), David Kaufman (HUC), Elder Gary Wilde, Marvin Sweeney (Claremont School of Theology), Rabbi Leon Wiener Dow (Shalom Hartman Institute, Jerusalem), Yossi Klein Halevi (Shalom

Hartman Institute, Jerusalem), Rabbi Dalia Marx (HUC-Jerusalem), Rabbi Shabtai Rappaport (Beit Midrash at the Jesselson Institute for Advanced Torah Studies, Bar-Ilan University, Tel Aviv) all played important roles in various aspects of this dialogue.

Special thanks must be given to Rabbi Ilana Schwartzman (now at Beth Haverim Shir Shalom, Mahwah, NJ), who was instrumental to the successful beginning of this dialogue project and an exemplary participant in the discussions between 2016 and 2018. Upon Rabbi Schwartzman's move across country, Rabbi Samuel L. Spector (Congregation Kol Ami) enthusiastically joined the group and has contributed in countless ways.

We particularly thank Rabbi Michael Melchior (Chief Rabbi of Norway and founder of the Mosaica Center for Inter-Religious Cooperation) and Elder Quentin L. Cook (Quorum of the Twelve Apostles for The Church of Jesus Christ of Latter-day Saints) for their willingness to participate in the dialogue sessions by giving the keynote addresses in Jerusalem in 2019. In connection with that trip and warm hospitality in Israel, we thank Jim Kearl, Eran Hayet, and Tawfic Alawi (BYU Jerusalem Center for Near Eastern Studies), Rabbi Naamah Kelman (HUC-Jerusalem), Ronit Dukofsky (Shalom Hartman Institute, Jerusalem), Sari Granitza (Yad Vashem), Bill Bernstein (American Society for Yad Vashem), and Jack Mayer and Tamar Shapira (Save a Child's Heart).

Throughout the entire dialogue effort, donors on both sides have generously contributed to what they view as an important project for the benefit of both religious communities in an environment of growing antagonism to religious belief. Those donors include Jake (of blessed memory) and Janet Farber, Irwin and Helgard Field, Stanley and Ilene Gold, Ken and Wendy Ruby, Alan Sieroty, Naomi Vanek, Roy Christensen, Brent and Jill Bishop, Helen Leon, Dave and Bianca Lisonbee, Bruce Winn, George and Joyce Hill, and Michael and Margie Draper.

Student participants in various dialogue sessions included Zoë Zafman, Sarah Markowitz, and Matthew Stirling (LMU), Maddie Blonquist and Jake Smith (BYU), numerous undergraduate and graduate students from Holli Levitsky, Mark Diamond, and Fr. Alexei Smith's 2019 Literature and Faith in the Holy Land seminar in Israel (LMU), Joshua Matson (PhD candidate, Florida State University), and Cameron Scott (PhD candidate, Ben-Gurion University of the Negev).

Institutional support and participation from BYU Religious Education and Religious Outreach Council, Loyola Marymount University, Academy for Jewish Religion CA, Brigham Young University, Hebrew Union College–Jewish Institute of Religion, the John A. Widtsoe Foundation at University of Southern California, Los Angeles Public Affairs Committee for The Church of Jesus Christ of Latter-day Saints, Leo Baeck Temple (Los Angeles), Adat Ari El (Valley Village, CA), Temple Ramat Zion (Northridge, CA), Brigham Young University Jerusalem Center, Shalom Hartman Institute, Congregation Kol Ami (Salt Lake City), HUC Skirball Archaeological Museum (Jerusalem), and Wolfson Medical Center and Save a Child's Heart (Holon, Israel) made this endeavor far more meaningful through their contributions.

We are grateful to graduate and undergraduate students Emily Larson, Spencer Clark, and Kelly Duncan (BYU), and Thalia Halpert Rodis (CCAR Press) for their work on the book at various stages and for Thalia's help with the discussion guide available at covenants.ccarpress.org. We also thank Tyler Hobson (BYU) and Rena Gallagher (LMU). Shirley Ricks (Religious Studies Center at BYU) and student intern Sarah Johnson proved invaluable in making this volume much better. Brent Nordgren's (RSC) thoughtful guidance with the design and production of the volume along with Carmen Cole's assistance during the design and typesetting process proved how important professional advice and technical skills are to the process as a whole. Scott Esplin (BYU) has been gracious and supportive in his role at the RSC every step along the way. Rabbi Hara Person, Chief Executive of the Central Conference of American Rabbis (CCAR) and former Chief Strategy Office and publisher of CCAR Press, enthusiastically encouraged the book project from the beginning. We are indebted to her for her leadership and the support of her dedicated colleagues at CCAR Press, Rabbi Sonja Pilz and Rafael Chaiken.

Lois Diamond and Kaylyn Reed both lent the most significant contributions to the coming forth of this volume as they provided constant encouragement, support, and love to us throughout this endeavor.

INTRODUCTION

***

MARK S. DIAMOND AND ANDREW C. REED, EDITORS

And this shall be My covenant with them, said the Lord: My spirit which is upon you, and the words which I have placed in your mouth, shall not be absent from your mouth, nor from the mouth of your children, nor from the mouth of your children's children—said the Lord—from now on, for all time.

—Isaiah 59:21[1]

This passage, an instructive connection for both Jewish and Latter-day Saint communities, speaks to the injunction to create generational bonds framed in terms of covenant. The work represented within these pages is the result of hard-earned discussions among Jewish and Latter-day Saint scholars.[2] These discussions began in 2016 and have carried forward to the present. The resulting dialogues provided space in which participants engaged with topics of common interest, including those that challenged our best thinking and required a true sense of patience and understanding.

The chapters contained in this volume draw upon some of the discussions and papers that framed much of the agenda during the first four academic dialogue sessions held between March 2016 and March 2018. From the beginning of the project, a common goal for participants and organizers was the production of a volume of essays that chronicle the history of this significant endeavor, that highlight the work of scholars in this area, and that provide good practices and lessons learned about successful interfaith dialogues. As participants, the sustained effort to develop strong ties academically and personally through this work has enlarged our sense of a community of scholars and pastorally engaged leaders to foster good in the world.

In our endeavor as scholars and adherents of particular traditions and cultures, we are bound together by something more profound than common academic interests. The deeply personal nature of this endeavor asks much of those who participate in the interfaith project. There is a degree of vulnerability in placing deeply held traditions, beliefs, and communal values on the table for examination, discussion, and inquiry. Yet in doing so a profound sense of the generosity of spirit pervades this work; glimpses of it are seen on the pages of this book. *Understanding Covenants and Communities* builds on the words penned by Henry David Thoreau that speak to the nature of our relationships that emerged through hours and days of discussions and shared experiences. "The Friend asks no return but that his Friend will religiously accept and wear and not disgrace his apotheosis of him. They cherish each other's hopes. They are kind to each other's dreams."[3] Rabbi Abraham Joshua Heschel further developed this notion of interreligious engagement with those of other traditions when he gave his landmark address at Union Theological Seminary in 1965. Heschel reflected on the encounter with those who hold religious views different from one's own. He noted:

> On what basis do we people of different religious commitments meet one another?
>
> First and foremost we meet as human beings who have so much in common: a heart, a face, a voice, the presence of a soul, fears, hope, the ability to trust, a capacity for compassion and understanding, the kinship of being human. My first task in every

encounter is to comprehend the personhood of the human being I face, to sense the kinship of being human, solidarity of being.

To meet a human being is a major challenge to mind and heart. I must recall what I normally forget. A person is not just a specimen of the species called *homo sapiens*. He is all of humanity in one, and whenever one man is hurt we are all injured. The human is disclosure of the divine, and all men are one in God's care for man. Many things on earth are precious, some are holy, humanity is holy of holies.[4]

While individual participants joined with this project at various times and for various reasons, the collective efforts to foster rich relationships among participants and among broader communities of Jews and Latter-day Saints remains the common goal for the Jewish–Latter-day Saint Academic Dialogue Project.

Academically, this book is designed to provide sound thinking on the endeavor of interfaith work—thematically and methodologically. Readers will encounter a wide range of disciplinary backgrounds—biblical studies, theology, practical theology, women's studies, history, literature, and political science. In addition to the academic participants, the experiences and voices of each person's pastoral and communal experiences emerge throughout this book. While academic perspectives guide the individual chapters, there is a strong desire to make these articles readily accessible to interested readers outside academia. Interfaith work only goes so far if it remains cloistered in ivory towers away from those in the communities for whom this work is intended. Each piece contained in this volume attempts to marry these two initiatives—speaking to scholars and lay people alike.

The volume is divided into four thematic parts: Foundations and Perspectives, Scripture, Lived Experience and Worship, and Culture and Politics. Each part contains articles by scholars who presented research and formal papers in closed-door dialogue meetings or in public venues as part of the community outreach in Los Angeles, California, or in Salt Lake City and Provo, Utah. Readers will notice the progression of themes and topics throughout the chapters from those in which the common goal of bridge building between the two communities is evident to those in which individual participants grapple with some of the more difficult topics internally and scholars respond, looking at these ideas from outside that particular tradition. The topics covered in this volume were selected by the organizers before each dialogue. Often, the papers were paired with a similar paper from the other perspective, as in the papers by Thomas Wayment and Joshua Garroway on Paul or by Brent Top and Mark Diamond on Sabbath observance. Methodologically, this framing of dialogue sessions permitted interlocutors to engage a common topic and allowed for comparisons of similarities and differences to emerge in the process of discussion and reflection.

In the end, while this volume is an important milestone in the history of the Jewish–Latter-day Saint dialogue, it represents just one step in the broader project. It documents the history and development of the process, structure, and accomplishments of this effort. At the same time, cloaked behind the written word on these pages are hundreds of combined hours of conversation and shared experiences that helped build the successful dialogue. No doubt some of this shared learning emerges through the tone and content found in this book. It speaks to the possibilities of careful, thoughtful engagement engineered to foster interfaith progress in our communities. As editors, we hope that this project inspires people interested in interfaith dialogue generally, but also that it specifically encourages those in our communities to find opportunities to develop understanding through lived, sustained contact with one another and through our historical, cultural, and theological narratives. It is our hope and prayer that the Jewish–Latter-day Saint Academic Dialogue Project will proceed "from strength to strength" in the spirit and vision of Rabbi Heschel:

What, then, is the purpose of interreligious cooperation? It is neither to flatter nor to refute one another, but to help one another; to share insight and learning, to cooperate in academic ventures on the highest scholarly level, and what is even more important to search in the wilderness for well-springs of devotion, for treasures of stillness, for the power of love and care for man.[5]

NOTES

1. *The Jewish Study Bible, Jewish Publication Society Tanakh Translation* (Oxford: Oxford University Press, 2004), 903.

2. In October 2018, Russell M. Nelson, president of The Church of Jesus Christ of Latter-day Saints, asked members of the Church and media outlets to respectfully revise the terms used to refer to the Church and its members. For more on this, see the Church's style guide at https://newsroom.churchofjesuschrist.org/style-guide. Where possible, we as editors have tried to accommodate this request.

3. Henry David Thoreau, *Friendship and Other Essays* (New York: Little Leather Library, 1923), 16.

4. Abraham Joshua Heschel, "No Religion Is an Island," *Union Seminary Quarterly Review* 21, no. 2 (January 1966): 120–21.

5. Heschel, "No Religion Is an Island," 133.

FOUNDATIONS AND PERSPECTIVES

PART ONE

In part one, "Foundations and Perspectives," the founders of the Jewish–Latter-day Saint Academic Dialogue—including Shon Hopkin, Mark Diamond, Steven Windmueller, and Andrew Reed—open the volume with a discussion about the history of this project from its inception in 2015 to the most recent sessions held in Israel. In order to show the importance of organization and structure in successful dialogues, they provide a history of the dialogue to orient readers generally about the project and its foundational goals and to reflect on lessons learned in the process.

In chapter 2, Shon Hopkin examines the historic ties (imagined and real) to show that for Latter-day Saints, perceived connections lead to a deep affinity that is both meaningful and oftentimes overly simplistic in its views of Jews and Judaism. Hopkin shows how the development of Latter-day Saint themes of priesthood, Zion, and covenant are often inlaid within a constructed, imagined community that depends on a relationship to biblical Judaism.

1

A History of the Jewish–Latter-day Saint Academic Dialogue

SHON D. HOPKIN, MARK S. DIAMOND,
STEVEN WINDMUELLER, AND ANDREW C. REED

This history of the Jewish–Latter-day Saint Academic Dialogue details how the relationship began and progressed and shares its goals and general methodology. We hope that this account will assist those who desire to understand the project better. At the same time, we trust that this short history will provide suggestions and offer lessons learned and modeled during the project that can help other dialogue efforts succeed.

EARLY BEGINNINGS

Although not a part of the Jewish–Latter-day Saint Academic Dialogue as it would eventually be created, The Church of Jesus Christ of Latter-day Saints maintains a group of public affairs volunteers in every location where there are enough Church members to warrant such efforts. The goals of Church public affairs offices include promoting positive awareness of the faith and building bridges of friendship and understanding with local government, community, and religious organizations.[1] Church public affairs in the Los Angeles area has been especially successful in building bridges with local Jewish, Muslim, Christian, and Eastern religious communities through tireless work for many years. One of the ways that public affairs offices encourage understanding of the Church is by bringing leaders of other faiths to visit Salt Lake City, Utah, the headquarters of The Church of Jesus Christ of Latter-day Saints. These visits include tours of Welfare Square, the center of welfare operations of the Church; tours of Temple Square, where the Salt Lake Temple, Church Headquarters, and the Church History Museum are located; a visit to Brigham Young University in Provo, Utah; and meetings with general Church leaders.

Rabbis and other Jewish leaders in the greater Los Angeles area had cooperated with Church public affairs on a variety of projects that involved their congregations and community organizations, including the Board of Rabbis of Southern California and the American Jewish Committee. Leaders of both communities had promoted interfaith and intergroup understanding and cooperation for many years. In May 2015, having developed a close relationship with members of Latter-day Saint Church public affairs leaders, Mark Diamond (Loyola Marymount University [LMU] and the Academy for Jewish Religion California [AJRCA]), Steven Windmueller (Hebrew Union College–Jewish Institute of Religion [HUC-JIR]), and other Jewish academics and rabbis were invited to visit Utah. During the trip, leaders attended the open house of the Latter-day Saint Payson Utah Temple prior to the temple's dedication and were hosted for a tour and luncheon at Brigham Young University (BYU). Shon Hopkin and Andrew Reed, part of BYU's newly formed Council of Religious Outreach, helped host the luncheon. Diamond and Hopkin struck up a friendship, and both mentioned an interest in beginning a formal dialogue effort between the two communities.

Following the initial meeting, Diamond and Hopkin remained in communication, continuing to explore the possibility of initiating an ongoing dialogue that would help Jews and Latter-day Saints better understand each other, increase awareness and cooperation, and reduce friction points between the two communities. These conversations led to a lunch visit in Los Angeles that included Hopkin and Reed from BYU along with Diamond, Windmueller, and Tamar Frankiel from Los Angeles institutions. The group brainstormed a number of approaches and decided that the dialogue project would be best served by starting cautiously, with a consistent composition and a numerically limited group, usually not more than six participants from each community. The founders decided that for the first two or three years the group would meet twice a year to build sufficient friendship and trust, that dialogue sessions would be held primarily in Utah and Los Angeles to reduce expenses, and that dialogue topics would extend over time from areas of commonality toward areas of challenge and potential friction.[2] Each semiannual dialogue would consist of two or more of these models of interfaith dialogue:

- closed-door, academic sessions to preserve the ability of dialogue participants to express themselves openly;
- public sessions to allow the dialogue effort to have a broad impact among students, faculty, and members of the religious communities; and
- joint cultural and religious activities to help dialogue participants experience the history and lived religious lives of the two communities.

Leaders of the dialogue subsequently decided that most closed-door academic sessions would include papers and responses from a member of each side of the dialogue team, followed by open discussion between all dialogue participants. This led to a fourth component of the dialogue effort—the publication of papers in an academic publication venue.

FIRST DIALOGUE SERIES, MARCH 2016, PROVO, UTAH

Diamond, Windmueller, Frankiel, Reed, and Hopkin returned to their respective academic communities to build dialogue teams that could balance academic integrity with respect, kindness, and warmth across the religious divide. The first meetings were planned for Brigham Young University in Provo, Utah, as the strongest center of potential student involvement in the two communities and thus as a good test case for the long-term viability of the project. Participants on the Jewish side included Mark Diamond of LMU and AJRCA, Tamar Frankiel of AJRCA, Ilana Schwartzman from Congregation Kol Ami in Salt Lake City, and Steven Windmueller from HUC-JIR in Los Angeles. The Latter-day Saint members of the dialogue team were all professors from BYU and included Richard Holzapfel, Shon Hopkin, Barbara Morgan Gardner, Jared Ludlow, Andrew Reed, and Brent Top (former dean of Religious Education at BYU), all of whom either had a background in some form of Jewish studies or were a part of BYU's Council of Religious Outreach.

This first dialogue series started with a set of topics of common interest, with academic papers and responses that detailed what Jews could learn from Latter-day Saints (in one session), and how Latter-day Saints build on concepts and imagery provided by their interpretation of ancient Judaism as found in the Hebrew Bible (in a second session). A third academic session presented various philosophies and approaches to interfaith dialogue over the past decades in an effort to help guide the new dialogue teams forward in their approaches. The three academic sessions were followed by a public evening session held on the BYU campus, which was attended by approximately 350 students and members of the community. This public session repeated abbreviated forms of the first two academic presentations, followed by a panel of the participants who responded to questions from a moderator and from the audience. The group's leaders left the dialogue satisfied that participants had interacted in productive and respectful ways, a necessity in building an interfaith relationship. The public session was especially helpful in communicating the ideas and success of the academic sessions to those outside the small group of academic dialogue participants.[3]

SECOND DIALOGUE SERIES, DECEMBER 2016, LOS ANGELES, CALIFORNIA

The Jewish dialogue participants hosted the second series of dialogues in Los Angeles in December 2016. The dialogue boasted an ambitious schedule of private academic dialogues, public interactions, and joint cultural and religious experiences. Jewish participants organized what was certainly the most intensive and impactful dialogue effort to date. In addition to the previous participants, the Jewish dialogue leaders added two colleagues who continued to participate in future dialogue efforts, along with two guest presenters who were experts in their respective fields. New or guest members of the dialogue included Joshua Garroway (HUC-JIR), David Kaufman (a visiting scholar at the the Los Angeles campus of HUC-JIR), Holli Levitsky (LMU), and Marvin Sweeney (AJRCA; Claremont School of Theology). The BYU dialogue leaders added Jacob Rennaker (John A. Widtsoe Foundation, University of Southern California) and Fred Woods (BYU).

This dialogue series continued to build on the foundation of the first, broaching relatively safe and comfortable topics of mutual interest to both Jews and Latter-day Saints in an effort to understand each other better and help new participants blend with the existing dialogue team. These included closed-door sessions (held mostly at the AJRCA campus) on covenant understanding, Latter-day Saints and Jews in literature, and liturgical understandings and approaches in the two communities. Public sessions also provided extensive interaction in both the Latter-day Saint and Jewish communities, including:

- Shabbat programs at area synagogues featuring Q&A sessions that allowed Jewish attendees to ask any question they wished regarding Latter-day Saint beliefs and practices;
- a Sunday public presentation at AJRCA on Latter-day Saints and Jews in film was attended by students, faculty, and members of the community; and
- a Sunday evening presentation and Q&A session in a Latter-day Saint chapel was attended by Latter-day Saint stake presidents (individuals who administer and coordinate multiple local congregations) in order to help members in the area better understand their Jewish neighbors.

Finally, dialogue participants enjoyed numerous joint religious and cultural events that enabled the Latter-day Saint guests to better understand Jewish history and religious practices. These included a traditional Shabbat dinner hosted by Mark and Lois Diamond in their home, Friday evening and Saturday morning Shabbat services, a tour of the Skirball Cultural Center, and a music recital by AJRCA cantorial students. The entire multiday series was enriching and memorable for all colleagues and helped solidify new and existing friendships among the dialogue participants while contributing to better interfaith understanding among both Jews and Latter-day Saints.

THIRD DIALOGUE SERIES, MARCH 2017, SALT LAKE CITY, OREM, AND PROVO, UTAH

The third series occurred approximately one year after the initial dialogue series. The dialogue teams returned to Utah, with two Jewish participants joining the effort from California, along with one new Latter-day Saint dialogue member and one guest presenter. Jewish participants included those from the first dialogue series at BYU, joined by Joshua Garroway and Holli Levitsky, both of whom had participated in the second dialogue series. The Latter-day Saint cohort added Quin Monson from BYU as a political scientist to complement Steven Windmueller's academic interests, along with Thomas Wayment from BYU as a guest presenter on the figure of Paul in the New Testament.

This series began to explore subjects of a more sensitive nature to both sides of the dialogue and led to numerous discoveries and "red button" topics on both sides.[4] These moments of heightened sensitivity and reflection were especially evident for the Latter-day Saint cohort as scholars discussed their views on Paul, which began to touch more precisely on their views of Jews and Judaism in relation to Christianity. Jewish participants experienced similarly vulnerable moments when discussing their views of Israel, Zion, and the Holy Land. Both cohorts openly shared their perceptions of their experience with a Latter-day Saint worship service, particularly as it related to women's participation in the service. These experiences helped move the dialogue effort forward into more challenging territory but also increased trust between the two groups as both did not hold back challenging questions and viewpoints. Instead they were able to voice and discuss those viewpoints in an atmosphere of academic and religious respect, preparing the way for more challenging topics in the future.

The third dialogue series included closed-door sessions on viewpoints of Paul, Sabbath-day practice in both religious traditions, and positions regarding Israel in both religious communities. A visit to Rabbi Schwartzman's synagogue, Congregation Kol Ami, was followed by a cultural and historical presentation on an aspect of Jewish history by Holli Levitsky. At the invitation of Shon Hopkin, then serving as bishop of the Orem 2nd Ward, Mark Diamond gave a talk on the Sabbath at a Latter-day Saint sacrament meeting service. Frankiel and Diamond were able to extend their Utah stay and teach two classes on Judaism in Reed's world religion classes. Joint cultural and religious experiences included attendance at Shabbat services at Kol Ami, a tour of Temple Square for new Jewish members of the dialogue team, and attendance of all three hours of Sunday services (sacrament meeting, Sunday School, and priesthood/Relief Society meetings) at Shon Hopkin's Latter-day Saint community by all the Jewish members of the dialogue. For those who were able to extend their visit, a traditional "Mormon" Sunday dinner was hosted by Brent and Wendy Top. This last experience especially provided for important comparison and contrast in the religious customs in the two communities. These viewpoints centered on heavy family participation in Latter-day Saint services, a perception of somewhat lower leadership participation for women in Latter-day Saint communities, and liturgy and teaching that are significantly different in temperament than Jewish liturgical practices and teaching styles.

FOURTH DIALOGUE SERIES, NOVEMBER 3, 2017, WEBCAST DIALOGUE, BRIGHAM YOUNG UNIVERSITY AND LOYOLA MARYMOUNT UNIVERSITY

After three intensive dialogue series in California and Utah, there was a desire to continue the semiannual schedule of the dialogue project without overscheduling the busy academic participants with preparing papers and presentations. This led to a decision to dialogue via webcast, with the two sides gathered in one room at BYU and another at LMU (and from a third location by Barbara Morgan Gardner). Since both cohorts remained in their home locations, no public events or joint cultural events were planned. Rather than papers, discussion leaders were chosen who provided a series of readings on a topic and then guided the participants through those readings and into an open dialogue. This style of academic session thus allowed participants to benefit from strong scholarship outside the dialogue teams, provided more discussion time, and also permitted students and other invited guests who would not have been able to travel for a typical dialogue series to participate. Students were included to train them, to gain insights from younger participants, and to begin to build a group that could perpetuate dialogues between the two religious traditions in the future. In addition to previous participants, Michael McNaught (invited faculty guest from LMU's Center for Religion and Spirituality), and LMU students Zoé Zafman, Sarah Markowitz, and Matthew Stirling joined the dialogue. Additional participants at the BYU location included Quin Monson (a recent addition to the dialogue team), Janiece Johnson (a visiting academic and discussion leader from BYU's Maxwell Institute), Eric Huntsman (a visiting guest), Jared Ludlow (who had been unable to participate since the first dialogue series), and BYU students Maddie Blonquist and Jake Smith. Topics in the three sessions continued to build on the previous session as participants addressed important documents and different models of Jewish-Christian interfaith engagement (including Latter-day Saint religious statements regarding Judaism), Latter-day Saint female authors and writings, and lived religion in Latter-day Saint and Jewish culture. These topics again allowed both sides to explore sensitive areas, particularly the attitude toward women in Orthodox Jewish and Latter-day Saint culture and some exclusivist historical Christian attitudes toward Judaism.

FIFTH DIALOGUE SERIES, MARCH 2018, LOYOLA MARYMOUNT UNIVERSITY, LOS ANGELES, CALIFORNIA

The fifth dialogue series, held two years from the beginning of the dialogue effort, returned to Los Angeles but this time was hosted at Loyola Marymount University. The benefits of modern religious tolerance and the progress of interfaith understanding were on display as a Roman-Catholic Jesuit institution hosted a group of Jewish and Latter-day Saint academics, a historic first for all three faith communities. This dialogue series returned to the style of paper presentations and continued to approach challenging subjects, but the schedule was abbreviated to accommodate busy teaching and research schedules. The shorter nature of this dialogue series did not allow for public sessions, but two students from LMU trained in interfaith work attended the first session, along with Robert Hurteau, director of the Center for Religion and Spirituality at LMU. Joint religious and cultural experiences included a tour of the LMU campus focused on its contributions to interfaith understanding and a Shabbat dinner hosted at the home of Steven and Michelle Windmueller. The group was saddened by Ilana Schwartzman's move to a synagogue in New Jersey. Rabbi Schwartzman contributed important perspectives as the only Jewish member of the team who lived among the Latter-day Saint communities of Utah. The group was pleased to welcome her replacement at Congregation Kol Ami, Rabbi Elect Sam Spector, who had been living and working in Los Angeles but moved to Utah to fulfill his new role during the summer of 2018. Rabbi Spector connected quickly and comfortably with the group and has become an important part of the dialogue effort. The Jewish cohort also added an expert on women in the Bible, Kristine Garroway, whose husband, Joshua Garroway, was already a dialogue participant.

This dialogue series approached the most sensitive of subjects, touched on in other sessions but receiving focused attention here, of Latter-day Saints and supersessionism, or the view that Judaism has been superseded by Christianity. Latter-day Saints have a type of supersessionism in their attitudes to Judaism and other religions, but it is in many respects softer or more inclusive than some traditional Christian attitudes have been. The two other academic sessions included important topics that had been touched on before—the religious experiences of Jewish and Latter-day Saint women and Latter-day Saint and Jewish political views on Israel and Zionism.

SIXTH DIALOGUE SERIES, JUNE 2019, ISRAEL

In June 2019 the dialogue project took a significant step forward as it achieved a goal that had represented a core objective from the outset—convening participants in the Holy Land. As previously envisioned, this dialogue took advantage of the wide array of Jewish academic expertise and cultural experiences available in Israel. Starting on June 4, dialogue members visited the Wolfson Medical Center in Holon, where participants met with representatives from the Israeli charity Save a Child's Heart, followed by a visit to the Save a Child's Heart Children's Home. This organization is committed to providing pro bono medical assistance to young patients from across the globe who need lifesaving cardiac surgery. In the afternoon, dialogue participants met with scholars at Bar-Ilan University. Rabbi Shabtai Rappaport, the head of the Beit Midrash at the Jesselson Institute for Advanced Torah Studies, led a Jewish text study.

Important and memorable activities on June 5 began with an archaeologically oriented exploration of the City of David led by dialogue member Kristi Garroway. This session was followed by a deeply moving visit to the Yad Vashem Holocaust Memorial Museum. This visit included a VIP tour, along with a wreath-laying ceremony in the Hall of Remembrance that was one of the more meaningful experiences of a lifetime for many of the Latter-day Saint and Jewish participants. After the museum visit, the dialogue team moved to the BYU Jerusalem Center for Near Eastern Studies, where Steven Windmueller and Quin Monson conducted an academic dialogue session analyzing and discussing the recent increases in global anti-Semitism. In a historic and possibly the most important bridge-building session since the inception of this project, a public event was held in the stunning auditorium of the BYU Jerusalem Center in which Elder Quentin L. Cook of the Quorum of the Twelve Apostles and Rabbi Michael Melchior, the chief rabbi of Norway and a founder of the interfaith organization Mosaica, were keynote speakers and expertly answered questions from the audience. A reception followed, permitting BYU students and many other invited guests to mingle with the keynote speakers, the dialogue participants, and one another.

On June 6, the final day of the program provided several strong academic experiences. The morning session was held at the Shalom Hartman Institute and consisted of guided, paired/*hevrutah* readings led by Rabbi Leon Wiener Dow. A discussion on the "Responses to the Moral Challenges of Zionism Today" followed with Yossi Klein Halevi, a senior fellow at the Hartman Institute and world-renowned author of *Letters to My Palestinian Neighbor* and other works. The afternoon saw a change of venue as the group moved to the Hebrew Union College, where Professor Dalia Marx (the Rabbi Aaron D. Panken Professor of Liturgy and Midrash) conducted a discussion of Jerusalem as a sacred site in Talmudic sources. Kristi Garroway led the group on a tour of the HUC Skirball Archaeological Museum. At a business meeting that followed, the participants had occasion to review the Israel experience and to plan for future dialogue activities. The formal program concluded with a dinner at a local Jerusalem restaurant, ending this most memorable of dialogue experiences. The participants felt united through their shared cultural and academic experiences to a greater degree than ever before.

FUTURE PLANS FOR 2020 AND BEYOND

At the planning session in Jerusalem the group decided that there were still significant topics to discuss and important goals to drive the dialogue effort forward. The model of the past three years was taken as a guide in planning for the next three years. The proposed format will include biannual dialogue gatherings, primarily held at BYU and in Los Angeles, hopefully leading to a second publication. The plan also includes the goal to host another significant public dialogue event at the end of this second three-year cycle, possibly culminating with a visit to a Latter-day Saint historical site in Illinois or New York, locations where there are also large Jewish population centers nearby. Dialogue organizers launched a new educational component of the project in November–December 2019 when Shon Hopkin and Andrew Reed came to Los Angeles to conduct seminars at HUC-JIR and LMU and Mark Diamond and Steven Windmueller visited Provo to teach classes at BYU. These programs advanced the shared goal of strengthening the project's outreach to Jewish and Latter-day Saint students, academics, and their respective communities.

CONCLUSIONS: STRENGTHS OF THE JEWISH–LATTER-DAY SAINT ACADEMIC DIALOGUE EFFORT

The history of the Jewish–Latter-day Saint Academic Dialogue project provides a number of successful approaches and suggestions to strengthen the choppy waters of interfaith understanding. They may be summarized in the following ten principles of interfaith dialogue:

1. *Choosing dialogue participants carefully is crucial.* One poor choice can undo years of careful work or even derail the effort entirely. Important attributes include a balanced ability to be both warm and respectful while being willing to be honest about the challenges in one's own religious tradition and open-minded when discussing another's. Combative or defensive personalities, those who are unwilling to recognize or be open about challenging realities in their own religious tradition, or those who do not believe that they can learn from the other side will undermine trust and the success of the endeavor.

2. Dialogue efforts tend to work best when the *numbers are kept relatively small.* This allows for increased individual participation, a greater ability to connect and build trust on a more personal level, and a heightened sense of commitment and perceived need of involvement from each of the participants.

3. *Attending worship services, cultural events, or historical sites* of each other's faith traditions also helps to build trust and understanding. Academics are at times inclined to focus on theoretical concepts and ignore the importance of lived religion in the lives of their academic counterparts. Experiencing worship together helps develop a deeper emotional bond that can help overcome the sensitive parts of dialogue between faiths. Eating and relaxing together also play a significant role in recognizing the fellow humanity of both faith cohorts and building genuine friendship that can withstand later disagreements. The relationships that have been formed in these intimate social settings are an especially critical ingredient in

personalizing and nurturing these interfaith connections beyond the formalities of prayers, papers, and publications.

4. Assigning presentation responsibilities in the dialogue sessions also maintains a sense of commitment and intellectual involvement. Participants feel a deeper connection to the project when they are *expected to share their academic expertise with fellow dialogue members and in public forums.*

5. An added benefit of presenting papers rather than simply discussing readings is the ability to turn the interfaith effort, which rarely garners much credit for academic advancement, into *publications* that can strengthen the scholar's portfolio. The sacrifices entailed by deep interfaith commitment can thereby be balanced by the academic benefits the scholar can gain from the engagement.

6. The writing and subsequent publishing of papers also helps ensure that scholars are not working in an academic silo that benefits only them. The knowledge and approaches explored by the dialogue can reach beyond the "ivory tower" environment of academia to benefit the community at large. Of additional importance, where possible, is that dialogue planning include efforts to *involve and educate the community* in public settings.

7. This type of broader community engagement via publications and public dialogue sessions also assists in *procuring financial assistance from donors.* Their efforts on behalf of the community can be publicized and acknowledged. In so doing, donors may appreciate that their assistance reaches beyond the academic community.

8. As important as public sessions and shared explorations of culture and religious experience are, *the core of the dialogue should be the closed-door academic sessions.* These seminars, wherever possible, should be free of outside oversight to allow participants to voice viewpoints freely and with full honesty. Creating this safe space is vital to the success of interfaith dialogues in general and of academic interfaith dialogues in particular.

9. In planning the closed-door sessions, we consciously decided to begin with topics that were designed to highlight shared beliefs and values between the communities. This understanding *builds a foundation of shared viewpoints that can then resist rapid disintegration* when addressing areas of fundamental disagreement. When both groups recognize the similarity of many goals and religious desires, they are more likely to give the benefit of the doubt when first confronting a foreign and seemingly unethical or contradictory practice or belief.[5]

10. As important as building upon commonalities is for the success of the dialogue effort, we believe *it is crucial to move as soon as reasonable and feasible to challenging and sensitive topics of potential disagreement and sensitivity.* This type of engagement, successfully navigated, continues to build a deeper level of trust and also provides meaning to the dialogue as an effort that can help communities coexist and cooperate in meaningful ways while navigating some of the most significant points of potential friction. From our perspective, getting to these topics and learning to understand and communicate with each other is one of the primary goals that makes academic interfaith dialogue a worthwhile and productive endeavor.

We believe we have designed a dialogue project that exhibits each of these ten characteristics. As we carefully and faithfully build and move forward, we are hopeful that the dialogue effort will continue to bear positive fruit for our respective academic and religious communities. May our work be a visible manifestation of our evolving, maturing relationship as brothers and sisters of faith.

NOTES

1. See "5.5 Stake Specialists," in *General Handbook: Serving in The Church of Jesus Christ of Latter-day Saints* (Salt Lake City: The Church of Jesus Christ of Latter-Day Saints, 2020), https://churchofjesuschrist.org/study/manual/general-handbook/5-stake-leadership?lang=eng #title_number22.

2. An abbreviated history of the dialogue can be accessed under initiatives at https://religiousoutreach.byu.edu.

3. The specific titles, presenters, and respondents for each session, along with accompanying images, are presented in appendix 2.

4. For an analysis of "red button" issues in interfaith dialogue, see Reuven Firestone's chapter "Jewish 'Red Buttons,'" in Leonard Swidler, Kahlid Duran, and Reuven Firestone, *Trialogue: Jews, Christians, and Muslims in Dialogue* (New London, CT: Twenty-Third Publications, 2007), 89–91.

5. "A dialogue among persons can be built only on personal trust. Hence it is wise not to tackle the most difficult problems in the beginning, but rather to approach first those issues most likely to provide some common ground, thereby establishing the basis of human trust." Leonard Swidler, in *Trialogue: Jews, Christians, and Muslims in Dialogue*, 30.

2

ANCIENT FOUNDATIONS OF A MODERN RELIGION: LATTER-DAY SAINTS AND THE HEBREW BIBLE

SHON D. HOPKIN

Many Jews feel confusion, skepticism, or even distrust when approached with enthusiasm and a sense of shared background by members of The Church of Jesus Christ of Latter-day Saints. Latter-day Saints often connect contemporary Jews to perceptions of Jews as ancient sisters and brothers and often maintain a belief—rarely subjected to critical examination—in a shared religious identity that will certainly allow Jews and Latter-day Saints to form the natural connection of extended relations who are meeting for the first time. This concept, of course, makes little sense to most Jews, who are aware of just how different their own history has been from their Christian neighbors and who have a fairly concrete view of their own ethnic identity. How can they understand this sense of deep connection felt by their Latter-day Saint acquaintances?

In his influential work *Imagined Communities*, Benedict Anderson presents an analysis of the strength of nationalism that may be useful for the study of religion.[1] While nations are a very modern phenomenon in historians' eyes, nationalists often feel that their nation's history extends back into antiquity. According to Anderson, modern communities often connect themselves to more ancient communities, adopting and adapting older stories to provide themselves with stability, legitimacy, and strength.[2] This tie to ancient identity, ideas, and symbols—such as the modern nation of Italy with the Colosseum and the Pantheon as symbols of its ancient Roman strength—ignites the imagination of the new community and unites its people.[3] Pride in the nation can bind a people together beyond the competing claims of individual families, cultural practices, and even religious identity.

Although outsiders might look with suspicion on these types of connections, closer examination reveals that the pattern has repeated itself again and again. A newer community adopts and adapts the symbols of an existing or earlier community, honoring the strength of that community while at the same time providing new life and vitality to its ancient practices. Ancient biblical authors, for example, sought to connect their own religious history with events of the past, leading back to the first parents of humankind.[4] Although the connections are much more organic, even the various strands of modern Judaism could be said to be an "imagined community" based on Second Temple Judaism, connecting with many of the practices of the earlier community, but giving those practices new life, vitality, and relevance in modernity.[5] New Testament authors reinterpreted the teachings of the biblical prophets, providing a foundation for their own position.[6] Christianity sprang from a foundation of Judaism, building upon prior practices but adapting them in ways that soon created an entirely distinct religion.[7]

As in early Christianity, efforts to show relevance include setting up the new religious tradition in contradistinction to the former, emphasizing or even exaggerating the weaknesses of the former, and showing how these weaknesses are resolved by the latter, even as the new faith continues to employ many of the practices of the former. Although this practice sets up the two faiths as competitors, it still defines the new in terms provided by the old. It is also important to remember that the new community's connection with older concepts does not seek to re-create the precise image of the previous community. Rather, it seeks to build on a foundation provided by that community, adapting concepts and practices in a way that creates an entirely new organism. In the comparative study of religions from an anthropological perspective, proving the reality of these connections is less fruitful than analyzing the *meaning* of those connections for religious participants.[8]

Because The Church of Jesus Christ of Latter-day Saints is a Christian faith, some who seek to understand Latter-day Saint approaches to Judaism view it through the lens of other Christian-Jewish relationships. These Christian traditions have at times viewed Judaism as part of antiquated Old Testament practices, with a strong demarcation between the less-developed faith of the Hebrew Bible and that faith's fulfillment in Christ as presented in the New Testament. In the New Testament, God's work as Christians define it finally commenced. The Old Testament may be useful for its inspiring stories, for providing the Ten Commandments, or for showing the anticipation of Jesus Christ, but it has been superseded.[9] Most Christians see themselves as continuations of New Testament communities, building on the foundations of early Christians.

Latter-day Saints instead view themselves as building on the foundations of the Hebrew Bible, and they see one unified program of God running through the two testaments. Joseph Smith's prophetic project has been described by one scholar as seeking to heal or restore the brokenness of history, including the healing of broken family lines, broken marriages, the broken state of relationships between the multitude of Christian communities, and the broken nature between God's biblical communities—Christians and Jews.[10] Part of that project included reuniting the two testaments and showing how they function as one great whole. Smith stated, for example:

> Some say the kingdom of God was not set up on the earth until the day of Pentecost; . . . but I say in the name of the Lord, that

the kingdom of God was set up on the earth from the days of Adam to the present time, whenever there has been a righteous man on earth unto whom God revealed his word and gave power and authority to administer in his name: and where there is a priest of God, a minister who has power and authority from God to administer in the ordinances of the Gospel, and officiate in the Priesthood of God, there is the kingdom of God.[11]

This concept is much more significant than simply acknowledging the importance of Old Testament communities. Ancient practices from the Hebrew Bible—at least as those practices are "imagined" and re-created in the Latter-day Saint faith—permeate Latter-day Saint religious thought and are embedded in the Church's religious practices. The ways in which the Latter-day Saint faith builds on the foundations of the Hebrew Bible can be briefly summarized under the following topics: patriarchs, prophets, and high priests; the Abrahamic covenant; revelation (leading to additional sacred texts); the temple; and the longing for Zion. All of these concepts find regular expression in Latter-day Saint worship and practice but are relatively absent from traditional Christian practices. These ideas and practices do not function as exact mirrors of ancient behaviors but rather build on ancient foundations—real or perceived—in new ways in modernity. All of these concepts are interwoven in both the Hebrew Bible and in modern Latter-day Saint practice and therefore must be discussed with considerable overlap.

PATRIARCHS, PROPHETS, AND HIGH PRIESTS

The first three topics—patriarchs, prophets, and high priests—are titles of three different types of Israelite leadership in antiquity. Following the guidance of Joseph Smith, Latter-day Saints traditionally read the pre-Sinai period leadership as one based primarily in family organizations, with the head of the family, the patriarch, functioning as the prophetic leader of God's community. Latter-day Saints thus describe Abraham as both patriarch and prophet.[12] The role of patriarch as head of the family continued even after the development of the priesthood hierarchy expressed in Exodus, Leviticus, and Numbers. Latter-day Saints also view these prophets/patriarchs functioning as high priests before the Mosaic covenant,[13] leading the community in ritual observances such as animal sacrifices performed in sacred spaces that these modern readers equate with later temple service. This view of the patriarchs functioning under the title of "high priest" is somewhat unfamiliar to many Jews, who instead understand the role of high priest as beginning with the tabernacle/temple priesthood hierarchy that was instituted with the Mosaic covenant.

With Moses, however, the role of prophet separated from and superseded the role of patriarch, uniting disparate family organizations into the broader Israelite family. Additionally, with the institution of the Mosaic covenant, the role of high priest was separated from the function of the prophet; thus Aaron was called to lead the ritual observances of the united community while the prophet continued to function outside the temple priesthood hierarchy.[14] Throughout the remainder of the Hebrew Bible, the relationship between the prophet and the high priest is not perfectly clear. Sometimes the prophet appears to work closely with the priestly organization, providing guidance and direction.[15] Other times, the prophet appears to stand almost outside the community, acting as an inspired goad to the establishment.[16] At times, as with Samuel, the role of prophet and high priest appear to reunite in one figure. Mirroring reasoning found in the Epistle to the Hebrews,[17] Latter-day Saints have typically viewed the high priest under the Mosaic covenant as functioning with Aaronic Priesthood authority, while the prophets functioned with Melchizedek Priesthood authority.[18] For Latter-day Saints, when Jesus told Peter in Matthew 16 that he would build upon "this rock" and promised that he would give Peter the keys of the kingdom of heaven, he was declaring that Peter would be the new prophet and high priest of the Christian faith, connecting these two biblical roles, and was providing Peter with both Melchizedek Priesthood and Aaronic Priesthood authority.[19] Jesus was calling Peter as his chief witness or apostle, the leader of his newly formed community.

This review of how Joseph Smith understood the Bible demonstrates how these ancient roles manifest themselves in The Church of Jesus Christ of Latter-day Saints. The Church is structured hierarchically, with the prophet standing at the head as the presiding high priest and chief apostle. Under the prophet and the First Presidency of the Church are twelve apostles, reflecting Jesus's New Testament organization that in its turn reflected the ancient covenant with the twelve tribes of Israel. All fifteen leaders, however, are not just viewed as New Testament apostles. They are sustained by Latter-day Saints as prophets, seers, and revelators, mirroring ancient descriptions of the prophetic gifts.[20] Serving under the First Presidency and the Twelve are Quorums of the Seventy, reflecting Jesus's New Testament organization,[21] which itself was connected to the "seventy elders" found in the Old Testament.[22]

Priesthood authority in the modern Church is available to all worthy males, who function in both Aaronic and Melchizedek Priesthood offices.[23] From a Latter-day Saint perspective, this fits the stated desire of God to Moses at Sinai: "And ye shall be unto me a kingdom of priests, and an holy nation" (Exodus 19:6).[24] All Latter-day Saints, females and males, whether they hold priesthood office or not, are encouraged to exercise the prophetic gift to receive guidance, knowledge, and direction from God.[25] Those with priesthood authority are to use that prophetic gift to lead and direct the work of the Church, administering authorized priesthood rituals (known by Latter-day Saints as ordinances—and similar to Catholic sacraments) and thus combining the ancient roles of prophet and priest, much as Samuel did.

The role of the patriarch has split into dual roles in the modern Church. First and most prevalently, fathers stand in the role of the ancient patriarch, functioning in general terms as the prophetic leader of the family but still operating under the organization of

God's community, as was the case for families under the Mosaic covenant. Through their priesthood authority, fathers can give priesthood blessings and inspired guidance to members of their families.[26]
Latter-day Saints believe that fathers stand as equal partners with
their wives at the head of their families.[27]

THE ABRAHAMIC COVENANT

In a second role, however, a priesthood office[28] exists for ordained
patriarchs in the modern organization of the Church, and a patriarch functions in each local division of the Church. These patriarchs
give official patriarchal blessings to members of the Church, with the
blessings recorded and held in repository by the Church. In addition
to inspired counsel understood as coming directly from God to the
Church member (mirroring the type of prophetic counsel provided
by the patriarch Jacob to his twelve sons in Genesis 49), the patriarch's primary function is to declare the lineage of the individual.
This lineage indicates through which of the twelve tribes of Israel
the individual is connected to Abraham, either by direct descent or
by adoption,[29] and through which ancestor the member can lay claim
to the promises and responsibilities of the Abrahamic covenant. This
proclamation designates the individual as a true and lineal recipient
of the early covenants made to the first patriarchs—Abraham, Isaac,
and Jacob—and brings to life those ancient lineages in the modern
Church. All Latter-day Saints who receive a patriarchal blessing
thereafter claim lineage from the tribe of Ephraim, Manasseh, Judah,
Naphtali, or one of the other tribes. This designation, a very real one
to Latter-day Saints, causes them to view themselves through the lens
of the Abrahamic covenant and the twelve tribes of Israel and helps
explain the kinship they feel with their Jewish brothers and sisters.

This, of course, is a very different approach to the Abrahamic covenant than that taken by most Christians, who typically view Jesus as
the fulfillment of that covenant. For many Christians, God's designation of the Israelites as a chosen people was subsumed in Christ, the

perfect Israelite, and all become spiritual Israelites—that is, adopted Israel—through faith in Jesus.[30] Latter-day Saints also believe that their covenants center in Christ but maintain the tenet that God's plan to bless all nations through Abraham's descendants remains in force.[31] Latter-day Saints interpret numerous prophetic statements in the Hebrew Bible as indicating that God has scattered and spread the house of Israel—including the lost ten tribes—throughout all nations, and that few people have remained untouched by that scattered and forgotten lineage over the course of the centuries.[32] One of God's grand projects, one of the ways that he plans to unite the world in the end time, is by revealing anew the importance and continued existence of that scattered people, reminding them of their covenantal identity, and gathering them back into a covenant relationship with him.[33] For Latter-day Saints, their missionaries are identifying and gathering true Israel together and bringing them to a modern organization that can reveal to them their ancient identity or adopt them into those lineages through the priesthood office of patriarch.[34]

This approach does not abandon the Christian reliance upon God/Christ, who gives the covenant its power, force, and authority. But neither does it abandon the ancient view of the Abrahamic covenant.[35] Latter-day Saints view themselves as responsible under that same covenant. Since Latter-day Saints equate Jesus Christ with the God of the Hebrew Bible, they believe that the covenantal relationship expressed in the Abrahamic covenant was essentially renewed in New Testament times but with a clarified understanding of the role and identity of the Messiah. They thus view Jews as their sisters and brothers[36] and believe that the ancient enmity between Judah (the Jews) and Ephraim (the lineage found primarily in the Church) will be healed in the last days.[37]

These viewpoints spring from Joseph Smith's prophetic efforts to unite the ancient with the modern and to turn the hearts of the children to their fathers, as taught in the words of Malachi.[38] At first contact, this type of connection with ancient lineages may seem terribly naive and presumptuous to outsiders. However, the connection is deeply meaningful and real for Latter-day Saints and in their minds allows for the functional fulfillment of ancient prophecies that appear lost or outdated to others, including the teaching that Gentiles would also be gathered and given a name and place among covenant Israel.[39]

An additional way in which the Abrahamic covenant becomes real and living for Latter-day Saints merits brief mention here. Latter-day Saint marriages, performed in temples that are built to celebrate religious rituals held sacred by them, are understood as creating an eternal bond between husband and wife that will last beyond death and throughout the eternities.[40] Children born or "sealed" into these eternal marriages are also understood as maintaining their family relationship, in some way, beyond death and into the eternities. The blessings pronounced upon the couple during the temple sealing or marriage ceremony mirror the blessings promised to Abraham and Sarah regarding their posterity and influence.[41] Latter-day Saints who are sealed in this way believe themselves full participants in the ancient promises, in effect becoming a new Abraham and a new Sarah to their posterity. Again, these beliefs may appear presumptuous and even audacious to outsiders, but they act as a stabilizing force in Latter-day Saint marriages, in which husband and wife seek to build a relationship with each other and with their children that will endure not only until death but that could remain satisfying and holy throughout all eternity. One 1999 study showed that Latter-day Saints who marry within their faith have the lowest rate of divorce in the United States after five years (13%).[42]

REVELATION (LEADING TO ADDITIONAL SCRIPTURAL TEXTS)

The Latter-day Saint understanding of the prophetic role leads to a discussion of modern-day revelation and the expanded canon of scripture in the Church. The prophetic utterance "thus saith the Lord" was powerful enough anciently that over time it was written down, leading to scripture that led to a scriptural canon.[43] If the prophetic gift (and, as Latter-day Saints see it, the prophetic office) has been restored, then it would be logical to find an expanding canon. In that sense, Joseph Smith stands in relation to the modern Church in a position similar to Moses at Sinai to the Israelites, a revealer (or restorer) of truths that help identify and unify God's community. Similar to the revelations to Moses found in Exodus and elsewhere that outline the covenantal identity of God's people, Doctrine and Covenants[44] is a record of God's revelations to Joseph Smith that show God's design for his modern Church.[45]

The first new scripture given by Joseph Smith, however, was not this compilation of his revelations but was rather the Book of Mormon. This book, published in 1829 before the new church was organized in 1830, surprisingly does not record God's words to Joseph Smith. Instead it is Smith's English translation (through the "gift and power of God")[46] of ancient records from an Israelite people who were separated from those living in the kingdom of Judah around 600 BCE, before the destruction of the First Temple. Why would an ancient record from a forgotten people be an important antecedent to the formation of the new religious faith?

Functionally, the Book of Mormon showed Smith and early Latter-day Saints how God interacts with humankind—he calls prophetic leaders with enough faith to converse with him and then uses those leaders to provide his will to groups of people invited into a covenant relationship with him. The Book of Mormon is an additional witness that God spoke to more than just those found in the land of Israel and that other divine stories occurred in antiquity (although still through connections with the Abrahamic line). For Latter-day Saints, then, the Bible ceased to be the final word of God and became instead an indication that God is willing to communicate with humankind through prophets, through the miraculous, and through temple rituals. Not only did the Book of Mormon affirm the Bible's ancient account, but it also brought that account to life in the history of a people on the opposite side of the world. These people were broken off from their homeland, but God continued to communicate with them. God's ancient covenant with Israel was affirmed in the Book of Mormon. At the same time, God's exodus pattern of leading his people to new lands of promise was brought to life in new ways. God's ability to reveal his truth in different times and to different peoples was demonstrated.

All of this laid the foundation for the modern understanding of Latter-day Saints as a new iteration of God's community, not abrogating the ancient covenant pattern but confirming it and bringing it back to life. New scripture was one of the evidences that God was working with his covenant community.[47]

THE TEMPLE

These concepts help frame the Latter-day Saint self-image and highlight other unique ways in which Church members see themselves connecting with God's ancient covenant people. Early on, Joseph Smith revealed that Latter-day Saints needed to gather to Zion, a physical location in Missouri where a temple would be built.[48] Understanding themselves as modern Israel and understanding from the Book of Mormon account that temples are part of how God works with his covenant people (rather than one structure designed to be located only in Jerusalem), Latter-day Saints built numerous temples (over time) in which they seek to interact with God.[49] It was not surprising for these temples to be places that reaffirmed ancient themes of sacrifice and covenant,[50] places where the ancient story of Adam and Eve's fall from the Garden of Eden and their efforts to return back to the presence of God were brought to life again in modernity, places where the generations were connected together,[51] places where the Abrahamic covenant was brought to life as modern husband and wife became new iterations of Abraham and Sarah through the covenant of eternal marriage, and places where ancient worship met Christian understandings of Jesus as the Messiah.[52] The temple is one of the best examples of how Joseph Smith built his prophetic view on ancient foundations, combined those foundations with Christian understandings, and provided an organization that would ground and give strength and vitality to the modern church he organized.

THE LONGING FOR ZION

Latter-day Saints were also not surprised to find a longing for Zion embedded in their self-identity. When they were driven from Missouri, the location of their first planned temple and their promised Zion,[53] they found solace in understanding themselves as modern Israel who would long for the return to Zion,[54] much as their Jewish sisters and brothers longed for their return to Jerusalem. When Joseph Smith was martyred, the Saints saw him as following a long line of biblical prophets who suffered for their teachings.[55] When they were driven from the then-current boundaries of the United States and made their home in the Rocky Mountains, they saw their journey as the exodus of modern Israel to a new promised land, led by their modern Moses—Brigham Young.[56] Their suffering seemed to them as part of the common lot of Israelites throughout time.

Latter-day Saints do not reject Jerusalem and its environs as Israel's promised land. Rather, they show a strong sense of affinity with biblical lands, modeling locations in Utah after the biblical pattern.[57] They pray for the return of Israel to their land in Jerusalem[58]—even sending an early apostle, Orson Hyde, to dedicate that land in 1841 for the return of the Jews[59]—and also pray for the New Jerusalem in Missouri. They seek to create Zion-like communities wherever they are spread throughout the earth.[60] For Latter-day Saints, as for ancient Jews, a Zion community is centered and strengthened by the sacred space that is found uniquely in the temple of God. Temples are the earthly center of the Latter-day Saint cosmos, providing stability and order to their society. Thus Latter-day Saints build temples whenever and wherever their prophet directs, seeking to build up Zion throughout the earth.

CONCLUSION

What does all of this mean for modern relations between Latter-day Saints and Jews? On the positive side, Latter-day Saints view their Jewish acquaintances as true inheritors of the Abrahamic covenant and firmly believe that the covenant is still in effect. They long to connect with and support those that they view as family members, those who have suffered at the hands of Christianity for centuries. They wish to help them prosper and, should they desire, return to their ancient lands of promise. They find these themes in their own religious thought and longing, themes that are not just of casual importance to them.

Latter-day Saints are sometimes surprised to find that their enthusiasm is mistrusted or found annoying or naively entertaining. They tell their Jewish friends that they love the Jewish religion; unfortunately, though, what that often means is that they love the Latter-day Saint version of Judaism, what Latter-day Saints have understood, re-created, and brought to life in their own ways from the Bible. They are shocked to find that their Jewish friends have beliefs that are significantly different from their own, having supposed that Jewish beliefs would be more or less similar to theirs, except for the small matter of how each group understands messianic prophecies. The "imagined Jew," beloved by most Latter-day Saints, does not prepare them for the actual living figures that they encounter, each with their own rich tapestry of beliefs, history, and developed understandings.

A text message I received from a relative painfully demonstrates this reality and the challenges to healthy Jewish–Latter-day Saint interfaith understandings. I had helped the daughter of a Jewish acquaintance find a place to stay in my relative's home during an internship in Utah. This text will be humorous or even shocking to most who have at least a small understanding of Judaism, but it might feel frustratingly familiar to Jews who have lived in Utah: "Do Jews not believe in a heaven? I might have not understood [the Jewish girl] correctly, but that is what I took from our discussion yesterday.

Anyway, it surprised me. And I always thought they believed in a Savior the way we did, just that he hasn't come yet. The Jesus she believes in is clearly not the Jesus I believe in. And no resurrection as well. Don't most Christians believe they will get their bodies back? Anyway, it has caused lot of questions."[61]

There is a surprising number of misunderstandings embedded in this short message from my kind-hearted, sincere relative. She enthusiastically expected to find a new Jewish friend and rejoice in just how similar the beliefs of two long-lost relatives turned out to be. Instead she discovered that modern Judaism has kept its traditions and beliefs alive on very different paths than she could have expected from her own religious beliefs. Second, she may still not realize that her own Latter-day Saint viewpoints reflect only one particular interpretation of a biblical foundation that has been brought to life in her church. Resolving those two issues is why Latter-day Saint–Jewish dialogue is so critical. The enthusiasm exists and can form a foundation. That foundation must lead to much more solid information. In the meantime, Latter-day Saints will remain indebted to early biblical Jews and will continue to feel that indebtedness to those who provided a sturdy foundation for their modern religious practices.

NOTES

1. See Benedict Anderson, *Imagined Communities: Reflections on the Origin and Spread of Nationalism* (New York: Verso, 1983), 15.
2. See Anderson, *Imagined Communities*, 4. Anderson discusses the desire of modern nations to connect their history to the histories of ancient empires and to see themselves as a continuation of that empire.
3. See Anderson, *Imagined Communities*, 6–7.
4. See Ithamar Gruenwald, "The Relevance of Myth for Understanding Ritual in Ancient Judaism," in *The Annual of Rabbinic Judaism: Ancient, Medieval, and Modern*, ed. Alan J. Avery-Peck (Leiden: Brill, 2000), 3:3–17; see also Ronald S. Hendel, "Genesis, Book of," in *Anchor-Yale*

Bible Dictionary, ed. David Noel Freedman (New York: Doubleday, 1992), 2:935–37.

5. For a discussion of the shift from Second Temple Judaism to rabbinic Judaism, see Shaye J. D. Cohen, "Judaism to the Mishnah: 135–220 C.E.," in *Christianity and Rabbinic Judaism: A Parallel History of Their Origins and Early Development*, ed. Hershel Shanks (Washington, DC: Biblical Archaeological Society, 1992), 195–223.

6. See G. K. Beale, *A Handbook on the New Testament Use of the Old Testament: Exegesis and Interpretation* (Grand Rapids, MI: Baker Academic, 2012), 97.

7. See D. L. Bock, "Scripture Citing Scripture," in *Interpreting the New Testament Text*, ed. D. L. Bock and B. M. Fanning (Wheaton: Crossway, 2006), 261–64; and Shaye J. D. Cohen, *From the Maccabees to the Mishnah* (Philadelphia: Westminster Press, 1987), 166–68.

8. See Anderson, *Imagined Communities*, 5–6.

9. As described by Jewish commentators Amy-Jill Levine and Marc Zvi Brettler, "Supersessionism (also sometimes called "replacement theology") is the claim, expressed in its starkest form, that by rejecting Jesus and then killing him, the Jews have lost their role as a people in covenant with God, and that the promises made to Abraham now apply only to the followers of Jesus. In other words, this view regards Jews and Judaism as having been superseded by or replaced with Christians and Christianity." *Jewish Annotated New Testament* (New York: Oxford University Press, 2011), xii.

10. See Philip Barlow, "To Mend a Fractured Reality: Joseph Smith's Project," *Journal of Mormon History* 38, no. 3 (2012): 28–50.

11. See Joseph Smith, "History, 1838–1856, volume D-1 [1 August 1842–1 July 1843] [addenda]," p. 4 [addenda], The Joseph Smith Papers, http://josephsmithpapers.org/paper-summary/history-1838-1856 -volume-d-1-1-august-1842-1-july-1843/285.

12. "Abraham: . . . A prophet of the Lord with whom the Lord made eternal covenants, through which all the nations of the earth are blessed." Guide to the Scriptures, "Abraham," https://churchofjesuschrist.org /scriptures/gs/abraham.

13. "Finding there was greater happiness and peace and rest for me, I [Abraham] sought for the blessings of the fathers, and the right whereunto I should be ordained to administer the same; . . . desiring . . . to be a father of many nations, a prince of peace, . . . I became a rightful heir, a High Priest, holding the right belonging to the fathers" (Abraham 1:2). The Book of Abraham was provided by Joseph Smith in 1842 and has become a canonized scriptural account for Latter-day Saints. The book, in which Abraham speaks in the first person, amplifies the biblical account of Abraham's life. See "Translation and Historicity of the Book of Abraham," originally published July 2014, https://churchofjesuschrist.org/topics/translation-and-historicity -of-the-book-of-abraham.

14. For the first biblical mention of the role of high priest, see Leviticus 21:10. See Deuteronomy 18:15–22 for the continued importance of the prophetic role.

15. See, for example, Nathan's role in the anointing of Solomon as king in 1 Kings 1:44–45.

16. See, for example, the critique in Isaiah 1:10–15.

17. See Hebrews 5:1–6, 10; 7:1–11.

18. See also Doctrine and Covenants 84:5–18. The Latter-day Saint understanding of the title "high priest" is more complicated than discussed in this chapter's generalized overview. This complexity includes an expression of the title under Melchizedek Priesthood authority, as with Abraham and modern Latter-day Saint high priests, and its expression under the Aaronic Priesthood, as with Aaron under the Mosaic covenant, a role that Latter-day Saints might view as corresponding most closely to the Latter-day Saint Aaronic Priesthood office of bishop.

19. See Shon D. Hopkin, "Peter, Stones, and Seers," in *The Ministry of Peter the Chief Apostle*, ed. Frank Judd, Eric Huntsman, and Shon Hopkin (Provo, UT: Religious Studies Center, Brigham Young University, 2014), 103–25.

20. See Doctrine and Covenants 21:1. Joseph Smith's use of the Urim and Thummim, also called seer stones, to gain revelation from God is

another interesting connection to the role of the high priest in antiquity that can be mentioned only briefly here. For the ancient use of the Urim and Thummim, see Exodus 28:30; Leviticus 8:8; Numbers 27:21; Deuteronomy 33:8; 1 Samuel 28:6; Ezra 2:63; and Nehemiah 7:65.

21. See Luke 10:1, 17.

22. See Exodus 24:1; Numbers 11:16.

23. The priesthood offices of the Church again demonstrate both Old and New Testament titles. In the Aaronic Priesthood, the offices are deacon (New Testament), teacher (primarily New Testament), priest (Old Testament), and bishop (New Testament). In the Melchizedek Priesthood, the offices are elder (Old Testament and New Testament), high priest (Old Testament), seventy (Old and New Testament), patriarch (Old Testament), and apostle (New Testament).

24. Since Latter-day Saints still use the King James Version as their official Bible version, all biblical passages quoted in this essay will be from the KJV unless otherwise noted.

25. See Revelation 19:10, which says, "For the testimony of Jesus is the spirit of prophecy."

26. See "Lesson 11: The Father as Patriarch," in *Duties and Blessings of the Priesthood: Basic Manual for Priesthood Holders, Part B* (Salt Lake City: The Church of Jesus Christ of Latter-day Saints, 2000), 96–104, https://churchofjesuschrist.org/manual/duties-and-blessings-of-the -priesthood-basic-manual-for-priesthood-holders-part-b/duties -and-blessings-of-the-priesthood.

27. "In these sacred responsibilities, fathers and mothers are obligated to help one another as equal partners." "The Family: A Proclamation to the World," first presented September 1995, https://churchofjesus christ.org/bc/content/shared/content/english/pdf/36035_000_24 _family.pdf.

28. The term *priesthood office* refers to a specific type of priesthood ordination in the Church, with accompanying responsibilities and authority. Some priesthood offices, such as the offices of deacon (usually ages 12–13), teacher (usually ages 14–15), priest (usually ages 16–17), and elder (usually ages 18 and over), are held by almost all men in the

Church at some point in their lives. Others, such as the offices of high priest, patriarch, bishop, seventy, and apostle, are held by relatively few.

29. See "Patriarchal Blessings," https://churchofjesuschrist.org/topics /patriarchal-blessings. "A patriarchal blessing includes a declaration of lineage, stating that the person is of the house of Israel—a descendant of Abraham, belonging to a specific tribe of Jacob. . . . It does not matter if a person's lineage in the house of Israel is through bloodlines or by adoption. Church members are counted as a descendant of Abraham and an heir to all the promises and blessings contained in the Abrahamic covenant."

30. See note 9 above on supersessionism. See also Hebrews 8:13 and Romans 9:8.

31. Responding at least in part to this Christian view of the Jewish people, the Book of Mormon proclaims, "O ye Gentiles [i.e., Christians], have ye remembered the Jews, mine ancient covenant people? Nay; but ye have cursed them, and have hated them, and have not sought to recover them. But behold, I will return all these things upon your own heads; for I the Lord have not forgotten my people" (2 Nephi 29:5).

32. For some of the scriptural texts used by Latter-day Saints to support the belief of a near-universal scattering and sifting of Israel among the nations of the world, see the following: Leviticus 26:33 ("I will scatter you among the heathen"); Deuteronomy 28:25 ("The Lord shall cause thee to be smitten before thine enemies: thou shalt be removed into all the kingdoms of the earth"); Deuteronomy 28:37 ("And thou shalt become an astonishment, a proverb, and a byword, among all nations whither the Lord shall lead thee"); Deuteronomy 28:64 ("And the Lord shall scatter thee among all people, from the one end of the earth even unto the other"); Amos 9:9 ("I will sift the house of Israel among all nations"); and Zechariah 10:9 ("I will sow them among the people"). And from the Book of Mormon, see 1 Nephi 22:3–4 ("The house of Israel, sooner or later, will be scattered upon all the face of the earth, and also among all nations. And behold, there are many who are already lost from the knowledge of those who are at Jerusalem. Yea, the more part of all the tribes have been led away; and they

are scattered to and fro upon the isles of the sea; and whither they are none of us knoweth, save that we know that they have been led away"). This collection of scriptures is found in Bruce R. McConkie, *Mormon Doctrine* (Salt Lake City: Bookcraft, 1966), 679.

33. This gathering is first viewed as spiritual, as individuals are brought into a covenant relationship with God, and eventually as physical, as individuals and groups are gathered to a land of inheritance during a millennial era of peace. For a few of the scriptural texts used by Latter-day Saints to support the belief of a miraculous gathering of Israel from among all the nations of the world, see the following: Deuteronomy 30:1–4 ("And it shall come to pass, when all these things are come upon thee, . . . and thou shalt call them to mind among all the nations, whither the Lord thy God hath driven thee, and shalt return unto the Lord thy God . . . that then the Lord thy God will turn thy captivity, and have compassion upon thee, and will return and gather thee from all the nations, whither the Lord thy God hath scattered thee. If any of thine be driven out unto the outmost parts of heaven, from thence will the Lord thy God gather thee, and from thence will he fetch thee"); Jeremiah 16:14–16 ("Therefore, behold, the days come, saith the Lord, that it shall no more be said, The Lord liveth, that brought up the children of Israel out of the land of Egypt; but, The Lord liveth, that brought up the children of Israel from the land of the north, and from all the lands whither he had driven them. . . . Behold, I will send for many fishers, saith the Lord, and they shall fish them; and after will I send for many hunters, and they shall hunt them from every mountain, and from every hill, and out of the holes of the rocks"); Jeremiah 23:3 ("I will gather the remnant of my flock out of all countries whither I have driven them"); Ezekiel 34:11–16 ("For thus saith the Lord God; Behold, I, even I, will both search my sheep, and seek them out. . . . And [I] will deliver them out of all places where they have been scattered in the cloudy and dark day. And I will bring them out from the people, and gather them from the countries. . . . I will seek that which was lost, and bring again that which was driven away").

34. Regarding the Latter-day Saint view of Israelites miraculously spring-
ing forth from forgotten lineages, see Isaiah 54:1–3: "Sing, O barren,
thou that didst not bear; break forth into singing, and cry aloud, thou
that didst not travail with child: for more are the children of the desolate than the children of the married wife, saith the Lord. Enlarge the
place of thy tent, and let them stretch forth the curtains of thine hab-
itations: spare not, lengthen thy cords, and strengthen thy stakes; for
thou shalt break forth on the right hand and on the left; and thy seed
shall inherit the Gentiles, and make the desolate cities to be inhabited."

35. For the conflation of these two views, see the title page of the Book
of Mormon: "Which is to show unto the remnant of the house of
Israel what great things the Lord hath done for their fathers; and that
they may know the covenants of the Lord, that they are not cast off
forever—And also to the convincing of the Jew and Gentile that Jesus
is the Christ, the Eternal God, manifesting himself unto all nations."

36. For a more comprehensive discussion of the Latter-day Saint understanding of the Jewish tradition and people, see Jared W. Ludlow,
Andrew C. Reed, and Shon D. Hopkin, "Supersessionsim and Latter-
day Saint Thought: An Appraisal," 89–137, in this volume.

37. See Isaiah 11:13: "The envy also of Ephraim shall depart, and the
adversaries of Judah shall be cut off: Ephraim shall not envy Judah,
and Judah shall not vex Ephraim." See also Ezekiel 37:19–22: "Thus
saith the Lord God; Behold, I will take the stick of Joseph, which is
in the hand of Ephraim, and the tribes of Israel his fellows, and will
put them with him, even with the stick of Judah, and make them one
stick, and they shall be one in mine hand. . . . And say unto them, Thus
saith the Lord God; Behold, I will take the children of Israel from
among the heathen, whither they be gone, and will gather them on
every side, and bring them into their own land: And I will make them
one nation in the land . . . and they shall be no more two nations, neither shall they be divided into two kingdoms any more at all."

38. See Malachi 4:5–6. This is one of the earliest texts referenced (as
early as 1823) in Joseph Smith's ministry and teachings. See Doctrine
and Covenants 2:1–3.

39. See Isaiah 56:3–8: "Neither let the son of the stranger, that hath joined himself to the Lord, speak, saying, The Lord hath utterly separated me from his people. . . . Even unto them will I give in mine house and within my walls a place and a name better than of sons and of daughters: I will give them an everlasting name, that shall not be cut off. Also the sons of the stranger, that join themselves to the Lord, . . . and taketh hold of my covenant; even them will I bring to my holy mountain, and make them joyful in my house of prayer. . . . The Lord God which gathereth the outcasts of Israel saith, Yet will I gather others to him, beside those that are gathered unto him."

40. See Doctrine and Covenants 131:1–4; see also "Marriage," Gospel Topics, https://churchofjesuschrist.org/topics/marriage.

41. See Genesis 22:16–18.

42. See Bob Mims, "Mormons: High Conservatism, Low Divorce, Big Growth," *Salt Lake Tribune*, March 6, 1999.

43. In the King James Version of the Old Testament, the phrase "thus saith the Lord" is found 415 times, including 10 times in Exodus and 349 times in the prophetic books.

44. Doctrine and Covenants contains 138 revelations given mostly to Joseph Smith (but includes a few given to succeeding prophets) that are viewed as canonical scripture by the Latter-day Saints, supplementing but not supplanting the biblical text.

45. Although rarely, if ever, used by current Church leaders, the phrase "thus saith the Lord" was frequently used in the early revelations to Joseph Smith, and is found sixty-two times in the Doctrine and Covenants.

46. See the title page of the Book of Mormon.

47. In 2 Nephi 29:1–10, a Book of Mormon prophet overtly demonstrates the importance of building on ancient foundations in order to give power and voice to a future religious group: "But behold, there shall be many—at that day when I shall proceed to do a marvelous work among them, that I may remember my covenants which I have made unto the children of men, that I may set my hand again the second time to recover my people, which are of the house of Israel.

... And because my words shall hiss forth—many of the Gentiles shall say: A Bible! A Bible! We have got a Bible, and there cannot be any more Bible. But thus saith the Lord God: O fools, they shall have a Bible; and it shall proceed forth from the Jews, mine ancient covenant people. And what thank they the Jews for the Bible which they receive from them? Yea, what do the Gentiles mean? Do they remember the travails, and the labors, and the pains of the Jews, and their diligence unto me, in bringing forth salvation unto the Gentiles? O ye Gentiles, have ye remembered the Jews, mine ancient covenant people? Nay; but ye have cursed them, and have hated them, and have not sought to recover them. . . . Know ye not that there are more nations than one? Know ye not that I, the Lord your God . . . bring forth my word unto the children of men, yea, even upon all the nations of the earth? . . . And I do this that I may prove unto many that I am the same yesterday, today, and forever; and that I speak forth my words according to mine own pleasure. And because that I have spoken one word ye need not suppose that I cannot speak another; for my work is not yet finished; neither shall it be until the end of man, neither from that time henceforth and forever."

48. See Doctrine and Covenants 42:35–36.

49. As of January 2020, there are over two hundred temples throughout the world either built or under planning and construction. See "Temple List," https://churchofjesuschrist.org/temples/list.

50. The Book of Mormon explains, using reasoning similar to that found in Hebrews 8–9, that blood or animal sacrifice is fulfilled in the offering of Jesus Christ (see Alma 34:13–14). The theme of sacrifice in Latter-day Saint temples centers on a willingness to give up anything of mortal interest that God might require.

51. Again, see the prophecy in Malachi 4:5–6, which is one of the earliest texts referenced (as early as 1823) in Joseph Smith's ministry and teachings (Doctrine and Covenants 2:1–3). "Behold, I will send you Elijah the prophet before the coming of the great and dreadful day of the Lord: And he shall turn the heart of the fathers to the children, and the heart of the children to their fathers, lest I come and smite the earth with a curse" (Malachi 4:5–6).

52. For a thorough discussion of the Latter-day Saint understanding and use of temples, see "Temple List," https://churchofjesuschrist.org /temples/list. The "About Temples" tab contains "Prophetic Teachings on Temples," "History of Temples," "Why Latter-day Saints Build Temples," "Inside Temples," "Draw Nearer to Christ," "Families and the Temple," "Ordinances and Covenants," and "Common Questions," demonstrating in the section titles alone the connections suggested in this essay.

53. See Doctrine and Covenants 57:3. See also the promise in Doctrine and Covenants 38:18–20: "I hold forth and deign to give unto you greater riches, even a land of promise, a land flowing with milk and honey . . . and I will give it unto you for the land of your inheritance, if you seek it with all your hearts. And this shall be my covenant with you, ye shall have it for the land of your inheritance, and for the inheritance of your children forever, while the earth shall stand."

54. See the promise in Doctrine and Covenants 100:13: "Zion shall be redeemed, although she is chastened for a little season." See a similar promise in Doctrine and Covenants 136:18: "Zion shall be redeemed in mine own due time." Latter-day Saints understand their loss of Zion as a consequence of both intense and unjustified persecution, but also as a consequence of their own rejection of God's commandments: "Verily I say unto you, concerning your brethren who have been afflicted, and persecuted, and cast out from the land of their inheritance—I, the Lord, have suffered the affliction to come upon them, wherewith they have been afflicted, in consequence of their transgressions" (Doctrine and Covenants 101:1–2).

55. See Doctrine and Covenants 136:34–36.

56. See the revelation received by Brigham Young to prepare for the trek west, in which the travelers are designated "the Camp of Israel." "The Word and Will of the Lord concerning the Camp of Israel in their journeyings to the West. . . . And this shall be our covenant—that we will walk in all the ordinances of the Lord" (Doctrine and Covenants 136:1, 4).

57. After they arrived in their new home in Utah, Latter-day Saints found that a body of fresh water (Utah Lake) flowed north into the saltiest

body of water on the Western Hemisphere (the Great Salt Lake). Their main temple was built just to the east of this body of salt water, and the river connecting the two lakes was named the Jordan River. The Utah map, of course, is an inverted model of the Holy Land, in which the River Jordan in the north flows into the Dead Sea in the south, and the temple was built just to the west of the saltiest large body of water in the world. Other city names such as Enoch, Ephraim, and Moab dot the Utah map, along with numerous city names taken from the Book of Mormon, such as Nephi, Lehi, and Manti.

58. See Joseph Smith's prayer at the dedication of the first Latter-day Saint temple in Kirtland, Ohio, in 1836: "But thou knowest that thou hast a great love for the children of Jacob, who have been scattered upon the mountains for a long time, in a cloudy and dark day. We therefore ask thee to have mercy upon the children of Jacob, that Jerusalem, from this hour, may begin to be redeemed; and the yoke of bondage may begin to be broken off from the house of David; and the children of Judah may begin to return to the lands which thou didst give to Abraham, their father" (Doctrine and Covenants 109:61–64).

59. For a description of Orson Hyde's mission and dedicatory prayer on the Mount of Olives, offered at a time when the young Church of Jesus Christ was struggling to survive, see David B. Galbraith, "Orson Hyde's 1841 Mission to the Holy Land," *Ensign*, October 1991, https://churchofjesuschrist.org/ensign/1991/10/orson-hydes-1841-mission-to-the-holy-land.

60. Following a definition provided in a scriptural text revealed to Joseph Smith known as the Book of Moses (an amplification or restoration of the biblical account of Genesis), Latter-day Saints use *Zion* to refer to God's people as much as to a specific location. According to Moses 7:18–19, "And the Lord called his people Zion, because they were of one heart and one mind, and dwelt in righteousness; and there was no poor among them. . . . And it came to pass in [Enoch's] days, that he built a city that was called the City of Holiness, even Zion."

61. Personal communication with the author, February 2016.

SCRIPTURE

PART TWO

In part two, "Scripture," scholars examine the ways in which scriptural interpretation plays out in the context of Jewish–Latter-day Saint dialogue. Thomas Wayment and Joshua Garroway use Latter-day Saint and Jewish interpretations of Paul to examine how our approach to this central figure in the New Testament might be understood through the lens of this dialogue. As was true of many of these subjects, the dialogue session in which these two papers were originally presented revealed that sometimes the most difficult discussions are held within a tradition and not between two traditions.

Drawing upon the foundation laid by Wayment and Garroway, three scholars detail and highlight the contours of historical Latter-day Saint thought on Jews and Judaism and explore how supersessionist thinking is both noticeably present but not always stridently developed in Latter-day Saint theological discourse. In response, Garroway offers his interpretation, as a New Testament scholar and rabbi, on supersessionism as a broad religious attitude and articulates why Latter-day Saint supersessionism is unique from other forms of the phenomenon within Christianity.

3

LATTER-DAY SAINT ENGAGEMENT WITH PAUL: STATUS QUAESTIONIS

THOMAS A. WAYMENT

Latter-day Saint scholarship on Paul has its origins in the translation of the Book of Mormon and in the twentieth-century debates about Paul and not, for example, in the New Testament or the academic discussion about Paul's foundational role in establishing Christianity.[1] Latter-day Saint scholars have promoted a reading of Paul that places him squarely within existing ecclesiastical structures organized by Peter and the first New Testament disciples that already anticipated a Gentile mission in Jesus's day. Jesus's disciples were required, according to the Latter-day Saint view, to delay the evangelization of Gentiles until after the resurrection of Jesus. Following this line of thinking, Paul's Damascus experience and mission strategy are then interpreted as logical steps in a sequence of an expanding church, organized to promote Jesus's teachings and belief in him as Messiah. One way to define the Latter-day Saint worldview is that it views Judaism and Christianity as sequentially connected with a shared purpose and worldview. Pauline scholars will see in this brief outline themes and topics already discussed and debated in the New Perspective.

To facilitate this discussion, the New Perspective on Paul is defined as a movement to avoid oversimplification in describing and engaging the intersection between Christianity and Judaism in the first century. The New Perspective focuses on Paul's Damascus vision in the context of Christian mission strategies and attempts to convert Jews to the new messianic faith. The vision is of central importance because it has been defined as a conversion away from, or a call to, and therefore is of major significance to defining the intent of the early Christian mission. To put it in other words, the New Perspective problematizes the notion that Paul converted away from his ancestral religion and has raised the important question of whether Paul, upon seeing the vision of the Lord, thereby expanded his beliefs or abandoned his tradition.

Today, scholars often articulate several different movements within Judaism or even assert several different Judaisms. E. P. Sanders was among the first to call attention to the notion that Pauline scholars in particular had interpreted Paul against a simplistic understanding of Judaism as a monolith.[2] Sanders pushed the Pauline conversation to differentiate between Hellenistic, Palestinian, and Judean forms of Judaism, which opened the way for the radical consideration that Paul remained Jewish his entire life—a Hellenistic Jew—and that the Gentile mission was part of an intentional strategy to evangelize Gentiles.

From the existing literature produced by Latter-day Saint scholars, the following broad categories of engagement with Pauline studies emerge as a reasonable general framework under which a conversation could begin. First, Paul's letters shaped early Latter-day Saint theology in important ways, particularly in the development of the Articles of Faith, an early Latter-day Saint statement of belief, and in the text of the Book of Mormon. Second, while Paul as a historical figure has been a point of interest for Latter-day Saint scholars, detailed exegetical work on his corpus of letters has not been at the forefront of that discussion. This approach will be shown to be foundational to Latter-day Saint interest in Paul because his letters have been used as critical building blocks in establishing the Latter-day Saint narrative of restoration and ecclesiastical authority, while the Pauline language of salvation-righteousness has largely been derived from modern Latter-day Saint works such as the Book of Mormon and the Doctrine and Covenants—the canonized collection of Joseph Smith's revelations from the 1830s and 1840s. Finally, a Latter-day Saint reading of Paul, inasmuch as one can be established, has consistently pushed against the findings of the New Perspective. The structure of this paper will be to engage these three categories in an attempt to quantify Latter-day Saint interest in Paul and thereby provide a starting conversation point of Latter-day Saint views concerning Judaism. In each of these three categories, I also propose to discuss some of the difficulties that have forced Latter-day Saint scholars to limit their engagement with Paul.

PAUL'S LETTERS AS A SOURCE FOR LATTER-DAY SAINT THEOLOGICAL DEVELOPMENT

One of Joseph Smith's strongest doctrinal statements comes from an 1842 letter written to John Wentworth of the *Chicago Democrat* that reported his own sketch of the "faith of the Latter-day Saints."[3] That letter set forth a series of creed-like statements that were themselves founded upon a tractate authored by Orson Pratt, an early Latter-day Saint leader, two years earlier.[4] The Pratt tractate draws fewer times on Pauline wording—although it references Romans 5:18 and Galatians 1:8—than Smith's Wentworth letter, and therefore the decidedly Pauline character of the Articles of Faith may be attributed to Smith.

Although the Wentworth letter offers only a limited description of Church beliefs, the thirteen declarations capture many of the ideas that Joseph Smith felt were unique to the Latter-day Saint movement. Those foundational, and later canonical, Articles of Faith are fundamentally Pauline in nature.[5] For example, the thirteenth article of faith declares, "We believe in being honest, true, chaste, benevolent, virtuous, and in doing good to all men; indeed, we may say that we follow the admonition of Paul—We believe all things, we hope all things, we have endured many things, and hope to be able to endure all things. If there is anything virtuous, lovely, or of good report or praiseworthy, we seek after these things." The statement is a mixture of language from 1 Corinthians 13:7 and Philippians 4:8, with expansions by Joseph Smith, one of which declares, "we have endured many things, and hope to be able to endure all things." The use of Paul's letters in composing an article of faith for the fledgling faith exemplifies how Pauline language would shape early Latter-day Saint theology. In the process of engaging Paul's letters, the language of virtue is connected with suffering, and thus this is interpreted as "chaste, virtuous, and . . . good" with respect to their recent suffering and persecution. Paul's words offered comfort and justification for the lived early Latter-day Saint experience.[6]

According to the *Encyclopedia of Mormonism,* "The language of Paul is discernible in most of the Articles of Faith (e.g., in A of F 4 on the first principles of the gospel [cf. Heb. 6:1–2]; in A of F 5 on ordination to the priesthood [cf. 1 Tim. 4:14]; in A of F 6 on the officers of the Primitive Church [cf. Eph. 4:11]; and in A of F 7 on the gifts of the spirit [cf. 1 Cor. 12:8–12]), and part of the sublime hymn to charity (1 Cor. 13:4–8) is also found in the Book of Mormon (Moro. 7:45–46)."[7] The parallels reveal shared scriptural language between the Articles of Faith and the Pauline, deutero-Pauline letters, and Hebrews, but little exegetical work has been done to unravel the intertextual details.[8] This merging of Pauline language with the development of Latter-day Saint theological concepts is prevalent also in the Book of Mormon and the Doctrine and Covenants. In a simple sense, some of Paul's letters provided language that helped Joseph Smith declare his own theological uniqueness.

On a more profound level, the Book of Mormon draws upon Pauline language and concepts, and as a result creates a rich tapestry of echoes, allusions, borrowed wording, and shared concepts. The Book of Mormon openly engages Pauline ideas while shaping them and allowing its own narratives to be shaped by Pauline concepts. For example, the Pauline language is unmistakable in Mosiah 16:10: "Even this mortal shall put on immortality, and this corruption shall put on incorruption." The passage closely follows the wording of the King James translation of 1 Corinthians 15:53: "For this corruptible must put on incorruption, and this mortal must put on immortality." Similar language occurs in other Book of Mormon passages like Alma 5:15 and Mormon 6:21, but such shared language presents Latter-day Saint scholars with a significant interpretive obstacle: if it is conceded that the language is Pauline in origin, then questions arise regarding the historical origins of the Book of Mormon. For the Latter-day Saint scholar, admitting that the language is Pauline is akin to acknowledging that the Book of Mormon is not an ancient work but rather a nineteenth-century production dependent upon the King James translation. But by rejecting the Pauline origins of the parallels, scholars overlook an opportunity to engage Paul and his letters.[9] Nicholas Frederick's recent work on New Testament language in the Book of Mormon has sought a way forward through this difficult terrain. And with literally hundreds of such parallels, Frederick's intertextual work may potentially yield valuable results.[10]

Paul's letters also make a significant appearance in the Doctrine and Covenants, the canonized collection of Joseph Smith's early revelations given as directives from the Lord. In them a general usage pattern emerges.[11] References to the books of Romans, 1–2 Corinthians, and Ephesians dominate with parallel language to single verses in Colossians 1:16; 1 Thessalonians 5:2; 1 Timothy 4:1; 2 Timothy 4:8; and Hebrews 12:23 appearing; Latter-day Saints accept all these writings as Pauline.[12] Usage patterns in the Doctrine and Covenants reveal that borrowing of soteriological language is infrequent, while the language of spiritual gifts and sealing tends to dominate.[13] Of particular interest is the way the Doctrine and Covenants engages 2 Corinthians 12:9, "And if you do these last commandments of mine, which I have given you, the gates of hell shall not prevail against you; *for my grace is sufficient for you*, and you shall be lifted up at the last day" (Doctrine and Covenants 17:8; emphasis added; compare 18:31). In the context of 2 Corinthians, the phrase was used in connection with Paul's "thorn in the flesh" (2 Corinthians 12:7), which was not relieved or taken away through prayer, at which point Paul declared that the Lord spoke to him, "My grace is sufficient for thee." The Lord extended his grace to Paul to remedy a prayer that had been answered negatively.[14] The Doctrine and Covenants turns this idea into a statement on works leading to righteousness, explicitly linking the commandments of God to receiving grace. The second usage of the same passage demonstrates an even clearer picture of works-righteousness: "And now I speak unto you, the Twelve—Behold, my grace is sufficient for you; you must walk uprightly before me and sin not" (Doctrine and Covenants 18:31). The coupling of *sin* and *grace* is quite removed from its 2 Corinthians context, but it demonstrates a strong grace-sin connection in early Latter-day Saint theology.

Pauline language is deeply embedded in the theological narratives of the Latter-day Saints, but recovering them has proven to be somewhat of an obstacle. One possible way forward in this discussion would be to acknowledge that Joseph Smith was more personally influential in the translation process, with the realization that the modern reader is engaging the King James translation of the Bible through the words of the translator. Open engagement with Pauline language in early Latter-day Saint teachings and revelations is sorely needed. Language from 1–2 Corinthians, Ephesians, and Romans dominates the parallels, and in this admittedly cursory examination of the issue, it seems that Pauline language in the Book of Mormon focuses on salvation, the fall of Adam, and works-righteousness.

PAUL IN HISTORY: PAUL THE APOSTLE

To date, the most widely sold work on Paul written to a Latter-day Saint audience has been Sidney Sperry's *Paul's Life and Letters*, published in 1955 and frequently cited in Church curricular materials.[15] The work is episodic, detailing Paul's life according to the major missionary journeys and placing discussions of the letters within a framework of a contextualized mission strategy. Each of the letters is diagrammed with brief commentary, and the study includes travel plans documenting the journeys of Paul. The work contains no footnotes, but a short bibliography at the end contains some curious omissions, particularly given the state of Pauline scholarship when he wrote.[16] Sperry's sources tend to side unequivocally with the very ideas that gave rise to the New Perspective as presented by E. P. Sanders in *Paul and Palestinian Judaism*, although it is difficult to determine precisely where those sources shaped his narrative.[17] Sperry's work was the watershed moment for Latter-day Saint historians who used the short study as an invitation to critically sift through the historical life of Paul and to examine the meaning of those writings through Restoration scripture.[18] But Sperry's publication and lack of academic engagement also seemed to point to a future when Latter-day Saint scholars avoided the academic discussion and turned inward toward their own Latter-day Saint community and interests.[19]

A more recent stage in the development of a subtle, growing interest in Paul is the intense scrutiny placed on Acts 15, referred to by Latter-day Saint scholars as the Jerusalem Conference, where matters of Jewish law and precedent were discussed in the context of the Pauline Gentile mission. Acts 15 is taken in these studies as indicative of Pauline influence on ecclesiastical decision-making and the beginnings of a church-wide rift.[20] Those who have probed this question argue that in the growth of the early church, the Gentile mission caused a deep rift between Gentile and Jewish factions, a rift that would set the stage for a general apostasy. For example, Robert

Matthews alludes to this when he says, "The decision of the council was favorable to Paul, Barnabas, Titus, and the Gentiles who were already in the Church and who would yet join, but it also left the Jewish members free to continue the practice of the law of Moses if they wished to."[21] Frank Judd makes obvious what Matthews implied: "The inability of some early disciples to accept new revelation concerning the Gentiles, however, would fracture the young Church."[22] But these same studies avoid investigating one of the fundamental issues of interest in articulating an overall approach to Paul: Was Peter the head of an organized church structure that approached questions of Gentile inclusion from an apostolic-ecclesiastical vantage point? Certainly, a significant debate is reported in Acts 15, but did the debate originate between competing factions within a church organization, or was Paul's view of Gentile inclusion competing with James's Jewish-centered organizational strategy? In other words, was the issue one of method or of factions competing to lead the early Christian movement?

The Damascus event is at the center of the debate in Pauline studies for Latter-day Saints, with special emphasis on questions such as Paul's supposed departure from his ancestral faith, his call or conversion as a gateway to a Gentile mission, and his own reporting of the event as a pivotal moment in his acceptance of Jesus Christ as the Messiah. Latter-day Saint scholars have interpreted the Damascus event by situating it on a trajectory beginning with Jesus's command to *not* evangelize Gentiles (Matthew 10:5), which was a temporary injunction that would later be resolved through Cornelius's conversion and Paul's conversion on his way to Damascus. Of primary concern is an interest to fit Paul into the apostleship and to create a link of continuity between the twelve disciples of Jesus's ministry and Paul as a newly called disciple to evangelize the Gentiles. Frank Judd draws this theme out forcefully with reference to the Gentile mission: "The Savior, however, never intended the disciples to permanently withhold the gospel from Gentiles, but was informing them that they were not to teach them *at that* time."[23] Thus the Gentile mission cannot have been a Pauline innovation, but instead it was always part of a linear proselytizing plan to take the gospel to Jews first and Gentiles later, following Paul's pattern in Acts. The Latter-day Saint viewpoint thus forces the question of when to begin the Gentile mission onto the historical Jesus, who had envisioned a time after his death when Gentiles would be permitted to enter the faith.[24]

The theme of ecclesiastical and doctrinal continuity between Jesus, Peter, and Paul has dominated the Latter-day Saint hermeneutic. This is important for a religion that declares itself to be similar to or even the same as the "Primitive Church."[25] As a fundamental concern, belief in organizational and practical continuity stretching from Jesus's day to the present has clearly shaped the way Latter-day Saint scholars interpret Paul. This approach has led to an increased interest in Acts 15 as the beginning point for the modern church, when the first signs of fracture resulting from ecclesiastical decisions hinted at a general church-wide apostasy. Indeed, Latter-day Saint scholarship on Acts 15, when coupled with the rebellion or apostasy language in 2 Thessalonians 2:3–5, demonstrates a continued interest to establish a model of an early Christian church in distress that was struggling with a Jewish-Gentile divide. But such a reading of Paul is also confirmed in the general patterns of usage of Paul's letters by Latter-day Saint scholars.

In a recent study on how the Pauline epistles have been used by ecclesiastical leaders, ten passages from Paul's letters were identified as being the most frequently referenced.[26] This evidence demonstrates a broad interest by Latter-day Saints leaders to draw upon Pauline literature to bolster current doctrinal positions, and these interests are parallel to the work being done by Latter-day Saint scholars. The study did not account for authorship questions relating to the deutero-Pauline epistles, but it did reveal an interesting trend in how Paul's writings currently shape Latter-day Saint belief. The passages demonstrate a collective criticism of denominational

Christianity from a Latter-day Saint perspective as well as an interest in establishing current ecclesiastical structures. The criticisms are quite overt, and the second most quoted passage is Ephesians 4:11–16, emphasizing the following sentences: "And he gave some, apostles; and some, prophets; and some, evangelists; and some, pastors and teachers; for the perfecting of the saints. . . . That we henceforth be no more children, tossed to and fro, and carried about with every wind of doctrine." A similar idea is presented in the fifth most referenced passage (2 Timothy 3:1–7), again a deutero-Pauline writing, and focuses on the phrase "ever learning, and never able to come to the knowledge of the truth" (3:7), coupled with the third most quoted passage, which emphasizes that the church is "built upon the foundation of the apostles and prophets" (Ephesians 2:20).

A second consistent theme identified in the study is the emphasis on the wisdom provided by the Restoration: "Eye hath not seen, nor ear heard, neither have entered into the heart of man, the things which God hath prepared for them that love him" (1 Corinthians 2:9), and this generation is "ever learning, and never able to come to the knowledge of the truth" (2 Timothy 3:7).[27] More examples could be drawn upon, but the themes that are engaged remain fairly consistent: the foundation of the Restoration and the blessings it provides. And herein lies a primary challenge of Latter-day Saint engagement with Paul. His letters are used as critical predictors providing descriptive support of the Restoration, but they are not formative in describing or supporting the Latter-day Saint view on salvation, righteousness, and a Christian life. For example, Latter-day Saints speak of grace, but their lack of indebtedness to or even awareness of the language of Paul's letters makes them shift to the Book of Mormon for the language of grace as outlined in 2 Nephi 25:23: "For we know that it is by grace that we are saved, after all we can do" (compare Mosiah 2:21). Romans comes close to capturing the opposite sentiment from the Latter-day Saint view by saying, "Therefore we conclude that a man is justified by faith without the deeds of the law"

(Romans 3:28). The law of Moses was in sight in the Pauline declaration, while the *Encyclopedia of Mormonism* makes clear the need for continued obedience to covenant and gospel, "A complete commitment to the gospel of Jesus Christ, the covenant of faith, automatically fulfills all previous obligations before God, including the obligations of the law of Moses."[28]

Several observations regarding Latter-day Saint usage of Paul are in order. First, Paul's words, as they relate to specific doctrinal or theological themes, make his letters continually relevant. Second, the context of Paul's statements has received almost no careful or thorough scrutiny in the Latter-day Saint tradition, perhaps because his words are seen as part of the prophetic tradition that is not typically subject to close scrutiny and critique by Latter-day Saints. Characterizing a letter as deutero-Pauline, or from a later school or from writers who mimicked Paul's style, does a disservice to authoritative discourse within the Latter-day Saint tradition. Third, and perhaps most importantly, Paul serves to document a moment in time of continued apostolic succession and authority in early Christianity.

SITUATING THE LATTER-DAY SAINT VIEW OF PAUL

In Latter-day Saint thought, Paul is thought to have developed a rationale for justification in faith that arose from his past experience with the law as a Pharisee and that was subsequently mitigated through his vision on the road to Damascus.[29] Paul was, following the Latter-day Saint vantage point, rooted in a salvation-by-works worldview only to have that worldview shaped by a revolutionary visionary experience, a position that is in some aspects remarkably close to that of the New Perspective.[30] This trajectory fits well within the Lutheran interpretation of Paul, namely that Luther's struggle with guilt pushed him to realize that Catholicism had developed a works-oriented religious consciousness that forced Luther to read Paul in search of a resolution. Grace was the gateway through which

Luther passed, resolved that his own struggle of conscious had received a necessary remedy. Latter-day Saints (inclusive of the various branches of Restorationist movements) have wrestled with the same questions that Luther faced, but unlike Luther's experience, their solution has been a more intimate coupling of grace and works.

Early Latter-day Saint theology resolved the conflict of grace and works through a concise definition of the "fulness of the gospel," in which belief in a clearly articulated plan and path to salvation made Luther's struggle seem smaller and less significant.[31] God had always planned not only for works connected with the law of Moses but also salvation by grace via Jesus Christ. Damascus, in this worldview, can be interpreted as a type of First Vision similar to Joseph Smith's, which dramatically changed Paul's views on the means of salvation. Joseph Smith already connected his own vision to Paul's in his 1838 retelling of the event: "I have thought since, that I felt much like Paul, when he made his defense before King Agrippa, and related the account of the vision he had when he saw a light" (Joseph Smith—History 1:24). Seeing Paul's vision in this light makes it possible to overlook, or significantly diminish, the question of the role that Judaism played in early Christian belief. Judaism, like Joseph Smith's early religious inclinations toward Methodism, placed Paul on a trajectory toward a new faith, one that required a revelatory event to awaken in him the realization of the importance of Christ and his proffered grace.[32] This viewpoint is evident in the following assessment of Paul's post-Damascus development: "In Damascus the governor under Aretas the king kept the city of the Damascenes with a garrison, desirous to apprehend me" (2 Corinthians 11:32). "He was so effective in preaching Christ that he provoked much Jewish opposition and was eventually compelled to flee for his life. Returning to Jerusalem after three years, he met briefly with Peter and James, the Lord's brother, and then went to Cilicia and Syria, where he spent approximately the next decade preaching the gospel."[33] Paul's provocation of Jewish opposition (Galatians 1:17) assumes an absolute

Christianity for Paul, no longer a Jew in any sense (besides ethnic) and now persecuted as an outsider.

Proponents of the New Perspective would be more than mildly surprised at such a quick turnaround from Paul the Pharisee to the persecuted Christian who seems to avoid Jerusalem when possible.[34] Fundamental to the Latter-day Saint view is the belief that Paul's Judaism had been fully and completely relegated to his past religious identity and that his new life as a Christian was fundamentally different and distinct. The Latter-day Saint view of Paul needs Judaism to be insufficient in some way, or to be more precise, it requires that Judaism reached a point at which it was no longer able to save God's people.[35] Christianity was the remedy to that problem, and Paul was, in the Latter-day Saint view, the most vocal and early proponent of declaring this message to Gentiles. But such a worldview faces significant headwind unless there is only one unified message presented by Paul, Peter, James, and others. In other words, Latter-day Saints will need to find productive ways to discuss Paul if it is conceded that Paul had views, beliefs, and practices that were at odds with Peter's.

The viewpoint that Paul did not depart from or leave his ancestral religion is one that has a number of vocal proponents.[36] But the Latter-day Saint position might have something important to say on the topic. If Paul's pre-Damascus faith influenced him in ways that are similar to the ways that Joseph Smith's Methodist-leaning Christianity influenced him, then there might be added meaning to be gained through comparison. It is clear that Joseph Smith was a Christian both before and after his First Vision, and with Paul it is possible that his pre-Damascus worldview continued to shape and color his post-Damascus Christianity. Latter-day Saints clearly blur the strong distinctions between Judaism and Christianity: they are, according to that viewpoint, two sides of the same coin. When evidence suggests that Paul maintained his Jewish faith, Latter-day Saints would see that as a strong indicator of the continuity between the law and its later corollary, the gospel. Donald Hagner has noted that "Judaism was not and is not a religion where acceptance with God is earned through the merit of righteousness based on works."[37] This is an interesting challenge, following Hagner, both for historical Pauline studies and for the view of Latter-day Saints. If righteousness connected to works is not the fundamental deficiency in Judaism, to use language familiar to Latter-day Saints, then some other causative source for righteous action must be identified.[38]

The Latter-day Saint view on Paul might find productive ways of engaging and rewriting the narrative of a depleted Judaism by reconsidering what Paul meant by "works of the law." Paul's declaration to the Galatians in 2:16—"for by the works of the law shall no flesh be justified"—is inherently negative in its assessment of the law according to this view. But as Hagner has claimed, Paul's arguments against doing "works of the law" do not concern rejection of the law but rather its tendency to promote one ethnic group over another and therefore to separate Jews from Gentiles.[39] Thus, Paul was not advocating the demolition and abandonment of Judaism but only its tendency to promote ethnic Jews above Gentiles. The proliferation of ethnic divisions was problematic to Paul, following this line of thinking, and such an avenue of discussion could help members of The Church of Jesus Christ of Latter-day Saints find more productive ways of promoting inclusion and greater continuity between Judaism and modern practices and beliefs. It could also help in the development of more sensitive narratives of ethnic inclusion and participation.

Some of the tensions that have been highlighted in the foregoing discussion are brought forward in the following summary of Paul's view of the law as presented in Galatians: "He [Paul] knew the requirements of the law of Moses. If any human could have been justified by it, Paul would have, but he knew that despite all of his efforts, he still lacked the righteousness he needed. The incident in Antioch when Peter and Barnabas stopped eating with Gentiles when 'certain [men] came from James' (Galatians 2:11–14) crystallized in Paul's mind that righteousness or justification could not be attained by worrying about issues of table fellowship or circumcision (see Galatians 5:1–12) or observing holy days (see Galatians 4:10–11). In Paul's day, these activities were viewed as the identifying marks of a follower of Judaism. Justification transcends such practices."[40] While allowing for further development in Paul's worldview after the Damascus experience, this interpretation promotes the idea that Paul came to see justification by faith as a solution when his own Christian table fellowship practices were suddenly challenged by Jewish norms. In that setting, Paul came to see the inadequacy of his former faith and the potential of the Christian message, but his former worldview is still described in terms that suggest a works-righteousness model was insufficient to save.

Hagner challenges this conclusion because it fails to grapple with the fundamental question of how central the message of justification was to Paul's teachings. Hagner has argued that "contrary to the Reformation understanding of Paul, *justification by faith is not the center of Paul's theology but instead represents a pragmatic tactic to facilitate the Gentile mission*. If Judaism is not a religion of works-righteousness, then it hardly needs to hear the message of justification by faith, whereas that message makes perfect sense if directed solely to Gentiles."[41] This assertion raises a legitimate point, one that could pose challenging questions to the Latter-day Saint view. Returning to the issue of how to introduce Book of Mormon evidence into debates about salvation through justification by faith, the following reference implies to the Latter-day Saint scholar that Judaism was a works-righteousness religion: "And by the law no flesh is justified; or, by the law men are cut off. Yea, by the temporal law they were cut off; and also, by the spiritual law they perish from that which is good, and become miserable forever" (2 Nephi 2:5).[42] The situation is not easily resolvable because the source in question is historical for one side and a nineteenth-century Christian document for the other side.

Finally, it is perhaps helpful to consider the Latter-day Saint view of justification and what Latter-day Saint scholars potentially mean when referring to justification by faith. There can be little doubt that Latter-day Saints inherited the justification versus works division from a Protestant American worldview. According to one Latter-day Saint scholar, "Though notionally separate, the two concepts were viewed as a complementary pair that could not be separated in describing the full work of salvation."[43] In other words, seeing a division between justification and works is to describe the relationship in unsatisfactory ways. Grant Underwood offers the following clarification: "Mormons view it as a synergistic balance between divine grace and human effort. The apostle Paul encouraged the Philippians: 'work out your own salvation,' but he did so with the clear acknowledgment in the very next verse that 'it is God which worketh in you both to will and to do' (Philip 2:12–13). We humans may be what the medieval Scholastics called the 'efficient cause' of righteous behavior, that is, the immediate agent in bringing it about, but at every step of the way from spiritual rebirth onward, an empowering, facilitating, gracious God is the real cause."[44]

This point has also been pursued by other Latter-day Saint scholars who note that the believer must have faith in Christ as Christ has faith in God's ability to save. This faith(fulness) of Christ has the danger of becoming a work, and therefore a type of earned salvation. Gaye Strathearn, in discussing the meaning of the Pauline phrase "the faith of Christ" (Philippians 3:9), maintains that the "faith of Christ" is the most logical reading, and Paul intends to signal a shift to the faith that believers have in Christ. Our *faith* has become our work, never mind the difficult theology of a faithful Christ.[45]

Early Latter-day Saints continued to pursue a works-leading-to-righteousness model by defining the requirement to earn salvation as dependent upon works while defining the power to save as grace. In the early Church's Articles and Covenants that were accepted during a conference on the day that the Church was officially organized, Joseph Smith offered a uniquely early Latter-day Saint view on justification, "And we know that all men must repent and believe on the name of Jesus Christ, and worship the Father in his name, and endure in faith on his name to the end, or they cannot be saved in the kingdom of God. And we know that justification through the grace of our Lord and Savior Jesus Christ is just and true" (Doctrine and Covenants 20:29–30).[46] One might argue like Paul did in Romans 11:6, "And if by grace, then is it no more of works: otherwise grace is no more grace. But if it be of works, then is it no more grace: otherwise work is no more work." But for Latter-day Saints, grace is one part of a process whereby a person is saved in recognition of faithful and enduring works.

Underwood conjectures that instead of speaking of grace, Latter-day Saints turn to scriptural passages such as, "Yea, I know that I am nothing; as to my strength I am weak; therefore I will not boast of myself, but I will boast of my God, for in his strength I can do all things; yea, behold, many mighty miracles we have wrought in this land, for which we will praise his name forever" (Alma 26:12).[47] This avowed nothingness is not without its own evidences of righteous actions. It is a deeply informed nothingness, one that has been carefully planned for, executed in humility with an open willingness to accept God's power in salvation. For the Latter-day Saint scholar on Paul, this will always be the challenge—seeing works-righteousness as an either-or proposition to justification by faith.

Criticisms, such as Hagner's and Francis Watson's, of those who describe the transition from Judaism to Christianity as a conversion from legalism to grace as a result of a "protestant schema" need further clarification.[48] Such a criticism comes close to isolating the fundamental challenge in accepting the New Perspective on Paul for Latter-day Saints. Their reading is also decidedly protestant in accepting a Judaism bound up in legalism and in the fundamental need to have a fallen, broken Judaism in need of a new life in the Spirit.

CONCLUSION

In this paper I have attempted to outline three areas of engagement with Pauline scholarship in which productive conversations might be possible. These three areas represent what may be the most significant trends of discussion on the Latter-day Saint side of the conversation. It appears that one of the most urgent needs is a careful and full consideration of how Latter-day Saint scholars will use Book of Mormon narratives in the discussion on Paul. And it seems that if the question of the historicity of the Book of Mormon can be separated from the conversation about how the Book of Mormon uses, adapts, and engages Paul, then several interesting threads of conversation can be pursued. Paul was fundamental to Joseph Smith when Smith articulated the Articles of Faith, which were themselves based on the writings of Orson Pratt. This study claims that the engagement with Paul is much more profound because of how intimately Paul's language is woven into Book of Mormon narratives.

Latter-day Saint scholars have also shown an intense interest in Acts 15 as a point of collision between a Jewish faction and a Gentile faction in the early Christian community. Multiple studies have seen the conflict as one signaling a decline in a central ecclesiastical authority that is challenged by evidences of Gentile conversion and Jewish resistance to accepting Pauline converts. It has been described as a moment of confrontation between a works-leading-to-righteousness model of salvation and a justification-by-faith worldview. The two factions strike an uneasy friendship, and Latter-day Saint scholars have seen this as a general sign of a church in decline.

Finally, it seems that Latter-day Saint scholarship will be resistant to the New Perspective on Paul if it means accepting Paul as a Jew who evangelized Gentiles under a belief in a two-covenant worldview. While such a characterization of the New Perspective is certainly overtly simple, it does highlight the fundamental challenge Latter-day Saint scholars will have with it. Latter-day Saints have been consistent in the viewpoint that the early church was a united organization dedicated to declaring Jesus to be the Messiah. That organization certainly faced significant challenges, but it was unified under Peter and the apostles. Paul was, according to the Latter-day Saint worldview, probably welcomed into the apostleship at some point in time, and he worked in harmony toward a more perfect kingdom of God on the earth. The law had become insufficient and unable to save, which remains one of the primary tenets of the Latter-day Saint view on Paul. But these scholars have not drilled down to describe precisely what was insufficient with respect to Judaism, and the suggestions offered by the New Perspective may offer a rich theological terrain to survey. A productive discussion might also be had with respect to uncovering the tensions that exist between the Pauline, deutero-Pauline, and later Pauline letters. Those dynamics have been overlooked, but they could be used to develop a healthy hermeneutic that shows theological development over time.

NOTES

1. Latter-day Saint scholars have almost completely avoided modern discussions of Paul and his impact on Christianity. Instead, as will become more obvious in the ensuing discussion, Latter-day Saint scholars frequently subordinate Pauline interests to theological positions advanced in the Book of Mormon.

2. E. P. Sanders, *Paul and Palestinian Judaism: A Comparison of Patterns of Religion* (Minneapolis: Fortress Press, 1977).

3. For a survey of the Articles of Faith in their historical contexts, see David J. Whittaker, "The 'Articles of Faith' in Early Mormon Literature and Thought," in *New Views of Mormon History: A Collection of Essays in Honor of Leonard J. Arrington*, ed. Davis Bitton and Maureen Ursenbach Beecher (Salt Lake City: University of Utah Press, 1987), 63–92. The Articles of Faith were republished in the *Times and Seasons*, March 1842.

4. Orson Pratt, A[n] Interesting Account of Several Remarkable Visions, and of the Late Discovery of Ancient American Records (Edinburgh: Ballantyne and Hughes, 1840), 24–31. Compare Peter Crawley, A Descriptive Bibliography of the Mormon Church, Volume One, 1830–1847 (Provo, UT: Religious Studies Center, Brigham Young University, 1997), 127–29.

5. John W. Welch, "Joseph Smith and Paul: Co-Authors of the Articles of Faith?," Instructor, November 1969, 422–26.

6. The Doctrine and Covenants is a canonical book of scripture that contains Joseph Smith's record of some of the revelations received during his lifetime. While it contains a few other historical and theological records, the great majority owe their provenance to Smith. A direct connection between Paul and early Latter-day Saint theology can be found in Doctrine and Covenants 27:15–18 and its usage of Ephesians 6:13–18 (compare Doctrine and Covenants 127:2 and Romans 5:3). The following quotation further demonstrates the coupling of Joseph Smith's experiences and those of Paul: "Follow the labors of this Apostle from the time of his conversion to the time of his death, and you will have a fair sample of industry and patience in promulgating the Gospel of Christ. Derided, whipped, and stoned, the moment he escaped the hands of his persecutors he as zealously as ever proclaimed the doctrine of the Savior. . . . Paul rested his hope in Christ, because he had kept the faith, and loved His appearing and from His hand he had a promise of receiving a crown of righteousness." "Letter to the Church, circa March 1834," p. 144, The Joseph Smith Papers, https://josephsmithpapers.org/paper-summary/letter-to-the-church-circa-march-1834/3.

7. J. Philip Schaelling, "Paul," in Encyclopedia of Mormonism, 1070; https://eom.byu.edu/index.php/Paul. Bracketed references appear in the original.

8. James E. Talmage, The Articles of Faith (Salt Lake City: Deseret News, 1915); Bruce R. McConkie, A New Witness to the Articles of Faith (Salt Lake City: Deseret Book, 1985).

9. Compare Mormon 6:21: "And the day soon cometh that your mortal must put on immortality, and these bodies which are now moldering

in corruption must soon become incorruptible bodies"; and Alma 5:15: "Do you look forward with an eye of faith, and view this mortal body raised in immortality, and this corruption raised in incorruption?"

10. An exception to this hesitancy to engage New Testament wording in the Book of Mormon is Nicholas Frederick's *The Bible, Mormon Scripture, and the Rhetoric of Allusivity* (Maryland: Fairleigh Dickinson University Press, 2016). A sampling of parallels includes 1 Nephi 2:10 = 1 Corinthians 15:58; 2 Nephi 2:5 = Romans 3:20 and Galatians 2:16; 2 Nephi 2:14 = Romans 4:15 (also Romans 5:13); 2 Nephi 4:17 = Romans 7:24; 2 Nephi 9:7 = 1 Corinthians 15:53; 2 Nephi 9:39 = Romans 8:6; 2 Nephi 26:33 = Galatians 3:28; 2 Nephi 28:11 = Romans 3:12; Mosiah 2:33 = 1 Corinthians 11:29; Mosiah 4:27 = 1 Corinthians 9:24; and 14:40; Mosiah 16:10 = 1 Corinthians 15:53 (Alma 5:15; Mormon 6:21).

11. Latter-day Saints recognize 138 different documents, referred to as "revelations" as canonically authoritative and instructive. These revelations were eventually canonized and collected in a book of scripture called the Doctrine and Covenants.

12. See Terrence L. Szink, "Authorship of the Epistle to the Hebrews," in *How the New Testament Came to Be*, ed. Kent P. Jackson and Frank F. Judd Jr. (Provo, UT: Religious Studies Center, Brigham Young University; Salt Lake City: Deseret Book, 2006), 243–59.

13. The "fulness of times" is frequently mentioned (Ephesians 1:10; Doctrine and Covenants 27:13; 76:106; 112:30; 121:31; 124:41; 128:18, 20; 138:48, 53.

14. So also Margaret E. Thrall, *The Second Epistle to the Corinthians*, 2 vols. (Edinburgh: T&T Clark, 2000), 2:821–22.

15. Sidney B. Sperry, *Paul's Life and Letters* (Salt Lake City: Bookcraft, 1955).

16. See, for example, Albert Schweitzer, *The Mysticism of Paul the Apostle* (Baltimore: Johns Hopkins University Press, 1998).

17. For example, J. Edgar Goodspeed, *An Introduction to the New Testament* (Chicago: University of Chicago Press, 1937), referred to by Sperry as "liberal." Sperry refers to Theodor Zahn's *Introduction to the New*

Testament, 3 vols. (Edinburgh: T&T Clark, 1909) as "possibly the best advanced conservative introduction." See also F. W. Farrar, *The Life and Work of St. Paul* (New York: E. P. Dutton, 1902); and F. A Spencer, *Beyond Damascus* (New York: Harper, 1934), of which Sperry declares, "Useful for background material. Notes are very useful. Written in a racy style. L.D.S. teachers should use with care." The prevalence of Goodspeed's work is not surprising given that Sperry had been instructed by Goodspeed during the latter's summer seminars in Utah. See "Chapter One: By Small and Simple Things, 1912–1935," in *By Study and Also by Faith: One Hundred Years of Seminaries and Institutes of Religion* (Salt Lake City: The Church of Jesus Christ of Latter-day Saints, 2015). Sperry's main intellectual inheritance may have come from his apostolic sponsor, James E. Talmage (d. July 27, 1933). Sperry's work shows an awareness of the sources favored by Talmage, particularly Alfred Edersheim, but also an interest to draw upon recent academic work on Paul.

18. This can be seen, for example, in the collection of essays from a conference that annually celebrates the legacy of Sidney Sperry: Ray L. Huntington et al., *Go You into All the World: Messages of the New Testament Apostles* (Salt Lake City: Deseret Book, 2002).

19. Although articles directed to a Latter-day Saint audience have continued to appear, the only other major treatment of Paul was Richard L. Anderson, *Understanding Paul*, rev. ed. (1983; Salt Lake City: Deseret Book, 2007).

20. Exemplary of this approach are Robert L. Millet, "The Saga of the Early Christian Church," in *Studies in Scripture: Volume Six: Acts to Revelation* (Salt Lake City: Deseret Book, 1987), 1–11; Robert J. Matthews, "The Jerusalem Council," in *Sperry Symposium Classics: The New Testament*, ed. Frank F. Judd Jr. and Gaye Strathearn (Provo, UT: Religious Studies Center, Brigham Young University; Salt Lake City: Deseret Book, 2006), 254–66; Frank F. Judd Jr., "The Jerusalem Conference: The First Council of the Christian Church," *Religious Educator* 12, no. 1 (2011): 55–71; Gaye Strathearn, "Fallible but Faithful: How Simon

the Fisherman Became Peter the Rock," in *The Ministry of Peter, the Chief Apostle*, ed. Frank F. Judd Jr., Eric D. Huntsman, and Shon D. Hopkin (Provo, UT: Religious Studies Center, Brigham Young University; Salt Lake City: Deseret Book, 2014), 226–46.

21. Matthews, "Jerusalem Council," 254–66.

22. Judd, "Jerusalem Conference," 58.

23. Judd, "Jerusalem Conference," 58; emphasis in original.

24. This theme is dealt with in W. D. Davies, "Israel, the Mormons and the Land," in *Reflections on Mormonism: Judaeo-Christian Parallels*, ed. Truman G. Madsen (Provo, UT: Religious Studies Center, Brigham Young University, 1978), 79–82 and n6.

25. The sixth article of faith declares, "We believe in the same organization that existed in the Primitive Church, namely, apostles, prophets, pastors, teachers, evangelists, and so forth."

26. Brad Farnsworth, John Hilton III, Jaclyn Nielson, and Jonathan Ogden, "Prophetic Use of the Pauline Epistles, 1970–2013," *Religious Educator* 16, no. 1 (2015): 77–103.

27. An important concept for Latter-day Saints is the notion that the current Church—its practices and beliefs— are built upon a foundation of truths that have been restored from ancient times. Latter-day Saints frequently speak of the restored gospel and restored truths and generally refer to the earliest period as the "Restoration."

28. Schaelling, "Paul," 1069.

29. For example, Edward J. Brandt, "The Law of Moses and the Law of Christ," in *Sperry Symposium Classics: The Old Testament*, ed. Paul Y. Hoskisson (Provo, UT: Religious Studies Center, Brigham Young University; Salt Lake City: Deseret Book, 2005), 133–53. He stated, "When the spirit of the law of Moses is really understood, can one teach of Christ? Paul did, and he used it in power while teaching."

30. Seyoon Kim, *Paul and the New Perspective* (Grand Rapids, MI: Eerdmans, 2002), is perhaps the most vocal opponent of the New Perspective and has argued that accepting it will ultimately ruin the foundations of Reformation faith in salvation through grace.

31. See Charles R. Harrell, *"This Is My Doctrine": The Development of Mormon Theology* (Salt Lake City: Greg Kofford Books, 2011), 303–7.

32. Joseph Smith was noted as saying that he had been inclined toward the Methodist faith prior to his First Vision. See John Matzko, "The Encounter of the Young Joseph Smith with Presbyterianism," *Dialogue: A Journal of Mormon Thought* 40, no. 3 (Fall 2007): 78. In the official published account of Joseph's early spiritual life, he declared, "In process of time my mind became somewhat partial to the Methodist sect" (Joseph Smith—History 1:8).

33. Schaelling, "Paul," 1069.

34. Donald A. Hagner, "Paul and Judaism. The Jewish Matrix of Early Christianity: Issues in the Current Debate," *Bulletin for Biblical Research* 3 (1993): 122–23, notes that many assume that Paul was problem-free as a Pharisee, but he may have already felt the problematic weight of Judaism (Acts 15:10). Stephen Westerholm, "The 'New Perspective' at Twenty-Five," in *Justification and Variegated Nomism: A Fresh Appraisal of Paul and Second Temple Judaism*, ed. D. A. Carson, Peter T. O'Brien, and Mark A. Seifrid, 2 vols. (Grand Rapids, MI: Baker, 2004), 2:1–38.

35. The struggle to make sense of this is evident in the following summary, "The result has been that justification has been viewed from an anthropological perspective rather than a christological one. In other words, justification has been understood as a function of human belief in isolation from the pivotal role played by the Savior." Gaye Strathearn, "The Faith of Christ," in *A Witness for the Restoration: Essays in Honor of Robert J. Matthews*, ed. Kent P. Jackson and Andrew Skinner (Provo, UT: Religious Studies Center, Brigham Young University, 2007), 112–13.

36. See Krister Stendahl, "Call Rather than Conversion," in *Paul among Jews and Gentiles and Other Essays* (Philadelphia: Fortress Press, 1976), 7–23; James Dunn, "'A Light to the Gentiles,' or 'The End of the Law?' The Significance of the Damascus Road Christophany for Paul," in *The Glory of Christ in the New Testament: Studies in Christology in Memory of George Bradford Caird*, ed. L. D. Hurst and N. T. Wright (Oxford: Clarendon Press, 1987), 251–66.

37. Hagner, "Paul and Judaism," 111–12.

38. This language draws upon the assessment of John Dillenberger, "Grace and Works in Martin Luther and Joseph Smith," in *Reflections on Mormonism: Judaeo-Christian Parallels*, ed. Truman G. Madsen (Provo, UT: Religious Studies Center, Brigham Young University, 1978), 175–86.

39. Hagner, "Paul and Judaism," 115. James D. G. Dunn, "Works of the Law and the Curse of the Law (Gal 3:10–14)," in *Jesus, Paul and the Law* (Louisville: Westminster/John Knox, 1990), 215–41; D. B. Garlington, *"The Obedience of Faith": A Pauline Phrase in Historical Perspective* (Tübingen: Mohr Siebeck, 1991). Such a view can lead to a two-covenant theology, namely one for the Gentiles and one for Jews. See John D. Gager, *The Origins of Anti-Semitism* (Oxford: Oxford University Press, 1983).

40. Strathearn, "Faith of Christ," 106.

41. Hagner, "Paul and Judaism," 112; emphasis in original.

42. This is the point made by Steven L. Olsen, "The Centrality of Nephi's Vision," *Religious Educator* 11, no. 2 (2010): 51–66.

43. Grant Underwood, "Justification, Theosis, and Grace in Early Christian, Lutheran, and Mormon Discourse," *International Journal of Mormon Studies* 2 (2009): 210.

44. Underwood, "Justification, Theosis, and Grace," 219.

45. Strathearn, "Faith of Christ," 100–104.

46. Underwood, "Justification, Theosis, and Grace," 208.

47. Underwood, "Justification, Theosis, and Grace," 220.

48. Hagner, "Paul and Judaism," 113; Francis Watson, *Paul, Judaism and the Gentiles: A Sociological Approach* (Cambridge: Cambridge University Press, 1986), 1–22.

4

A JEWISH VIEW OF PAUL

JOSHUA D. GARROWAY

"What is the Jewish view of Paul?"

As a rabbi who studies Paul professionally, I encounter this question routinely from Jews and Christians alike. My unhelpful answer invariably finds interlocutors dissatisfied: "Is there a Jewish view on anything?" A touch of sarcasm tinges this response, to be sure, but there is also something uncomfortably true about it. Ask most rabbis in the United States, and they will report that questions about "the Jewish view" on this or that are par for the course: "What is the Jewish view of the afterlife? The soul? The Messiah?" There is no end to the subjects about which people inquire, and likewise no end to the variety of ways in which rabbis, at least those who appreciate the complexity of Judaism, explain that consensus among Jews, presently or in the past, proves difficult to come by.

Arriving at a Jewish view on Paul presents an even more vexing problem. The afterlife, the soul, the Messiah—these are issues with which Jews have occupied themselves at length through the ages. Lack of consensus has hardly resulted from a lack of interest. When it comes to Paul, one reason no Jewish view prevails is that Jews gave such little thought to Paul for nearly eighteen centuries. Only by scouring the tradition can one scare up the scant Jewish statements about Paul from the medieval or early modern periods.[1]

It is true that since the Enlightenment Jews have turned their attention to Paul in increasing numbers. Daniel R. Langton has written extensively on the dozen or so Jews from the nineteenth or early-twentieth century who wrote about Paul from an interested Jewish perspective.[2] The likes of Isaac Mayer Wise, Heinrich Graetz, Kaufmann Kohler, Martin Buber, Claude Montefiore, and Leo Baeck were not professional New Testament scholars but leading Jewish thinkers who recognized in the figure of Paul a useful vehicle for European and American Jews to wrestle with the implications of the open society brought about by emancipation. As Langton reveals, these writers utilized Paul as a tool for negotiating, on one hand, the modern relationship between Judaism and Christianity and, on the other, the threat posed by post-Enlightenment apostasy or religious reform. Paul might be seen, for example, as a forerunner to the emancipated Jews' hope to share the message of Israel with the nations (per Wise), or as a forerunner to apostates who abandon Judaism in their headlong jump to embrace the extraneous sentiments prevailing in the wider world (per Kohler).[3] Among these writers, however, there was hardly a consensus assessment regarding Paul, his thought, or his significance.

Nor has a consensus developed in recent years among the handful of Jews who have penetrated the highest ranks of New Testament scholarship. Jewish writers like Alan Segal, Mark Nanos, Paula Fredriksen, Daniel Boyarin, and Pamela Eisenbaum, among others, who approach Paul as professionally trained historians, hardly subscribe to a singular perspective that could aptly be dubbed a Jewish view of Paul.[4]

With due respect to well-meaning Jews (and others) who ask after it, there is simply no such a thing as *the* Jewish view of Paul. To make matters worse, I am not even certain what characterizes any particular approach to Paul as a Jewish view. Is an approach to Paul considered Jewish if a Jew expresses it? Is it Jewish if it prioritizes a confessional Jewish perspective over a putatively objective historical one? Is it Jewish if it construes Paul as more rather than less loyal to the Judaism of his day? All this is to say that any essay purporting to offer a Jewish view of Paul, or a survey of Jewish views of Paul, must begin by explaining why the perspectives presented qualify as Jewish.

CHARACTERISTICS OF A JEWISH PERSPECTIVE ON PAUL

This essay offers three approaches to Pauline interpretation that I consider Jewish, albeit for different reasons. First is what has been called "the traditional Jewish view of Paul," the generally (but not uniformly) negative assessment of Paul put forward by those nineteenth- and early twentieth-century rabbis and scholars of Judaism who, despite lacking expertise in New Testament studies, endeavored to account for Paul and his thought *from a confessional Jewish perspective*. Seeing as these Jews read Paul *as Jews* (rather than as historians) and *in the interest of Judaism* (rather than as contributions to academic knowledge), I deem their approach to be Jewish.

The second is what is known as the Radical New Perspective on Paul, or more recently as the Paul within Judaism perspective, a contemporary scholarly approach to Paul that upends nearly all Pauline scholarship prior to the 1970s. To the extent that this perspective pursues a Paul who embraces rather than rejects ancient Judaism, I call it Jewish in its orientation, even if the majority of its adherents are non-Jewish scholars.

Finally, I offer my own understanding of Paul, which, like the Paul within Judaism perspective, presents Paul as a Jew committed to thinking Jewishly about implications of the death and professed resurrection of Jesus. Paul was very much "within Judaism," I argue, but not in the way the Paul within Judaism perspective typically proposes.

THE PAUL VERSUS JUDAISM PARADIGM

Both the (so-called) traditional Jewish view of Paul and the Radical New Perspective aim to undermine the view of Paul that prevailed among Christian scholars for most of the twentieth century, aptly identified with the expression "Paul versus Judaism." Though its contours were refined after World War II by Günther Bornkamm, Ernst Käsemann, and other disciples of Rudolf Bultmann, this view trades on theological currents in Catholicism and especially in Lutheranism stretching back centuries.[5] In sum, this standard approach construes Paul as the lead prosecutor in an unmitigated exposé of Judaism's inherent badness. According to most scholarship prior to 1970, Paul impugns Judaism as the futile attempt to gain God's favor through obedience to the commandments of the Torah, the so-called works of the Law. Try as they may, Paul insists, Jews invariably fall short of full obedience, and their lifelong struggle leads ineluctably to sin, condemnation, and death. Paul's gospel represents the alternative to this failed legalistic system. Through faith in Christ and the transformation it affords, a person can be "justified by faith" (Romans 5:1), as Paul puts it—to wit, granted the righteousness necessary to withstand the eventual judgment of God. Gospel, faith, and Christianity, on this reckoning, are the superior alternatives to Torah, works, and Judaism.

No shortage of passages from Paul's epistles to the Romans, Galatians, Corinthians, and Philippians might be adduced to buttress this view. Writing to the Philippians, for example, Paul boasts of his Jewish lineage, his circumcision, and his erstwhile observance of Jewish law only to dismiss them as *skubala*, "trash" (see Philippians 3:1–11). To the Romans, Paul says things like "Israel, who did strive for the righteousness that is based on the law, did not succeed in fulfilling that law ... because they did not strive for it on the basis of faith, but as if it were based on works" (Romans 9:31–32 New Revised Standard Version), a statement suggesting that faith, not the Torah, leads to righteousness. Paul appears to spell out this notion more clearly to the Galatians, saying, "We know that a person is justified not by the works of the law but through faith in Jesus Christ. And we have come to believe in Christ Jesus, so that we might be justified by faith in Christ, and not by doing the works of the law, because no one will be justified by the works of the law (Galatians 2:16 NRSV). Elsewhere, in Galatians 3:23–29, Paul seems to indicate that the Torah has become obsolete, an assertion he also makes to the Corinthians by contrasting the "ministry of condemnation" provided to Moses with "ministry of justification" that comes through Christ (2 Corinthians 3:7–18). These passages are not unique. Scores more could be presented as evidence that Paul not only abandoned the Judaism in which he was raised but also turned against it with scorn. No wonder Käsemann could describe Paul's gospel of justification as "eine antijudaistische Kampfeslehre"—a battling doctrine against Judaism.[6]

A PARADIGM REVERSED: JUDAISM VERSUS PAUL

Nor is it any wonder that more recently Rabbi Nancy Fuchs Kreimer could tell Paul in an imagined correspondence that "most of my coreligionists, from your era right up till mine, see you as the archetype of the Jewish heretic, the prototypical Jew who abandons the faith and then unjustly criticizes it in a way our enemies can use against us, to put it bluntly—a traitor."[7] This oft-heard Jewish indictment of Paul taps into the same assumption that informs the Lutheran approach to Paul just described: Paul and Judaism are mortal enemies. Rabbi Fuchs Kreimer's comment simply reflects an opposite view of the combatants: Judaism is the superior alternative to Paul.

This approach to Paul was forged by the pioneering Jewish intellectuals who turned their attention to Paul more than a century ago, among them the historians Heinrich Graetz (d. 1891) and Joseph Klausner (d. 1958), as well as the influential rabbi Kaufmann Kohler (d. 1926) and renowned philosopher Martin Buber (d. 1965).

Informing their perspective was the reclamation of Jesus occurring especially in liberal Jewish circles beginning in the nineteenth century, when many Jews latched on to the portraits of Jesus offered up by liberal Christians like Albrecht Ritschl and Adolf von Harnack, who emphasized the piety and ethics of Jesus over his supernaturality.[8] Jesus was merely a man, these Jews naturally insisted, but he exhibited "spotless moral purity," as Graetz puts it.[9]

The reclamation of Jesus as a Jew meant, in turn, that these Jews had to hold someone else responsible for making Christianity into what they saw as a bastardized version of Judaism. As Langton explains, Paul became for them "Jewish public enemy number one."[10] They fashioned Paul as the weak-minded, ignorant, opportunistic, diaspora Jew who invented Christianity by corrupting authentic Judaism with sundry pagan ideas. Paul's gospel was "half pagan and half Jewish," according to Kohler;[11] for Klausner, "the complete antithesis of Judaism";[12] and for Graetz, "the very opposite of Judaism."[13] Buber identified Paul's notion of faith (Greek *pistis*) with the inferior I-It relationship, while the faith of Jesus (Hebrew *emunah*) represented the superior I-Thou. Put bluntly, these thinkers reclaimed Jesus as a pious, faithful, Galilean Jew, while they rebuffed Paul as the traitor responsible for pushing Christianity outside the bounds of Judaism.

Calling this perspective on Paul the traditional Jewish view is problematic, however. In the first place, a late nineteenth-century vintage hardly merits "traditional" status. More importantly, it is not as though every Jew in these generations looked upon Paul with such unbridled hostility. Balanced against the negative portrait of Paul was a measure of praise, especially from classical Reform rabbis like Isaac Mayer Wise (d. 1900) and Joseph Krauskopf (d. 1923).[14] For American Reform Jews at the turn of the century, Paul's spiritualization of the law and his expressed desire to bring Gentiles closer to God resonated with their own antinomian and universalistic aspirations. Wise, for example, wished to reclaim Paul no less than Jesus as a great Jew, proclaiming that "all Jews of all ages hoped and expected that the kingdom of heaven should be extended to all nations and tongues; but Paul went forth to do it."[15]

To be fair, in North America at least, this more generous estimation of Paul does not appear to have penetrated the popular Jewish consciousness with nearly the same vigor as the negative representations typically identified as the traditional Jewish perspective. I am not aware of any scholarly surveys that have explored the way(s) the average American Jew in the last fifty years views Paul, but my own experience suggests that American Jews are typically more hostile to Paul than to Jesus. The trend in twentieth-century research to see Jesus as a loyal Jew seems to have seeped into the Jewish imagination.[16] When it comes to Paul, however, Jews attending my lectures in a synagogue or Jewish community center come steeled to learn about a figure against whom they already harbor prejudice. He is, in many of their minds, the unscrupulous salesman who sold out his native religion in favor of the bogus imitation of Judaism that appealed to his Gentile devotees.

Thus, the traditional Christian view of Paul and the traditional Jewish view—putting aside the question of whether they ought to be called traditional—actually trade on the same basic paradigm. In each, Paul and Judaism are pitted against each other. Whereas Christians advocated on behalf of the apostle and against his native faith, Jews looked to the other side of the ledger, defending Judaism against a pernicious apostate. But whether it was "Paul versus Judaism" or "Judaism versus Paul," rarely the twain did meet.

A PARADIGM DISMANTLED: PAUL WITHIN JUDAISM

Until the twenty-first century, that is. A recent trend in New Testament scholarship has begun to challenge the traditional paradigm by outright dismantling it. According to a handful of prominent scholars of the last three decades, Paul should not be pitted *against* Judaism, but situated *within* Judaism.

This approach to Paul, also called the Radical New Perspective, developed out of the (not yet radical) New Perspective on Paul that hatched in the 1970s with the pioneering work of E. P. Sanders.[17] Sanders undertook an exhaustive survey of Jewish literature from the Second Temple period, including the early rabbis, and concluded that the time-honored Christian assessment of ancient Judaism as an ossified, works-righteousness legalism is a canard. Ancient Judaism was rather a "covenantal nomism," as Sanders called it, a religion in which Jews thrilled in legal observance (hence, "nomism") not as a way to gain salvation, but to maintain a secure place in their established covenant with God (hence, "covenantal"). Since ancient Judaism did not advocate works-righteousness legalism, Paul could not have inveighed against Judaism as such. Instead of legalism, Sanders and his contemporaries (James D. G. Dunn, N. T. Wright, and others) held that Paul disapproved of Jewish nationalism or ethnocentrism and those legal practices whose primary function was to separate Jews from other people—for example, circumcision, dietary laws, or Sabbath observance. Ethnic chauvinism, not legalism, became the Jewish blight Paul railed against.[18]

Concerned that the New Perspective persists in pitting Paul against Judaism (albeit in new terms), interpreters investigating Paul from the Radical New Perspective call upon scholars to move beyond the entrenched assumption that Paul objected to Judaism at all. Paul rather should be viewed as a Jew, a loyal Jew, whose gospel presumes no inadequacy in Judaism. The origins of this groundbreaking perspective are found in the landmark 1963 essay by Krister Stendahl, "The Apostle Paul and the Introspective Conscience of the West," in which the acclaimed Swedish bishop argued that the principal concern in Paul's epistles is not the inadequacy of Judaism or even Judaism itself, but Paul's preoccupation with reconciling Gentiles to the Jewish God.[19] The only thing wrong with Judaism, for Paul, was that not enough Gentiles had realized how important it was for them to reconcile themselves with the Jews' God. A half century later, a spate of scholars both Jewish (e.g., Pamela Eisenbaum, Paula Fredriksen, Mark Nanos) and non-Jewish (e.g., Magnus Zetterholm, Caroline Johnson Hodge) have taken Stendahl's lead by portraying Paul as a Jew "within Judaism," as they put it, a pious Jew who crisscrossed the Mediterranean to bring a form of Judaism, centered around the messiahship of Jesus, specifically to Gentiles.[20] Paul found nothing wrong with Judaism per se, and he ought to be viewed as a representative, not an opponent, of ancient Judaism.

This new approach to Paul enjoys several advantages. On ecumenical terms, it introduces a Paul who might be considered a point of contact rather than contention in Christian-Jewish relations. On historical terms, it offers an appropriate correction to one of the tenacious anachronisms in New Testament scholarship. Christians have historically read Paul's letters as though they were intended for a general audience, even though Paul explicitly addresses only Gentile recipients. In his epistle to the Romans, for example, Paul tells readers of his hope "that I may reap some harvest among you as I have among the rest of the Gentiles" (Romans 1:13 NRSV). Later in the letter, he likewise says, "I am speaking to you Gentiles, inasmuch as I am an apostle to the Gentiles" (Romans 11:13 NRSV adapted). Acknowledging that Paul may not be speaking to Jewish readers in his own day, much less Christian readers in the centuries to follow, has enabled interpreters from the Radical New Perspective to suppose that Paul's apparently hostile statements about Judaism were relevant only for Gentiles. They did not constitute indictments of Judaism per se. Paul, in other words, opposed Judaism *only* as a recourse for Gentiles. He said that the Torah has become obsolete (Galatians 3:6–29) *only* for Gentiles. He considered the Torah a "ministry of condemnation" (2 Corinthians 3:9; my translations) that "promotes sin" (Romans 5:20) and even kills (2 Corinthians 3:6), but *only* for Gentiles. For Jews baptized into Christ, including himself, Paul thought the covenant at Sinai and the laws that maintain it remained valid and salutary. Paul thus appears to be "within Judaism," on this approach.

MY JEWISH VIEW OF PAUL

Colleagues often assume that I too, as a Jew who studies Paul, subscribe to the Radical New Perspective. After all, it seems so Jewish in its orientation. Why would I not want to see in Paul a loyal Jew, a defender of the Torah and its ongoing authority for Jews, an apostle whose writings should not be construed by Christians as a "battling doctrine against Judaism"? To be sure, it would be nice to encounter such a Paul. I simply do not find this Paul in his epistles. There are just too many passages in which I fail to see how Paul's apparent disparagement of the Torah or the observance of its laws is anything other than it has seemed through ages, even if Gentiles were indeed his only intended audience.

His argument in Galatians 3:1–29, for example, reads like a replacement of the Torah with Christ, not just for Gentiles but for all humanity. Especially revealing in this regard is his likening the Torah to a *paidagogos*, the custodian who supervised aristocratic boys (Galatians 3:24–25). Just as a young man no longer needs the *paidagogos* once he has come of age, Paul intimates, so those who were subject to the Torah no longer need the Torah once the covenant safeguarded by the Torah has been fulfilled through the death and resurrection of Christ. Since Jews, and not Gentiles, were subject to the Torah in ages past, Paul appears to be saying that the Torah, in the wake of Christ, is no longer authoritative for Jews.

Paul's description of the Torah as a "ministry of death" and a "ministry of condemnation" in 2 Corinthians 3:7–9 likewise seems to indicate that Jews, no less than Gentiles, should abandon Jewish law, especially after he caps the argument with a peculiar interpretation of the veil worn by Moses. In 2 Corinthians 3:12–15, Paul explains that Moses wore the veil to conceal his fading glory from the Israelites. In his own day, Paul goes on to say, Jews themselves wear a veil of ignorance because they read the Torah without recognizing it as a ministry of condemnation and death. Galatians 3 and 2 Corinthians 3, among other passages, therefore suggest to me that Paul believed that the Torah had been rendered generally obsolete by the death and resurrection of Christ and that ongoing Torah observance by Jews was useless at best, repugnant at worst.

That having been said, I am not opposed to reading Paul as a Jew "within Judaism," a representative of Second Temple Judaism fully committed to Judaism as he understood it. We simply need to reconsider what Judaism constitutes and how Paul's loyalty to Judaism should be evaluated. In short, we need to recognize that Paul's negotiation with the ongoing significance of the Torah and other Jewish ideas in response to transformative historical events is not unparalleled in Jewish history. Jews whom we recognize as Jews have wrestled with similar issues.

In this vein, I proposed in a recent study that one way to contextualize Paul as a Jew might be to look beyond his contemporaries in the Second Temple period and toward a Jew from an entirely different era, a Jew who dealt with social, intellectual, and theological conundrums similar to what Paul experienced, albeit under different circumstances. The figure I put forth was the nineteenth-century German rabbi Samuel Holdheim.[21] Holdheim was an articulate spokesman for the small number of European Jews who believed that the Enlightenment and the dawn of democracy and Jewish emancipation in Europe signaled the final hour of history envisioned by the prophets.[22] These Jews, who comprised the radical wing of the Reform movement in Europe and slightly later in the United States, were wholly messianic in their outlook—not because they believed that a messiah had come, as Paul did, nor because they thought a messiah might soon arrive, but rather because of their conviction that humanity was on the brink of redeeming itself through liberalism, science, democracy, love, and other Enlightenment achievements.[23] They expected the struggles of history soon to give way to a world at last united in universal brotherhood.

Accordingly, Jews like Holdheim believed that the present messianic age demanded a new sort of Judaism. Obsolete was the medieval Judaism of yesteryear that laid heavy emphasis on the Talmud and
ceremonial Jewish law. A modern Judaism, argued Holdheim, should
aspire to liberate the pure kernel of Jewish tradition—specifically the
moral precepts of the Torah and the Prophets—from the rabbinic
husk that had accreted over the ages. To persist in Orthodox Judaism
would represent a regression to what Holdheim called the "embry-
onic stage of Judaism," a far cry from the mature Jewish consciousness he envisioned.[24] Moreover, Holdheim insisted, the peculiar rites
of Talmudic Judaism would impede progress toward the ultimate
Jewish vision of redemption—to wit, the unification of all humanity
in love for God and one's fellow, the root of all genuine religion.

Did this radical interpretation of Judaism make Holdheim a
controversial figure? Of course it did. Opponents of the Reformers
balked at the dramatic reorientation of Judaism away from the Talmud and Jewish particularism. Graetz, for example, said of Holdheim
that "since Paul of Tarsus Judaism had not known such an enemy in
its midst, who shook the whole edifice to its very foundation."[25] Even
his fellow Reformers expressed concern over the extent to which he
envisioned the abandonment of Jewish rites; at the same time, however, they still saw in Holdheim a loyal Jew—a Jew who harbored
an overly universalistic, naive vision of Judaism, but a Jew "within
Judaism" nevertheless. As Rabbi David Philipson, the colleague of
Isaac Mayer Wise and one of the first American-born rabbis, put it:
"Whatever [Holdheim] may or may not have been, he was certainly
a Jew with all his heart and soul; he had no intention or purpose to
undermine Judaism and replace it by another religion as did Paul."[26]

I agree with Philipson's assessment of Holdheim. He was indeed
a Jew "with all his heart and soul" who endeavored to rethink what
Judaism ought to be in the wake of the profound societal changes
introduced by enlightenment and emancipation in Europe. With
due respect to Philipson, however, I fail to see why Paul cannot be

understood similarly. Philipson probably feared acknowledging what detractors of Reform Judaism so often claimed (and continue to claim)—namely, that Reform is akin to Christianity. In my view, a nuanced view of the relationship between Reform Judaism and Christianity does not see them as the same or different *tout court*, but similar in some respects while different in others. Indeed, when it comes to important Christian tenets like resurrection from the dead or mystical union with God, Reform Judaism would seem far more antithetical than Orthodox Judaism to Christianity. On the other hand, when it comes to the historic Christian, specifically Pauline, attempt to reconceptualize its relationship to Jewish history and the law in the light of a radically new perspective on the world, Reform Judaism is indeed similar.

Similar, but hardly identical, for the event(s) that sparked the change in perspective of the first-century Paul and the nineteenth-century Holdheim were wildly different. Paul's reorientation of Judaism was not sparked by the dawn of what seemed like a messianic utopia in Europe, but what seemed to him the experience of a risen messiah. Paul believed with unshakeable conviction that God had sent the long-awaited Messiah of Israel, who died and was raised from the dead. Paul could no more un-know this experience than Holdheim could un-know his own experience of modernity. Like Holdheim, Paul spent the remainder of his days contemplating how Judaism ought to change in advance of the final hour; and, like Holdheim, he concluded that the present messianic age rendered the ceremonial aspects of the Torah obsolete and that the principal priority of Judaism had become the realization of the prophetic vision in which Jew and Gentile are reconciled in advance of the end.

No less than Holdheim, then, Paul preached this vision of a refined Judaism as a loyal Jew. True, the inheritors of Paul's reoriented Judaism eventually determined that it comprised a new and superior religion in opposition to Judaism, but this subsequent development should not alter our appreciation of Paul as a Jew, a Jew within Judaism, who nonetheless believed that Judaism required a radical reinterpretation in order to accommodate the radically new circumstances of the present age.

NOTES

1. For a listing of premodern Jewish authors who discuss Paul, see Daniel R. Langton, "The Myth of the 'Traditional View of Paul' and the Role of the Apostle in Modern Jewish-Christian Polemics," *Journal for the Study of the New Testament* 28, no. 1 (2005): 70n2; and his slightly longer treatment of those sources in his monograph, *The Apostle Paul in the Jewish Imagination: A Study in Modern Jewish-Christian Relations* (Cambridge: Cambridge University Press, 2010), 24–30. Among the figures he considers are the ninth-century philosopher al-Mukammis, the tenth-century Karaite Jacob Kirkisani, Judah Ben Elijah Hadassi of Constantinople, Benedict Spinoza, and Jacob Emden. Langton, *Apostle Paul*, 24–25, also notes with appropriate suspicion those modern scholars who have discerned cryptic references to Paul in rabbinic literature.

2. Langton, *Apostle Paul*, 57–96; Langton, "Myth of the 'Traditional View of Paul,'" 69–104; Daniel R. Langton, "Modern Jewish Identity and the Apostle Paul: Pauline Studies as an Intra-Jewish Ideological Battleground," *Journal for the Study of the New Testament* 28, no. 2 (2005): 217–58.

3. Isaac Mayer Wise, "Paul and the Mystics," in *Three Lectures on the Origin of Christianity* (Cincinnati: Bloch, 1883), 53–75; Kaufmann Kohler, "Saul of Tarsus," in *The Jewish Encyclopedia* (New York: Funk & Wagnalls, 1906), 79–87.

4. For a sampling of their respective work, see Alan F. Segal, *Paul the Convert: The Apostolate and Apostasy of Saul the Pharisee* (New Haven: Yale University Press, 1990); Mark D. Nanos, *The Mystery of Romans: The Jewish Context of Paul's Letter* (Minneapolis: Fortress, 1996); Paula Fredriksen, *Paul: The Pagans' Apostle* (New Haven: Yale University

Press, 2017); Daniel Boyarin, *A Radical Jew: Paul and the Politics of Identity* (Berkeley: University of California Press, 1994); Pamela Eisenbaum, *Paul Was Not a Christian: The Original Message of a Misunderstood Apostle* (New York: HarperOne, 2009). To include my own work would only add to the diversity: Joshua D. Garroway, *Paul's Gentile-Jews: Neither Jew nor Gentile, but Both* (New York: Palgrave, 2012); *The Beginning of the Gospel: Paul, Philippi, and the Origins of Christianity* (New York: Palgrave, 2018). In particular, Pamela Eisenbaum, "Following in the Footnotes of the Apostle Paul," in *Identity and the Politics of Scholarship in the Study of Religion,* ed. José Ignacio Cabezón and Sheila Greeve Davaney (New York: Routledge, 2004), 77–97, has emphasized the putative objectivity of professional Jewish New Testament scholars, insisting that a Jewish scholar of the New Testament, no less and no more than a Christian (or Muslim or Atheist) scholar, is held to the rigorous academic standards of evidence and argumentation.

5. For representative works, see Rudolf Bultmann, *Theology of the New Testament,* 2 vols., trans. K. Grobel, (New York: Scribner, 1951–55); Günther Bornkamm, *Paul,* trans. D. M. G. Stalker (Minneapolis: Fortress, 1995); Ernst Käsemann, *Commentary on Romans,* trans. G. W. Bromiley (Grand Rapids, MI: Eerdmans, 1980). For an instructive analysis of these figures and their approach to Paul, see Magnus Zetterholm, *Approaches to Paul: A Student's Guide to Recent Scholarship* (Minneapolis: Fortress, 2009), 69–94.

6. Ernst Käsemann, *Perspectives on Paul,* trans. Margaret Kohl (Philadelphia: Fortress, 1971), 70.

7. As represented in Langton, "Myth of the 'Traditional View of Paul,'" 70. He cites Nancy Fuchs Kreimer, "Seven Extant Letters of Rabbi Nancy Fuchs Kreimer of Philadelphia to Rabbi Paul of Tarsus: Letter 1," The Institute for Christian-Jewish Studies, http://icjs.org/scholars/letters .html, but that site is no longer active.

8. Adolf von Harnack, *History of Dogma,* trans. Neil Buchanan (New York: Dover, 1961); Albrecht Ritschl, *The Christian Doctrine of Justification and Reconciliation,* trans. H. R. Mackintosh and A. B. Macaulay (Clifton, NJ: Reference Book Publishers, 1966).

9. Heinrich Graetz, *History of the Jews from the Earliest Ties to the Present Day*, ed. and trans. Bella Loewy (London, 1901), 2:149.

10. Langton, "Myth of the 'Traditional View of Paul,'" 76.

11. Kohler, "Saul of Tarsus," 79–87.

12. Joseph Klausner, *From Jesus to Paul*, trans. William Stinespring (New York: Menorah, 1979), 443.

13. Graetz, *History of the Jews*, 2:231.

14. Wise, "Paul and the Mystics"; Joseph Krauskopf, *A Rabbi's Impressions of the Oberammergau Passion Play* (Philadelphia: Edward Stern, 1908).

15. Wise, "Paul and the Mystics," 67.

16. Among the many such treatments, see E. P. Sanders, *Jesus and Judaism* (Philadelphia: Fortress, 1985); Paula Fredriksen, *Jesus of Nazareth: King of the Jews* (New York: Vintage, 1999); and Bart D. Ehrman, *Jesus: Apocalyptic Prophet of the New Millennium* (Oxford: Oxford University Press, 1999).

17. E. P. Sanders, *Paul and Palestinian Judaism: A Comparison of Patterns of Religion* (Philadelphia: Fortress, 1977).

18. Works representative of the New Perspective on Paul include James D. G. Dunn, *The Theology of Paul the Apostle* (Grand Rapids, MI: Eerdmans, 1998); N. T. Wright, *The Climax of the Covenant* (London: T & T Clark, 1991). See further Zetterholm, *Approaches to Paul*, 95–126.

19. Krister Stendahl, "The Apostle Paul and the Introspective Conscience of the West," *Harvard Theological Review* 56 (1963): 199–215.

20. Among the works by these scholars are the essays compiled in Mark D. Nanos and Magnus Zetterholm, eds., *Paul within Judaism: Restoring the First-Century Context to the Apostle* (Minneapolis: Fortress, 2015).

21. Joshua Garroway, "Paul: Within Judaism, without Law," in *Law and Lawlessness in Early Judaism and Early Christianity*, ed. David Lincicum, Ruth Sheridan, and Charles M. Stang (Tübingen: Mohr Siebeck, 2019), 49–66.

22. Many of the standard works devoted to the life and thought of Holdheim are now more than one hundred years old: Immanuel Heinrich Ritter, *Samuel Holdheim: Sein Leben und seine Werke* (Berlin, 1865); David

Philipson, *Samuel Holdheim, Jewish Reformer (1806–1860)* (Cincinnati, 1906). The most recent, and possibly the most valuable, treatment of Holdheim is found in Christian Wiese, ed., *Redefining Judaism in an Age of Emancipation: Comparative Perspectives on Samuel Holdheim (1806–1860)* (Leiden: Brill, 2007).

23. As an example of this reevaluation of messianism among early Reform Jews, see the transcript from the 1845 Frankfurt Conference in Paul Mendes-Flohr and Jehuda Reinharz, *The Jew in the Modern World: A Documentary History*, 3rd ed. (Oxford: Oxford University Press, 1995), 183–85.

24. Samuel Holdheim, *Das Ceremonialgesetz im Messiasreich; als Vorläufer einer grössern Schrift über die religiöse Reform des Judenthums* (Schwerin: C. Kürschner, 1845), 7.

25. Graetz, *History of the Jews*, 5:680.

26. Philipson, *Samuel Holdheim*, 12.

5

Supersessionism and Latter-day Saint Thought: An Appraisal

JARED W. LUDLOW, ANDREW C. REED,
AND SHON D. HOPKIN

Since 2016 Jewish–Latter-day Saint dialogue participants have engaged in discussions of numerous topics and ideas that mark significant steps toward the establishment of a functional and productive cooperation and have fostered true friendships and greater understanding. Over the course of several dialogue sessions, the topic of supersessionism in Latter-day Saint thought remained in the background. There is good reason for this. First, supersessionism, or replacement theology,[1] looms so large in any dialogue between Jews and Christians that our delay in addressing it may well have helped to establish deep-seated trust in the dialogue team and a patient willingness to build common goals before tackling this topic. Second, Latter-day Saint thought on the subject has historically vacillated between abrasive supersessionist rhetoric and softer, more generous thought in both official and individual statements. As a result, summarizing a Latter-day Saint view is a daunting task, even with fewer than two hundred years of Latter-day Saint existence. We recognize that the topic of supersessionism will spark a great deal of debate, but the expectation is that this will open critical lines of questioning and offer clarity and understanding by exploring the shifting tides and trends within Latter-day Saint thought and teaching.

As a beginning point, the cautionary adage of Jon Levenson serves as a useful reminder that this topic is not easily brushed aside or glossed over. As Latter-day Saints and Jews engage with one another in honest dialogue, they must eventually encounter the hard parts of the theological differences. Levenson makes a case:

> An interreligious dialogue in which the parties ignore, water down, or explain away their distinctive truth claims can help to improve the relations among the participants as individuals, but it does so at a great cost: it requires them to ignore the theological core of their own tradition or to take so critical a view of it that it is no longer a meaningful and productive aspect of their identities. In my experience, that cost usually does not seem so great to my fellow Jews. They tend to go into Jewish-Christian dialogue out of a concern to correct prejudices and prevent persecutions—both without question worthy and necessary goals. But such a dialogue, while it is intercommunal, is not truly interreligious so long as it brackets the distinctive truth claims of each tradition or imagines that those truths speak to no reality outside the respective communities themselves. When the pursuit of good human relations and social justice is the controlling factor in the dialogue, mutual affirmation becomes the goal, and religious relativism soon takes over. The future of any religious community that accepts such a model is not very bright.[2]

This chapter traces three distinct points of impact on the broader shape of Latter-day Saint thinking about Jews and God's covenant with Israel: scriptural frames, nineteenth-century thought, and contemporary views (from the twentieth and twenty-first centuries). The challenge of dealing with the subject is that elements that led to overtly supersessionist teachings in Christian thought also influenced Latter-day Saint thought, broadly speaking.[3] At the same time, Latter-day Saint thought often mutes or tones down these supersessionist tendencies because of strong theological viewpoints that maintain and protect the ancient covenantal status of Israel in God's grand plan for humankind. Within this chapter, we follow Levenson's guidance and try to avoid any bracketing of particular Latter-day Saint truth claims. At the same time, when supersessionist ideas exist, we try to acknowledge them without downplaying their significance.

Supersessionism exists in all religious traditions in one form or another. Edward Kessler suggests that Islamic supersessionism of both Judaism and Christianity could productively remind Christians how their own form of thought about superseding Judaism feels when the point of view is flipped and they become the superseded.[4] Christian supersessionism, as Christopher Leighton argues, suggests that God's new covenant belongs to Christians, and more specifically to "the Church," since the covenant made anciently to Israel expired because of unworthiness, rejection, or irrelevance after the life of Jesus.[5] David Novak maintains that within contemporary Judaism and Christianity today, there are hard and soft forms of supersessionism. The divide between hard supersessionism and its soft form stems from the insistence of eradication rather than accommodation. By Novak's estimation, hard Christian supersessionists demand that "the only option for Jews is conversion to Christianity," while soft supersessionism allows for a kind of theological and practical validity for Judaism that fosters dialogue.[6] The history of Christian scripture posits a unique challenge to those who seek to eradicate supersessionist thinking from Christianity because of the insistence upon christological readings of the Hebrew Bible that must confront Matthew's fulfillment passages and Paul's contested impact upon Christianity.[7] As one commentator on the place of supersessionism in the Catholic lectionary readings for the Second Sunday of Advent noted, "We need some kind of supersessionism."[8] Likewise,

Novak argues that supersessionism (whether Jewish or Christian in origin), appropriately "stands as an *inner* Christian and an *inner* Jewish matter." That is, the individual community engagement with supersessionism requires that each community find purpose in their supersessionist tendencies to improve their community. Thus the Christian community "need[s] to be able to answer to themselves why they ought to remain Christian and not become Jewish; and we Jews need from time to time to be able to explain to ourselves why we remain Jewish and do not become Christian."[9] The deeply entrenched notions of supersessionism go beyond reading scripture to interpreting scripture within theological frames and delimit the applicability of our answers. This is the difficult work of fitting religious tenets into practical necessity—the two can work together, but occasionally this requires significant acknowledgment of the issues preventing productive relational development among religious traditions and concerted effort to view the possibilities in a fresh light. This article is an effort in that direction.

ELECTION AS A CENTRAL PROBLEM IN SUPERSESSIONISM

The subject of election is at the heart of Jewish and Christian historical worldviews. Both religious traditions couch their lived religion and their communal memories on the notion that God has, in some merciful way, elected them to do something in the world. The biblical narrative highlights moments of this concept of election. The late scholar Jacob Neusner reflected on Christian claims and rightly noted that among a number of distinctions, Jews and Christians diverge on the notion of election. "The Christian emphasis on faith over works and on the individual, indeed unique, man who is also God yields a different cultural ethos. For Christianity, the emphasis is on the individual worshipper. Each individual Christian enters into the Church individually, through baptism. Election is a personal matter." On the other hand, Neusner believed that among Jews "election

... is a communal matter. Jews are a people, tracing an ancestry back to Abraham and Sarah, Isaac and Rebekah, and Jacob and his wives. Jacob, whose name was changed to Israel, is the father of the people Israel."[10] For many Jews, the passage from Isaiah 49:5–8 makes clear that Israel was appointed as a "covenant people." Further, the communal nature of Israel's election rested in the call to service and to "be a light of nations."[11] Christians often look to certain passages to make the case for followers of Jesus as having taken on that role of God's people (1 Peter 1:4–10; Galatians 4:22–5:1).

While The Church of Jesus Christ of Latter-day Saints is a new religious movement (est. 1830), it draws heavily upon biblical narratives and frames its existence within the textual history of Judaism and Christianity. Supersessionism, as developed in Christian thought, required exclusion of other religious alternatives as incomplete or incorrect in their worldview. Thus exclusive claims to truth required subsequent exclusive claims to relationship with God. Within Latter-day Saint thought, such ideas are poignantly present at times, but so too are ideas that trade exclusion for inclusion in God's working out of the divine plan. The Book of Mormon serves both purposes at times, depending upon the reading and approach taken by scholars, students, and believers. For example, the Book of Mormon sometimes castigates the waywardness of God's early covenant people, warning them of forfeited blessings and revoking their identification as God's people. Yet at other times, often through tree imagery, Book of Mormon passages portray the original roots as life-giving and ever central to God's dealings with his children on earth.[12] Beyond the Book of Mormon as a text, The Church of Jesus Christ of Latter-day Saints also builds upon a foundation of contemporary prophetic leaders who speak for the Church as a whole. Latter-day Saints believe that God continues to speak through modern prophets, so they study modern revelations as contained in a book known as the Doctrine and Covenants as well as pronouncements made by Church leaders in general conferences twice a year.

Additionally, Latter-day Saints tend to use Paul as a way of framing early Christianity. They also study the Hebrew Bible or Old Testament and employ it in their attempt to understand God and covenantal relations.

These multivalent sources of revelation and inspiration mean that Latter-day Saints are encouraged to accept truth from many sources and that they recognize that truth originates in God. One of the early Latter-day Saint Church presidents, John Taylor (1808–1887), suggested:

> We are open for the reception of all truth, of whatever nature it may be, and are desirous to obtain and possess it, to search after it as we would for hidden treasures; and to use all the knowledge God gives to us to possess ourselves of all the intelligence that he has given to others; and to ask at his hands to reveal unto us his will, in regard to things that are the best calculated to promote the happiness and well-being of human society. If there are any good principles, any moral philosophy that we have not yet attained to we are desirous to learn them. . . . If there are any religious ideas, any theological truths, any principles pertaining to God, that we have not learned, we ask mankind, and we pray God, our heavenly Father, to enlighten our minds that we may comprehend, realize, embrace and live up to them as part of our religious faith.[13]

In practical terms, Latter-day Saints recognize through the Book of Mormon that "God is mindful of every people, whatsoever land they may be in; yea, he numbereth his people, and his bowels of mercy are over all the earth" (Alma 26:37). There is ample room within Latter-day Saint thought for multiple covenants and multiple ways through which God works with people over time. Latter-day Saints look to the Book of Mormon as a foundation for that space of openness. All of this being said, historically there are noticeable strands of thought that have claimed a more exclusionary approach to election and salvation—that is, one can be saved only through the work of and belief in Jesus Christ. This doctrinal point is significant because it is the message that is taught to all members of the Church from the youngest children to the most senior of Church leaders.

However, there is a unique perspective on Jews and Judaism among Latter-day Saints that often seems (or *is*) philo-Semitic in nature. Anecdotally, when Latter-day Saints meet Jews, they often claim a distinctive relationship based on assumptions framed through the Book of Mormon. The Book of Mormon teaches that Jews are God's covenant people who have a special mission to complete in the world today and that there will be an eventual reconciliation of God to his covenant people. In 1978 the First Presidency of the Church produced a statement on "God's Love for All Mankind" in which they maintained that "the Hebrew prophets prepared the way for the coming of Jesus Christ, the promised Messiah, who should provide salvation for all mankind who believe in the gospel. Consistent with these truths we believe that God has given and will give to all peoples sufficient knowledge to help them on their way to eternal salvation, either in this life or in the life to come."[14] This statement has not received the kind of sustained treatment that it might have, but it does promote a different take on God's work in the world than many Latter-day Saints have traditionally espoused. In 1921 Heber J. Grant (then President of the Church) prodded members to remember that God's covenant people need support. He commented in a periodical meant for all members of the Church:

> Some of you may be familiar with the agitation that is going on at the present time, in the publications, against the Jewish peo-ple. . . . By the authority of the Holy Priesthood of God, that has again been restored to the earth, and by the ministration, under the direction of the Prophet of God, Apostles of the Lord Jesus Christ have been to the Holy Land and have dedicated that country for the return of the Jews; and we believe that in the due

time of the Lord they shall be in the favor of God again. And let no Latter-day Saint be guilty of taking any part in any crusade against these people.[15]

Latter-day Saint leaders throughout their history have suggested many things about the place of Jews within God's providential plan. Thus in trying to sketch the landscape, we hope that both positive and negative sides are recognized for being part of a multivalent and evolving story. In the following pages, we provide snapshots (with due weight given to the Book of Mormon) of Latter-day Saint thought historically and theologically regarding Jews and Judaism.

CONCEPTIONS OF THE JEWS IN THE BOOK OF MORMON

Latter-day Saints share conceptions of Jews common to other Christians based on the New Testament and particularly from Paul's teachings vis-à-vis Jews. However, Latter-day Saint conceptions of Jews are based not only on these writings but are especially influenced by the Book of Mormon.[16] In this section we will examine some of these Book of Mormon teachings about Jews to see how they are presented in light of God's covenant. Do Jews remain God's covenant people throughout time, or have they somehow been replaced by another group? The Book of Mormon's discussion of the Jews is lengthy and varied, so unsurprisingly this overview can highlight only major aspects of the Book of Mormon's conceptions of the Jews. We hope our discussion will demonstrate the variety of considerations and reveal why Latter-day Saints feel a closeness to the Jews and their role in God's salvation history, including what things Latter-day Saints believe will happen among the Jews in the last days for God to fully unfold his plan for his children here on earth.

To understand the perspective of the Book of Mormon, perhaps it would be helpful to review possibly the most important assumption about this text for a typical Latter-day Saint reader: this text is viewed as an ancient document transmitted *through* Joseph Smith and not simply created ex nihilo by him in the 1820s. As such, this book is believed to be a record of the events and history of a people closely connected with the house of Israel and originating from Jerusalem and its environs. The people, who leave Jerusalem and eventually settle in the Americas, are seen as a remnant of the house of Israel, a true branch of the original tree. Some of the record's stated purposes from its title page are to show the modern descendants of these people the great things God has done for their fathers and to teach them the covenants of the Lord, that they are not cast off forever. Despite being separated geographically from the other branches or tribes of the house of Israel, the Book of Mormon peoples maintain a spiritual rootedness in God's promises made to his Israelite prophets before 600 BCE (the time of departure from Jerusalem). For this reason, the teachings of Hebrew prophets, principally Isaiah, remain influential throughout the Book of Mormon—the covenant promises have not yet all been fulfilled.

The departure from Jerusalem results in two important outcomes: the idea of another promised land besides the land of Israel and new prophetic leaders called among their people. Thus while the Book of Mormon peoples feel connected to the Abrahamic covenant and the teachings of preexilic prophets, they proceed on a new trajectory into their own promised land in the Americas and receive additional divine instruction for their unique situation. While some of these instructions are practical guides for living their covenants in new circumstances, some are eschatological and point them to the future gathering of the house of Israel as a fulfillment of the promises made to their fathers, even if that means their land of inheritance remains in the Americas. They simply see themselves as planted in a different part of the Lord's vineyard, a perceived fulfillment of Joseph's promise to be a fruitful bough whose branches run over the wall (see Genesis 49:22).[17]

Another important Latter-day Saint belief gleaned from the Book of Mormon is that Jesus appeared among that people following his resurrection in Jerusalem. Though the Book of Mormon peoples had no contact with Jesus during his earthly ministry, his appearance among them as a resurrected being led to his imparting some teachings from his earthly ministry as well as additional commandments for them in a post–law of Moses setting.[18] Though he appeared and remained with them only a few days, Latter-day Saints view this as the zenith of the record. The earlier prophets had looked forward to this pivotal event, which strongly influenced subsequent generations as well. In this way the Book of Mormon reveals many messianic prophecies before Christ's mortal ministry, gives a brief account of his visit as a resurrected being, and includes some reflections on Jesus's teachings until around 400 CE. The Book of Mormon is therefore wholly Christian throughout and is considered another testament of Jesus Christ, or another witness of his role in God's plan of salvation alongside the Bible, even though, ironically, the book does not narrate anything from Christ's mortal ministry.

When discussing Jews, the Book of Mormon generally speaks about them in three different time periods: the preexilic period shortly before the Babylonian conquest, the time of Jesus's earthly ministry, and the last days. Therefore, one can see the remembrance of the Jews for their inheritance fading in the distance in the centuries following 600 BCE after the initial group leaves Jerusalem. They no longer have any contact with the Jews in Jerusalem, and Jews basically exist only as a historical memory. When the Jews are mentioned later in the text, they are primarily discussed in *prophecy* during Jesus's day and the last days with the exception of Jesus's own words in his brief post-Resurrection appearance (Jesus is the only Book of Mormon figure to have physical contact with the Jews after the sixth century BCE).[19] In the first two periods, the Jews' wicked actions are noted as the causes for their forfeiture of covenant blessings, such as military protection and abiding in the land; therefore, they are scattered into exile and diaspora. When discussing the last days, the Book of Mormon focuses on the scattered state of the Jews and the role of the Gentiles to help gather them back. Therefore, the Book of Mormon takes the perspective that its prophecies and teachings are primarily an inner house of Israel dialogue; the "Jews" are treated as one branch or part of the house of Israel, and the Book of Mormon peoples are yet another.[20] Thus when criticisms and condemnations are aimed toward the Jews, it is akin to Israelite prophets reproving their people for their wickedness and warning them of God's punishments rather than outsiders rejecting them as covenant people. They have temporarily broken the covenant, and thus God must turn away for a time and allow them to be scattered; however, God will never completely forsake nor forget them (see Isaiah 49:14–15 and 1 Nephi 21:14–15).

The Book of Mormon prophets make some specific critiques of the Jews, the people from whence they were taken, to help their people avoid some of the Jews' existing and impending wickedness (but of course the Book of Mormon peoples then fall into their own wickedness at various times in their new land). Lehi, the initial prophet who left Jerusalem, and two of his sons outline—through their own experience in Jerusalem and through prophetic vision—what they believe will happen to the people they recently left around 600 BCE. At the beginning of the record, Nephi, the first record keeper of what came to be the Book of Mormon, recounts why Lehi's family left Jerusalem: the people were warned they must repent or Jerusalem would be destroyed—no one repented, so they departed. Lehi prophesied to and warned the inhabitants of Jerusalem, but they mocked him and angrily rejected his condemnation of their wickedness and his teachings of a Messiah who would come to redeem the world (see 1 Nephi 1:19–20). Nephi also states that although he was taught in the learning of the Jews, he did not readily share that learning with his people because "their works were works of darkness, and their doings were doings of abominations" (2 Nephi 25:2). Nephi yearns "for those who are at Jerusalem" but is grateful he was taken out of Jerusalem before his family also perished (see 1 Nephi 19:20).

Jacob, one of Nephi's brothers, also taught that the Jews were a stiffnecked people who "despised the words of plainness, and killed the prophets, and sought for things that they could not understand. Wherefore, because of their blindness, which blindness came by looking beyond the mark, they must needs fall" (Jacob 4:14). Their stumbling, Jacob taught, would lead them to reject the stone and sure foundation of the Messiah. He presented a lengthy allegory in Jacob 5 to explain how the Jews may go from once rejecting to later building upon the sure foundation. In the allegory, the roots of the main tame olive tree represent the covenant promises made to the fathers, but the tops of the branches, representing the house of Israel, begin to decay because of disobedience and corruption. The master of the vineyard, therefore, destroys some branches, scatters others to various parts of the vineyard, and grafts in new, wild branches (Gentiles). Eventually this process essentially gets reversed to preserve the original roots and restore branches to their original trees.

Lehi gives one of the early prophecies about the Jews that seems to be a common vision that others will also see and relate. They view a historical progression that comprises elements such as the Jews' Babylonian exile and return, prophecies of the coming Messiah, rejection of the Messiah, scattering among the Gentiles, Gentiles as instruments in their gathering, and eventual acceptance of the Messiah (see 1 Nephi 10:3–5, 11–14).

One of the strongest condemnations of those "at Jerusalem" is a prophecy that they will be "scourged by all people, because they crucify the God of Israel" (1 Nephi 19:13), and that Jerusalem will be destroyed *again* (see 2 Nephi 25:14), the first time being by the Babylonians. As a result of despising the Holy One of Israel, "they shall wander in the flesh, and perish, and become a hiss and a byword, and be hated among all nations" (1 Nephi 19:14; see 2 Nephi 6:9–10). "Wherefore, the Jews shall be scattered among all nations; yea, and also Babylon shall be destroyed; wherefore, the Jews shall be scattered by other nations" (2 Nephi 25:15). In even stronger language, the Book of Mormon points out that the Messiah will come among his people and that no other people would crucify their God (see 2 Nephi 10:3–6).

Yet despite these wicked conditions, the promise of mercy is always extended for when they no longer turn aside their hearts. "Then will he [God] remember the covenants which he made to their fathers. Yea, then will he remember the isles of the sea; yea, and all the people who are of the house of Israel, will I gather in" (1 Nephi 19:15–16). God will not allow them to completely perish so that he can show his mercy, and "they shall be gathered together again to the lands of their inheritance" (2 Nephi 6:11; see 2 Nephi 9:2).[21]

In a subsequent chapter, Nephi teaches his brothers that the house of Israel will be scattered upon all the face of the earth among all nations. In fact, some were already lost from the knowledge of those at Jerusalem. Yet the scattered tribes, through the instrumentality of the Gentiles who initially scattered them, would be nurtured and gathered back to the lands of their inheritance (see 1 Nephi 22:6–12; 2 Nephi 6:12). The covenants made to Abraham and others will thereby be remembered and fulfilled. Near the end of the Book of Mormon, Mormon declared to the future Gentiles that "ye need not any longer hiss, nor spurn, nor make game of the Jews, nor any of the remnant of the house of Israel; for behold, the Lord remembereth his covenant unto them, and he will do unto them according to that which he hath sworn" (3 Nephi 29:8).

Despite some of the negative portrayals of the Jews or those at Jerusalem, particularly regarding the consequences that befall them because of their unfaithfulness to the covenant, the Book of Mormon does praise the Jews, especially in the area of scripture and prophecy. Nephi, though he said he did not teach his people the manner of the Jews, still acknowledges that they have, in fact, a great understanding of Isaiah and prophecy (see 2 Nephi 25:5). In a vision of the future,

Nephi states that a book (the Bible) would proceed forth from the mouth of a Jew containing the fullness of the gospel of the Lord. It would "go forth from the Jews in purity unto the Gentiles" (1 Nephi 13:25). Then, after going among the Gentiles, the scriptural text would be corrupted by the "great and abominable church," which would take away many plain and precious parts "and also many covenants of the Lord" (1 Nephi 13:26). Eventually the Gentiles would carry this book, "which had proceeded forth from the mouth of a Jew" (1 Nephi 13:29), and other books unto a remnant of the seed of the Book of Mormon peoples "unto the convincing of the Gentiles and the remnant of the seed of my brethren, and also the Jews who were scattered upon all the face of the earth, that the records of the prophets and of the twelve apostles of the Lamb are true" (1 Nephi 13:39). In a strong warning to the Gentiles, the Lord emphasizes the vital role the Jews played in bringing forth scripture (the Bible).

> O fools, they shall have a Bible; and it shall proceed forth from the Jews, mine ancient covenant people. And what thank they the Jews for the Bible which they receive from them? Yea, what do the Gentiles mean? Do they remember the travails, and the labors, and the pains of the Jews, and their diligence unto me, in bringing forth salvation unto the Gentiles? O ye Gentiles, have ye remembered the Jews, mine ancient covenant people? Nay; but ye have cursed them, and have hated them, and have not sought to recover them. But behold, I will return all these things upon your own heads; for I the Lord have not forgotten my people. (2 Nephi 29:4–5)[22]

The Gentiles' relationship with the Jews as outlined in the Book of Mormon is a complicated one. Part of this complication arises because the Book of Mormon seems to use a different definition of Gentile from that of the Hebrew Bible. Whereas the Hebrew Bible tends to use *Gentile* for any stranger in the land or foreigner—in other words, a non-Israelite by blood—the Book of Mormon seems to use more of a cultural definition. Usually in prophecy and future visions, the Book of Mormon describes the Gentiles as those living away from the land of Israel who do not observe Israelite cultic practices. On the surface they look like Gentiles whether they may happen to be Israelite descendants or not (and it seems some Gentiles mentioned in the Book of Mormon were actually scattered Israelites now living among the Gentiles). Within the Book of Mormon, the Gentiles are both the primary aggressors against the house of Israel (similar to the role of the Assyrians in the eighth century BCE against the Israelites—tools in God's hands, but not envisioned as righteous) as well as the chief instruments in gathering them back to the lands of their inheritance (e.g., 2 Nephi 10:18). The Gentiles thus become instruments of God both in exacting justice on his wayward children *and* in delivering scripture, teachings, and support needed to help them return to the covenant path (see 1 Nephi 22:7–11). They have "care for the house of Israel" and "will sorrow for the calamity of the house of Israel" (Mormon 5:10–11).

The Book of Mormon teaches that in the pre-Christian world the people kept the law of Moses and by so doing could reach salvation because it was all they could do at that point. Various Book of Mormon writers taught that the purpose and intent of the law of Moses was to look forward to the Messiah and believe in him "as though he already was" (see Jarom 1:11). Latter-day Saint interpretation, therefore, follows the common Christian hermeneutic in viewing the Hebrew Bible through the lens of messianic prophecy. More particularly, however, Latter-day Saints believe that the Book of Mormon people saw *Jesus* as the very Messiah and the divine Son and Jehovah of the Hebrew Bible—these people kept the law of Moses because it pointed to him.[23] The Book of Mormon prophets taught that Jesus played a role as a premortal God in appearing to prophets and giving commandments to the people. Jesus continued to play a direct role both among the Jews during his mortal ministry and among this relocated branch when he appeared to them after his resurrection and taught them the commandments they must now follow—sometimes it was a continuation of what was previously taught, but other times he presented new interpretations or foci that differed from other Jewish teachings of his day. In the risen Jesus's own words, the Book of Mormon clearly states that the law that was given to Moses was fulfilled in him; however, all the words of the prophets must be fulfilled but had not yet been, and thus the covenant made with his people was not all fulfilled (3 Nephi 15:4–8). The risen Jesus supersedes and becomes the replacement for the law since he was the one who initially gave it to Moses (15:5), but he also continues to work toward fulfilling all the covenant promises made through prophets such as the final gathering of the house of Israel. It is a lengthy salvation history with many twists, turns, rejections, and returns, but ultimately it is an everlasting plan, a single path, intended to bring as many of God's children to salvation as possible.

The Book of Mormon consistently teaches the necessity for all, both Jew and Gentile, to accept Jesus as the Messiah. In a lengthy prophecy after quoting from multiple chapters of Isaiah, Nephi states that the Jews will be scattered and scourged by other nations for the space of many generations until they shall be persuaded to believe in Christ and his Atonement.[24] The Lord will restore his people from their lost and fallen state and bring forth scripture to convince them of the true Messiah (see 2 Nephi 26:16–19). Mormon, one of the last writers in the Book of Mormon, wrote around 360 CE that every person from the whole human family of Adam must stand before the judgment seat. He also declared that "the Jews, the covenant people of the Lord, shall have other witness besides him whom they saw and heard, that Jesus, whom they slew, was the very Christ and the very God" (Mormon 3:21).

A key event in facilitating the acceptance of Jesus as the Messiah consists of bringing together various records of the scattered branches of the house of Israel. In this narrative, Jews will eventually have the writings of the Nephites, and they both will have the writings of the other tribes of the house of Israel. This amassing of God's word matches the physical gathering of the house of Israel to the lands of their possessions (see 2 Nephi 29:12–14).

Several Book of Mormon writers proclaimed that their writings, though hidden for a while to preserve and protect them, would come forth in the last days unto a remnant of the house of Jacob and go among the unbelieving of the Jews. For what purpose? To persuade them that Jesus is the Christ, the Son of the living God, and that thereby God, in fulfillment of his covenant, could restore the Jews and all the house of Israel to the land of their inheritance (see Mormon 5:14).

The Book of Mormon prophesies that the Lamb of God will "manifest himself unto all nations, both unto the Jews and also unto the Gentiles; and after he has manifested himself unto the Jews and also unto the Gentiles, then he shall manifest himself unto the Gentiles and also unto the Jews, and the last shall be first, and the first shall be last" (1 Nephi 13:42). "The last shall be first, and the first shall be last" is a concept found repeatedly in the Book of Mormon and describes the chronology of God's salvation history in which the Jews are given the first opportunity as God's covenant people in ancient times, but because they reject the Messiah, the covenant and authority pass to the Gentiles. In the last days, the Gentiles have the initial responsibility and instrumentality of carrying forth God's covenant purposes and bringing the Jews and others of the house of Israel back into the covenant and to the lands of their inheritance. This period is sometimes referred to as the times of the Gentiles.[25] As long as the Gentiles remain humble and repentant, they can partake of the covenant blessings, but if not, they will be trodden down while the Jews and other scattered remnants return to God's full covenant blessings.[26]

So in the end, who constitutes the covenant people of the Lord? The Book of Mormon does not identify the covenant people solely by blood or lineage. According to one definition, those who repent and believe in God's Son are numbered among the Lord's chosen.

"As many of the Gentiles as will repent are the covenant people of the Lord; and as many of the Jews as will not repent shall be cast off; for the Lord covenanteth with none save it be with them that repent and believe in his Son, who is the Holy One of Israel" (2 Nephi 30:2). Before his death, Nephi concludes with this counsel:

> I have charity for the Jew—I say Jew, because I mean them from whence I came. I also have charity for the Gentiles. But behold, for none of these can I hope except they shall be reconciled unto Christ, and enter into the narrow gate, and walk in the strait path which leads to life, and continue in the path until the end of the day of probation. And now, my beloved brethren, and also Jew, and all ye ends of the earth, hearken unto these words and believe in Christ; and if ye believe not in these words believe in Christ. And if ye shall believe in Christ ye will believe in these words, for they are the words of Christ, and he hath given them unto me; and they teach all men that they should do good. (2 Nephi 33:8–10)

Nephi ends with a stern warning. "You that will not partake of the goodness of God, and respect the words of the Jews, and also my words, and the words which shall proceed forth out of the mouth of the Lamb of God, behold, I bid you an everlasting farewell, for these words shall condemn you at the last day" (2 Nephi 33:14).

The Book of Mormon clearly and consistently teaches that Jesus is the Messiah and must be accepted as such for ultimate salvation. The Book of Mormon can be seen as the model of how some members of the house of Israel were living in accordance with the law of Moses while also putting their faith in prophecies of Jesus as the Messiah even before he fulfilled his mortal ministry. Others in the Book of Mormon lambasted and opposed this view, leading some to fall away, but some remained faithful to the messianic prophecies. The Book of Mormon also asserts that the ancient records such as the Bible and the Book of Mormon will come forth to bear witness of the need to accept Jesus as the Messiah. Thus for the Book of Mormon, the covenant people are neither the Jews nor the Gentiles, but those who repent and believe in Jesus as the Messiah and God's Son. The same requirements for achieving salvation pertain to all, both Jew and Gentile. However, *who* plays the primary role in bringing forth God's word to the remnants of the house of Israel varies through time depending on the faithfulness of the people: first the Jews, then the Gentiles.

THE JEWS IN THE DOCTRINE AND COVENANTS

The terms *Jew(s)* and *children of Judah* appear twenty-five times in the Latter-day Saint book of scripture known as the Doctrine and Covenants, which is primarily a record of the teachings and revelations of Joseph Smith.[27] These references follow three main themes. First, the majority of the instances speak of God's work as being both for the Gentiles and for the Jews, repeating themes first found in the Book of Mormon and almost always using the two terms (*Gentiles* and *Jews*) in conjunction.[28] Second, the terms are sometimes used when describing aspects of biblical history (often as that history is understood through a uniquely Christian or Latter-day Saint lens) or when naming the Jews as the authors of the biblical text.[29]

Finally, references to Jews in the Doctrine and Covenants prophesy of the role the Jews will play in the last days leading up to and including the end of times.[30] Some of these prophecies mirror other strands of Christian thought that interpreted prophetic texts from the Hebrew Bible—and from the book of Revelation in the New Testament, which builds on those texts—as referring to a future time when two prophets will rise up in Jerusalem.[31] These figures will prophesy to the Jewish people (see Doctrine and Covenants 77:15) and work miracles to prevent the nations of the world from destroying the Jews. The two prophets will eventually be slain, but Jesus will return to rescue his covenant people, the Jews. He will set foot upon the Mount of Olives, and an earthquake will ensue that will rock the entire area and split the mount in two (see Doctrine and Covenants 45:48; 133:18–20). The Jews will notice the wounds in their rescuer's hands, recognize Jesus as the Messiah for whom they had waited, and weep with the recognition (see Doctrine and Covenants 45:51–53).[32]

Although Latter-day Saint prophetic voices anticipate the fulfillment of biblical prophecy in ways that mirror some strands of Christian thought, other prophetic texts in the Doctrine and Covenants make clear that God's covenant relationship with the Jews remains intact and that they continue to play a central role in the unfolding of his plans. In Smith's dedicatory prayer of the Kirtland Temple, he prayed and prophesied "that Jerusalem, from this hour, may begin to be redeemed; and the yoke of bondage may begin to be broken off from the house of David; and the children of Judah may begin to return to the lands which thou didst give to Abraham, their father" (Doctrine and Covenants 109:62–64). This 1836 prayer is closely associated with Smith's decision to send one of his most trusted leaders, Orson Hyde, on a mission to Jerusalem to dedicate that land for the return of the Jews, a mission that was accomplished by Hyde in 1841.[33] A later prophecy focused on the end time encourages the Gentiles to flee to Zion (probably understood as the then-center of the Church in Missouri) and for the Jews to flee to Jerusalem, going "out from among the nations, even from Babylon, from the midst of wickedness" (Doctrine and Covenants 133:14). A statement from the same prophecy indicates that the Jews will continue beyond the end time and into the millennial era as God's covenant people: "And they also of the tribe of Judah, after their pain, shall be sanctified in holiness before the Lord, to dwell in his presence day and night, forever and ever" (Doctrine and Covenants 133:35). Although the prophecies in the Doctrine and Covenants envision the Jews as eventually being converted to Christ, they strongly affirm the Book of Mormon teachings that God's covenant purposes will continue with the Jewish people.

LATTER-DAY SAINTS BETWEEN NAUVOO AND UTAH

Views and statements by later Latter-day Saints regarding the Jews continued to follow the main outlines provided by the Book of Mormon and Doctrine and Covenants. They also showed two other strands of thought. First, in the early Utah years, Brigham Young and subsequent Church leaders continued to rely on Joseph Smith's Nauvoo expressions of the importance of religious tolerance and of protecting the great variety of religious expressions. Smith had summarized these views in two of his thirteen Articles of Faith. The eleventh article of faith states, "We claim the privilege of worshiping Almighty God according to the dictates of our own conscience, and allow all men the same privilege, let them worship how, where, or what they may." The thirteenth article of faith proclaims, "If there is anything virtuous, lovely, or of good report or praiseworthy, we seek after these things." Although the city of Nauvoo was fully dominated by Latter-day Saints, Smith ensured that freedom of religious expression was encoded in a Nauvoo City Ordinance.[34]

Second, the statements of Brigham Young and others seem designed to explain the lack of Jewish conversions to the great Latter-day Saint project in Utah. The Latter-day Saints were greatly isolated in their new mountain home, but their missionaries continued to depart and return, having interacted with those of all faiths and religious persuasions. Latter-day Saint views from the pulpit not only express respect for the covenant status of the Jews but also critically contemplate the impossibility of converting them. This inability to convert Jews leaves the task in the hands of God and does not seek to focus on Jewish conversion at the time, viewing the lack of Jewish incomers as further evidence that the "time of the Gentiles" was still in force. Further, prophetic statements from the Doctrine and Covenants were interpreted as a likely indication that God's plan for the Jews would include a delay in their conversion to the gospel until the time of Jesus's coming to the Mount of Olives.

Statements of religious tolerance toward the Jews (and other religions) typically contained within them a strong flavor of Latter-day Saint superiority. For example, Brigham Young taught that there would be many religions on the earth after the coming of Jesus but also taught that all would confess to the Savior (a potential contradiction that he does not elucidate further).[35]

In one statement, Church leader Parley P. Pratt combined the position of the thirteenth article of faith, that Latter-day Saints would seek after every good thing, with a view of the particular chosen status of the Jewish people:

> If I were a Jew, you might cry to me and preach to me until doomsday, and then take a sword, and hold it over me to sever my head from my body, but I should say, "I will not move one step to the standard that is not Abraham's, nor from the everlasting covenant in which my fathers Abraham, Isaac, and Jacob, and all the holy Prophets will come and sit down in the presence of God, upon the same principles with their modern children. I am a Jew, and my hope is in the covenants of the fathers. "Well," says one, "I am a Jew; I guess I can get up a quarrel with you." No, you cannot. I shall not contend with you, for the Jews have got true principles, and they possess no truth but what belongs to "Mormonism"; for there is not a truth on earth or in heaven, that is not embraced in "Mormonism."[36]

Pratt affirms that the Jewish people are part of the covenant and that, apparently, this status provides them unique access to true principles. His admiration for Jewish religious intractability is also apparent, although that admiration was expressed more critically at other times.

Later, Wilford Woodruff reiterated Book of Mormon teachings of the chosen status of the Jewish people: "I thank God that the day is at hand when the Jews will be restored. I have felt to pray for them; I feel interested in their behalf, for they are of the seed of Abraham and a branch of the house of Israel, and the promises of God still remain with them."[37]

Both Young and Woodruff, however, declared that Jews could not be converted, with Young making it clear that this intractability did not just stem from their loyalty to the covenant but that it also stemmed from their ancient decision to reject Jesus. Although it was commonly taught that the time of the Jews' conversion would not arrive until the time of the Gentiles was fulfilled, Young, in what was one of his strongest statements concerning the Jews, went so far as to state that they would be the last of all of God's people who would be converted to a belief:

> Can you make a Christian of a Jew? I tell you, nay. If a Jew comes into this Church, and honestly professes to be a Saint, a follower of Christ, and if the blood of Judah is in his veins, he will apostatize. Jerusalem is not to be redeemed by the soft still voice of the preacher of the Gospel of peace. Why? Because they were once the blessed of the Lord, the chosen of the Lord, the promised seed. They were the people from among whom should spring the Messiah; and salvation could be found only through that tribe. The Messiah came through them, and they killed him; and they will be the last of all the seed of Abraham to have the privilege of receiving the New and Everlasting Covenant. You may hand out to them gold, you may feed and clothe them, but it is impossible to convert the Jews, until the Lord God Almighty does it; . . . they will be the last of all the seed of Abraham to have the privilege of receiving the New and Everlasting Covenant.[38]

Although Young's remarks attribute the inability to convert as a hallmark of early rejection of the Messiah, they also remove Jews as a Latter-day Saint object of conversion, leaving that conversion in the hands of God for the appropriate time.

Woodruff took a similar approach, although not speaking as negatively as Young: "You cannot convert a Jew, you may as well try to convert this house of solid walls as to convert them into the faith of Christ. They are set in their feelings, and they will be until the time of their redemption."³⁹ Thus early in their history as a separate people, Church leaders were already helping to place the Jewish people in a category set apart—not being fully subject to proselytizing because of their intractable natures; being subject to conversion by God rather than by evangelizing; holding a special place as one of God's covenant people in possession of truth; but also being considered (at least in the Young statement cited above) the last people who would become converted to Christ. It was not until the Latter-day Saints began to emerge from isolation in the twentieth century that their discourse regarding the Jewish people significantly shifted.

TWENTIETH CENTURY TO THE PRESENT DAY

The development of a scriptural canon that became tightly constructed as the standard works of the Church by the first decades of the twentieth century presented new opportunities for extrascriptural theological development.⁴⁰ Further, the gradual centralization of the Church hierarchy in the Salt Lake Valley, coupled with a new age of stability, allowed for more concerted efforts toward the production of books that would aid Latter-day Saints in their study of scripture and history. Even then, the importance of and influence of "bookish academics," or trained theologians, was marginal at best in the early decades of the twentieth century.⁴¹ Those who generated Latter-day Saint thought with regard to practical, eschatological, and spiritual matters were the result of several generations of individuals whose influence overlapped in ecclesiological and intellectual arenas. When members of the Church talk of "Latter-day Saint thought" in the twentieth century, they most often refer to those comments and writings produced by Church leaders known as General Authorities. These include members of the First Presidency and Quorum of the Twelve Apostles and other leaders with close connections to Church headquarters. Latter-day Saints do not have trained theologians who do the intellectual and spiritual work of generating theological trac-tates. While members look to Church leaders as spiritual heads of the institution, they do so not because of theological or scholarly acu-men but rather because they view them as uniquely chosen for work within the global church by God. These individuals often come from backgrounds in business, medicine, law, or education. Thus an assess-ment of Latter-day Saint thought requires one to situate the diver-sity of comments, teachings, and writings of these individuals within their particular settings. Some writings are understood as authorita-tive to Latter-day Saints, while others (because of their more esoteric or unsubstantiated claims) are less so.[42]

Within twentieth-century thought on this subject, a number of important figures naturally rise to the top because of their engage-ment with the topic of Judaism and the immense popularity of their writings on all subjects. There are many books that belong in the corpus of Latter-day Saint writings that members generally under-stand as scholarship. James E. Talmage, Church apostle and scholar (geologist), wrote a number of books that are still widely appreciated by Latter-day Saints.[43] His most important and lasting books include *Jesus the Christ* (1915), *The Great Apostasy* (1909), and *The Articles of Faith* (1899). Of these, the first two contain long passages that are exam-ined here only in part for the sake of brevity.

In part, we might see Talmage as the father of Latter-day Saint biblical interpretation in the twentieth century and the preemi-nent doctrinal scholar for generations of Church members. Talmage regarded the biblical record with high esteem in part because he sought to show how it prophesied of Jesus as the Messiah. Further, he strove to articulate particular Latter-day Saint doctrines through his careful study of the New Testament. Thus he attempted to show how the gradual accumulation of sacred texts and historical records in the Bible were both prophecy of and partial fulfillment of the narrative explained in the Book of Mormon about additional records of Jesus as Messiah. Talmage described the value of various records:

> To these earlier writings were added the utterances of divinely commissioned prophets, the records of appointed historians, and the songs of inspired poets, as the centuries passed; so that at the time of our Lord's ministry the Jews possessed a great accumulation of writings accepted and revered by them as authoritative. These records are rich in prediction and promise respecting the earthly advent of the Messiah, as are other scriptures to which the Israel of old had not access.[44]

In other places Talmage attempted to explain the reason for a needed gathering. "Needless to say, the Jews took not kindly to alien domination, though for many generations they had been trained in that experience, their reduced status having ranged from nominal vassalage to servile bondage. They were already largely a dispersed people. All the Jews in Palestine at the time of Christ's birth constituted but a small remnant of the great Davidic nation. The Ten Tribes, distinctively the aforementioned kingdom of Israel, had then long been lost to history, and the people of Judah had been widely scattered among the nations."[45] Elsewhere, Talmage takes a strident tone of accusation and condemnation, although he does pause to particularize that by "the Jews . . . we mean the priestly officials and rulers of the people." About the episode at the cleansing of the temple recorded in Luke 19:45–47, he wrote,

> The Jews, by which term we mean the priestly officials and rulers of the people, dared not protest this vigorous action on the ground of unrighteousness; they, learned in the law, stood self-convicted of corruption, avarice, and of personal responsibility for the temple's defilement. That the sacred premises were in sore need of a cleansing they all knew; the one point upon which they dared question the Cleanser was as to why He should

thus take to Himself the doing of what was their duty. . . . Their tentative submission was based on fear, and that in turn upon their sin-convicted consciences. Christ prevailed over those haggling Jews by virtue of the eternal principle that right is mightier than wrong, and of the psychological fact that consciousness of guilt robs the culprit of valor when the imminence of retribution is apparent to his soul.[46]

Thus in his effort to explain and find faith in the life of Jesus, Talmage could be fair and seemingly even in his evaluation of Jews at the time of Christ, but in other contexts he echoed centuries of anti-Judaic sentiment and imbued such rhetoric with authoritative condemnatory fervor. As Matthew Grey has shown, extensive elements of previous British scholarship are evident in Talmage's writing, notably the work of Frederic Farrar, Alfred Edersheim, and others.[47] The heavy imprint of their writings on Talmage's thinking is clear, and his methodology was shaped by their interpretive lenses. However, by the time Talmage engaged with their work, it was already outdated by forty years or more. Further, the continental biblical scholarship from Germany, France, and elsewhere had moved dramatically away from the strong anti-Semitic tones and articulations present in the work cited most heavily by Talmage.[48] Thus what Latter-day Saints inherited via Talmage was an outdated supersessionism that overemphasized Jewish legalism in contrast to a supposed Christian spiritualism and downplayed the existence of Judaisms of the Christian first century. In this way, the Jews became synonymous with opponents of Jesus and Christians in highly unnuanced ways that left Latter-day Saint readers with a very negative view of first-century Judaism. Such views were countered or softened to varying degrees by individuals such as Julius Wellhausen and others in continental Europe, though those views were largely ignored or remained undiscovered among Latter-day Saint readers.[49] The heavy impact of Farrar and others on the viewpoints of some of the most significant histories written by

Latter-day Saints in the early twentieth century projected a strong anti-Judaic stance, particularly when they read the New Testament and searched for the first-century contexts from which it emerged.

The continued life of Talmage's mode of thinking à la Farrar and Edersheim continued until nearly the end of the twentieth century in the work of Bruce R. McConkie. In the 1960s to 1980s, Elder Bruce R. McConkie played a dominant role in theological writing for the Saints. McConkie was called as an apostle in 1972 and continued in that position until his death in 1985. McConkie most famously wrote an encyclopedic text titled *Mormon Doctrine* that served as an important pedagogical text for decades.[50] McConkie also wrote a multivolume series on the life of Jesus known as the Messiah series.[51] McConkie, like Talmage before him, sought to outline the life of Jesus to help Latter-day Saints interpret and understand the divine mission of Jesus Christ as the Savior of the world. He employed much of the same scholarship as Talmage and looked to similar non–Latter-day Saint scholars. He also employed his own *Doctrinal New Testament Commentary* (1965).

McConkie was widely quoted and read by Latter-day Saints, and so his writings deserve a greater in-depth treatment than we will make here. However, a few of McConkie's statements stand out in the context of how Latter-day Saints today read the biblical and Book of Mormon text. In *Mormon Doctrine*, McConkie included within his entry on circumcision the following commentary: "By the time of Paul, the apostate Jews, as with the people of Abraham's day, had lost the knowledge 'that children are not accountable . . . until they are eight years old.' Rather they had a tradition that little children were unholy and that circumcision was essential to their cleansing. Those thus circumcised were then 'brought up in subjection to the law of Moses,' and giving 'heed to the traditions of their fathers,' they 'believed not the gospel of Christ, wherein they became unholy.'"[52] In his entry on deafness, he suggested that "the gathering of Israel in the last days shall consist in bringing together 'the blind people that have eyes, and the deaf that have ears,' that is, the spiritually blind and deaf shall come to a knowledge of the things of God and they shall see and hear (Isa. 43). In large part the opening of the eyes of the blind and the unstopping of the ears of the deaf shall take place by means of the Book of Mormon." McConkie used Isaiah 29:18 to defend this assertion, "And in that day shall the deaf hear the words of the book, and the eyes of the blind shall see out of obscurity, and out of darkness."[53] For McConkie, the idea of gathering shaped his theological view. The divine working out of gathering scattered Israel (in its very broadest sense) framed every aspect of his thought by making all things lead back through Christ to covenantal fulfillment.

> The purpose of the gathering of Israel is twofold: 1. To put the peoples of living Israel in that environment where they may the better work out their salvation, where they may have the Gentile and worldly views erased from them, and where they may be molded into that pattern of perfect righteousness which will please the Almighty; and 2. To enable the gathered remnants of the chosen lineage to build temples and perform the ordinances of salvation and exaltation for their Israelitish ancestors who lived when the gospel was not had on earth.[54]

He further wrote that "the glory of Israel's latter-day gathering is beginning to appear, and it will not be long before the Ten Tribes and all things incident to this great work will be fulfilled."

In the twentieth century, it wasn't just biblical scholarship and Latter-day Saint thought that shaped the way members of the Church envisioned their Jewish neighbors. By midcentury Israel's establishment as a political entity encouraged some Latter-day Saints to see prophesied precursors to the Second Coming of Jesus found in the Bible, Book of Mormon, and Doctrine and Covenants as imminent. One movement that specifically encouraged the idea of gathering in the form of proselytization had a lasting impact on Jewish and Latter-day Saint relations. In the early 1950s there was a concerted effort in the Los Angeles area to bring Jews to a greater awareness of and belief in the restoration message promoted by the Church. The movement started with Elder LeGrand Richards (1886–1983) and Rose Marie Reid (1906–1978). The two met in 1953 and immediately found a common interest in Judaism and in efforts to draw connections between the world events (establishment of Israel) and the ongoing restoration spoken of by Latter-day Saints. LeGrand Richards (a member of the Quorum of the Twelve Apostles) wrote a book titled *Israel! Do You Know?*, which was geared toward a Jewish audience and showed how the flourishing of Israel as a country and as a home for Jews was a central component of the gathering of Israel spoken of in the biblical text and the Book of Mormon.

Rose Marie Reid, perhaps the most successful businessperson of the 1950s, designed swimsuits, ran her company, and in her free time sought out potential Jewish converts to the Church of Jesus Christ. Reid and Richards sought to create a missionary tract system specific to Jews in the Los Angeles and New York areas. Rose Marie Reid created a self-published pamphlet titled *Attention Israel*, which cited on its cover the passage from Jeremiah 3:18: "In those days the house of Judah shall walk with the house of Israel." Her efforts included creating fictional discussions with Jews in which she walked Latter-day Saints through potential trouble areas that might arise when approaching Jewish friends with the message of the restored Church.[55] In creating her program, Reid sought to help avoid such areas. For example, she wrote, "I found one serious problem in giving out the whole book (i.e., Richards's *Israel! Do You Know?*) that they read ahead at once, and want to discuss Christ in an argumentive [*sic*] manner. I really feel that the book should not be given until Lesson Four."[56] For a short period (ca. 1953–1960) the Church allowed (though not entirely supported) Reid and Richards to continue their efforts. In the late 1950s and early 1960s, internal disagreements among Church leadership caused the First Presidency to stop their efforts to evangelize specifically to Jews in targeted locations.

These efforts continued somewhat privately and inconsistently over the next twenty years until the Church officially ended proselytization to Jews in Israel in connection with the creation of the BYU Jerusalem Center and the controversies that accompanied the establishment of a branch/satellite campus for study abroad programs of the university in Israel. Today, students who travel abroad to Israel as part of the BYU program commit to avoiding any activity others may perceive or construe as proselytization. The seriousness of this commitment has consistently been encouraged through official Church channels and through the BYU Jerusalem Center's administration.[57]

The final area to which we might look to understand current trends in Latter-day Saint relations with Jews and Judaism is in the current writings of lay authors who publish through presses geared toward Latter-day Saints. To understand why this area is useful as a category of analysis, a few words regarding the curriculum used in Church teaching today will help make this connection clear. Latter-day Saints follow an annual curriculum prescribed through central Church headquarters in Salt Lake City. In 2018, this curriculum was greatly modified to include an at-home component that mirrored the Sunday School curriculum. For example, in 2019 the text of study was the New Testament. Given the subject matter, teachers and learners needed the very best thinking about how to make sense of the historical, cultural, religious, and interpretive backdrops of Latter-day Saint understandings of the text. The Church produces for all members everywhere a common core set of lessons that are to be used in teaching at home and in Church settings. While this is an ambitious program, the curricular material provided is limited so as to be accessible for Saints globally and to make translation work possible. As such, many Latter-day Saints often look to outside resources to better understand scriptural texts, especially books published through Latter-day Saint venues.

With this adjustment in the curriculum, a broad range of new texts were released both through publishers connected to the

Church as well as those who publish to Latter-day Saint audiences. These books include highly responsible texts that serve to clarify and encourage careful readings of the New Testament. For example, Thomas A. Wayment's *The New Testament: A New Translation for Latter-day Saints* stands out as a premier example of such responsible scholarship.[58] Wayment tries to carefully balance his reading of the New Testament while allowing the difficult passages of the text to stand on their own and does not try to reconcile them in haphazard or sloppy ways. When the text appears irreconcilable, Wayment allows the reader to grapple with scriptural passages in light of helpful notes and references.

Likewise, other recent publications exhibit sincere efforts to benefit members. While many authors' work encourages a robust study of the scriptural text by adding useful and insightful commentaries and interpretations, not all Latter-day Saint publications adequately meet the standards of scholarship. Like many of their earlier predecessors (Talmage, McConkie, and others), some continue to perpetuate overgeneralizations and stereotypes about Jews and Jewish law that can also be found in hard supersessionist Christian discussions of Judaism.

Latter-day Saint publishers actively seek to put useful scholarship into the hands of interested readers. The problem occurs, however, when poor scholarship obscures well-intentioned gospel messages. *Christ's Emancipation of Women in the New Testament* is one such book that seeks to emphasize the good news of the gospel of Jesus Christ with respect to women in Christ's day. Despite the good intentions of the author, the book is built on a flawed framework and dangerous interpretations and assumptions. To be fair, the book is written for a popular audience and not for an academic readership, which creates problems.[59] While finding greater application for members of the Church and greater appreciation for the role of women in the New Testament text is ambitious and necessary, the book exhibits a dangerous form of textual reading. The book's framework is as problematic as the actual interpretive work highlighted throughout the text. The author framed the first chapter, "Women Released from Their Cultural Baggage," by subtopics that define the "Cultural Background and Baggage" in opposition to "Changes by Jesus." Such language couches the principal teachings of Judaism within very negative notions of baggage that must be shed to attain Christian standards of acceptability. *Christ's Emancipation of Women in the New Testament* never fully explains the parameters or methodologies that define the use of negative/positive comparisons.

The central thesis of the text points to the radical nature of Jesus Christ's teachings to and about women that ruptured a supposedly misogynistic Judaism. The book begins by positing that "Jewish records spanning two centuries before and after the New Testament express little evidence that their authors understood the benefits of a mutually supportive, sensitive, affection-based companionship with one's spouse—let alone the relationship's eternal importance."[60] Further, the author adds,

> By the time of the New Testament, respect, cooperation, and love between spouses was not necessarily the aim of marriage. Righting these wrongs was one of the powerful legacies of Jesus' ministry. By placing the cultural background adjacent to Jesus' teachings, one can see the emancipation he offered. The truths He taught transformed the cultural worth of women.[61]

The book reaffirms anti-Judaic sentiments by improperly contrasting a seemingly benevolent Christian worldview with an oppressive, legally fixated Judaism. To further complicate the narrative, academic and Latter-day Saint sources are poorly contextualized and are used to prooftext a narrative that becomes compelling because of its contempt against Judaism. In working to revitalize an important interpretive lens for Latter-day Saints, *Christ's Emancipation of Women in the New Testament* unfortunately perpetuates some of the heavy-handed anti-Semitism of the nineteenth- and early twentieth-century writers.[62]

In another variation on this theme, several Latter-day Saint Church Educational System employees and curriculum writers compiled *The New Testament Study Guide* that aims to enhance Latter-day Saint study of the 2019 curriculum. The book uses the Church's accepted King James Version of the New Testament as its core text and then in a side-by-side format adds quotations from Latter-day Saint scholars and Latter-day Saint General Authorities to answer questions posed by the editors. Additionally, the compilers refer extensively to Edersheim and Farrar. Although many of the uses of Edersheim and Farrar are benign, one example illustrates how these sources are sometimes used in problematic ways. In the commentary for Matthew 28:11–15, the editors pose the question "Why did Matthew include the story of the soldiers accepting bribes and lying?" The answer, according to *The New Testament Study Guide* (citing Farrar), is "Discovering the empty tomb, the Roman guards 'fled to the members of the Sanhedrin who had given them their secret commission. To these hardened hearts, belief and investigation were alike out of the question. Their only refuge seemed to be in lies. They instantly tried to hush up the whole matter.'"[63] While Matthew's account does not place the Sanhedrin's leaders in positive light, Farrar imbues them with dark internal goals that are not available through the text itself. The *New Testament Study Guide* perpetuates such negative portrayals without attempting to show the nuance needed to understand the context of the scriptural text.

The editors of *The New Testament Study Guide* unfortunately failed to consistently employ scholarship from the past fifty or sixty years to help readers learn how they might more accurately depict the social, religious, and political culture and context of the New Testament setting. So, for example, readers are given a table affixed to the pages of Matthew 5:22–44 that shows "Jesus' New Law Transcends the Old" with subheadings "The Old Law (of Moses)" with "The New Law (of Jesus Christ)." There is no effort to contextualize the commentary when the table includes ideas such as "Take an eye for an eye—justice (Lev. 24:20)" and "Hate thine enemy (Micah 3:2)" under the heading "Old Law" juxtaposed against "Turn the other cheek (Matthew 5:39–42)" and "Love your enemies (Matthew 5:44)" under the "New Law." Further complicating the interpretation of the New Testament are selections from Church leaders without regard for how this might lead Latter-day Saints to read the text. A striking example here is the use of Bruce R. McConkie's statement that is freely brought to the modern reader without reservation or critique. In Acts 13:46 (a difficult passage in its own right), McConkie is cited to interpret the scriptural passage. The editorial question posed in the commentary is "What happens to the Jews because they rejected the gospel? (13:46)." McConkie's quotation from his *Millennial Messiah* is presented here as it appears in the *New Testament Study Guide*:

> Let this fact be engraved in the eternal records with a pen of steel: the Jews were cursed, smitten, and cursed anew because they rejected the gospel, cast out their Messiah, and crucified their King. Let the spiritually illiterate suppose what they may, it was the Jewish denial and rejection of the Holy One of Israel, whom their fathers worshipped in the beauty of holiness, that has made them a hiss and a byword in all nations and that has taken millions of their fair sons and daughters to untimely graves.[64]

McConkie's effort draws forward New Testament accusations against Jews of Jesus's day to the Holocaust-perpetuated medieval arguments that Jews served as eternal reminders of the rejection of Jesus as Messiah.[65] Without caution, the editors of *The New Testament Study Guide* ignorantly thrust that sword one more time into efforts to improve and build strong bonds with Jews as Jews today. The inclusion of these types of quotations without any effort to mitigate against such anti-Semitic thought is both academically and religiously irresponsible. Latter-day Saint thinking on the question of where and how Jews fit theologically into their framework has dramatically changed in recent decades—such changes need to be more boldly included in works to help overturn earlier theological and historical claims against Jews and Judaism. This is of great importance particularly when such publications are channeled through publishing houses like Deseret Book that are tangentially, or at least perceived as being, affiliated with The Church of Jesus Christ of Latter-day Saints. More importantly, how generations of students of Latter-day Saint scriptural texts study them is of great importance. A renewed commitment to understanding how scholars' work can be better utilized in that process will require greater attention to these issues.

CONCLUSION

This brief overview of Latter-day Saint perceptions and teachings about Jews highlights the variety of perspectives toward Jews and their former and continued role as God's covenant people. Some common threads persist in Restoration scripture, among Latter-day Saints in early Utah, and in twentieth-century Latter-day Saint thought. While certainly some of these perspectives are supersessionist in the belief that God is for now working through different instruments to fulfill his covenant purposes because of perceived past covenantal failures, they also do not push for a complete replacement of the Jews since God's covenant with the Jews has not expired. The gathering of Israel and support for the return of the Jews to the land of their inheritance are constant among Latter-day Saint sources. Earlier stories, covenants, and scripture from the Hebrew Bible continue to be seen as relevant and formative for Latter-day Saint beliefs, particularly of their adoption into prior covenant promises, even while additional scripture is produced that not only guides Latter-day Saints but is sometimes aimed at future Jews as well. One area in which there might be significant room for improvement among Latter-day Saints is to more fully understand the complexity of Jewish history, particularly the development of rabbinic Judaism and the varieties of Judaism in the modern world. Latter-day Saint usage almost always refers to biblical Jews and Judaism—which misleads many Latter-day Saints when they encounter Jews in their neighborhoods, schools, or businesses.[66] A more developed awareness of the shapes of modern Judaism and Jewish communities could prove a major step forward in the improvement of Jewish–Latter-day Saint relations.

Latter-day Saint thought often highlights the continued importance, relevance, and potential of Jews within God's salvific work with humankind, while also acknowledging the centrality of Jesus as the Messiah in carrying out God's plan of salvation. How these seemingly contradictory notions can or will be resolved is largely unknown at this time and seems to be in God's hands. The acceptance or rejection of Jesus as the Messiah and the possible consequent effect on salvation seems to be an intractable tenet that neither side of us participating in this dialogue would want to force upon the other or ignore at risk of reducing the other's core beliefs. This may be another instance of agreeing to disagree, but we trust that a better understanding of where Latter-day Saints are coming from in some of their stances toward Judaism can be gained from this overview.

NOTES

1. Replacement theology developed out of a reading of the New Testament that attempted to elevate the followers of Jesus over the Jewish nonfollowers. Challenged by the assumed essentialness of the Hebrew Bible to the Christian narrative and the complexity of incorporating and interpreting the text in light of New Testament narratives, Christians fought over whether the Old Testament text was one that Christians ought to continue to use in their theology. An early Christian bishop named Irenaeus (ca. 130–ca. 202) ultimately won a doctrinal battle against his rival Marcion that led to the Christian adoption of the "Old Testament" text as a companion to the New Testament. The effort to maintain the Old Testament as a central text led Christians to insist upon a stark difference between the two biblical texts, and the

result was a firm belief that Christ had provided a new way, a new covenant that superseded (hence supersessionism) God's covenant with ancient Israel.

2. Jon D. Levenson responds to Steven Englund in "Getting Past Supersessionism: An Exchange on Catholic-Jewish Dialogue," *Commonweal*, February 21, 2014, 20–21.

3. Matthew J. Grey, "Latter-day Saint Perceptions of Jewish Apostasy in the Time of Jesus," in *Standing Apart: Mormon Historical Consciousness and the Concept of Apostasy*, ed. Miranda Wilcox and John D. Young (Oxford: Oxford University Press, 2014), 149–50.

4. Edward Kessler, *An Introduction to Jewish-Christian Relations* (Cambridge: Cambridge University Press, 2010).

5. Christopher M. Leighton, "Christian Theology after the Shoah," in *Christianity in Jewish Terms*, ed. Tikva Frymer-Kensky et al., (Boulder, CO: Westview, 2000), 38.

6. David Novak, "Supersessionism Hard and Soft," *First Things* (February 2019), https://firstthings.com/article/2019/02/supersessionism-hard-and-soft. Novak defines supersessionism broadly as "the theological conviction that the Christian Church has superseded the Jewish people, assuming their role as God's covenanted people, Israel."

7. For examples of Jewish interpretations of Paul, see the cursory overview provided by Daniel R. Langton, "Paul in Jewish Thought" in *The Jewish Annotated New Testament*, 2nd ed., ed. Amy-Jill Levine and Marc Zvi Brettler (Oxford: Oxford University Press, 2017), 741–44. For a more sustained argument for the damage caused by Paul within the Jewish-Christian world, see Jonathan Sacks, *Not in God's Name: Confronting Religious Violence* (New York: Schocken, 2015), 92–100; Kessler, *Introduction to Jewish-Christian Relations*, 177–79. See also Heinrich Graetz, *History of the Jews* (Philadelphia: Jewish Publication Society, 1893), 2:221–32; and E. P. Sanders, *Paul and Palestinian Judaism* (Philadelphia: Fortress Press, 1977). See also the treatment of the topic by Joshua D. Garroway and Thomas A. Wayment contained herein.

8. Hans Boersma, "On Supersessionism," *First Things* (December 5, 2019), https://firstthings.com/web-exclusives/2019/12/on-supersession ism#print. It should be noted that while Boersma values a particular form of supersessionism within Catholic teaching, it is one that is nuanced by three caveats: (1) "though universalism supersedes particularism, there's no Gentile church replacing Jewish synagogue"; (2) "the universal reach of the gospel under the new dispensation does not contract but fulfills the promises made to Abraham"; (3) "Jesus makes clear that the monikers 'brood of vipers' and 'children of Abraham' were always in flux." Thus, "it is one thing to follow Saint Paul in referring to the church as the 'seed of Abraham'; it is another to turn John's juxtaposition between the two groups into an immutable us-versus-them framework."

9. Novak, "Supersessionism Hard and Soft."

10. Jacob Neusner, "A Jewish Reflection on Christian Claims," in *Jewish Annotated New Testament*, 725.

11. Isaiah 49:5–8 Jewish Publication Society Tanakh Translation. The KJV translates this as "a light unto the Gentiles."

12. See, for example, Jacob 5. The Book of Mormon focuses on the *restoration* of the house of Israel and the Jews. A restoration implies something that is diminished or broken but then restored to what it was before. It is not something replaced with a new product. Speaking in botanical terms, which is often how the Lord speaks about his vineyard, what the Book of Mormon describes is not so much *supplanting* what was there previously, but rather *grafting in* or *tending to* new branches. The earlier roots and branches still have strength, covenants, and relevance, yet because some of the fruits have gone bad, God is working through new branches as his primary instruments for salvation history to restore the production of the branches to what it was before. In the end, God is tending his vineyard so that he can produce the best fruit possible from as many branches and trees as possible.

13. John Taylor (1872), *Journal of Discourses*, 26 vols. (Liverpool: F. D. Richards and Sons, 1851–86), 14:337.

14. "Statement of the First Presidency of The Church of Jesus Christ of Latter-day Saints regarding "God's Love for All Mankind" (February 15, 1978).

15. Heber J. Grant, "Attitude of the Latter-day Saints towards the Jews," *Improvement Era*, 1921, 747.

16. The Book of Mormon consistently uses the term *the Jews* in describing inhabitants of Judea, but it is unclear whether some of the writers also assumed a notion of a corporate religious body since the book does not deal with rabbinic Judaism and its later developments but treats the Jews as a collective branch from the preexilic period, Jesus's time, and as a scattered remnant in the last days to be regathered. We recognize the difficulty of terminology and that at times such language has allowed for Christian supersessionist rhetoric to gloss over diverse groups of people with this simplistic construction. On the subject, Cynthia Baker has argued, "The most persistent meanings and force of the term *Jew(s)* derive, then, from an antique Christian worldview in which *the Jews* functions foundationally as a kind of originary and constitutional alterity, or otherness. *The Jews* serves as the alpha to the Christian omega; the 'Old' to the Christian 'New'; the 'particular' to the Christian 'universal'; grounded and bound materialism to visionary, redeemed spirituality; deicide to self-sacrificial love—at best, the sainted or moribund 'ancestor'; at worst, the evil 'spawn of Satan' to a godly, good, and triumphantly immortal Christianity. *The Jews*, in other words, serves instrumentally to name the key *other* out of which *and* over against which the Christian *self* was and is constituted." Cynthia Baker, *Jew (Key Words in Jewish Studies)* (New Brunswick, NJ: Rutgers University Press, 2017), 4. Further, she asserted, "*The Jews*, like *the Jew*, can and does function in a similar fashion, as described above, most often in polemical contexts." Andrew Bush claimed that "Biale [an editor of *Cultures of the Jews*] rewrites 'the culture' as the plural 'cultures' in his title, but it will require a new key in Jewish Studies to learn to eliminate the 'the' that so frequently universalizes some Jews as 'the Jews.'" *Jewish*

Studies: A Theoretical Introduction (New Brunswick, NJ: Rutgers University Press, 2011), 89.

17. Admittedly, the translation and meaning of the Hebrew text is debated, but this rendition is comparable to the KJV with which Latter-day Saints are most familiar.

18. The term *law of Moses* is used purposefully here, since the Book of Mormon speaks of the "law of Moses" (see 2 Nephi 25:24, 25) as something that would be or has been fulfilled but also indicates that the covenant remains in force (see Mormon 3:21).

19. During the visit of the resurrected Jesus among the Nephites, Jesus gave a few teachings about the Jews from whom he had recently departed. After some spiritual experiences among the Nephites, Jesus declared that he had never seen such great faith among the Jews, "wherefore I could not show unto them so great miracles, because of their unbelief" (3 Nephi 19:35). This is a somewhat similar sentiment that he sometimes shared during his mortal ministry as recorded in the Gospels about the lack of faith in Israel, including among those in his hometown (see Matthew 8:10; 13:57–58).

20. The Northern Kingdom tribes, or lost ten tribes, are also sometimes referred to in the Book of Mormon; however, the Book of Mormon peoples have no contact with them and provide allusions only to their being lost and to future prophecies of their return to the land of their inheritance with their own collection of scriptural records.

21. The Jews are believed to be scattered and punished because of their stiffneckedness and rejection of the prophets and the Messiah, but they are never completely abandoned or forgotten. Many Book of Mormon prophecies outline their eventual glorious restoration and gathering back to the lands of their inheritance, chiefly through the instrumentality of the Gentiles. Because the Jews are the ancient covenant people and God had made promises to their forefathers, he will continue to work on their behalf.

22. Even though the Jews' diligence helped bring forth scripture and salvation to the Gentiles, it will be the Gentiles who will then bring forth

scripture and salvation to the Jews. The first shall be last and the last shall be first. The Gentiles will be blessed and numbered among the house of Israel so long as they remain repentant and obedient. According to the Book of Mormon, the Gentiles will be both the aggressors and the restorers to the house of Israel. In other words, they will be the catalyst for God's dealings with his ancient covenant people—to scatter them and then to gather them. The strong language here in 2 Nephi 29:5 helps Latter-day Saints recognize the need for a more appreciative language and approach to Jews today and also opens (as do other places in the Book of Mormon text) space for theological justification of both Jews and Christians as eternally important to the covenantal relationship with God. More importantly in terms of lived practical relations, Jews and those who value the Book of Mormon as a sacred text must find avenues toward productive relationships in the present while leaving the eschatological determinations for later.

23. Abinadi's thoroughly christological interpretation of Isaiah 53 (see Mosiah 14–15) also has significant influence both within the Book of Mormon narrative and on modern Latter-day Saint readers.

24. While the Book of Mormon's portrayal of the Jews may seem predominantly negative, this results from the fact that the two primary time periods it discusses about the Jews are shortly before the Babylonian conquest, when the Jews' wickedness and idolatry led to their downfall, and the later Jews' rejection of Jesus as the Messiah, which, like other Christian teachings, the Book of Mormon sees as a major failing. The rejection of Jesus as Messiah is an accusation made against many groups within the Book of Mormon and against many Gentiles as well.

25. Although the precise phrase "times of the Gentiles" (Luke 21:24) is not found in the Book of Mormon, it does occur in Doctrine and Covenants 45:25, 28, 30, and the Book of Mormon does develop the concept of a time when the Gentiles would have great power and influence, preparing for a subsequent time when God's covenant people would return to power and influence (as discussed in the body of the paper).

26. Another last days prophecy involving the Messiah and the Jews is that he will defend them against any who fight against Zion and the covenant people of the Lord. The Messiah "will set himself again the second time to recover them" and destroy their enemies "when that day cometh when they shall believe in him; and none will he destroy that believe in him" (2 Nephi 6:14; see 10:16).

27. See Doctrine and Covenants 3:16; 18:26; 19:27; 20:9; 21:12; 45:21, 51; 57:4; 74:2, 6; 77:15; 84:28; 90:9; 98:17 (2); 107:33; 107:34, 35, 97; 109:64; 112:4; 133:8, 13, 35; 138:25.

28. See Doctrine and Covenants 18:26; 19:27; 20:9; 21:12; 57:4; 90:9; 98:17 (2); 107:33, 34, 35, 97; 112:4; 133:8.

29. See Doctrine and Covenants 3:16; 74:2, 6; 84:28; 138:25.

30. See Doctrine and Covenants 45:21, 51; 77:15; 109:64; 133:13, 35.

31. For an overview of various Christian views of end-time prophecies, see Timothy Paul Jones, David Gundersen, and Benjamin Galan, *The Rose Guide to End of Times Prophecy* (Torrance, CA: Rose, 2011). The pages that provide a description of the concepts mentioned in this paragraph are 104, 192, 216–17, 236, and 307.

32. Some of the biblical texts that provide imagery for these concepts are found in Zechariah 4:14; Isaiah 51:19 (interpretation, particularly as provided in Revelation 11: two holy ones will rise up to prophesy and to protect the Jews); Zechariah 12:2–3 (interpretation: all nations will be gathered against the Jews in Jerusalem); Zechariah 12:9–10 (interpretation: the nations gathered against the Jews will eventually be destroyed and the Jews will mourn when they look upon the one they have pierced); Zechariah 13:6 (interpretation: the Jews ask about the wounds they see in their rescuer's—Jesus's—hands and are told he received them in the house of his friends); and Zechariah 14:4–6 (interpretation: Jesus stands on the Mount of Olives and it cleaves in two).

33. For a description of Orson Hyde's mission and dedicatory prayer on the Mount of Olives, see David B. Galbraith, "Orson Hyde's 1841 Mission to the Holy Land," *Ensign*, October 1991, 16–19. See also Andrew

Reed, "Framing the Restoration and Gathering: Orson Hyde and Early Mormon Understandings of Israel, Jews, and the Second Coming," in *Foundations of the Restoration: Fulfillment of the Covenant Purposes*, ed. Craig J. Ostler, Michael H. MacKay, and Barbara Morgan Gardner (Provo, UT: Religious Studies Center, Brigham Young University, 2016), 225–44.

34. The city ordinance stated, "Be it ordained by the City Council of the City of Nauvoo, that the Catholics, Presbyterians, Methodists, Baptists, Latter-day Saints, Quakers, Episcopals, Universali[s]ts, Unitarians, Mohammedans [Muslims], and all other religious sects and denominations whatever, shall have free toleration, and equal privileges in this city." "Nauvoo City Council Minute Book, 3 February 1841–8 February 1845," p. 14, The Joseph Smith Papers, https://josephsmith papers.org/paper-summary/nauvoo-city-council-minute-book-3 -february-1841-8-february-1845/19.

35. Brigham Young (1855), in *Journal of Discourses*, 2:185.

36. Parley P. Pratt (1854), in *Journal of Discourses*, 1:180.

37. Wilford Woodruff (1857), in *Journal of Discourses*, 4:230.

38. Brigham Young (1854), in *Journal of Discourses*, 2:140.

39. Wilford Woodruff (1857), in *Journal of Discources*, 4:230.

40. Between 1876 and 1920, the Book of Mormon and Doctrine and Covenants were standardized by Church leaders. These changes included modifying the texts into two-column pages, expanding notes, and providing historical and thematic headings for individual chapters. Additionally, the *Lectures on Faith*, a series of theological lessons were removed from the Doctrine and Covenants in 1921. For more on this history, see Richard E. Turley Jr. and William W. Slaughter, *How We Got the Doctrine and Covenants* (Salt Lake City: Deseret Book, 2012), 81–109.

41. Philip L. Barlow, *Mormons and the Bible: The Place of the Latter-day Saints in American Religion* (Oxford: Oxford University Press, 2013), 119.

42. While there is not an exact formula to aid members of the Church in navigating which statements are authoritative, the longevity and repetitious nature of certain statements, along with continued reference to and endorsement of particular writings, become a measure of their

acceptance by Church leaders and members. For more on how members of The Church of Jesus Christ of Latter-day Saints seek to understand what is and what is not doctrine, see "Approaching Mormon Doctrine," Newsroom, May 4, 2007, https://newsroom.churchofjesuschrist.org /article/approaching-mormon-doctrine.

43. When Latter-day Saint missionaries embark on their missions, they take with them only a few books outside of canonized scripture. These volumes comprise the missionary reference library, which currently includes James E. Talmage, *Jesus the Christ* (Salt Lake City: Deseret Book, 1981); M. Russell Ballard, *Our Search for Happiness: An Invitation to Understand the Church of Jesus Christ of Latter-day Saints* (Salt Lake City: Deseret Book, 1993); *Our Heritage* (Salt Lake City: Deseret Book, 1996); and *True to the Faith* (Salt Lake City: Deseret Book, 2004). These volumes continue to be essential reading for Latter-day Saint missionaries well into the twenty-first century. As such, they are usually read without reference to other scholarship as they belong to a corpus of essential texts. Talmage's *Jesus the Christ* was recently updated by scholars to include more nuanced readings and updated citations. See Lincoln Blumell, Gaye Strathearn, and Thomas Wayment, *Jesus the Christ* (Springville, UT: Cedar Fort, 2015); and Richard Neitzel Holzapfel and Thomas Wayment, *James E. Talmage's Jesus the Christ: Study Guide* (Salt Lake City: Deseret Book, 2014). These two volumes have helped clarify Talmage's place in early twentieth-century Latter-day Saint writing and may add nuance to the ways that Latter-day Saint readers study his text.

44. Talmage, *Jesus the Christ*, 40.

45. Talmage, *Jesus the Christ*, 58.

46. Talmage, *Jesus the Christ*, 146.

47. Grey, "Latter-day Saint Perceptions of Jewish Apostasy." The relevant citations for the nineteenth-century works employed heavily by Talmage are Frederic Farrar, *Life of Christ*, 2 vols. (New York: E. P. Dutton, 1875); Cunningham Geikie, *The Life and Words of Christ* (New York: Columbian, 1891); and Alfred Edersheim, *Life and Times of Jesus the Messiah*, 2 vols. (London: Longmans, Green, 1883).

48. Grey, "Latter-day Saint Perceptions of Jewish Apostasy," 150.

49. For a well-balanced description of the impact of Wellhausen on continental biblical criticism and scholarship, see Yaacov Shavit and Mardechai Eran, *The Hebrew Bible Reborn: From Holy Scripture to the Book of Books: A History of Biblical Culture and the Battles over the Bible in Modern Judaism*, trans. Chaya Naor (Berlin: Walter de Gruyter, 2007), 85–155.

50. Bruce R. McConkie, *Mormon Doctrine* (Salt Lake City: Bookcraft, 1966).

51. Bruce R. McConkie, *The Mortal Messiah: From Bethlehem to Calvary*, vols. 1–4 (Salt Lake City: Deseret Book, 1979).

52. McConkie, *Mormon Doctrine*, 144.

53. McConkie, *Mormon Doctrine*, 184.

54. McConkie, *Mormon Doctrine*, 306.

55. Reid on occasion would have discussions with Jews (including her future son-in-law) to test out her approach and refine it. One such conversation is recorded in her pamphlet *Attention Israel*. Andrew Reed has conducted interviews with Eugene Freedman and his wife, Claire (Reid's niece). Freedman indicated the intensity of Reid's personality in this endeavor by explaining her insistence on getting her point across even when her interlocutors were uninterested or lacking energy to continue the conversation.

56. Rose Marie Reid to LeGrand Richards, August 5, 1956, Rose Marie Reid Collection, MS 8044, series 3, box 16, folder 3, L. Tom Perry Special Collections, Brigham Young University.

57. Another related arena where there is a serious commitment to engagement with Jewish communities is the practice of posthumous baptism. The Church of Jesus Christ of Latter-day Saints has reaffirmed a strong commitment to prevent members from doing genealogical research on victims of the Holocaust that leads to posthumous baptism, a religious rite that Latter-day Saints view as an offering in behalf of their deceased ancestors, one that may be accepted or rejected according to the desires of the deceased in the next life. In February 2012, the First Presidency of the Church responded to renewed critiques of the Church for some evidence of such baptisms with a letter that was read in sacrament meet-

ings across the global church. It suggested, "Without exception, church members *must not* submit for proxy temple ordinances any names from unauthorized groups, such as celebrities and Jewish Holocaust victims. If members do so, they may forfeit their New FamilySearch privileges. Other corrective action may also be taken." See "Names Submitted for Temple Ordinances," *Letter from First Presidency of The Church of Jesus Christ of Latter-day Saints* (February 29, 2012).

58. Thomas A. Wayment, *The New Testament: A New Translation for Latter-day Saints* (Provo, UT: Religious Studies Center, Brigham Young University; Salt Lake City: Deseret Book, 2018). Wayment's translation has been favorably reviewed and recommended for Latter-day Saint readers of the New Testament. See for example, Joshua M. Sears, "Study Bibles: An Introduction for Latter-day Saints," *Religious Educator* 20, no. 3 (2019): 27–57.

59. Lynne Hilton Wilson, *Christ's Emancipation of Women in the New Testament* (Palo Alto: Good Sound Publishing, 2015). Wilson's book is interesting in part because it shows a wide range of sources to help the author interpret the New Testament world through Jewish, Christian, and Latter-day Saint lenses. The author displays some awareness of the breadth of possible sources and readings, but the tone of the book reflects a very negative portrayal of Judaism.

60. Wilson, *Christ's Emancipation of Women*, 3.

61. Wilson, *Christ's Emancipation of Women*, 5.

62. Wilson cites McConkie's *Mortal Messiah* and Frederic W. Farrar's *The Life of Christ* with only marginal regularity but extensively cites Edersheim's *The Life and Times of Jesus the Messiah* (notably with the wrong publication information given) and his *The Temple: Its Ministry and Services as They Were at the Time of Christ* (London: Religious Tract Society, 1874).

63. Thomas R. Valletta, ed., *The New Testament Study Guide* (Salt Lake City: Deseret Book, 2018), 128–29. The Farrar citation, according to Valletta, is from *Life of Christ*, 663–64. It seems that Valletta is using the 1980 reprint of *The Life of Christ*. The same printing and pagination can

be found in Frederic W. Farrar, *The Life of Christ* (Portland, OR: Fountain, 1976), 663–64.

64. Valletta, *New Testament Study Guide*, 492. Original source in Bruce R. McConkie, *The Millennial Messiah: The Second Coming of the Son of Man* (Salt Lake City: Deseret Book, 1982), 224–25.

65. The use of passages like this one by the editors of *The New Testament Study Guide* ignores the guidance provided to Catholics in Vatican II's "Declaration on the Relation of the Church to Non-Christian Religions *Nostra Aetate*" (October 28, 1965). In this landmark document, the Catholic Church suggested, "True, the Jewish authorities and those who followed their lead pressed for the death of Christ; still, what happened in His passion cannot be charged against all the Jews, without distinction, then alive, nor against the Jews of today. Although the Church is the new people of God, the Jews should not be presented as rejected or accursed by God, as if this followed from the Holy Scriptures." See the dialogue between Reverend Thomas F. Stransky and Rabbi Marc H. Tannenbaum on this document in *Vatican II: An Interfaith Appraisal* (Notre Dame: University of Notre Dame, 1966), 335–74.

One recent attempt to reread the Book of Mormon with respect to latent anti-Semitism and find a more positive narrative within its pages is Bradley J. Kramer's work in his two published books. In *Beholding the Tree of Life: A Rabbinic Approach to the Book of Mormon* (Salt Lake City: Greg Kofford, 2014), Kramer introduced readers of the Book of Mormon to a new way of reading the scriptural text by employing traditional rabbinic questions and methods to find deeper meaning. This effort prepares Kramer's readers to think differently about the text and his approach to argue for a different outcome in terms of Jewish-Christian relations through the Book of Mormon. In his second volume, *Gathered in One: How the Book of Mormon Counters Anti-Semitism in the New Testament* (Salt Lake City: Greg Kofford, 2019), Kramer argues that the Book of Mormon "counters anti-Semitism the same way the New Testament supports it—*literarily*, using artistic devices common to novels, short stories, and tales, and it does so *respectfully*, without chal-

lenging the New Testament's text or undermining its religious authority, reliability, or credibility. As a result, the elements in the New Testament that foster anti-Semitic attitudes and behaviors are not deleted
or destroyed; they are instead detoxified, their poison either diluted
or eliminated entirely by a flood of similar elements from the Book of
Mormon, elements that promote a more positive view of Jews, Judaism,
and the Mosaic Law" (preface). Taken together, these books reflect an
overtly philo-Semitic Latter-day Saint approach to Judaism.

66. The traditional Latter-day Saint narrative of what is often referred to
as the Great Apostasy tends to dictate the overlooking of a significant
portion of Jewish and Christian development. This traditional narrative suggests that between the middle of the second century to the early
nineteenth century CE, there was a noticeable absence of divine authority. The restoration narrative, commenced in 1820 with Joseph Smith's
theophany, suggests that from that point forward, proper authority to
carry out sacramental rites was again restored. For one perspective, see
Robert L. Millet, "Apostasy, Great," in LDS Beliefs: A Doctrinal Reference,
ed. Robert L. Millet et al. (Salt Lake City: Deseret Book, 2011), 46–50.
Thus the lack of discussion or engagement with the rabbinic period in
Judaism by Latter-day Saints is also mirrored by their lack of engagement with Christian church fathers and church development during the
same period.

6

SUPERSESSIONISM IN THE CHURCH OF JESUS CHRIST OF LATTER-DAY SAINTS: A JEWISH RESPONSE

JOSHUA D. GARROWAY

As a Jewish scholar who specializes in ancient Christian litera-ture, I am often asked about my perspective on Christian supersessionism.[1] I usually begin my response, as I will do here now, with the following observation: every religion with which I am famil-iar manifests supersessionism in one manner or another. That Chris-tianity and Islam have traditionally done so goes without saying; each of those traditions has seen itself in relation to God's covenant with Abraham as a belated, yet superior, dispensation that renders for-mer dispensations at best insufficient, at worst obsolete. But Judaism too, especially in its expressions of strident monotheism emerging in the seventh and sixth centuries BCE, dismisses previous manifesta-tions of Canaanite religion and aggressively posits itself as the newer, superior alternative.[2] And just to show that I, as a Reform Jew, stand doubly accused, I note that when Reform Judaism emerged in the nineteenth century, and as it thrived in the twentieth century, it rou-tinely presented itself as the superior, final form of Judaism that ren-dered obsolete what it considered to be the ossified, medieval relic known as Orthodox Judaism.[3] I would, therefore, be astonished if The Church of Jesus Christ of Latter-day Saints, as a religion that emerged in the Christian context of early nineteenth-century America, didn't exhibit supersessionist tendencies both with respect to the Christianity it sought to update and by extension with respect to the Judaism that Christianity already claimed to have updated. All of us religionists—Catholics, Protestants, Muslims, Jews, Latter-day Saints—are in our own way supersessionists.

Nevertheless, we cannot fail to acknowledge that traditional Christian expressions of supersession over Judaism have proven uniquely pernicious, especially as they were expressed in the medieval ideologies of towering intellectuals like Augustine and Aquinas and manifested in European social and political arrangements for more than a millennium.[4] I am pleased to say that, judging by the appraisal of supersessionism offered by my Latter-day Saint colleagues, their community has exhibited a notably milder brand of supersessionism toward Judaism—certainly less invidious than the supersessionism of its medieval Christian forebears, but also milder than the so-called replacement theologies in other forms of contemporary Christianity.

This milder version of Latter-day Saint supersession over Judaism results from its not being grounded in an ideology that insists upon either the complete rejection of the Jewish people by God or the complete replacement of the Jewish people by a new spiritual elect. In Augustine's classic expression of Jewish subjugation, Jews are comparable to the biblical Cain, dismissed from their ancestral home and forced to wander the earth perpetually, forever unable to gain sustenance from the earth. The ongoing existence of the Jewish people, moreover, is not for their own sake or because of any lingering relationship with God; rather, Jews are permitted to survive, albeit in abased condition, for the sole purpose of bearing testimony to the truth of Christianity and to the terrible price paid by a people who rejects God.[5]

To be sure, the Book of Mormon does not shy away from casting reproach upon Jews for their disobedience to God in preexilic Judah, and likewise for their rejection of Jesus as the Messiah. But Latter-day Saint teachings, if I understand them correctly, do not present that rejection as permanent. Jews remain one of the covenant peoples of God, however obstinate they have temporarily become. Yet no less confident are Latter-day Saints in the currently unfortunate condition of Jews than they are in the prospect of Jews one day accepting Jesus and reclaiming the pride of place they once enjoyed. The Latter-day Saint view is therefore triumphalist, if not supersessionist, insofar as believing that Jews will gain their inevitable restoration by realizing their error. Triumphalism is hardly so condemnable, however. After all, we Jews harbor our own triumphalist aspirations, expressed in prayers and prophecies that envision the day when non-Jews will recognize the deficiency in their thinking and swear fidelity to the God of Israel.[6]

Even as the Latter-day Saints' perspective on Jews appears less supersessionist, I find unnerving one particular aspect of their faith, however, that in my view continues in the mold of its Christian forebears. Here I am speaking about the historic Christian tendency to view Jews one-dimensionally as a theological construction of the past and the future, rather than as a vibrant, dynamic religious community of the present that has trotted its way through the last two millennia and continues to prosper today.[7] The Book of Mormon does not deal with rabbinic Judaism whatsoever, nor do Latter-day Saint writers of the last two centuries in any significant way. The result, I fear, is that Jews today are not seen as people in the fullest sense, nor Judaism as a living, breathing religion; both are seen more so as avatars that stand in for the real Jewish people who either lived in the hoary past or will live again in an ideal future. To put it in the terms of contemporary cultural studies, Latter-day Saints still appear to cast upon Jews the domineering Christian gaze accompanied by the certainty that Jews are not who they think they are. Jews are rather who Latter-day Saints think they are, and who they need them to be in order for Latter-day Saint theology and history to make sense.

The pitfalls resulting from Christians viewing Jews as an idealized caricature from the past or the future have been seen in history time and again. On the one hand, it leads to one-dimensionally negative characterizations in which Jews are seen as incorrigibly bad for one reason or another. For Latter-day Saints like Brigham Young, Wilford Woodruff, and I assume, other General Authorities of the past two centuries, the hallmark of Jewish badness is their unique intractability, ingrained in them by their rejection of Jesus, an ancient event that nevertheless becomes the prototype for defining Jews for all time. True, members of The Church of Jesus Christ of Latter-day Saints hardly invented this perspective. The stubborn, unmovable, willfully ignorant Jew has been a staple of Christian (mis)representation since antiquity. When mixed with political power or religious zeal, however, this Christian tendency to see Jews as one-dimensional and incorrigible has led to mistreatment of the sort I need not describe. Dehumanization, after all, often goes hand in hand with cruelty and abuse. I suspect I speak for many other Jews when I say that I would rather a Christian try to convert me than think I am so incapable of conversion that it is not even worth the try.

This desire to be evangelized—or, at least, to be deemed evangelizable—exposes the other side of the coin, the other pitfall resulting from Christians viewing Jews in idealized terms. Here I am speaking of the fetishism so often expressed in contemporary evangelical circles. Already in the seventeenth century, English and Dutch Protestants were expressing a certain affection for Jews—again, not for Jews as they actually are, but for Jews as an idealized actor in the eschatological drama they expected soon to unfold. This Protestant infatuation with Jews has manifested sporadically over the past four centuries, but in American evangelicalism of the last two generations, the fetish appears be rising to a high tide. It is hardly uncommon nowadays to hear evangelicals proclaim their love for the Jews, in some cases evangelicals who have never actually interacted with a Jew in any serious way, or who know little to nothing about Judaism as a lived religion of the twenty-first century. Jews are seen one-dimensionally as the theological construction necessary to proclaim the fidelity of the Christian God and the imminent onset of Christian redemption.

In Latter-day Saint circles, based on what I gather from the previous chapter, the fetishistic interest in Jews was represented by the targeted missionary endeavors of LeGrand Richards and Rose Marie Reid. Like the Southern Baptists and other groups, they placed special value on the conversion of Jewish souls.[8] While such efforts to target Jews have been abandoned by Latter-day Saints in recent years, I suspect that many Jews still find themselves in some settings feeling gazed upon as though they are not simply non–Latter-day Saints, but non–Latter-day Saints of peculiar interest—gazed upon not like a person in the fullest sense but as a human manifestation of a necessary theological category.

This is not to say that being viewed one-dimensionally is entirely unpleasant. To be ogled and admired simply because I have the title "Jew" can admittedly feel good sometimes, and certainly it is better than being spat on or thrown into a ghetto on account of the same title. Ultimately, however, I think Jews would like to be seen by Christians, and Christians by Jews, and all people by all other people, as living, breathing, people with the same sorts of struggles, fears, and aspirations as anyone else—that is to say, to be seen as a Jew of the present, in all three dimensions, rather than as a token caricature of an idealized past or future Jew.

What has pleased me thus far about our Jewish–Latter-day Saint dialogues is my confidence that the participants on both sides aspire to exactly that sort of perspective when regarding one another.

NOTES

1. The library of recent literature on Christian supersessionism is vast. Among the helpful places to get started, see R. Kendall Soulen, *The God of Israel and Christian Theology* (Minneapolis: Fortress, 1996); John Howard Yoder, *The Jewish-Christian Schism Revisited*, ed. Michael G. Cartwright and Peter Ochs (Grand Rapids, MI: Eerdmans, 2003); Michael J. Vlach, *The Church as a Replacement of Israel: An Analysis of Supersessionism* (Frankfurt am Main: Peter Lang, 2009); Philip A. Cunningham et al., eds., *Christ Jesus and the Jewish People Today: New Explorations of Theological Interrelationships* (Grand Rapids, MI: Eerdmans, 2011); Peter Ochs, *Another Reformation: Postliberal Christianity and the Jews* (Grand Rapids, MI: Baker, 2011); George Hunsinger, "What Christians Owe Jews: The Case for 'Soft Supersessionism,'" *Commonweal*, February 20, 2015, 12–17; Shaul Magid, "Christian Supersessionism, Zionism, and the Contemporary Scene: A Critical Reading of Peter Ochs's Reading of John Howard Yoder," *Journal of Religious Ethics* 45, no. 1 (2017): 104–41.
2. Regarding ancient Israel, see also the recent study by Joshua Berman, "Supersessionist or Complementary? Reassessing the Nature of Legal Revision in the Pentateuchal Law Collections," *Journal of Biblical Literature* 135, no. 2 (2016): 201–22, who evaluates the extent to which certain legal portions of Exodus, Leviticus, and Deuteronomy were composed with the intention of superseding previous law collections.
3. For dismissive statements about previous iterations of Judaism from Reform rabbis in Europe (e.g., Samuel Holdheim) and the United States (e.g., Isaac Mayer Wise and Kaufmann Kohler), see Michael A. Meyer, *Response to Modernity* (Detroit: Wayne State University Press, 1988), 80–84, 251–52, 264–95.
4. On Augustine, see note 5. On Aquinas, see the recent treatments of supersessionism in his writings offered by Bruce D. Marshall, "Postscript and Prospect," *Nova et Vetera* 7, no. 2 (2009): 505–22; Fainche Ryan, "'Salvation Is from the Jews' (Jn 4:22): Aquinas, God, and the People of God," *Studies in Christian-Jewish Relations* 5, no. 1 (2010): 1–14; Steven C. Boguslawski, *Thomas Aquinas on the Jews: Insights into His Com-*

mentary on Romans 9–11, Studies in Judaism and Christianity (New York: Paulist Press, 2008); Jeremy Cohen, "Supersessionism, the Epistle to the Romans, Thomas Aquinas, and the Jews of the Eschaton," *Journal of Ecumenical Studies* 52, no. 4 (2017): 527–53.

5.   Among the best recent treatments of Augustine and his view of Jews and Judaism, see Jeremy Cohen, *Living Letters of the Law: Ideas of the Jew in Medieval Christianity* (Berkeley: University of California Press, 1999); and Paula Fredriksen, *Augustine and the Jews: A Christian Defense of Jews and Judaism* (New Haven: Yale University Press, 2008).

6.   Consider, for example, the Aleinu prayer from the daily liturgy, which proclaims, "Therefore we hope in you, Lord our God, that we will soon see the glory of your might. False gods will be removed from the earth and idols will be utterly cut off. The world will be perfected in the kingdom of God. All humanity will call upon your name, and all the wicked of the earth will turn to you. All inhabitants of the world will recognize and know that to you every knee must bend, and every tongue swear loyalty."

7.   Even the groundbreakingly open-minded *Nostra Aetate* that issued form the Second Vatican Council in 1965 fails to acknowledge the development of Judaism since the time of Jesus or its rich expressions in the contemporary world. The statement links Jews and Judaism of the past—the biblical patriarchs, covenants, and prophets—to Jews of the future, who one day will worship the Lord alongside Christians. That having been said, there can be no doubt that the decades of Christian-Jewish dialogue resulting from *Nostra Aetate* have fostered Christian appreciation for rabbinic Judaism as a historical religion and for Jews as multidimensional persons, rather than as mere theological categories.

8.   A humorous aside: targeted conversion reminds me of an episode from *The Simpsons* in which the evangelical Flanders family owns a video game called Billy Graham's Bible Blaster. Players shoot heathens to make them Christians. When Bart merely wings one, a Flanders child laments, "You made him a Unitarian!" I have long wondered if shooting/converting a Jew might, on the contrary, secure bonus points.

LIVED EXPERIENCE AND WORSHIP

PART THREE

In part three, "Lived Experience and Worship," five scholars model the framework used in many of the Jewish–Latter-day Saint academic dialogue sessions. In a comparative model, scholars from each tradition use specific themes to identify where Jews and Latter-day Saints have shared themes and where they diverge in terms of lived religious experience and worship. Tamar Frankiel examines the experiences of women within Judaism and Jewish communities. Frankiel highlights the constant negotiation of space and place in religious communities by women who contribute to the development of communal and familial practices and relations. In response to the work of Frankiel on women's experiences in community, Kristine Garroway reflects on the subject by thinking about women's experience in ancient Israel. Garroway shows how the dichotomy of secular/religious experience is not new and how we might rethink it in light of comparative ancient experiences.

During the dialogue, one of the foundational goals that quickly became important to participants was to experience community worship. As part of this, Latter-day Saints were given opportunities to speak in synagogues, seminaries, and community settings in Los Angeles, and Mark Diamond spoke in a gathering of Latter-day Saint leaders in Los Angeles and a Latter-day Saint sacrament meeting in Orem, Utah. As the Sabbath is a central moment of weekly worship in both Jewish and Latter-day Saint communities, Diamond and Brent Top individually worked through the meaning of sacred time and space in their respective chapters on the Sabbath. Both authors provide good evidence for historical importance while drawing their gaze into the present and also address areas where improvement might be needed and also where each community's experience might help the other strengthen Sabbath participation and observance. In connection with Sabbath worship, Frankiel and Hopkin further contribute to the discussion through their examinations of liturgy as a common element to both religions. Both authors use "religious imagination" as a way to think about the construction and reinforcement of a deep sense of religious community through liturgical development.

7

EXPLORING THE LIVED EXPERIENCE OF JEWISH WOMEN

TAMAR FRANKIEL

When we speak of the lived experience of Jewish women, we are, by the terms employed here, limited to modern times, in which women have been able and willing to write and speak about their experience and their reflections on it (for experience is known publicly only through reflection). Previous historical experiences of Jewish women, with few exceptions, have had to be reconstructed at second hand through either the archaeological record or the writings of men, so we will not be considering them except insofar as historic traditions impinge on women's lives today.

MODERNITY: DIFFICULT CHOICES FOR JEWISH WOMEN

In this context, we must note some significant modern developments that affect our understanding of Jewish women. While women's lives were always diverse, before the nineteenth century their differences were likely to relate to geography, language, ethnicity within Judaism, economic class, and marital status. After the Enlightenment—especially in the particular forms Judaism took in

Germany and America—women (and men) could make very different choices while claiming to represent an authentic Jewish identity. In religious institutions, this was represented largely in dichotomous fashion by the Reform movement on the one hand and traditionalist responses on the other.[1] Over the generations, the more traditional became officially Orthodox and tended to create inward-turning communities, while the Reform and other liberals—including most Conservatives—welcomed and advocated participation in the larger society. The organization of synagogue life and rabbinical authority were peripheral to most Jewish women because the home was their primary focus, and by extension areas like child care, education, and health. Yet the more that Jewish women participated in general non-Jewish society, the more likely they were to be affected by feminism, which led them to challenge and examine their roles and status vis-à-vis men. If they were in more self-enclosed Orthodox communities, they were likely to reject the claims of feminism out of hand.

But feminism did not always march hand-in-hand even with secular Jewish women. While some Jews were engaged in the fight for women's suffrage—indeed the National Women's Suffrage Association was formed by Susan B. Anthony and Elizabeth Cady Stanton and by their Jewish associate Ernestine Rose—many Jewish women were more engaged in general social welfare concerns.[2] They created major national and international women's organizations that were neither specifically religious nor political as in the fight for women's suffrage, but were focused on good works such as assisting poor or exploited women and improving women's health, education, or working conditions. They also were concerned about anti-Semitism and supporting immigrants to Israel. Among the best-known from that era are the National Council of Jewish Women (1896), Hadassah (1912), and Women's International Zionist Organization (1920).[3] Secular Jewish women were very active in the labor movement, for example, the International Ladies' Garment Workers' Union (1900), the first predominantly female labor union.[4]

On the other hand, women who were opting for a religious lifestyle increasingly chose not to join the general Jewish charitable societies but rather created their own, usually in local communities where the poor or disadvantaged were helped directly. This was typical of many immigrant communities, but the religious Jews who came from Eastern Europe in the early twentieth century had additional reason to keep to themselves: American society was *treif*—an expression meaning forbidden (usually applied to food). The newcomers meant also to exclude cultural habits they saw as dangerous, such as mixing of men and women and enjoying new forms of leisure and entertainment.

Additionally, the twentieth century saw a growing divide between women who participated in secular education and those who did not. Less religious Jewish women joined their American middle-class counterparts in going to college—for the first time in large numbers—after World War II, but religious Jewish women lagged behind in advanced education. Orthodox rabbis discouraged women of marriageable age from attending college at all and particularly opposed coeducational schools. The same was true when women made choices for their children's education. Orthodox Jews still sent their children to public schools, the great equalizer in America, in the early twentieth century. But after World War II and the Holocaust, Orthodox Jewish communities devoted much energy and money to setting up parochial schools to revive traditional Jewish culture. Not until 1967 did a Conservative system, the Solomon Schechter Day School network, begin educating elementary school boys and girls together.

In short, a divide had opened between two Jewish identities for women: one a strongly religious identity with commitment to living according to Jewish law, clearly identified as Orthodox; the other "liberal," ranging from secular to Reform to Conservative in institutional affiliation, but participating fully and freely in the larger culture. A historical note on the denominations may be helpful here.

Before the 1830s the Jewish population in the United States was quite small and quite traditional, including Sephardic and Ashkenazic Jews known by their place of origin. Beginning with a large German immigration in the 1830s, Reform Judaism gained a notable presence. As in Germany, Reform saw itself as freeing Judaism from obsolete laws and customs and espousing an Enlightenment ethical monotheism, while maintaining symbols of Jewish identity and a sense of mission. The movement became centralized with the establishment of the Hebrew Union College as its rabbinical training seminary in 1875.

Reform's outspoken American opponents were originally observant Jews who recognized some need for modernization but felt Reform had gone too far. They established the Jewish Theological Seminary (JTS, 1886) and later the United Synagogue of America (1913) as a centralizing organization; this came to be known as the Conservative movement. At that time most of its leaders would have been considered orthodox (with a lowercase o) in practice; the movement continued to have a strong interest in maintaining Jewish law as foundational, but modified it for contemporary situations.

The immigrations of 1890–1915 brought tens of thousands of East European Jews to America; they were more strictly observant than their American cousins, and their rabbis opposed the study of secular subjects, especially historical and biblical criticism, that characterized JTS. East European Jews followed the customs of their countries and did not create a seminary, although they established several rabbinical organizations, the most influential of which has been the Union of Orthodox Congregations (or Orthodox Union, OU), formed in 1898 as a platform for issues of common concern. By drawing sharp lines between themselves and less observant Jews, the Orthodox movement (with an uppercase O) established itself as a third force even though it was the smallest and least centralized of the three main groups.

Other much smaller denominations emerged later, including Reconstructionism (1920s), Jewish Humanism (1960s), and Jewish Renewal (1970s). Reconstructionism was an offshoot of Conservative Judaism that understood Judaism more as a civilization than a religion and was also Zionist. Humanism was similar in its emphasis on Jewish community but was more agnostic if not atheist. Jewish Renewal—influenced by growing interest in meditation, yoga, and personal spirituality—created congregations that emphasized the inner dimension of Jewish practice. In terms of women's participation, all these, along with Reform Judaism, would also be classed as liberal. Conservative Judaism was still quite traditional until, beginning in the 1950s, its law committee began to break with certain Orthodox rulings by, for example, allowing the use of electricity on Shabbat, or driving on Shabbat with some restrictions.

In the 1950s all women across the spectrum would still have had mostly Jewish friends (outside the workplace). Nearly all would have experienced anti-Semitism. Yet because traditional Jews lived ritually differentiated lives, most prominently by observance of Shabbat and dietary laws, the two broad divisions (liberal and traditional) mixed less and less often.[5] An educational divide emerged as well: women from the liberal denominations usually had a public school education and if possible went to college, whereas their religious education (if any) ended before high school. Orthodox women would have gone to parochial schools and rarely attended college before the 1990s. The traditionally observant group was much smaller than the liberal-secular, but it still held a significant place since what was now officially labeled Orthodoxy also represented the faith of the ancestors in most people's minds. Yet the gap in women's perceptions of one another was about to become still larger after 1970 as specifically religious issues about women were opened to public debate.

FEMINIST CRITIQUES OF TRADITIONAL PRACTICE

In the 1970s and 1980s, critiques of the received Jewish wisdom about women and their roles began to erupt openly. Judaism was criticized for not allowing women to be counted in a minyan (quorum for prayer), to say the Kaddish prayer for a deceased relative, or to sing publicly with or in the presence of men. Women began to write about the ways in which they felt treated as second-class members of their own families, as boys studied more and were honored at bar mitzvah celebrations, while many girls had only a birthday party. Girls who liked studying were told it ruined their chances for marriage. A woman could not become a rabbi in any denomination before 1970, and most Jewish institutions were run by men, except the women's charitable organizations mentioned earlier. Women complained there were no distinctively Jewish female role models other than wife and mother.

Reform Judaism, because of its reduction of Jewish ritual law to a minimum, had long ago vitiated some of women's complaints. But positions of authority still largely went to men, and there were no female rabbis. Other denominations that now call themselves part of liberal Judaism (including most Conservatives), eventually followed feminist thinkers in their critiques of male bias, but it took time to implement changes. The Reform movement ordained its first female rabbi in 1972, and the Reconstructionist movement in 1974, but the Conservative movement took ten more years, finally ordaining a female rabbi in 1985. The Cantors Assembly, officially a nondenominational group but dominated by cantors of the Conservative movement, did not accept women until 1990, and even then it took a special vote by the leaders that avoided a membership vote to change the bylaws. (Many Conservatives still held to the *halachah* that prohibited women from leading prayer services.)

The resistance to women's leadership should not be understood merely as men's fear of sharing power. While many men did feel personally uncomfortable with women in authority over men (as evidenced in many areas of American life), Judaism also had traditions, established for centuries and even millennia in some cases, of law and practice wherein women's religious desires were acknowledged, but their public participation was nevertheless forbidden. Often the overriding issue was to create a fence against immorality. For example, the issue with women serving as cantors in the Conservative movement was a halachic restriction that forbade them from leading a minyan, since public prayer is a time-bound obligation traditionally reserved for men alone. For a woman to be a rabbi might have been less problematic, except that women were normally ineligible to be witnesses in court and therefore could not adjudicate legal documents—a common task of a traditional rabbi—and also were not counted in a minyan because they were exempt from the requirement of being present for public prayer. Women therefore had to argue for admission to official leadership not only on the basis of personal ability, but also on broader grounds, both legal and institutional.

Nevertheless, the lack of female models in religious leadership was being rectified in significant branches of Jewish synagogue life—Reform, Reconstructionist, and Conservative denominations, as well as later offshoots. This was part of first-wave feminism: enfranchisement, which in Judaism meant being counted in a minyan, and access to positions of authority.

Other issues have arisen in Jewish settings that are also part of secular feminist concerns: equal pay for equal work, egalitarian hiring standards, representation of women on synagogue boards, and effective measures against sexual harassment.[6] Matters of personal autonomy—such as in health-care decisions, abortion, accepting gay marriage, and redefining gender—are areas where liberal and secular Jewish women hold more variable positions, not necessarily determined by their denomination or even by Jewish identity at all.

Generalizing broadly, liberal Jewish women tend to be closer to secular American women than they are to their Orthodox sisters on issues of personal autonomy and egalitarianism. However, they have not abandoned Jewish values of community, and they also care deeply about participation in Jewish rituals while wanting to make them more accessible to women and more affirming of women as full participants. One person who articulated these desires was Professor Judith Plaskow in her 1990 book *Standing Again at Sinai*.[7] She reviewed many Jewish traditions about women and delivered a stinging critique of male bias and negative attitudes toward women as purveyed by the rabbinic tradition. Women in the liberal movements, following her lead, criticized masculine God-language in the siddur, paving the way for revisions in many denominational prayer books.

Moreover, for some liberal women, these were not just issues in American Jewish denominations, but ones that should concern Jewish women everywhere. This is illustrated in the movement in Israel called Women of the Wall, in which some American women have joined with their Israeli counterparts, not along denominational lines but simply as feminists.

Some background may be helpful to understand this issue. Prayer at the Kotel, or Western Wall, is a precious expression of Jewish devotion because this wall is the only segment remaining from the ancient Second Temple—not actually the temple itself, but a surrounding outer wall constructed when Herod (late first century BCE) undertook major expansion and upgrading of the temple site. In modern times, after Jews began to return to the land but before Israel became an independent nation, Jews prayed there under the protection of the governing authorities—the Turks before World War I and the British under the Protectorate. However, the settlement after the War of Independence in 1948 left Jordan in control, and Jews were no longer allowed to pray at the Wall. After the Six-Day War in 1967, Israel repossessed the Wall and opened it to prayer, and it again became a pilgrimage site, attracting Jews from all over the world.

Orthodox officials in charge of ritual observance at the Wall then constructed a *mechitzah*, or separation barrier, so that men could pray separately from women, in accordance with Jewish law. (In the ancient temple, there were also separate men's and women's areas.) This was disappointing to some groups but largely uncontested until women began to organize in groups to pray as a minyan, that is, a quorum of ten for prayer.[8] This was an upsurge of women's desire to pray communally, at a site where previously they had come as individuals. (On the men's side of the wall, men did gather in minyanim, and it was not uncommon to hold small communal celebrations such as bar mitzvahs.) In rabbinic law there are some opinions that women cannot constitute a minyan themselves even if no men are in the group, and other opinions that they may do so, with certain restrictions. In any case, at first there was no objection from the authorities.

However, other people praying at the Wall did object. In 1987 a women's group that attempted to pray and read Torah in Orthodox fashion were pushed away and verbally attacked by traditional worshippers. Subsequently the women formed a regular group to meet on Rosh Chodesh (the New Moon holiday, which is traditionally special to women).[9] At some point they adopted the name Women of the Wall. The women at these gatherings pray in accordance with the liturgy, including reading the Torah; some women also wear the traditional *tallit* or prayer shawl, which the Orthodox regard as a garment for men only. Sometimes there has been little or no opposition; sometimes violence or arrests. The struggle has continued to this day, with varying attempts at compromise, which have been affected by Israeli politics.[10] The significance continues to be the desire for recognition of women's ability to function as equals to men in their ability to create and lead Jewish ritual communities.

FEMINISM AND ORTHODOX WOMEN

Orthodox women's writings were beginning to be published around the same time as the more liberal stances appeared in print. In 1990 my book *The Voice of Sarah* appeared, arguing that recent feminist discussions went too far in blaming Judaism for all the sins of patriarchy

while ignoring the real Jewish heroines in our tradition.[11] In addition, the book pointed out that while home and family had long been
regarded as the woman's domain in a restrictive sense, our role in
anchoring the home was regarded in traditional literature as one of
honor and beauty. In 1981 Blu Greenberg's book *On Women and Judaism: A View from Tradition* tackled some of the key issues of feminist
concern.[12] She too admitted that traditional Judaism had institutionalized some negative stereotypes and needed updating but proposed
ways that the most pressing issues could be addressed. Both of these
books were welcomed by Orthodox women but were questioned by
liberals for stances that seemed mere apologetics. Nevertheless, they
carved out a more nuanced framework for discussion of Jewish wom-
en's experience of being Jewish and offered different perspectives on
how women's experiences were related to their choices (or lack of
free choice) in religious belief and practice.

Nearly thirty years later, much to the surprise of prognostica-
tors who thought Orthodoxy would die off as "enlightenment" proceeded, Jewish observance has been growing significantly. While the
Orthodox percentage of the Jewish population remains small (10%
in the United States in 2013), Orthodox Jews usually marry within
the faith, marry younger and have more children than their liberal
counterparts, and are far more likely to provide a Jewish education
and strong religious environment. If Orthodox Jewish families continue to bear twice as many children and their children marry ten
years earlier than their non-Orthodox counterparts, the Orthodox percentage of the total Jewish population will increase rapidly.
Among the young adult sector of the Jewish population (age 18–29),
the Orthodox sector was estimated at 25% in 2015.[13]

Moreover, the trends seem to indicate that despite the attrac-
tions of secular culture, Jewish women value many aspects of Orthodox life, either because they were brought up happily in the tradition
or because it promises to satisfy significant needs in their lives. One
might ask, if Orthodox women are "happy with the way things are,"
perhaps feminism is simply not relevant to their lived experience.

But that is not quite the case. As Greenberg and I argued in differ-ent ways, feminism has continued to raise significant issues. I will focus on three elements: women's learning, women's ordination as congregational leaders (not usually called rabbis in Orthodoxy), and women's theology or religious worldview.

WOMEN LEARNING TORAH

Judaism, as it has manifested over the past two thousand years at least, is focused on learning, defined specifically as Torah study. One of the disadvantages women experienced if they wanted to argue against the prevailing order of things was lack of knowledge and textual skill in the Jewish textual tradition; and therefore, one of the key entry points to different positions (especially, but not only, the rabbinate) was to acquire that knowledge and skill. Women were not explicitly forbidden to study, though it was questionable whether they should aspire to study Talmud. A strong traditional view held that women needed to learn *halachah*, Jewish law, in order to maintain a Jewish household and instruct their children properly at home. This was no small matter—the *halachah of kashrut* (dietary laws); laws surrounding Shabbat, holidays, and memorials; laws of intimacy in marriage, as well as basic regulations of social behavior constituted an impres-sive set of practical and intellectual skills. However, women rarely had time to do more unless the family was wealthy enough to allow leisure and the head of the household approved of wives and daugh-ters learning. Before the nineteenth century, this did occur in some families and regions.[14] But modernity brought changes to the ways of the old world, such that opportunities for learning were altered even among those who intended to maintain a traditional religious life.

In the nineteenth century, one of the most dramatic changes, noted by Shoshanah Zolty's research, was that families began to send promising young men away from home to learn in newer, larger *yeshivot* for what would now be considered high school (and perhaps an additional year or two until they were married). With fewer older boys at home, there was less Torah learning in the home environment, and opportunities for women to "listen in," so to speak, also decreased.

In Europe by the time of World War I, it was more likely that a young woman from a family of means would have an advanced secular education than an advanced Jewish one. In a story that is famous in Orthodox circles, a seamstress named Sarah Schenirer decided that this situation had to change. She campaigned and raised money for a girls' high school in Poland, and while meeting resistance in many quarters, eventually obtained the approval of important rabbis, including the outstanding ethicist Rabbi Yisroel Meir Ha-Cohen, known as the Chafetz Chaim.[15] He later wrote that "ancestral tradition has become exceptionally weak," and so it would be a great *mitzvah* to teach women Tanakh (Bible) and ethical teachings of the sages "so that they will internalize our sacred faith, lest they be prone to abandon the path of God."[16] Sarah Schenirer's school, established in Krakow in 1918, was the first of many Orthodox women's schools outside the home that would constitute the Bais Yaakov high school movement.[17]

Still, women were expected to marry early and not to spend much time learning once they began having children. A few schools were established for women after World War II, notably New York's Stern College of Yeshiva University and in Israel, the Jerusalem College for Women (*Michlalah*), established in the 1960s by Tziporah Pincus Cooperman. But in the 1980s there emerged a new generation of female *ba'alot teshuvah* (returnees to traditional Judaism), and schools were needed for them—first in the basics but, since many of them had strong secular education backgrounds, also serious study that would challenge them intellectually. Further, teachers were needed in existing Orthodox schools that would bring the schools up to par with secular competitors. While debates raged inside Orthodox school systems as to how much science or humanities should be studied, the levels of traditional Jewish education rose rapidly, with women studying traditional commentators and availing themselves of a growing number of female scholars.

In twenty years the landscape was transformed. Rochelle Furstenberg wrote in 2000 about the conferences being held to bring women together to study Torah in Israel:

> The scholars who taught at these mass learn-ins were themselves learned women, *talmidot hachamot,* who teach at the scores of institutions for women's study that have mushroomed in the last decade. "It is clear," said one scholar, "that the energy in religious Jewish life in Israel today revolves around women's study of Jewish sources." This energy radiates from institutions in the religious Zionist sector, and the women involved are primarily of orthodox orientation, but it embraces and influences women from all parts of the Jewish spectrum. It is generating a chain reaction that is changing the quality of Jewish life.[18]

Elements of the chain reaction eventually included women studying for positions as halachic advisors, rabbinical court advocates for women, and groups working with rabbinic authorities on women's issues, such as divorce. Rabbinic authorities have expressed stiff resistance to having women serve as rabbinic judges, but that is a goal for the future. In general, women do not seek congregational leadership positions in Israel as they do in the United States, but congregational rabbis are less significant there in any case, for a variety of sociological reasons that we will not discuss here. What is interesting is that women's search for opportunities to learn did not necessarily come from a desire for a certain Jewish career objective (e.g., to become a rabbi), but from either the desire to learn Torah *lishma,* "Torah for its own sake," or to help solve particular problems faced by Jewish women who need helpers, mentors, or legal advocates.

The question often raised by those who opposed advanced study for women was whether study would distract a woman from her primary role and lead to dilution of traditional Jewish values. Furstenberg cites Malka Bina, a pioneer Talmud teacher and founder of Matan, a women's institute in Israel representing many who had the same question at first but who have reached the conclusion that study does not undermine traditional Judaism:

The women involved are deeply and sincerely religious. The movement did not undermine their religiosity. *Their desire to study emerges from their religiosity and strengthens it.* Most of all, after twenty years of women's study, we see that it does not undermine the value of family in Jewish life. Many of our women scholars combine career and family. Many of the young men are also studying. It forces young couples to work out new family patterns together. Women must juggle priorities. But the family also gives the woman-scholar support. She can allow herself this new, innovative way of life because she is anchored in a Jewish family situation.[19]

The idea that family life and women's scholarly aspirations can be mutually supportive rather than competitive is also a highly significant development. Of course, this had begun to happen already as women sought professional training to enhance family income as well as to pursue their own interests.[20] But in the traditional Judaism of earlier generations, only the man's aspirations for study deserved support.

Perhaps it is appropriate to note here, based on my personal experience and what other Orthodox women have reported to me, that rabbis who advise families generally do not oppose women seeking personal fulfillment in study, whether Torah study or attaining a personal or professional goal. Her satisfaction with her life is considered essential to the health of the family.

ORDINATION OF WOMEN AS RABBIS

One aspiration cannot (yet) be fulfilled: occupying an unquestioned position of communal authority within Orthodoxy. This has emerged as one of the chief issues in American Orthodoxy as learned Orthodox women have sought the recognition that is accorded their sisters in the liberal movements—namely, ordination as clergy, but usually under another title than that of rabbi, such as "rabba" or "rabbanit."

While occasionally in the recent past a woman might have received private *s'michah* (ordination) from one rabbi, now there is an Orthodox institution, Yeshivat Maharat, offering a course of rabbinic studies that leads directly to ordination. (The consonants of Maharat stand for *Manhigah Hilchatit Ruchanit Toranit*, meaning "[female] leader of law, spirituality, Torah.") Founded in 2009 by Rabbi Avi Weiss and Rabba Sara Hurwitz, who was previously ordained by Weiss, the school, by the end of 2019, had produced twenty-six graduates with the title "Rabbanit" and had about two dozen more students in various stages of its program. All these women are committed to halachic observance within Orthodox parameters and do not seek to break down Jewish law and custom (for example, they do not question separate seating for men and women). They have asked only to be recognized as having earned their title by accomplishments in Torah studies equivalent to men who are accorded the title of rabbi and therefore to be eligible for rabbinic leadership positions within appropriate parameters. Quietly, these graduates have occupied positions as teachers or communal leaders in various synagogues or agencies. However, the opposition to these appointments by rabbis representing the Orthodox center, where there had been some hope for change, has been intense.

The public declarations of the Orthodox Union (OU), the largest centrist Orthodox organization, affirmed in September 2017 the results from a Rabbinic Panel (whose task was to present findings, not to adjudicate law as with a court) assigned the task of investigating the issue of ordination and women's authority. The panel held that while no explicit law has been handed down about female rabbis, the normative practice has been to exclude women from the rabbinate and similar positions. Women scholars in the past were acknowledged and appreciated, but they had impact upon and guided the community without rabbinic titles or ordination. Through the centuries, Jewish law repeatedly ruled against women exercising communal authority in a formal way. This practice "reflects a baseline truth that must be grappled with," said the rabbis, who described this baseline as a "halackic ethos" that must be further elaborated in each generation by rulings on actual behavior. The status quo, said the panel, is "meaningful and intentional," and therefore the burden of proof rests on those who seek change.

On the one hand, the panel asserted that men and women are held to be absolutely equal in value as individuals and as servants of God; personal spiritual achievement does not differ between the genders; and most halachic obligations apply equally to women and men. On the other hand, role differentiation on the basis of male and female genders expresses two different paths by which the two halves of humanity serve God and perpetuate the Jewish people. The panel's report quoted Rabbi Joseph Soloveitchik, one of the great thinkers of modern Orthodoxy: "Two humans were created who differ from each other metaphysically, not only physiologically."[21] Appointing women to positions of communal authority contradicts this ethos.

How are we to understand this? A legal ruling would require a legal precedent, one which ultimately could be traced back to the Mosaic Torah or to early rabbinic law, and there was no such law for or against. (The existence of female prophets and once even a judge—Devora—did not count for the panel as a law since those were divinely chosen individuals for specific times, not constitutive of a continuing justice system.) The repeated practice over dozens of generations was *not* to appoint women to formal leadership positions, and Jewish law frequently stipulates that the customs of one's community represent a form of wisdom that should not be lightly overturned, even if it is difficult to observe them. The panel translated this well-known principle into modern parlance with the terms *baseline* and *ethos*, probably because modern usage interprets the idea of customs more lightly than does traditional Jewish law.

The panel went on to detail the kinds of higher-level positions women can occupy and the services many are already performing in synagogues: working in managerial and administrative positions; directing programming and religious education; teaching as institutional scholars to supplement the community's educational opportunities; serving in professional counseling roles as synagogue staff members; serving as mentors and teachers to women undergoing conversion; and being advisers to women on halachic matters relating to personal health and intimacy. However, women should not officiate at life-cycle events, regularly deliver sermons from the pulpit, lead prayer services at a minyan, or serve as the synagogue's primary religious mentor, teacher, and spiritual guide—all of which constitute the norm for the position of congregational rabbi in America.[22]

The examples of legal rulings, the description of duties allowed and proscribed, and the argument from ethos mostly revolve around the idea that women should not be placed in authority over men, at least not in the sphere of religion. This is held to be the case despite what may be an extensive range of intellectual, managerial, interpersonal, and educational skills. Essentially, the Orthodox Union position stands on a "metaphysical" difference, as in Rabbi Soloveitchik's claim above, that overrides all the ways in which a woman candidate for a rabbinic position may be equal to a man. Perhaps most surprising is a piece that goes beyond organizational communal authority and authoritative teaching—namely, forbidding women from officiating at life-cycle events: baby namings (of girls), *brit milah* (circumcision for boys), bar and bat mitzvah, weddings, and funerals. The male rabbi is, presumably, "metaphysically" suited to this role. That seems particularly odd in that the Tanakh describes, in ancient Israelite times, women as singers and "lamenters" and women naming their babies (and even, in the case of Moses's wife Tziporah, circumcising one).

The extent to which this sharp ruling will affect Yeshivat Maharat and similar efforts is yet to be seen. Some were forecasting a schism within Orthodoxy over this issue, but that has been forestalled by the OU allowing the four Orthodox Union synagogues who have hired Yeshivat Maharat graduates to continue membership in the organization. Rabbi Weiss continues to hold that the exclusion of women from the rabbinate is "not halakhic, but sociological," but he has also expressed concern over the OU's effort to centralize and control in areas where synagogues have till now been autonomous, particularly the area of defining the role of rabbi.[23] This concern is not without ground. In Britain, the United Synagogue is a centralized institution with power to prevent a synagogue from hiring a woman rabbi simply because the Chief Rabbi and the London Beth Din (court) forbid it.[24] Nevertheless, Orthodox thinkers generally see the surge in women's learning as the key to change across the board, though that change may come slowly. As Miriam Shaviv has observed, Blu Greenberg writing in the late 1980s had spoken of changes that might take two or three generations to achieve, but "the milestones she predicted were all achieved in less than a decade."[25]

COMMUNAL AUTHORITY

I want to be a bit more provocative and point to a dimension that these descriptions seem to be carefully avoiding. A couple of decades ago, Jewish feminists were accused of "trying to be like men" (by wearing the *tallit* and leading services, for example), of imitating the status-seeking of the secular world, or of wanting only their own honor rather than the service of God. Most Orthodox rabbis, unless on the extreme right, no longer use that kind of language. Rather, like the OU's Rabbinic Panel, they offer apparently rational outlines of the types of jobs appropriate to women, distinguishing them from inappropriate ones. When one examines the two sets closely, however, the underlying differences cannot be about ability or talent, because the kinds of skills needed for the jobs women are allowed to perform are virtually the same skills as would be listed in a rabbinic candidate's résumé, with the possible exception of public speaking. As far as I can tell, the bottom line is honor, title, the public face of the top leader.

The flip side of this is that women should not want honor or final authority; to expect it or ask for it is considered inappropriate. Actually, in rabbinic Judaism, men are warned not to seek honor either.[26] However, while one may roll one's eyes about a man who openly revels in being honored, a woman who insists on honor is more likely to be shamed. Rabbi Lila Kagedan, a Yeshivat Maharat graduate who now leads a Massachusetts congregation, reports that when she decided to use the title "rabbi" instead of "rabba," she was met with "devastating . . . hate and pushback."[27]

Honest self-examination is the only process I can suggest for those struggling with these issues. What is authority? Why is it difficult to share authority? Do women and men have different ways of expressing authority? Am I uncomfortable with those differences? Is my reaction mere habit or something deeper? Are the differences situational, cultural, or essential, and how do we know?

Rabbinic tradition has a way of approaching difficult and uncomfortable questions that allows us to step back and look at them. It is called midrash. So I offer here a famous midrash that occurs in a few places in ancient literature. This is my favorite version:

> In a portion of tractate Hullin (60b) where the Sages are discussing various passages in the Torah, Rabbi Shimon ben Pei asks:
>
> It is written, "G-d made two great lights," then it is written, "the great light and the smaller light." [Genesis 1:16] What happened here? [The text seems to contradict itself.]
>
> The moon said before the Holy One, Blessed Be He, "Master of the Universe, is it possible that two kings can wear one crown?"
>
> "Right!" He replied. "Make yourself smaller."
>
> "Master of the Universe," the moon cried, "just because I suggested a proper thing, I should diminish myself?"
>
> "Right," He replied. "But you shall rule both by day and by night."
>
> She said to Him, "What is a little light of the candle in the daylight?"

He tried to appease her, saying, "By you Israel will count the days and years."

She said, "It's impossible to count without the sun. It is written, 'And they will be for lights, for seasons and days and years.'"

He replied, "The righteous will be named after you [you who are *katanah*, the smaller light]: Yaakov HaKatan, Shmuel HaKatan, David HaKatan. [Jacob, Samuel, and David were all the "younger," which in Hebrew is expressed by the same word as "smaller."]

She was not consoled, and the Holy One Blessed Be He said that He would bring an atonement sacrifice for diminishing the moon. [Where do we find this?] Reish Lakish said, What is different about the goat [offering] of Rosh Chodesh?—that it says, "for the Lord"[28]—God said that this goat would be an atonement for diminishing the moon.

The issue of ruling has deep roots. According to this midrash, even God, the Holy One, Blessed Be He, had difficulty answering why an entity originally created equal, the Moon, could justly be diminished; and he sought atonement. Is anyone seeking atonement nowadays, perhaps on Yom Kippur, for disallowing women from positions of communal authority?

ORTHODOX WOMEN AND TRADITIONAL BELIEF

What remains clear through all the controversy is that women express in their lived experience the great value for them of Torah learning. They continue to want more of it, for themselves and their daughters, even when they do not necessarily desire a career in a specifically religious profession. Many discover (or, for those raised in the tradition, continue to feel) that commitment to a Torah-based life contributes to their personal fulfillment and spiritual growth. Professor Susan Handelman, a well-known scholar of literature and a representative of the theological position of Chabad-Lubavitch, points out that the search for knowledge today includes spiritual knowledge, which in turn includes a search for God. Women "partake of the spiritual quest occurring in the contemporary world. And because of the strength of that desire they, too, seek their place before G-d in synagogues and learning institutions, and look back to foundational texts for what these can tell them about their lives."[29]

This brings us to the further question of theology and philosophy in the broadest sense—of women reflecting on their own lived experience in light of "foundational texts," spiritual insights from others, and insights they have come to on their own. Handelman advises that we drop many of the categories in which we have defined women's issues, including autonomy versus heteronomous law, and independent reasoning versus dogma. Even arguing about secular versus Torah learning is, in her view, an outdated debate. She writes further, "I would like to see feminist thought itself challenged, in its turn, by Torah—to examine its own presuppositions, values, goals, in light of criteria such as the service of Hashem [God], awe of Heaven, humility, modesty, acceptance of the yoke of Torah and so forth. In other words, to be discerning about what philosophical and cultural categories it employs for its critique."[30]

In this regard, many female scholars are lending their voice to a search that goes deeper than the surface battles, even while recognizing that battles are still necessary to unlock certain doors for women. A few examples:

- Among theologians, Tamar Ross, a philosophy professor at Bar-Ilan University in Israel, is developing a process theology of revelation that is dynamic and allows for biblical criticism while strongly affirming a belief in God. She is known for her work in feminist theology—radically feminist and Orthodox. She traces among her most important formative influences the work of Rabbi Abraham Isaac Kook, chief rabbi of Palestine until 1935, who had an open-ended view of creation and revelation.[31]

- In a respectful but not Orthodox mode, Rachel Adler has developed a theory of law that could remove the authoritarian bias of rabbinic law, replacing it with a *halachah* that is egalitarian, founded on mutuality between men and women.[32]
- Among biblical commentators, Dr. Avivah Gottlieb Zornberg writes as an Orthodox scholar exploring biblical texts as authoritative but open to inquiry as she addresses fundamental human questions of doubt and authenticity. She brings attention to the presence of women in the Bible while ranging far beyond women's issues. In particular, her ability to move from psychoanalytical and literary theorists to classical Midrash and Hasidic thinkers provides a profound model for women seeking other approaches to foundational texts.[33]
- Sarah Idit Schneider wrote *Kabbalistic Writings on the Nature of Masculine and Feminine*, arguing that evolution as expressed in the changes encountered by women in the modern world are part of a deeper plan for human history.[34] The feminine can be understood symbolically as well as literally, and as midrashic tradition has suggested, as representative of the Jewish people's situation in the world.

Indeed, we must recognize that we are always traversing a multitude of bridges between reflection and experience, ideals and reality. Ideals sometimes seem oversimplified—for example, the traditional version of the Jewish woman sanctifying the home and men protecting the home by ruling the external world. Lived experience, we might object, is far more confusing and complex. Let it be said clearly that Jewish men also struggle with this problem: Devotion to Torah study is their proclaimed ideal, protecting and preserving the Jewish community by ensuring the continuity of our collective relationship to God. But in lived experience, the world demands ordinary work to put food on the table, as well as a multitude of other responsibilities.

Nevertheless, such ideals elevate one's perspective in the midst of the difficulties of ordinary life. Philosophical and theological reflection, taking account of lived experience in the present and recent past, can elaborate and improve on inherited ideals. "In every generation," we say at Passover, "each person must see herself as having come out of Egypt"—the trauma of Egyptian slavery from which we are continuously liberated by our connection to the Divine creative force in the world and within us. The additionally traumatic effect of difficult and sometimes oppressive male/female dynamics may be one of those residues that still needs healing.

At the same time, in lived experience, every week Jews sanctify Shabbat and the holidays with the *kiddush* prayer over wine "as a memorial of the Exodus from Egypt" (compare Exodus 12:14), confirming that, over thousands of years of social, cultural, and geographical change, the ideal of a relation to God that is nurturing, creative, and liberating can be eternal, or as near to eternal as human life allows.

POSTFEMINISM: WOMEN AND THE FAMILY

As mentioned above, the traditional Jewish family is making room for women's aspirations, whether in learning or career. Additionally, younger Orthodox women are no longer fighting the battle of earlier feminism, believing they are chained to the stove or smothered by motherhood. Precisely because they do have other options, many see family and motherhood as a positive choice. Professor Handelman calls today's young women "post-feminist"[35]—not, of course, on issues of abuse or harassment or equal pay, but in the sense that they feel confident enough to adopt an independent perspective that values family as part of their growth and fulfillment.

Regarding the comparisons we are making between Jewish and Latter-day Saint women, I would suggest that one thing we share is a spiritual ideal of the family, a connection known and felt across generations and extended, in hope, across to the future. In Jewish homes (and I include here many nonobservant women), this is symbolized by the woman lighting Shabbat candles in the home each Friday night, as women have done for millennia even though there is no biblical law prescribing it. Family is in many ways the sacred place of origin, before the temple and before Sinai, via our stories of the lives of Avraham and Sarah and the other patriarchs and matriarchs in Genesis. Since the destruction of the temple, family remains the fundamental embodiment of Judaism even while Torah is its intellectual ground.[36] Under the guidance of the family ideal, moral behavior is prioritized to preserve the family. Anything that threatens women or children receives attention. Caring for widows and orphans, which became the biblical paradigm for ethical behavior to all the unprotected, is founded on a concern for those who do not have the blessings of a normal family. Even today, when family appears to be undergoing redefinition by groups that were once marginalized and when families are spread all over the globe, family still serves as a core ideal to which Jews aspire and as a bulwark of Jewish communal life—even in a world in which social media aspire to define society.

Jewish women live this ideal in ushering Shabbat into the home each Friday night, in cherishing partnership, and in tending to the future of their own children and the community's children by nurturing body, mind, and soul. They follow the path of Sarah our Mother, who confronted difficult decisions about her own personal life and about the future of her and Avraham's offspring. She spoke with insight and authority, and was honored by God saying, "In all that Sarah says to you, listen to her voice" (Genesis 21:12, my translation). May Sarah's voice be our inspiration as we continue to work for the dignity of all women and men, made together in the image of God.

COMPARISONS

This leaves us, I think, with three points of discussion for comparison between traditional Jewish and Latter-day Saint women, collectively speaking.

One area of both similarity and difference concerns authority. This has been a primary battleground in Jewish responses to feminism, perhaps less so among Latter-day Saints. But every religious tradition today must face the question of whether, to what extent, and why women are excluded from positions of authority.

In Jewish tradition, authority is stated to depend on Torah knowledge, including knowledge not only of law and precedents but of what has been good for Jewish life, from the lived experience accumulated and passed down from generation to generation. I am persuaded by the argument that women's experience and reflection ought to be part of that knowledge and tradition—and specifically spoken from their own mouths, not just secondhand via their husbands or rabbis. Because authority rests on knowledge, it does seem that communal authority structures should be expanded to include the voices of women at all levels, and further, that a true and firm base of knowledge has to allow for shared authority.

By way of comparison, authority is not quite the same with Latter-day Saints, who ultimately claim prophetic authority that is safeguarded to men in matters affecting the community. This, however, deflects the question to another level—namely, why do women not have access to prophecy for the community, given precedents like Miriam and Devora in the Hebrew Bible? In any case, heirs of rabbinic Judaism, having declared that prophecy ended and authority rests in the hands of the sages who are Torah scholars, do not have the option of claiming direct access to the divine. As suggested earlier in this paper, we should also be examining what underlying attitudes and concerns, besides existing traditions of authority, make it so difficult to accept women's authority or to share authority equally.

A second area is one of curiosity for me, regarding an institution that may be unique to Latter-day Saints. Barbara Morgan Gardner raised the point in one of the dialogue sessions that priesthood in the Latter-day Saint temple involves women mentoring women, women sharing the foundational stories and rituals to guide women on their spiritual journey.[37] Judaism does not have an institution like this. In some Hasidic sects, women are specifically advised to find spiritual mentors as well as halachic advisors, but there is little formal organization of the process. This is, to borrow a phrase from another contribution to this volume, one of the things that "Jews could learn from Latter-day Saints."

A third area is to test my suggestion above that our traditions share many commonalities in our ideal of the family. How are our ideals similar or different? How important are theology and eschatology in this comparison? How are these ideals lived practically, and can we help each other improve on them? This could provide grounds for interesting and fruitful conversations in the future.

NOTES

1. *Traditional* and *traditionalist* are terms used in the last few decades to differentiate the various congregations and individuals who have stood apart from Reform and more recent liberal movements but are not recognized as, nor would they term themselves as, strictly Orthodox. Occasionally congregations will describe themselves as "traditional and egalitarian," meaning that they are halachically observant but liberal on women's (or gender) issues. Opponents of Reform in the early twentieth century would be described today as "traditionalist."

2. Bonnie S. Anderson, *The Rabbi's Atheist Daughter: Ernestine Rose, International Feminist Pioneer* (New York: Oxford University Press, 2017); Carol A. Kolmerton, *The American Life of Ernestine L. Rose* (Syracuse: Syracuse University Press, 1999).

3. See the online Jewish Women's Archive, https://jwa.org, for articles on these organizations and their leaders. Also, at the same site, "Feminism in the United States" identifies important Jewish women who contributed to feminist and working women's causes while also struggling with anti-Semitism in the feminist movement. For more on these movements, see Mary McCune, *The Whole Wide World, Without Limits: International Relief, Gender Politics, and American Jewish Women, 1893–1930* (Detroit: Wayne State University Press, 2005); Mirah Katsburg-Yungman, *Hadassah: American Women Zionists and the Rebirth of Israel*

(Cambridge: Littman Library of Jewish Civilization, 2014); Faith Rogow, *Gone to Another Meeting: The National Council of Jewish Women, 1893–1993* (Tuscaloosa: University of Alabama Press, 1993); Pamela Nadell, *America's Jewish Women: A History from Colonial Times to Today* (New York: Norton, 2019).

4. Gus Tyler, *Look for the Union Label: A History of the International Ladies' Garment Workers' Union* (Armonk, NY: Sharpe, 1995).

5. Because full observance of Shabbat precludes driving a car, this also separated the groups geographically. Orthodox Jews clustered in certain neighborhoods around a number of synagogues, while members of liberal Jewish denominations tended to spread throughout the suburbs. In the first half of the twentieth century, Conservative Jews were also forbidden to drive on Shabbat, but in 1950 the law was modified to permit driving only to synagogue services.

6. *Lilith* magazine (founded 1976 for discussion of feminist issues among Jews) devoted portions of its Spring 2018 issue to the questions generated by the #MeToo movement, following on a series of revelations of sexual harassment beginning in December 2017 in *Jewish Week* and other media. The most relevant articles were Sarah Seltzer's "The Hazards of Working in the Jewish Community"; Sarah Blustain's "#Me Too in the Media"; and Alice Sparberg Alexiou's "Child Molestation."

7. Judith Plaskow, *Standing Again at Sinai: Judaism from a Feminist Perspective* (New York: Harper and Row, 1990).

8. Certain prayers can be said only at a minyan, such as Kaddish (recited by mourners to honor the dead), the full Kedushah (responsive praise of God's holiness), and the public reading of the Torah on designated days.

9. Rosh Chodesh (New Moon) has attracted women of different denominations who wish to galvanize women's joint action for learning, deepening spirituality, or community building. Here are samples of resources that women might access for themselves online: https://reformjudaism .org/practice/ask-rabbi/why-rosh-chodesh-special-women (Reform); http://hirhurim.blogspot.com/2009/02/women-rosh-chodesh.html

(Orthodox); http://wlcj.org/resources/resources-for-members-and
-friends/guidelines-for-rosh-chodesh-groups/ (Conservative); https://
ritualwell.org/rosh-hodesh (Reconstructionist).

10. See http://womenofthewall.org.il/mission/ and http://womenofthewall
.org.il/rosh-hodesh/. For a history of prayer at the Wall, see Amanda
Borschel-Dan, "When Men and Women Prayed Together," *Times of
Israel,* June 29, 2017, https://timesofisrael.com/when-men-and-women
-prayed-together-at-the-western-wall/.

11. Tamar Frankiel, *The Voice of Sarah: Feminine Spirituality and Traditional
Judaism* (New York: Block, 1990).

12. Blu Greenberg, *On Women and Judaism: A View from Tradition* (Philadelphia: Jewish Publication Society, 1981).

13. For in-depth statistics, see the extracted information on the Orthodox from the 2013 Pew Report on American Jews, http://pewforum
.org/2015/08/26/a-portrait-of-american-orthodox-jews/. See also the
more recent Public Religion Research Institute report on American
religious identity, specifically the section on Jewish identity, https://
prri.org/research/american-religious-landscape-christian-religiously
-unaffiliated/.

14. Shoshanah Zolty's superb book, *And All Your Children Shall Be Learned:
Women and the Study of Torah in Jewish Law and History* (Northvale, NJ:
Aronson, 1993), details what can be known of women's learning before
the twentieth century.

15. The Chafetz Chaim ("Desiring Life," from one of the titles of his
books—a customary way of honoring Jewish scholars with a new cog-
nomen) is best known among the general Jewish populace as an expert
in laws concerning gossip and slander. "Who is the man that desires life
and loves length of days that he may see good? Guard your tongue from
evil and your lips from speaking deceit" (Psalm 34:12–13).

16. Quoted from Likutei Halachot, vol. 2, Masechet Sotah, p. 21, by Mayer
Twersky, "Women and Torah Study," in *Jewish Action: The Magazine of the
Orthodox Union* (Summer 1997), accessible at https://jewishaction.com
/religion/shabbat-holidays/siyum-hashas/women-and-torah-study/.

17. See Naomi Seidman, *Sarah Schenirer and the Bais Yaakov Movement: A Revolution in the Name of Tradition* (Liverpool: Littman Library of Jewish Civilization, 2019).

18. Rochelle Furstenberg, "The Flourishing of Higher Jewish Learning for Women," Jerusalem Center for Public Affairs, May 2000 (Letter #429), http://jcpa.org/jl/jl429.htm.

19. Furstenberg, "Flourishing of Higher Jewish Learning for Women"; emphasis added.

20. Orthodox women are working in professional positions far more than they did thirty years ago, in both Israel and the United States, as the stigma on most kinds of higher education has been lifted. Even in more extreme haredi communities, programs for women to learn secular skills in a safe, single-gender environment are mushrooming. The Haredi College of Jerusalem, for example, offers separate classes for men and women—and the CEO is a woman.

21. As quoted in Abraham R. Besdin, *Man of Faith in the Modern World: Reflections of the Rav* (Jerusalem: KTAV, 1989), 2:84–85.

22. The Orthodox Union accepted the "Responses of Rabbinic Panel" in a brief summary, https://ou.org/assets/OU-Statement.pdf. The full report is at https://ou.org/assets/Responses-of-Rabbinic-Panel.pdf.

23. A sampling of articles published discussing the ban includes Josh Nathan-Kazis, "Are the Orthodox Facing a Schism?," *Forward,* September 28, 2017, http://forward.com/news/national/383736/are-the-orthodox-facing-a-schism-over-female-rabbis/; Noam Stadlan, "An Analysis of the Ban on Women Rabbis," *Jewish Week,* September 26, 2017; http://jewishweek.timesofisrael.com/sneak-peek-an-analysis-of-the-ban-on-women-rabbis/; Ari L. Noonan, "OU Decision on Women Clergy Draws Controversy," February 2, 2018, http://jewishjournal.com/culture/religion/230404/ou-decision-women-clergy-draws-controversy/.

24. Miriam Shaviv, "Orthodox Women Rabbis? It's a Certainty," *Jewish Chronicle* (UK), January 30, 2017, https://thejc.com/judaism/features/orthodox-women-rabbis-it-s-a-certainty-1.431524, reporting on the

Jewish Orthodox Feminists Association conference (JOFA) in New York.

25. Shaviv, "Orthodox Women Rabbis?"

26. Pirke Avot 6:5: "Do not seek honor."

27. Quoted by Shaviv, "Orthodox Women Rabbis?"

28. This refers to the special *korban*, or sacrifice, described in Musaf Rosh Chodesh, an *olat l'Hashem*.

29. Susan Handelman, "Feminism and Orthodoxy: What It's All About," The Jewish Woman, Chabad-Lubavitch Media Center, http://chabad .org/theJewishWoman/article_cdo/aid/371261/jewish/Feminism -and-Orthodoxy.htm. Some observant Jews write G-d rather than God as an extension of a rabbinic prohibition of erasing or destroying God's name in a written Torah text. Most Jewish legal authorities limit this proscription to names of God written in Hebrew but not other languages.

30. Handelman, "Feminism and Orthodoxy."

31. Tamar Ross, *Expanding the Palace of Torah: Orthodoxy and Feminism* (Waltham, MA: Brandeis University Press, 2004). For summaries, see https:// hadassahmagazine.org/2008/08/02/profile-tamar-ross and https:// kavvanah.wordpress.com/2013/06/12/prof-tamar-ross-on-revelation -and-biblical-criticism.

32. Rachel Adler, *Engendering Judaism: An Inclusive Theology and Ethics* (Philadelphia: Jewish Publication Society, 1998); for a review, see https:// brandeis.edu/projects/fse/judaism/docs/lit-reviews/adler-engender ing-judaism.pdf. An interview that captures some of Adler's lived experience is at http://velveteenrabbi.blogs.com/blog/2013/01/reprint -interview-with-rachel-adler-in-anticipation-of-ohalah.html.

33. Avivah Gottlieb Zornberg, *Genesis: The Beginning of Desire* (Philadelphia: Jewish Publication Society, 1995); *The Particulars of Rapture: Reflections on Exodus* (New York: Doubleday, 2001); *Bewilderments: Reflections on the Book of Numbers* (New York: Schocken, 2015); *The Murmuring Deep: Reflections on the Biblical Unconscious* (New York: Schocken, 2011); and *Moses: A Human Life* (New Haven: Yale University Press, 2016).

34. Sarah Idit Schneider, *Kabbalistic Writings on the Nature of Masculine and Feminine* (Northvale, NJ: Aronson, 2001).

35. Handelman, "Feminism and Orthodoxy."

36. Jewish literature and archaeology suggest that sometimes ordinary families' practices were at odds with the ideals promoted by prophets and priests, particularly in the early centuries of settlement in Canaan, but that is more a matter of elite versus popular culture, not a reflection of possible weakness in family structure. The idea survived that we derived from one family and twelve tribes. As Judaism became cosmopolitan in the Persian and Greco-Roman periods, the temple and other allegiances may have dominated collective consciousness. But at least since the destruction of the temple, families again became nodes of social organization; the Passover came into the foreground as a family celebration, and rabbinic Judaism promoted strong families and protections for women.

37. Morgan Gardner has subsequently revised and expanded the research presented in our dialogues into a book, *The Priesthood Power of Women: In the Temple, Church, and Family* (Salt Lake City: Deseret Book, 2019). I am most grateful to Barbara for the personal conversations that helped me immensely in shaping my essay.

8

Women and Religion in Ancient Israel

KRISTINE GARROWAY

————

T amar Frankiel and Barbara Morgan Gardner address the conundrum some contemporary Jewish and Latter-day Saint women face as they grapple with how to adapt traditional religious beliefs to a nontraditional, more secular lifestyle.[1] For Jewish women, this means potentially divesting their religious *neshama* "soul" from its traditional place: the home. With the desacralization of the home, Jewish women need to reconceptualize what it means to be religious. For Latter-day Saint women, the complication lies not in the doctrine that *is* being taught but in the doctrine that *is not* being taught. Women have more equality within the Church and their priesthood authority than they are often aware of.[2] A major issue for both groups is how women conceive of their own religious practice and how their religion is transmitted to the next generation.

SOCIALIZATION AND ENCULTURATION

Religious beliefs and practices are an integral part of Jewish and Latter-day Saint culture and as such must be taught to the next generation. Jews have a term for the concept of passing on the chain of tradition: *shalshelet ha-kabbalah*. From a theoretical perspective, this process is what sociologists call enculturation, the process by which a culture trains up the next generation.[3] As children are socialized, they begin to learn and internalize aspects of their identity. Current studies of parental religious socialization (PRS) have identified multiple ways by which religious information is transferred to the child. Three relevant models are useful for consideration here. The traditional model is the unilateral model. In this model religious socialization is a one-way street; religious beliefs, practices, and behaviors are taught by the parent and reproduced by the child.[4] A newer approach recognizes the child as having agency. The parents model religion, but the child himself can also question, challenge, and begin conversations about religion. The process of religious socialization is therefore bidirectional.[5] The last model is called channeling. One might understand this model as the "village model," in which society *en large* plays a part in the religious socialization of the child.[6]

Researchers have interviewed children and parents to follow the development of the religious socialization process.[7] Studies have shown that the frequency with which PRS takes place has fallen. Researchers in Belgium hypothesize this might have to do with the increasing secularization of Western-European society.[8] Perhaps the outcomes of these studies touch upon some of the same sentiments Frankiel and Morgan Gardner have identified: the desacralization of the home leading to a hiccup in the transmission of religious education. The outcomes of the studies also demonstrate that people are reconceptualizing what it means to be religious. The religion of one generation might be completely different from that of the next.

AN ANCIENT DICHOTOMY: RELIGIONS OF ANCIENT ISRAEL

The dichotomy addressed by Morgan Gardner and Frankiel is not unique to the modern world. The tension between officially recognized religious practices and the reconceptualized religious practices can be seen already in the Hebrew Bible, which is perhaps fitting as the world of the ancient Israelites serves as a foundation of both The Church of Jesus Christ of Latter-day Saints and Judaism. By ancient Israel, I am referring to the period between 1200 and 586 BCE, from the time that we first find an "early Israel" reflected in the archaeological record to the destruction of the First Temple by the Babylonians.[9] This period is reflected in the books of the former and latter prophets of the Hebrew Bible.[10]

Before moving further, we must address what exactly is meant by the terms *Israelite* and *religion* and define how they will be used in this essay. The category of religion is a modern invention created during the Enlightenment, when people began to understand their personal beliefs and rituals as separate from other realms of experience. There was a need to set apart the "us" Christians from the "them" pagans. Jonathan Z. Smith has noted that this concern arose when Christians went beyond imagining "deities and modes of interaction with them" and began imagining about the many different ways people imagine such things.[11] Terms such as *polytheism/monotheism* or *Israelite/pagan* are modern twentieth-century concepts, also created to separate the "us" from "them." Ancient Israelites did not consider themselves monotheists or polytheists. As Mark Smith states, "monotheism's importance perhaps derived in part from contact between modern Europeans and non-Westerners, as a way of defining the Western religious traditions in contrast to non-European cultures."[12] Most likely the people of antiquity did not think of their daily offering or prayers for rain as religious acts, but rather viewed these as a part of life, simply something one does, like baking bread or paying taxes. These things had to be done; without them the universe would be unbalanced, and life would cease as they knew it.

The use of the term *religion* to describe the acts of ancient Israelites may seem anachronistic, for it is not possible to disengage "religion" in the ancient Near East (ANE) from other aspects of human experience, be it politics, law, economics, or daily life. Yet there is no other word to encapsulate what is known today as "religion." Despite its modern origins, we do not need to discard this term. As Philip Esler observed, "The whole process of translation between cultures necessitates that one culture use its concepts in relation to the other; . . . there must be a reasonable correspondence between the etic concept and the emic data upon which it will be employed, to avoid doing violence to the latter."[13] In order to talk about something that "looks like, smells like, and acts like" religion, we must use the term *religion*. In light of this, the term *religion* is used here to mean an "action or conduct indicating belief in, obedience to, reverence for a god, gods, or similar superhuman power; the performance of religious rites or observances."[14]

Religion in ancient Israel was not a monolithic concept; rather scholars talk of religions of ancient Israel.[15] There was indeed a tension between the officially sanctioned "national" cult presented in the Hebrew Bible and the religion practiced domestically. While there are many instructions for what to do at the central shrine in Jerusalem, the Hebrew Bible does not provide guidelines for religious activities that took place in the home.[16] Rather than jumping to the conclusion that nothing religious took place outside of the Temple because the Hebrew Bible did not dictate what happened in the home, scholars of household religion use a comparative method to fill in the missing pieces.[17] This method draws upon biblical allusions, ancient Near Eastern texts, archaeology, sociology, and ethnography.[18] The field of household religion sheds light on the way ancient Israelite families practiced religion. The practices, beliefs, and behaviors were often at odds with the way the state cult conceptualized religion. Important for the present discussion is the recognition that women played a central role in household religion.[19] Like contemporary Latter-day Saint and Jewish women, ancient Israelite women were purveyors of religion.

HOUSEHOLD RELIGION: A CASE STUDY (JEREMIAH 7:18)

> The children gather wood, and the fathers kindle the fire, and the women knead their dough, to make cakes to the queen of heaven, and to pour out drink unto other gods, that they may provoke me to anger. (Jeremiah 7:18)

Jeremiah 7:18 serves as an excellent case study for examining Israelite household religion and hypothesizing what PRS might have looked like in ancient Israel. The practices described here are definitely not a description of religious practices sanctioned by the official cult of Israel. In fact, the verse raises many issues, four of which will be briefly addressed here.

Issue one: Location

The activity was taking place in the home, not at the Temple in Jerusalem. The preceding verse, Jeremiah 7:17, says, "Seest thou not what they do in the cities of Judah and in the streets of Jerusalem?" The location of the house is important. As Carol Meyers points out, the people were not "saving up" all their religious needs for a trip to the Temple.[20] Religious practices were taking place in the house, practices that likely differed from household to household. What did that household look like? The pervasive familial structure throughout the Mediterranean for both city and village was the *bet 'av*, "house of the father."[21] The social or "people" component of the *bet 'av* consisted of a patrilocal extended or joint family.[22] Most ancient Israelite families were agrarian, meaning men worked the fields and women worked in and around the domicile.[23]

While the children were young they were under the care of the women in the house. During a child's early years this collective group of women would have the chance to model religious practices for the children. Household religion focused on issues concerning women's health and reproductive issues such as fertility, pregnancy, lactation, and infant survival. These issues, while specific to females, also affected the men. Having children who did not die but grew up to inherit was a primary focus of both men and women.[24] Thus, women carried out religious activities daily to ensure divine favor over the household and all the members in it.[25] The location of these religious activities is a question worth exploring. Archaeologists have done much to uncover the kinds of houses in which women would have been carrying out domestic religion.[26] The ancient Israelite house had multiple rooms that surrounded an open space where the fire pit was located. Religious activities connected to meals would have taken place there. Other religious activities took place in the meal preparation area in and around the house. The combination of things profane and cultic has an impact on the other three issues as well.

Issue two: Religious practices

A major question in Jeremiah 7:18 is the identity of the queen of heaven. Clearly a female deity, she is not YHWH. Suggestions for her identification range from Astarte (an Ugaritic goddess), to Astheroth (also Ugaritic), to Asherah (Canaanite), to Ishtar (Mesopotamian/later Egyptian). These suggestions are all raised based on comparative texts that link them to astral goddesses or provide the title "Lady," "Queen of Heaven," or "Great Lady." In addition, some of these goddesses have symbols associated with them—like stars—again with an astral connection.[27] Worshipping someone other than YHWH was forbidden (Exodus 20:4–5; Deuteronomy 5:8–9; 1 Samuel 7:3; 1 Kings 11:33; Psalm 106:38). However, archaeology shows that houses within ancient Israelite territory often contained plaques and figurines of women. These have been thought to be goddesses, specifically ones who watch over the family, provide fertility, and guard the children.[28]

The female/goddess figurines have been found in clear domestic contexts. At times they are found *in situ*, but most are found on floors or in a destruction layer, fill, or even garbage dumps. Unlike idols from ANE temples, these figurines were not made of precious materials. Rather, they were made of clay and were either fashioned

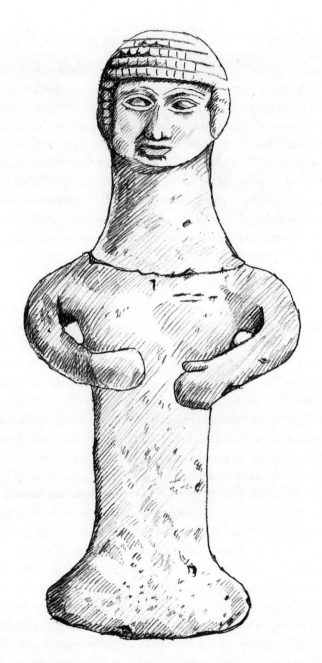

Judean pillar figurine from Tell Duweir. Metropolitan Museum of Art, gift of H. P. and D. Colt, 1934. Copyright Paul Butler, 2014.

by hand or by molds. The fact that some the figurines and plaques were not ritually disposed of in *favissae* raises questions whether there was the need to ritually deactivate the figurines before they went out of use.[29] Some of these figurines may have corresponded to the queen of heaven. Whatever their identity, we have no guidebook as to how they were used. It might be that women used the figurines differently based on geography, time of year, or stage of life. Furthermore, it seems reasonable that women within each household individually tailored their use of the figurines based on their own needs, thereby attesting to the multiplicity of religious practices taking place in the house.

Issue three: The juxtaposition of the sacred with the mundane

Most Israelite houses did not come with a separate cultic area, which means that sacred activities were juxtaposed with the mundane.[30] Jeremiah reminds us of this by pointing out that the women baked cakes for religious rituals. Ethnographic reports have demonstrated that in societies similar to ancient Israel bread preparation was done by women. It is estimated that women spent up to three hours a day grinding grain into flour to prepare bread for a family of six.[31] Bread was both part of the daily meal and an item used in ritual. Jeremiah makes a reference to special cakes, and the word used is a loanword that has been linked to the Akkadian word for sweetbread (Hebrew *kavan* > Akkadian *kamānu*). If similar to the Akkadian breads, they would contain special fruits or sweeteners.[32] Scholars have suggested these cakes might have been baked in bread molds that were shaped like a goddess or shaped like a symbol of the goddess.[33] If used in domestic religion, women would have been preparing these cakes in their houses in the same place daily bread preparation took place.

With respect to the daily bread itself, the *terumah* offering provides a strong link between the mundane and secular.[34] The biblical text states Israelites have a responsibility for returning some of the daily food to God (Numbers 15:17–21). Similarly, Babylonian prayers state that people gave a portion, called the *kispu*, of every meal to the gods. In return, the gods would maintain their protection over the family. Those who did not give a share to the gods were punished for their impudence.[35] The *kispu* ritual of breaking bread was also important in the Mesopotamian cult of the ancestors.[36] Here the point is that the daily meal was not simply a mundane activity but was infused with religious meaning. Women who prepared the meal would find religious activities, such as preparing cakes for the queen of heaven, a part of daily life.

Issue four: The role of the women and PRS

The previous point touched upon the actions of women, but here I want to shift the focus to the role of women in PRS. If we understand children as being enculturated into Israelite religion through the household practices, then they would have witnessed their mothers preparing bread on a daily basis. Children would see them prepare fancy bread for a special offering, like the queen of heaven cakes, or taking a portion of the daily bread and giving it as a *terumah* offering. As Jeremiah 7:18 suggests, children may also have been directed by their mothers to fetch kindling used to bake the bread, in this way making children active participants in the household cult.[37] Watching the mothers and following instructions regarding religious activities conforms to the unilateral model. If there was indeed a belief that carrying out certain actions curried the favor of a deity, it seems likely that children would have been expected to follow the actions taught to them.[38] The degree to which ancient Israelite children were able to change religious practices, or even question them is unknown. Thus, it is difficult to say if PRS was bidirectional. Envisioning PRS as a channeling model might be the most accurate. Combining the facts that ancient Israel was patriarchal and kinship based and that most families lived in close proximity, it seems natural that like-minded groups would religiously socialize the next generation in the same manner.

SUMMARY

The ancient world offers a useful model for addressing the dichotomy presented by Frankiel and Morgan Gardner. Their essays address a uniformity in Judaism and the faith of the Latter-day Saints, in which x, y, and z are expected. While it is often thought that the Hebrew Bible, a formative text for both religions, presents a standardized religion, this essay has shown that such a statement is a misnomer. Ancient Israelite women were not conformists to the state cult. They were perhaps ancient protofeminists. Household archaeology shows us that religious practices were not limited to the temple. The temple was for official state religion; the home was for domestic religion. In fact, the study of household religion attests to the multiplicity of religious activities that took place in ancient Israel. Jeremiah 7:18 is only one text; many other places in the Hebrew Bible attest to this fact: Micah's mother builds a shrine in her house (Judges 7:15), families celebrated Passover in the house (Exodus 12), women prayed for fertility and held figurines (e.g., the teraphim of Rachel and Michal). Far from being suppressed or repressed by the patriarchal world in which they lived, the women of ancient Israel created and participated in a meaningful religious life for themselves and for their families. Women of today might heed the example of their ancient counterparts and, like them, define their own religious options.

NOTES

1. See Tamar Frankiel, "Exploring the Lived Experience of Jewish Women," 149–79, in this volume, as well as Barbara Morgan Gardner's *The Priesthood Power of Women: In the Temple, Church, and Family* (Salt Lake City: Deseret Book, 2019).
2. Morgan Gardner addresses the seemingly lost power of the priesthood and addresses questions of assumed gender roles. She asks hard questions, like why mothers call upon the males in their families to pray (chapter 2) and provides enlightened answers regarding a woman's

access to priesthood, not just in the temple but in the home (chapter 5). She discusses the power taken from the temple for one's own life, as well as the ways in which the home then becomes the testing ground for religion. Morgan Gardner, *Priesthood Power*, 88.

3. Pierre Bourdieu, *The Logic of Practice* (Stanford, CA: Stanford University Press, 1990); Jeffery Jensen Arnett, "Broad and Narrow Socialization: Family in the Context of a Cultural Theory," *Journal of Marriage and Family* 57, no. 3 (1995): 617–28.

4. Neal Krause, "Parental Religious Socialization Practices, Connectedness with Others, and Depressive Symptoms in Late Life," *International Journal for the Psychology of Religion* 22, no. 2 (2012): 135–54.

5. Chris J. Boyatzis and Denise L. Janicki, "Parent-Child Communication about Religion; Survey and Diary Data on Unilateral Transmissions and Bi-directional Reciprocity Styles," *Review of Religious Research* 44, no. 3 (2003): 252–70.

6. Mark D. Regnerus, Christian Smith, and Brad Smith, "Social Context in the Development of Adolescent Religiosity," *Applied Developmental Science* 8 (2004): 27–38.

7. Neda Bebiroglu, Isabelle Roskam, and Nastasya van der Straten Waillet, "Discussing Religion: Exploring the Link between Parental Religious Socialization Messages and Youth Outcomes," *Review of Religious Research* 57, no. 4 (2015): 555–73.

8. Bebiroglu, Roskam, and Waillet, "Discussing Religion," 568.

9. Matthieu Richelle, *The Bible and Archaeology* (Peabody, MA: Hendrickson, 2018).

10. The former prophets of the Hebrew Bible are Joshua, Judges, 1 and 2 Samuel, and 1 and 2 Kings. The latter prophets are Isaiah, Jeremiah, Ezekiel, and the twelve minor prophets: Hosea, Joel, Amos, Obadiah, Jonah, Micah, Nahum, Habbakuk, Zephaniah, Haggai, Zechariah, Malachi.

11. Jonathan Z. Smith, *Imagining Religion* (Chicago: University of Chicago Press, 1982), xi.

12. Mark S. Smith, *The Origins of Biblical Monotheism: Israel's Polytheistic Background and the Ugaritic Texts* (Oxford: Oxford University Press, 2001), 11.

13. Philip Esler, *Conflict and Identity in Romans* (Minneapolis: Fortress, 2003), 8.

14. R. W. Burchfield, ed., "Religion 3a," OED 8:569.

15. Ziony Zevit, *The Religions of Ancient Israel: A Synthesis of Paralletic Approaches* (New York: Continuum, 2003).

16. Carol Meyers, "Household Religion," in *Religious Diversity in Ancient Israel and Judah*, ed. Francesca Stavrakopoulou and John Barton (London: Bloomsbury T&T Clark, 2010), 118.

17. Meyers, "Household Religion," 118. "The dearth of biblical information about what people did in their homes is probably a consequence of the Hebrew Bible's general focus on Israel's 'national' existence and its corporate or royal cults. It is thus unremarkable that it lacks detailed descriptions of other forms of religious life."

18. Lawrence Stager, "The Archaeology of the Family in Ancient Israel," *BASOR* 260 (1985): 1–35. For more on the comparative method and its benefits, see Carol Meyers, *Rediscovering Eve* (Oxford: Oxford University Press, 2013); Stanley K. Stowers, "Theorizing Ancient Household Religion," in *Household and Family Religion in Antiquity*, ed. John Bodel and Saul M. Olyan (Malden, MA: Wiley-Blackwell, 2008), 7, 16.

19. Susan Ackerman, "Household Religion, Family Religion, and Women's Religion in Ancient Israel," in Bodel and Olyan, *Household and Family Religion in Antiquity*, 127–56; Phyllis Bird, "The Place of Women in the Israelite Cultus," *in Ancient Israelite Religion: Essays in Honor of Frank Moore Cross*, ed. Patrick D. Miller, Paul D. Hanson, and S. Dean McBride (Philadelphia: Fortress, 1987), 397–419; Meyers, *Rediscovering Eve*.

20. Meyers, "Household Religion," 218.

21. J. D. Schloen, *The House of the Father as Fact and Symbol: Patrimonialism in Ugarit and the Ancient Near East* (Winona Lake, IN: Eisenbrauns, 2001).

22. Households are made up of the social (people), behavioral (activities), and spatial (physical) components. Richard Wilk and William

Rathje, "Household Archaeology," *American Behavioral Scientist* 25 (1982): 617–39; James Hardin, "Understanding Houses, Households and the Levantine Archaeological Record," in *Household Archaeology in Ancient Israel and Beyond*, ed. Laura B. Mazow, Jennie Ebeling, and Assaf Yasur-Landau (Leiden: Brill, 2011), 9–25.

23. Meyers, "Household Religion," 219.

24. Kristine Garroway, "Does the Birthright Law Apply to Reuben? What About Ishmael?," https://thetorah.com/article/does-the-birthright-law -apply-to-reuben-what-about-ishmael.

25. While men may also have participated in the household religion, they were also the ones called to the temple (Exodus 23:14–17; Deuteronomy 16:16).

26. Much has been written on the subject. Stager's work was one of the initial forays; see Stager, "Archaeology of the Family," 1–35. Other works, such as the collective volume of Mazow et al., approach the household from many perspectives. Mazow, Ebeling, and Yasur-Landau, *Household Archaeology in Ancient Israel*.

27. Philip Schmitz, "Queen of Heaven," in *ABD* 5:586–88. For alternate readings, see the suggestions offered by William Holladay, *Jeremiah 1: A Commentary on the Book of the Prophet Jeremiah Chapters, 1–2*, ed. Paul Hanson (Philadelphia: Fortress, 1986), 251.

28. Susan Ackerman, *Under Every Green Tree: Popular Religion in Sixth-Century Judah* (Winona Lake, IN: Eisenbrauns, 1992); Beth Alpert Nakhai, "Mother-and-Child Figurines in the Levant from the Late Bronze Age through the Persian Period," in *Material Culture Matters: Essays on the Archaeology of the Southern Levant in Honor of Seymour Gitin*, ed. John R. Spencer, Robert A. Mullins, and Aaron J. Brody (Winona Lake, IN: Eisenbrauns, 2014), 165–98.

29. Raz Kletter, *The Judean Pillar-Figurines and the Archaeology of Asherah* (Oxford: Tempus Reparatum, 1996), 73. For examples of *favissae*, see Ephraim Stern, "The Beginnings of Greek Settlement in Palestine in Light of the Excavations at Tel Dor," in *Recent Excavations in Israel:*

Studies in Iron Age Archaeology, ed. Seymour Gitin and William G. Dever (Winona Lake, IN: Eisenbrauns, 1989), 107–24.

30. For example, see James Hardin, *Lahav II: Households and the Use of Domestic Space at Iron II Tell Halif: An Archaeology of Destruction* (Winona Lake, IN: Eisenbrauns, 2010).

31. Carol Meyers, "From Household to House of Yahweh: Women's Religious Culture in Ancient Israel," in *Congress Volume Basel 2001*, ed. A. Lemaire (Leiden: Brill, 2002), 21. For an overview on theories and methods used to reconstruct archaeological populations, see Andrew Chamberlain, *Demography in Archaeology* (Cambridge: Cambridge University Press, 2006).

32. Holladay, *Jeremiah 1*, 254; Jack Lundbom, *Jeremiah 1–20: A New Translation with Introduction and Commentary* (New York: Doubleday, 1999), 476.

33. Such molds were found at Mari, while the *Epic of Gilgamesh* refers to cakes shaped like the goddess Ishtar. Lundbom, *Jeremiah 1–20*, 476.

34. The link between the daily meal and sacrifice was noticed early on in biblical scholarship. Since then the link has been explored by anthropologists, theologians, and scholars alike. Meyers, *Rediscovering Eve*, 165–68.

35. Meyers, *Rediscovering Eve, 167.*

36. Karel van der Toorn, *From Her Cradle to Her Grave: The Role of Religion in the Life of the Israelite and Babylonian Woman*, trans. S. J. Denning-Bolle (Sheffield: JSOT, 1994), 32; Karel van der Toorn, "Family Religion in Second Millennium West Asia (Mesopotamia, Emar, Nuzi)," in Bodel and Olyan, *Household and Family Religion in Antiquity*, 25–26.

37. Kristine Garroway, "Children and Religion in the Archaeological Record of Ancient Israel," *Journal of Ancient Near Eastern Religions* 17, no. 2 (2017): 116–39.

38. Jeremiah 44:18–19 states that the women noticed bad things happening to them when they stopped worshipping the queen of heaven. This is the explanation they give to Jeremiah when he asks why they began worshipping her again.

9

Shabbat in Jewish
Thought and Practice

MARK S. DIAMOND

The conceptual and practical framework of Shabbat is arguably the greatest gift biblical and rabbinic Judaism have bestowed upon the Jewish people and the world at large. In an oft-quoted reflection on the institution of the Sabbath, philosopher Ahad Ha'am wrote: "More than Jews have kept Shabbat, Shabbat has kept the Jews."[1] Throughout history, fealty to the laws and customs of Shabbat has been a prime indicator of traditional Jewish identity and the raison d'être for the formation and growth of close-knit neighborhoods and communities of observant Jews.[2]

The dawn of the twenty-first century in America has witnessed a sharp decline in institutional religious affiliation among large segments of the US population.[3] Christian and Jewish leaders search for new methods to reinvigorate time-honored norms and practices. What role does Jewish Sabbath observance play in contemporary Jewish identity? What conceptual and practical lessons does Shabbat offer for other faith traditions? In this essay, I will provide an overview of selected perspectives on Shabbat in classical and modern

Jewish thought, current patterns of Shabbat observance in America, and pedagogical insights Jewish Sabbath observance may hold for The Church of Jesus Christ of Latter-day Saints and my own Jewish community.

BIBLICAL AND RABBINIC NORMS

The institution of a weekly day of rest derives from several biblical passages, including two versions of the Ten Commandments as found in the books of Exodus and Deuteronomy:

> The heaven and the earth were finished, and all their array. On the seventh day God finished the work that He had been doing, and He ceased [*JPS translator's note* "or 'rested'"] on the seventh day from all the work that He had done. And God blessed the seventh day and declared it holy, because on it God ceased from all the work of creation that He had done. (Genesis 2:1–3)[4]

> *Remember* the Sabbath day and keep it holy. Six days you shall labor and do all your work, but the seventh day is a sabbath of the Lord, your God: you shall not do any work—you, your son or daughter, your male or female slave, or your cattle, or the stranger who is within your settlements. For in six days the Lord made heaven and earth and sea, and all that is in them, and He rested on the seventh day; therefore the Lord blessed the Sabbath day and hallowed it. (Exodus 20:8–11)

> *Observe* the Sabbath day and keep it holy, as the Lord your God has commanded you. Six days you shall labor and do all your work, but the seventh day is a sabbath of the Lord your God: you shall not do any work—you, your son or your daughter, your male or female slave, your ox or your ass, or any of your cattle, or the stranger in your settlements, so that your male and female slave may rest as you do. Remember that you were a slave in the land of Egypt and that the Lord your God freed you from there with

a mighty hand and an outstretched arm; therefore the Lord your God has commanded you to observe the sabbath day. (Deuteronomy 5:12–15)

It is noteworthy that these and other Torah citations mention the positive obligation of Sabbath rest without enumerating the activities associated with this injunction. The prohibition of working on Shabbat, on the other hand, receives greater attention and elaboration, with special emphasis on the broad nature of the ban for all living creatures in the community.

These verses also lay out the theological and practical implications of the day of rest. Shabbat observance is *imitatio dei*—we are bidden to rest on the Sabbath because God rested on the seventh day *and* because God freed the Israelites from bondage in Egypt. Free men and women may refrain from work on the Sabbath, a luxury not afforded to slaves who are subject to their master's commands and schedule. Having been redeemed from servitude, the truly free human being becomes a servant of God and thereby obeys the divine command to keep the Sabbath. The medieval philosopher and legalist Moses Maimonides derives two themes—one metaphysical, the other physical—from the creation and exodus motifs:

> God commanded us to abstain from work on the Sabbath, and to rest, for two purposes; namely, (1) That we might confirm the true theory, that of the Creation, which at once and clearly leads to the theory of the existence of God. (2) That we might remember how kind God has been in freeing us from the burden of the Egyptians—The Sabbath is therefore a double blessing: it gives us correct notions, and also promotes the well-being of our bodies.[5]

According to Maimonides, Shabbat observance nourishes the body and the soul, affirming God's role as Creator and bestowing restorative, weekly rest on its practitioners. Jewish liturgy reinforces the dual nature of the Sabbath commandment. The Friday evening *kiddush* (sanctification), a familiar ritual recited both in the home and in the synagogue, reads in part:

> Praise to You, Lord our God, Sovereign of the universe who finding favor with us, sanctified us with mitzvot. In love and favor, You made the holy Shabbat our heritage as *a reminder of the work of Creation.* As first among our sacred days, it *recalls the Exodus from Egypt.*[6]

Much is made in Jewish exegetical tradition of the key word change in the Sabbath precepts of Exodus, chapter 20, and Deuteronomy, chapter 5.[7] *Remember* and *observe* are two distinct directives; one can *remember* the Sabbath without performing any special rituals or refraining from any specific labors. Jewish commentators perceive several facets in the command to *remember*:

- Recall the twin imperatives to remember that God rested on the seventh day and freed our ancestors from servitude;
- Verbally declare Shabbat to be a holy day by reciting the Friday evening *kiddush.*

Remembering Shabbat is associated with positive *mitzvot* (commandments) to mark the seventh day. Observing the Sabbath, on the other hand, is associated with the negative commandments of the holy day. The edict to *observe* Shabbat is generally interpreted as the mandate to keep the Sabbath laws with their intricate prohibitions of performing any labor. Shabbat observance is seen as a strict requirement with severe consequences for those who perform forbidden labor:

> You shall keep the sabbath, for it is holy for you. He who profanes it shall be put to death: whoever does work on it, that person shall be cut off from among his kin. Six days may work be done, but on the seventh day there shall be a sabbath of complete rest, holy to the Lord; whoever does work on the sabbath day shall be put to death. The Israelite people shall keep the sabbath, observing the sabbath throughout the ages as a covenant for all time: it shall be

a sign for all time between Me and the people of Israel. For in six days the Lord made heaven and earth, and on the seventh day He ceased from work and was refreshed. (Exodus 31:14–17)

The severity of the punishment for willful violation of sabbath laws is one indication of their preeminent role in the life of the Israelite community. Specific mention is made in the Torah of labors prohibited on Shabbat—plowing, harvesting, kindling a fire, gathering food or wood.[8] The sages of the Mishnah and Gemara expand this list by deriving thirty-nine proscribed activities (*melachot*) associated with the preparation and construction of the *mishkan*, the portable tabernacle of Israelite worship:

THE 39 MELACHOT OF SHABBAT[9]

Fieldwork
- sowing
- plowing
- reaping
- binding sheaves
- threshing
- winnowing
- selecting
- grinding
- sifting
- kneading
- baking

Making material curtains
- shearing wool
- cleaning
- combing
- dyeing
- spinning
- stretching the threads

- making loops
- weaving threads
- separating the threads
- tying a knot
- untying a knot
- sewing
- tearing

Making leather curtains
- trapping
- slaughtering
- skinning
- tanning
- smoothing
- ruling lines
- cutting

Making the beams of the *mishkan*
- writing
- erasing

The putting up and taking down of the *mishkan*
- building
- breaking down

The *mishkan*'s final touches
- extinguishing a fire
- kindling a fire
- striking the final hammer blow
- carrying

In addition to their association with the work of the tabernacle, these *melachot* may be grouped into two broad categories—acts of exploiting nature and acts of creating or improving upon matter. Any work that involves even the most minute form of creating, improving, or destroying an object is prohibited according to traditional *halachah* (Jewish law). This helps us to understand why some Sabbath restrictions bear little relation to conventional explanations of what constitutes work. Put another way, the most accurate translation of the Hebrew term *melachah* as used in Jewish law is *Sabbath-prohibited labor* rather than *work*.

SHABBAT: BURDEN OR JOY?

Commentators offer diverse views on the challenges of keeping the detailed laws of Shabbat. We note in multiple sources hints of just how challenging it was (is?) for the people of Israel to scrupulously adhere to the Sabbath restrictions.[10] Promises of ultimate redemption and life in the world to come are often associated in exegetical circles with *mitzvot* that were most difficult to observe faithfully and continually.[11] Such is the case with the laws of Shabbat:

> Rabbi Yochanan said in the name of Rabbi Shimon ben Yochai: "If the Israelites were to keep two Sabbaths according to their prescribed law, they would immediately be redeemed." (Babylonian Talmud *Shabbat* 118b)

> Though I (God) have set a limit to "the end," that it will happen in its time regardless of whether they will do *teshuvah* or not . . . the scion of David (*Mashiach*) will come if they keep just one Shabbat, because the Shabbat is equivalent to all the *mitzvot*. (Exodus Rabbah 25:12)[12]

In contrast to biblical laws that mandate the death penalty and excision (*karet*) for Sabbath violators, these rabbinic texts offer the ultimate spiritual prize for a people that keep the Sabbath.[13] While the Torah admonishes the people of Israel to follow the Sabbath laws or pay the consequences for nonconformance, the Talmud and other rabbinic texts exhort the people to observe the Sabbath twice or even just once as a communal enterprise and reap the reward of messianic redemption. If the promise of severe punishments and lofty rewards is indicative of the spiritual import and practical challenges of keeping a set of laws, Shabbat observance ranks at the very top of the Jewish legal echelon.

When one views the laws of Shabbat from outside the halachic corpus, it is not uncommon to conclude that keeping the Sabbath is arduous and onerous. With a long list of don'ts and a much shorter list of dos, Shabbat observance can seem unduly legalistic and unspiritual. Abraham Millgram, author of a classic digest of Shabbat laws, customs, and narratives, argues otherwise:

> Non-Jews frequently describe the law of the Sabbath as harsh and burdensome. They usually point to the innumerable minutiae which suggest rigidity and pettiness. But the impression given by an enumeration of the many Sabbath prohibitions is altogether misleading. In practice, the observance of the Sabbath was always a joyful experience which led the Jew to regard the Sabbath as the greatest of divine gifts to Israel. The Sabbath was a day of physical relaxation and spiritual stimulation. The devout Jew, although he observed all the minute details of the Sabbath law, was conscious solely of the cheerful aspects of the Sabbath. To him the Sabbath laws were not burdensome. On the contrary, so great and unique was the joy which he reaped from their observance that he found it necessary to explain his delightful experience in terms of possessing an additional soul on the Sabbath.[14]

While Jewish texts are replete with lengthy discussions of *hilchot Shabbat* (the Sabbath laws), Jewish tradition also highlights the positive, joyful aspects of Sabbath observance. Shabbat home rituals—including meals with special foods, candle lighting, family blessings, prayers over wine and challah, table songs, *birkat ha-mazon* (blessings after the meal), and *havdalah* ("separation"—blessings over wine, spices, and a braided candle to conclude Shabbat)—serve to reinforce bonds with family and friends and enhance the Sabbath experience.[15] Synagogue rituals—such as additional prayers on Friday evening and Saturday, the public reading of passages from Torah and Prophets (*haftarah*), and a homily on the weekly scriptural portion—serve to strengthen communal bonds and collective allegiance to norms of prayer, learning, and observance. The "additional Sabbath soul" is nourished by other time-honored Shabbat activities—reading, taking a nap, strolling through the neighborhood, playing games with family and friends, enjoying the outdoors, and appreciating moments of peace and quiet that nurture the mind, body, and spirit.

Traditional metaphors and narratives that speak of the majestic, regal image of the Sabbath underscore the joyful aspects of the Shabbat experience. Shabbat is at once a queen (*malkah*) and a bride (*kallah*), dual images found in Midrashim and classical liturgical poems (*piyyutim*) chanted in synagogues and homes.[16] Shabbat is even described as a secret ingredient added to foods prepared for the Sabbath table, as we learn in an ancient, much-loved Jewish legend:

> Our Teacher, Rabbi Yehuda HaNasi, made a meal for Antoninus, the Roman king, on the Sabbath. Cold dishes were set before him; he ate them and found them delicious. On another occasion, Rabbi Yehuda made a meal for him during the week, when hot dishes were set before him.
>
> Antoninus said to Rabbi Yehuda, "Those others I enjoyed more. What was different?"
>
> Rabbi Yehuda replied, "These lack a certain spice."
>
> "Does then the royal pantry lack anything?" the King answered. "Tell me what you need, and I'll command to have it brought!"
>
> "They lack the spice we Jews call the Sabbath," said Rabbi Yehuda. "For on the seventh day we are commanded by God to rest from labor, both man and beast. Although there is no fire in the ovens on the Sabbath, the food on this day is flavored by a special Sabbath spice. Do you indeed possess the Sabbath?"

After that, Antoninus returned many times to eat at Rabbi Yehuda's table, and always on Shabbat, for only then was the proper spice not lacking. (Genesis Rabbah 11:4)

In times of relentless persecution and intolerance, in conditions of extreme poverty and suffering, Jews sought refuge in the simple, quiet joys of a Sabbath of peace and harmony. On Shabbat, Jews were transformed from tenuous subjects of church and state to the noblest of royalty. The existential loneliness of weekday living gave way to the hopes and dreams of brides and grooms wedded to one another, to their God, and to the holy Shabbat. In Jewish households, wherein husbands and wives struggled to put food on the table six days a week, somehow the Shabbat table glowed with a special spice—a favorite food reserved for the Sabbath, a loaf of challah, a pot of *cholent* (Sabbath stew) with a treasured piece of meat or two. Sabbath queen; Sabbath bride; Sabbath spice—three metaphors for the holiness and mystery of Shabbat in classical Jewish thought and practice.

SHABBAT IN MODERN JEWISH THOUGHT

Modern Jewish philosophers write extensively about the preeminent role of Shabbat in Jewish life and thought and its import for other peoples and religious traditions. German Jewish philosopher Hermann Cohen echoed and expanded upon Ahad Ha'am's premise that Shabbat is the foundation of Jewish survival:

The Sabbath is the most authentic and the most intimate exemplification of the Jewish law. It was this Day of Rest, with its law expressive of the Unique God who loves mankind, that preserved both Judaism and the Jews. Both were sustained by the mission of diffusing monotheism over all the earth, and of continually deepening its meaning and spirit, and thereby establishing true love for man among all the peoples of the earth. It is in the Sabbath that the God of love showed Himself to be the Unique God of Love for all mankind.[17]

According to Cohen, the institution of the Sabbath is both particularistic and universal. It preserved the Jewish people and their faith tradition and inspired Jews to bring the concept of a holy Sabbath ordained by a loving God to all humankind. Rabbi Pinchas Peli, a widely admired Orthodox rabbi and professor of Jewish thought and literature at Israel's Ben Gurion University of the Negev, similarly saw the universal character of Shabbat as an extension of biblical and Jewish thought:

> The Sabbath is, like the Bible itself, not merely a "Jewish" entity. While it partakes of an added "particularistic" dimension, it remains first and foremost universal. It offers the biblical and "Jewish" answer to questions which are not necessarily Jewish. They are the ultimate questions concerned with life and death, with the meaning (if it indeed possesses meaning) of the world; with human frailty versus the power of Nature and the glory of God; and other such intrinsically human questions.[18]

Enamored as he was of the Sabbath, Peli wrote an entire volume devoted to his love affair with the institution and experience of Shabbat. "If we were to condense all of Judaism—its faith, thought, life, poetry and dreams—into a single word, there is but one word which could be used—*Shabbat*," he wrote.[19] In a modern gloss, Peli infused the *mitzvot* to *keep (observe) Shabbat* and *remember Shabbat* with renewed meaning:

> While "keep" stands for the Law, without which there is no Sabbath notwithstanding noble sentiments, "remember" stands for love. While "keep" is the body of the Sabbath, "remember" is its soul—yearning and longing for the Sabbath. . . . To "remember" one day out of all days sounds an easy assignment, but it is not as simple as it may sound. . . . The act of sanctification, or setting aside, of that day takes place solely within—inspired by a secret shared revelation between God and the individual. Nothing external serves to remind us of the day and we could overlook it.

... "Remember the Sabbath!" This despite the pressures of work, business or play which engulf us and make it all too simple to forget that another week of life has passed and that it is time to pause before a new beginning.[20]

Peli extolled the virtues of observing and remembering Shabbat and recognized the modern-day pressures that work against setting aside one day each week for rest and renewal. A contemporary of Pinchas Peli, Orthodox scholar Dr. Emanuel Rackman, lived and taught in the United States and Israel, where he served for more than three decades as the president and chancellor of Bar-Ilan University. Rackman wrote that the six other days of the week are merely a prelude to the seventh day of rest:

Using the terminology of means and ends, it can be said that the six days of toil are concerned with the means of life and the Sabbath with its ends. The six days of toil represent the temporal and transitory; the Sabbath represents the eternal and the enduring. That is why the Hebrew language has no names for the days of the week. They are all the first day, or the second day, or the third day, "to the Sabbath"—the Sabbath is the goal toward which time itself moves.[21]

While most modern thinkers share an appreciation of Shabbat as an enduring signpost of religious identity, they express widely divergent views on how to enhance Sabbath observance in a post-Emancipation world. Progressive Jewish clergy have introduced new forms of synagogue prayer and home practices, prompting Rackman to offer a sharp critique of innovations in Shabbat worship and observance:

The Sabbath ... would long ago have lost its meaning and value but for the resistance of the traditionalists. Even the innovators are recognizing the folly of their license with the tradition, and ancestral forms and techniques are being refurbished for the greater bliss of beleaguered moderns. Psychiatrists too are now helping to give the Sabbath new significance in the face of that hedonistic philosophy in whose name they once whittled away all of its prohibitions.[22]

Taking aim at both liberal and conservative Jewish thinkers who elevate human needs over divine dictates, Rackman wrote:

> That the Sabbath was meant to be a day of rest and relaxation becomes an acceptable postulate (for these theologians). Therefore, what constitutes rest and relaxation for the individual Jew becomes the measure of Sabbath observance—golf for the sportsman, music for the aesthete, dancing for the teen-ager, cigar-smoking for the addict. Is that all these Jewish spiritual heirs of the historical jurists can find in a three-thousand-year tradition of scholarship on the Sabbath? Did they really probe the depths and come up with so tiny a pearl—that the Sabbath is a day of rest and relaxation? The answer is that they did not probe. History becomes an excuse to make the Halachah suit one's desires and not the means to fathom God's will.[23]

For Rackman, Shabbat is much more than a day of rest to be defined according to the varying needs and interests of individual Jews. He sounded a spiritual alarm in response to those who would strip the Sabbath of its firm halachic foundation. For others, especially non-Orthodox Jewish thinkers and practitioners, the very challenge of keeping Shabbat amidst the frenetic pace of modern living offers fresh opportunities and blessings. Rabbi Rona Shapiro writes:

> I do not think the Torah could have anticipated the busied, hurried lives we lead today, but it nonetheless provides an incredible antidote. According to the Torah, after creating the world in 6 days, God rested. We are enjoined to do the same. We refrain from recreating the world on Shabbat and we sit back and enjoy what we have been given. Literally, we smell the roses. Too many

of us, to paraphrase John Bradshaw, have become "human doings" who define ourselves by what we do in the world. Shabbat teaches us to remember our true essence as "human beings" and to practice the art of simply being. For some of us, this has become difficult. Accustomed as we are to our palm pilots and filofaxes, we hardly know how to slow down. Even our children are so busy with soccer practice, violin lessons, and homework that they too lack experience in doing nothing.

On Shabbat, we let time unfold. There is time to sing and to nap, to make love and to talk without a deadline or goal. There is time to watch an inchworm ease its way up toward the leaf and time to jump in leaf piles. Shabbat enables us to reconnect to ourselves, to one another, and to God, and to appreciate our blessings.[24]

Shapiro is one of many rabbis who advocate for the corrective of Shabbat rest in a high-tech, electronics-filled world. Another is Rabbi Arthur Green, former president of the Reconstructionist Rabbinical College and Boston's Hebrew College. He notes,

The root of the word "Shabbat" means to "cease" or "desist." To observe Shabbat means to cease our work life and break our daily routine every seventh day, making that day holy. Shabbat is to be a day of enjoying the world rather than doing battle with it; a day of relaxation rather than struggle, a time to live in harmony rather than to achieve domination.

Part of each Shabbat's celebration is based on our admitting that we are still slaves to work, oppressed today by the fast pace of our work lives and the pressures of living in a highly achievement-oriented society. Our taskmasters today may be electronic rather than human, tempting us rather than whipping us to work just a little faster and harder. Our ability to leave them behind once a week is our proclamation of freedom, a true cause for celebration.[25]

Shapiro and Green call attention to the practical benefits of keeping the Sabbath in the world today. Other theologians seek to fuse traditional Jewish observance and modern philosophical thought. Preeminent among these thinkers was Rabbi Abraham Joshua Heschel, whose poetic writing is an exquisite wrapping for the priceless gift of Shabbat that lies within. For Heschel, the Sabbath is an island in time, a precious glimpse of the world to come to combat the existential loneliness of a broken world. Here are two pearls from Heschel's classic work, *The Sabbath: Its Meaning for Modern Man*, reflections that need no further commentary:

> The meaning of the Sabbath is to celebrate time rather than space. Six days a week we live under the tyranny of things of space; on the Sabbath we try to become attuned to holiness in time. It is a day on which we are called upon to share in what is eternal in time, to turn from the results of creation to the mystery of creation; from the world of creation to the creation of the world.
>
> Six days a week we wrestle with the world, wringing profit from the earth; on the Sabbath we especially care for the seed of eternity planted in the soul. The world has our hands, but our soul belongs to Someone Else. Six days a week we seek to dominate the world, on the seventh day we try to dominate the self.[26]

PATTERNS OF SHABBAT OBSERVANCE

What does the Sabbath mean for Jews today? In an age marked by unparalleled resources, comforts, and conveniences, most Jews can readily set aside one day a week for complete rest and renewal. Nonetheless, Shabbat observance has declined markedly among American Jews, as witnessed by recent demographic surveys of the US Jewish population. In these studies, researchers ask questions about specific indicators of Jewish observance, including lighting Sabbath candles and attending Sabbath services. According to the 2013 Pew Research Center's study of American Jewry:

Regularly lighting candles to mark the start of the Sabbath is less common among Jews than participating in a Seder or fasting on Yom Kippur, as is keeping a kosher home. Nearly a quarter of Jews (23%) say they always or usually light Sabbath candles (down slightly from 28% in the 2000–2001 NJPS),[27] and a similar number say they keep kosher in their home (22%). As with other traditional practices, Orthodox Jews are much more likely than other Jews to say they regularly light Sabbath candles and keep kosher homes.[28]

Of special note in the Pew study is the statistically small difference in patterns of observance among Jews of different ages within a given parameter. However, clear differences emerge among Jews who self-identify as Orthodox, Conservative, Reform, and nondenominational. Orthodox Jews are nearly three times more likely to light Shabbat candles than Conservative Jews, who in turn are three times more likely to do so than Reform and nondenominational Jews. Likewise, Orthodox respondents are six times more likely to refrain from handling money on Shabbat than Conservative Jews, whose adherence to this Sabbath restriction is three times greater than that of Reform and nondenominational Jews (see table, right).[29]

While traditional Jews often invoke fealty to halachic norms as the primary reason for their regular Shabbat observance, many other Jews invoke personal motivations for how and how often they keep the Sabbath. Professors Steven M. Cohen and Arnold Eisen researched patterns of Jewish observance and concluded the following:

> The pattern of selective observance—the individual practices chosen according to personal preference, within constraints given by the environment (e.g., the need to work late on Friday or on Saturday), and endowed with personal meaning—is nearly universal. The more active Jews in our sample do more of the prescribed rituals, and do them with greater regularity. For them too, however, the meaning given Sabbath observance is almost

TABLE. JEWISH PRACTICES AND TRADITIONS

	Participated in Seder last year %	Fasted all/ part of 2012 Yom Kippur %	Always/ Usually light Sabbath candles %	Keep kosher in home %	Avoid handling money on Sabbath %
Net Jewish	70	53	23	22	13
Jews by religion	78	62	28	25	16
Jews of no religion	42	22	6	11	5
Age 18–49	68	54	25	28	15
18–29	73	55	24	27	13
30–49	65	53	25	28	17
Age 50+	71	53	21	16	12
50–64	68	56	20	17	12
65+	75	48	22	15	12
College graduate +	73	53	20	16	10
Post-grad degree	74	53	19	15	9
BA/BS	71	54	20	17	10
Some college	69	51	23	22	14
HS or less	59	56	32	41	26
Married	75	57	28	21	16
Spouse Jewish	91	75	45	35	24
Spouse not Jewish	54	34	7	4	6
Not married	64	49	17	22	11
Orthodox	99	95	90	92	77
Ultra-Orthodox	100	98	99	98	76
Modern	98	90	78	83	81
Conservative	80	76	34	31	13
Reform	76	56	10	7	4
No denomination	47	25	9	10	4

always personal rather than prescribed. It is a time to pause, a moment for quality time with family. Less observant Jews seem more content to have the day pass without any marking whatever. Our survey sample split almost evenly on the statement, "Even if I don't observe every aspect of the Sabbath, I do try to make it a special day": 47 percent agreed; 49 percent did not.[30]

Faced with a drop in parameters of observance among Jews in America, Jewish leaders expend great resources on formal and informal educational projects designed to foster greater allegiance to traditional Jewish practices. Rabbis, educators, and communal leaders champion programs that offer intensive Jewish experiences—summer camps, retreats, leadership seminars, study tours at home and abroad—as effective means to instill loyalty to Shabbat practices.

A 2016 study highlighted the value of one of these projects. The study's lead author, Professor Steven M. Cohen, and his associates surveyed alumni of the Conservative Jewish movement's Ramah camp system, which offers summer camp experiences in a network of sites across the United States and Canada. Ramah camps feature a mix of traditional camp activities—sports, arts and crafts, swimming, hiking, and the like—coupled with informal classes in Hebrew and Judaica and an immersive, uplifting Shabbat experience marked by communal singing, dancing, learning, and prayer. For many campers (and staff members), Shabbat at Ramah is the highlight of each week and offers a sharp contrast to the staid, formal Shabbat services they often encounter at their home synagogues.

Cohen's research compared and contrasted the religious practices of Camp Ramah alumni to data from two other recent demographic studies—the aforementioned *A Portrait of Jewish Americans* (Pew Research Forum, 2013) and *The Jewish Community Study of New York* (UJA-Federation of New York, 2012). Among his findings:

- Shabbat candle-lighting rates among camper alumni are about three times the NY and US rates (for those with in-married Conservative parents).[31]

Does your household usually light Shabbat candles?[32]

	Ramah	New York	Pew (US)
Yes	72%	27%	23%

- Nearly two-thirds of camp alumni attend religious services at least monthly. By any standard, alumni report high rates of service attendance. Over a third report attending synagogue services weekly, and almost two-thirds do so at least monthly. The percentage of Ramah alumni who attend religious services weekly is double that of children of Conservative in-married parents in NY and triple the US average (Pew).

How often do you attend Jewish religious services?[33]

	Ramah	New York	Pew (US)
Once a week or more	34%	15%	10%
Once or twice a month	30%	22%	17%
A few times a year, such as for High Holidays	29%	40%	45%
Seldom	5%		
Never	2%		

Large numbers of Ramah alumni take on liturgical leadership activities that demand high levels of religious skill and expertise. While we have no comparative data with New York or the United States, it's intuitively impressive that a third have chanted Torah in the last year.[34]

Which activities have you engaged in during the last year?

	Ramah
Led services (as the cantor or "shaliach tzibbur")	34%
Gave a "d'var torah" or sermon	27%
Chanted Torah	32%
Chanted a *haftarah*	22%
Any of the above	48%

Cohen's portrait of Ramah alumni demonstrates that this network of Jewish summer camps appears to have a positive impact on the Jewish engagement of its former campers. Alumni of Camp Ramah light Shabbat candles, attend Shabbat services, and actively participate in synagogue liturgical roles with much greater frequency than other American Jews. This should come as welcome news to advocates of intensive, informal Jewish education, as well as to families and funders who expend considerable resources to offer these opportunities for Jewish children and young adults.

CAMPAIGNS TO REVITALIZE SHABBAT

Jewish summer camps are one method to inculcate love for and observance of Shabbat. Campaigns to revitalize Shabbat are another response to the decline in frequency of Sabbath observance. In these regional, national, and international programs, organizers typically select one or more *Shabbatot* (plural of *Shabbat*) during the month or year when large cohorts of Jews are invited to "make *Shabbos*" or "do Shabbat." The worldwide network of Chabad houses, organized by the Lubavitch Hasidic movement, welcomes young Jews on college campuses and Jews in cities around the world to join their *shaluchim* (rabbinic emissaries) for *Shabbat at Chabad*—each week, each month, or as often as they can make *Shabbos*. Hillel Jewish centers on college and university campuses conduct similar programs for undergraduate and graduate students. Jewish congregations and federations in many cities sponsor annual projects of Shabbat dinners across the community, when hundreds of Jews in a given city celebrate Friday evening together in homes and synagogues.

Two prominent campaigns to revitalize Shabbat are highlighted below. The first, *Shabbat Across America* (and its northern neighbor *Shabbat Across Canada*), is con-ducted by National Jewish Outreach Program (NJOP), a national Orthodox Jewish out-reach organization that invites Jews of diverse backgrounds, interests, and affiliations (or no affiliation) to join together for festive Shabbat dinners hosted by local synagogues. "Turn an ordinary Friday night into something extraordinary!" NJOP leaders promise.[35] High-lights of these annual *Shab-bat Across America* experiences include delicious food, good conversation, and informal, creative instruction in candle lighting, family blessings, ritual handwashing, and other basic Shabbat rituals.

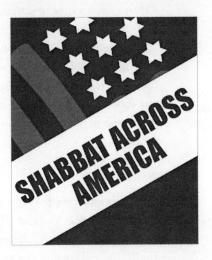

Shabbat Across America

- "On Friday night, March 3, 2017, hundreds of synagogues across the continent will take part in an historic national Jew-ish event to celebrate what unifies all Jews—Shabbat! Every-one is invited . . . singles, couples, families—all ages."
- "Turn an ordinary Friday night into something extraordinary!"
- "That's the magic of *Shabbat Across America* and *Shabbat Across Canada*. By participating in this continent wide event, you will

not only have the opportunity to experience Shabbat, but you will be sharing your experience with tens of thousands of Jews across North America."

- "No matter what your affiliation or which *Shabbat Across America* or *Shabbat Across Canada* location you choose to attend, NJOP's annual Shabbat program will give you a "taste" of Shabbat. Explanatory services, traditional rituals, delicious meals and lively discussions are all important components of the Shabbat experience, as well as the opportunity to spend the evening with like-minded people, friends and family."
- "*Shabbat Across America* or *Shabbat Across Canada* is for every Jew, and those who are unable to go to a registered location can participate in their own homes or in gatherings with friends/family."[36]

Jewish Reboot

The Jewish Reboot network offers its own innovative programs and campaigns to revitalize Shabbat. Reboot was founded in 2002 by and for creative young Jews; the organization affirms the value of Jewish traditions and creates new ways for people to make them their own.[37] To that end, Reboot spearheads several cutting-edge projects to make Shabbat more relevant for younger Jews and the community at large. These projects include:

- *The Sabbath Manifesto*, ten principles (commandments?) to enhance the Shabbat experience. These principles conform to traditional norms of Shabbat observance but are framed and publicized in contemporary language. One popular outgrowth of the *Sabbath Manifesto* is the *National Day of Unplugging*.
- The *National Day of Unplugging* occurs on the first Shabbat in March each year. For 24 hours, participants are asked to unplug their iPhones, iPads, computers, and other electronic devices and renew, reflect, and reconnect with family and friends. The project is an outgrowth of the *Sabbath Manifesto*,

THE SABBATH MANIFESTO

10 WAYS TO TAKE A DAY OFF

1. Avoid technology
2. Connect with loved ones
3. Nurture your health
4. Get outside
5. Avoid commerce
6. Light candles
7. Drink wine
8. Eat bread
9. Find silence
10. Give back

Above left: The Sabbath Manifesto. Above right: The National Day of Unplugging is a 24-hour period—running from sunset to sunset—and starts on the first Friday in March.

an adaptation of our ancestors' ritual carving out one day per week to unwind, unplug, relax, reflect, get outdoors, and connect with loved ones. Reboot distributes charming "sleeping bags" for cell phones to facilitate participation in the *National Day of Unplugging*.[38]

- The FRIDAY App, a free mobile application that creatively and colorfully marks the transition to Shabbat on Friday. It offers a distinctive invitation—a warm welcome and open door to unplugging, mindfulness, and connection. "Each Friday, 30 minutes before sunset, your phone's screen recedes into a blissful twilight and serves up a short thought-provoking story and question to prompt a pause for personal reflection and lively discussion,"[39] promises Reboot. Using head, heart, and humor, FRIDAY helps transition us from the stressful week into a more restful weekend state of mind.[40]

30 MINUTES BEFORE SUNSET, FRIDAY HELPS YOU UNWIND.
Friday available free in the App Store.

FRIDAY is a free mobile app designed and produced by Reboot + IDEO, for the iPhone.

This analysis of campaigns to revitalize Shabbat prompts several questions:

- How do we measure the long-term success of these engagement projects, especially those that present one annual Shabbat devoted to intensive Jewish experiential living?
- Echoing Rabbi Rackman, are these "Shabbat PR campaigns" merely slick contemporary innovations that traditionalists should avoid at all costs? Put another way, have the innovators removed the Divine from the Sabbath?
- Dr. Ron Wolfson, Fingerhut Professor of Education at American Jewish University, makes a strong case for transforming Jewish life through "relational Judaism." In a 2013 work, he contended that Jewish engagement is "not about programs, marketing, branding or institutions. It's about relationships."[41] Most campaigns to revitalize Shabbat have outstanding programs, first-rate marketing, and creative branding. Do they create long-term relationships that can truly transform Jewish congregations and institutions?

WHAT THE CHURCH OF JESUS CHRIST OF LATTER-DAY SAINTS CAN LEARN ABOUT/FROM SHABBAT

In recent years, Latter-day Saint leaders have devoted significant communal resources to a church-wide project to elevate the spirit and power of the Sabbath. Launched in 2015 by the Quorum of the Twelve Apostles, this campaign to revitalize Latter-day Saint Sabbath observance seeks to make the Sunday experience more meaningful for families and individuals at church and in their homes. What potential lessons, if any, can The Church of Jesus Christ of Latter-day Saints learn about and from the Jewish Sabbath? Are there parallels we may draw from the 3,000-year biblical and Jewish encounter with Shabbat? How might Latter-day Saint leaders revitalize Sunday worship and home observances to foster increased reverence for the weekly Sabbath? I offer these preliminary thoughts and further questions for study and reflection:

- *Shabbat restrictions help foster intensive, close-knit clusters of Sabbath observers.* To cite one example, halachic strictures prohibiting driving on Shabbat mandate that traditional, observant Jews live in walking distance of a synagogue. Fealty to halachic norms serves to create new synagogues and communities of observant Jews living in close proximity to one another. What does "Latter-day Saint *halachah*" do to increase Sabbath observance in stakes and wards? What additional Sabbath guidelines might strengthen the Latter-day Saint Sabbath campaign?
- While Shabbat restrictions are key components of traditional Shabbat observance, *don't focus exclusively on the Sabbath restrictions.* Remember to stress the activities faithful Latter-day Saints can and should do on the Sabbath, especially those that reinforce familial and communal bonds.
- *Develop, cultivate, and broaden experiential learning*, including summer camps, retreats, and skill-building opportunities (preaching, leading sacrament meetings, vocal and instrumental music, etc.).

- As the Church grows around the world, *plan and implement strategies to enhance Sabbath observance for Church members who live in the Latter-day Saint diaspora.* What new strategies and technologies can Church leaders utilize to enhance the Sabbath experience for members of the Church living outside the major Latter-day Saint population centers?
- Church (synagogue) rituals are a key component of the Sabbath. *Explore new modes of prayer and study for Sunday sacrament meetings.* Does the prevailing framework beautify and glorify the Sabbath?[42] Do younger and older Latter-day Saints, men and women, children of different ages, feel enriched by the Sunday communal experience? What innovations might be introduced slowly and judiciously into sacrament meetings to intensify the sweet aroma of the *Latter-day Saint Sabbath spice*?[43]
- Don't focus only on the Church! *Remember to stress the central role of the home.* Experiment with creative home customs and symbols that distinguish the Sunday Sabbath from Monday family home evenings.
- *Consider new leadership roles for women in Sabbath church and home programs.* The role of women in every Jewish movement—Conservative, Hasidic, Orthodox, Reconstructionist, Reform, Renewal, ultra-Orthodox, and nondenominational—continues to evolve and expand in religious life and communal leadership. Are there lessons here for Latter-day Saint Church leaders?

WHAT JEWS CAN LEARN ABOUT/FROM SHABBAT

I share these closing reflections on Shabbat for clergy, communal leaders, and members of my own Jewish community:

- *Keep it spiritual and succinct* (KISS). While traditionalists may remain loyal to lengthy Shabbat morning services, many others find three hours of worship each week to be unduly repetitive and uninspiring. Consider reducing and eliminating repetitive prayers; explore new ways to involve Jews in synagogue leadership roles. Experiment with introducing Friday evening prayer innovations into the Shabbat morning service.
- *Stress the dos more than the don'ts for those who are new to Sabbath observance or are estranged from it.* Teach and practice home customs and rituals for Friday evening, Saturday morning, and Saturday evening (e.g., the uplifting *havdalah* service to mark the conclusion of Shabbat). Adopt and adapt Reboot's strategies for breathing new life into the ancient institution of Shabbat. And please remember: Shabbat doesn't end on Friday night!
- *Details matter!* Personal grooming and clothing may enhance or diminish *k'vod Shabbat* (honoring the Sabbath). Food and drink served at home and in the synagogue may contribute to or detract from Shabbat *oneg* (joy). Standards matter!
- Keeping Shabbat can be a lonely experience without family, friends, and a supportive community that observes the Sabbath. *Create and nurture Shabbat-intensive, relational communities in homes and other venues outside synagogues.*
- *Make your Shabbat celebrations respectful and inclusive of the diversity of your Jewish community.* Welcome and honor Jews of all ages, backgrounds, and interests; born Jews and Jews by Choice; Jews who are married, single, divorced, or widowed; "religious Jews" and "Jewish nones."
- *Bring God back to Shabbat!* With all the good reasons for observing Shabbat, remember to include the Divine, holy mitzvah part of the Sabbath equation.

- *Take a lesson from our Latter-day Saint brothers and sisters. If they have holy envy of the Jewish Sabbath, perhaps it's time for Jews to take a second look at Shabbat!*

NOTES

1. Ahad Ha'am (Asher Ginsberg), *Al Parashat Derakhim*, vol. 3, chap. 30, cited in http://yivoencyclopedia.org/article.aspx/Sabbath.

2. It is often said that Judaism is a religion of deed, not creed. While this is an overstatement, it reflects a time-honored Jewish preoccupation with practice rather than belief. Indeed, traditional Jews rarely inquire about their coreligionists' theological views. Instead, they may query new Jewish acquaintances: "Are you *shomer Shabbat* (Sabbath observant)?"

3. Compare Pew Research Center, "America's Changing Religious Landscape," May 12, 2015; Pew Research Center, "A Portrait of Jewish Americans," October 1, 2013.

4. Unless noted otherwise, translations of biblical verses are from *Tanakh—The Holy Scriptures, The New JPS Translation according to the Traditional Hebrew Text* (Philadelphia: Jewish Publication Society, 1988).

5. Moses Maimonides, *The Guide for the Perplexed*, trans. M. Friedlander (New York: Dover Publications, 1956), 219.

6. Friday evening *kiddush*, translation adapted from "Sabbath Evening Blessings," ReformJudaism.org, https://reformjudaism.org/practice /prayers-blessings/shabbat-evening-blessings-kiddush-blessing-over -wine.

7. A well-known midrash posits the theological query of how God could have issued two different Shabbat commandments. The midrashic author answers: "Remember and observe were said together in a way that no mouth is capable of pronouncing and no ear is capable of hearing" (Talmud *Rosh HaShanah* 27a; see also Talmud *Shvu'ot* 20b), a phrase that in inverted fashion ("Observe and remember were said together") forms one line of Solomon HaLevi Alkabetz's sixteenth-century hymn *Lecha Dodi* chanted on Friday evenings in synagogues across the globe.

8. Exodus 34:21; 35:3; 16:29–30; Numbers 15:32–36.

9. "The 39 Melachot," Chabad.org, https://chabad.org/library/article
   _cdo/aid/102032/jewish/The-39-Melachot.htm. Based on Mishnah
   Shabbat 7:2.

10. See, for example, Numbers 15:32–36, the biblical narrative of a man who
    gathered wood on Shabbat. See also Talmud *Shabbat* 112a and numer-
    ous other accounts in the Talmud of rabbinic debates over meticulous
    observance of the laws of Shabbat.

11. Notes from classroom lectures in my rabbinical school studies at the
    Jewish Theological Seminary of America, New York, 1977–1982.

12. See also Jerusalem Talmud *Ta'anit* 1:10.

13. A foundational passage in Isaiah 58:13–14 likewise promises abundant
    rewards for those who keep the Sabbath:

    > If you refrain from trampling the sabbath,
    > From pursuing your affairs on My holy day;
    > If you call the sabbath "delight" (*oneg*),
    > The Lord's holy day "honored";
    > And if you honor it and go your ways,
    > Nor look to your affairs nor strike bargains—
    > Then you can seek the favor of the Lord.
    > I will set you astride the heights of the earth,
    > And let you enjoy the heritage of your father Jacob—
    > For the mouth of the Lord has spoken.

14. Abraham Millgram, *Sabbath: The Day of Delight* (Philadelphia: The Jew-
    ish Publication Society, 1965), 172. The concept of an extra soul on
    Shabbat is found in the Babylonian Talmud *Beitzah* 16a: "Rabbi Shimon
    ben Lakish said, 'On the eve of the Sabbath the Holy One, Blessed be
    He, gives man an extra soul. At the conclusion of the Sabbath, this extra
    soul is taken away from him, as it is written in Scripture, *shavat vayinafash*
    (Ex. 31:17), i.e., as soon as He finished the Sabbath, it is woe, because
    the soul is gone.'"

15. A popular tradition holds that Friday night is an especially propitious
    time for marital relations between husband and wife. The Babylonian
    Talmud *Ktubot* 62b notes: "How often are scholars to perform their

marital duties? Rabbi Judah in the name of Samuel replied: 'Every Friday night.' . . . Judah the son of Rabbi Hiyya and son-in-law of Rabbi Yannai would spend all his time in the schoolhouse but every Sabbath eve he came home."

16. Compare *Lecha Dodi* chanted in the Kabbalat Shabbat (Friday evening) service and other piyyutim found in Jewish liturgy.

17. Hermann Cohen, "The Jewish Sabbath as the Fundamental Law of Social Ethics in Western Culture," in *Contemporary Jewish Thought: A Reader*, ed. Simon Noveck (Washington, DC: B'nai B'rith Books, 1963), 148.

18. Pinchas H. Peli, *Shabbat Shalom: A Renewed Encounter with the Sabbath* (Washington, DC: B'nai B'rith Books, 1988) 4.

19. Peli, *Shabbat Shalom*, 1.

20. Peli, *Shabbat Shalom*, 53–55.

21. Emanuel Rackman, *One Man's Judaism* (New York: Philosophical Library, 1970), 53–54.

22. Rackman, *One Man's Judaism*, 11.

23. Rackman, *One Man's Judaism*, 46–47.

24. Rona Shapiro, "Making Shabbat," ritualwell.org, https://ritualwell.org /ritual/making-shabbat.

25. Arthur Green, *These Are the Words: A Vocabulary of Jewish Spiritual Life*, 2nd ed. (Woodstock: Jewish Lights Publishing, 2012), quoted at https:// myjewishlearning.com/article/observing-shabbat/.

26. Abraham Joshua Heschel, *The Sabbath: Its Meaning for Modern Man* (New York: Farrar Straus & Giroux, 2005), 10, 13.

27. Berman Jewish Databank, National Jewish Population Survey 2000–2001, https://jewishdatabank.org/content/upload/bjdb/NJPS2000 _Strength_Challenge_and_Diversity_in_the_American_Jewish_ Population.pdf.

28. "A Portrait of Jewish Americans," Pew Research Center, October 1, 2013, 71.

29. "A Portrait of Jewish Americans." Pew Research Center 2013 Survey of U.S. Jews, February 20–June 13, 2013.

30. Steven Cohen and Arnold Eisen, *The Jew Within: Self, Family, and Community in America* (Bloomington: Indiana University Press, 2000), 86.

31. This refers to "born Jews" married to other "born Jews," as opposed to Jews married to non-Jews.

32. New York: "How often, if at all (do you/does anyone in the household): light Sabbath candles on Friday night?" Pew: "How often, if at all, does anyone in your household light Sabbath candles on Friday night?"

33. New York: "About how often do you personally attend any type of synagogue, temple, or organized Jewish religious service?" Pew: "Aside from special occasions like weddings, funerals and bar mitzvahs, how often do you attend Jewish religious services at a synagogue, temple, minyan or Havurah?" Steven M. Cohen, "The Alumni of Ramah Camps: A Long-Term Portrait of Jewish Engagement," Berman Jewish Policy Archive, February 2017.

34. Cohen, "Alumni of Ramah Camps."

35. "Shabbat Across America," NJOP, https://njop.org/programs/shabbat /saac/.

36. "Shabbat Across America."

37. "Reboot," at rebooters.net.

38. "National Day of Unplugging," Reboot, https://nationaldayofunplug ging.com.

39. "The FRIDAY App," Reboot, http://thefridayapp.com.

40. "The FRIDAY App."

41. Ron Wolfson, *Relational Judaism: Using the Power of Relationships to Transform the Jewish Community* (Woodstock, VT: Jewish Lights, 2013), 1.

42. I note with admiration (and some degree of holy envy) the January 2019 change in Sunday sacrament meetings instituted by Church leaders. The former three-hour format of worship, study, and fellowship has been changed to two hours each Sunday with study and fellowship filling the second hour.

43. Videos of remarks delivered by Church elders and posted on the Church's website (https://churchofjesuschrist.org/study/manual/gospel -topics/sabbath-day) highlight numerous practical Sabbath concerns that are reminiscent of similar discussions in Jewish circles about Shabbat services:

- The order of worship (Latter-day Saint bishops and ward councils are now strongly encouraged to hold the weekly sacrament meetings during the first of the two-hour Sunday gatherings)
- The role of music in the Sabbath service
- Selecting and preparing participants for the worship experience
- Ushering (welcoming and greeting Sabbath service attendees has received lavish attention in debates about synagogue renewal)
- The challenges and opportunities of having young children at Sabbath services (separate children's services or one communal service; joyful noise or annoying disruptions for adults)
- The use of electronic devices

10

GUARDIAN OF FAITH: THE SABBATH IN LATTER-DAY SAINT THEOLOGY, HISTORY, AND PRACTICE

BRENT L. TOP

The late Krister Stendahl, who served as Lutheran bishop of Stockholm, Sweden, and later as a professor and dean of the Harvard Divinity School, was a noted champion of religious understanding and tolerance. Amid vocal opposition to the building of the Latter-day Saint temple in Stockholm, Stendahl came to the defense of members of The Church of Jesus Christ of Latter-day Saints. At a press conference in 1985 about the Church's intent to build a temple in Sweden—attended by many opponents of the Church—Stendahl proposed what has become known as "Stendahl's Three Rules of Religious Understanding." Beyond his comments to the press, Stendahl's life and ministry genuinely reflected these principles.

1. When you are trying to understand another religion, you should seek information from the adherents of that religion and not its enemies.
2. Don't compare your best to their worst.
3. Leave room for "holy envy."

By "holy envy," Stendahl meant that we should be willing to recognize elements in other religious traditions that we admire and wish could be part of our own faith or religious practice.[1]

For many Latter-day Saints—myself included—there is a degree of holy envy for the Jewish understanding of and practices relating to the Sabbath. A high-level expression of such holy envy regarding the Jewish Sabbath recently occurred at a general conference of The Church of Jesus Christ of Latter-day Saints. Elder Quentin L. Cook, a member of the Church's Quorum of the Twelve Apostles, stated,

> My wife and I, and two of my colleagues and their wives, recently participated in a Jewish Shabbat (Sabbath) at the invitation of a dear friend, Robert Abrams and his wife, Diane, in their New York home. It commenced at the beginning of the Jewish Sabbath on a Friday evening. The focus was honoring God as the Creator. It began by blessing the family and singing a Sabbath hymn. We joined in the ceremonial washing of hands, the blessing of the bread, the prayers, the kosher meal, the recitation of scripture, and singing Sabbath songs in a celebratory mood. We listened to the Hebrew words, following along with English translations. The most poignant scriptures read from the Old Testament, which are also dear to us, were from Isaiah, declaring the Sabbath a delight (see Isaiah 58:13–14), and from Ezekiel, that the Sabbath "shall be a sign between me and you, that ye may know that I am the Lord your God" (Ezekiel 20:20).
>
> The overwhelming impression from this wonderful evening was of family love, devotion, and accountability to God. As I thought about this event, I reflected on the extreme persecution that the Jews have experienced over centuries. Clearly, honoring the Sabbath has been "a perpetual covenant," preserving and blessing the Jewish people in fulfillment of scripture (see Exodus 31:16–17). It has also contributed to the extraordinary family life and happiness that are evident in the lives of many Jewish people.[2]

As Elder Cook stated, faithful Latter-day Saints and devout Jews share a love for and commitment to the teachings—admonitions, warnings, and promised blessings—found in the Hebrew Bible regarding the Sabbath. Like devout Jews, committed Latter-day Saints accept and are bound by the very command etched in stone tablets by the finger of God and delivered to Moses and the Israelites at Mount Sinai:

> Remember the sabbath day, to keep it holy. Six days shalt thou labour, and do all thy work: But the seventh day is the sabbath of the Lord thy God: in it thou shalt not do any work, thou, nor thy son, nor thy daughter, thy manservant, nor thy maidservant, nor thy cattle, nor thy stranger that is within thy gates: For in six days the Lord made heaven and earth, the sea, and all that in them is, and rested the seventh day: wherefore the Lord blessed the sabbath day, and hallowed it. (Exodus 20:8–11)

Latter-day Saints often cite in their worship services, instructional settings, and homes some of the same passages from the Hebrew Bible regarding the Sabbath that are taught in Jewish synagogues, schools, and homes. The Jewish understanding of the Sabbath informs Latter-day Saint thought and practice in meaningful ways. The purpose of this paper is to show the development of the Latter-day Saint doctrine of Sabbath observance, with special attention to the current emphasis by Church leaders.

One of the guiding principles for this dialogue team from the outset is to acknowledge points where deep appreciation for the other's traditions, faith, and practice affect us. In this spirit, such moments are at times highlighted in this chapter. For example, most Latter-day Saints have holy envy for the Jewish view of the Sabbath as a time of joy and celebration. Rarely do Latter-day Saints speak of "celebrating" the Sabbath, even though that is exactly what God has commanded his people to do (see Leviticus 23:32). Instead of *celebrate*, the word most often used today within Latter-day Saint culture would be *observe*. To Jews these words may be synonymous or certainly closely related because of their rich Sabbath traditions and teachings, but to many modern Latter-day Saints, *observing* the Sabbath connotes "putting up with" restrictions and a different kind of busyness and stress rather than *celebrating*. There is holy envy of the Jewish view of the Sabbath as a queen—"a precious gift from [God], a day of great joy eagerly awaited throughout the week."[3] There is holy envy of the Jewish view of the holy Sabbath as a holy gift, "the most precious mankind has received from the treasure house of God"[4]—a means whereby man can experience what Rabbi Abraham Joshua Heschel called "holiness in time," or a degree of God's holiness on earth. "Six days a week a week we live under the tyranny of things in space, on the Sabbath we try to become attuned to *holiness in time*."[5]

HISTORICAL OVERVIEW

Most of the early converts to The Church of Jesus Christ of Latter-day Saints came from strong puritanical Christian backgrounds in which honoring the Sabbath day was a religious and cultural expectation. There wasn't a great need for fiery sermons on the importance of keeping the Sabbath day holy. Yet in this setting, Joseph Smith, the founder and first prophet of the Church, reiterated the importance of the Ten Commandments, particularly keeping the Sabbath day holy. In his sermons, journals, and revelations, the Sabbath is seen as a day of joy,[6] a day of gospel instruction,[7] a day of reflection, meditation and revelation,[8] a day of ministering to the sick and confirming the faith of others.[9]

As these early Latter-day Saints sought to establish a "new Zion" on the American continent, keeping the Sabbath day holy was considered essential to the realization of that objective. A familiar hymn entitled "Gently Raise the Sacred Strain," written during the time of Joseph Smith by one of the prominent Church leaders, William W. Phelps, poetically declared the relationship between Sabbath obser-

vance, personal holiness, and the establishment of the "new Zion."
Phelps was reflecting what he had been taught by Joseph Smith while
in Missouri in 1831. The revelation found in Doctrine and Covenants
section 59 was of particular significance in showing the relationship
between Sabbath observance, personal holiness, and the eventual
establishment of "Zion."[10] This hymn was included in the Church's
first hymnbook in 1835.[11]

> Gently raise the sacred strain,
> For the Sabbath's come again
> That man may rest,
> And return his thanks to God
> For his blessings to the blest.
>
> Holy day, devoid of strife—
> Let us seek eternal life,
> That great reward,
> And partake the sacrament
> In remembrance of our Lord.
>
> Sweetly swells the solemn sound
> While we bring our gifts around
> Of broken hearts,
> As a willing sacrifice,
> Showing what his grace imparts.
>
> Holy, holy is the Lord.
> Precious, precious is his word:
> Repent and live;
> Tho your sins be crimson red,
> Oh, repent, and he'll forgive.

After the exodus of the Latter-day Saints from Nauvoo, the pioneer crossing of the central plains, and the subsequent establishment

of communities in the Utah territory, Latter-day Saint observance of the Sabbath declined, along with a general decline in religiosity and adherence to Church standards. This prompted Brigham Young, the successor to Joseph Smith and second prophet/president of the Church, and other leaders to call the members to repentance and a return to their covenants. This period of time has been called by historians the "Mormon Reformation."[12] Sabbath observance was central to the call to spiritual reformation and personal holiness. Brigham Young taught that honoring the Sabbath would be "for our own temporal good and spiritual welfare." Keeping the Sabbath holy acts as a "guardian of faith," a protective power, and the means whereby we keep in remembrance "our God and our holy religion." In a manner like ancient Israel's prophets, Young warned the Latter-day Saints that without a Sabbath—a day wholly set apart from others, an entire day consecrated to God, "we are liable to forget—so prone to wander that we need to have the Gospel sounded in our ears, once, twice, thrice a week, or behold, we will turn again to our idols."[13] Those who dishonor the Sabbath, he declared "are weak in the faith" because "gradually, little by little, little by little, the spirit of their religion leaks out of their hearts and their affections."[14]

From the latter part of the nineteenth century to the present, Church leaders continued to teach the importance of keeping the Sabbath holy and the resulting blessings that would come therefrom. For many decades, however, Church leaders focused a great deal on what activities should be avoided on the Sabbath, just as Brigham Young had decried "skating, buggy riding," and going "on excursions on the Sabbath day."[15]

> When we see a farmer in such a hurry, that he has to attend to his harvest, and to haying, fence-making, or to gathering his cattle on the Sabbath day, as far as I am concerned, I count him weak in the faith. He has lost the spirit of his religion, more or less. Six days are enough for us to work, and if we wish to play, play within

the six days; if we wish to go on excursions, take one of those six days, but on the seventh day, come to the place of worship, attend to the Sacrament, confess your faults one to another and to our God, and pay attention to the ordinances of the house of God.[16]

At the end of the nineteenth and beginning of the twentieth centuries, Church leaders continued to call upon the members to keep the Sabbath holy by remembering its sacred purpose and by avoiding those activities that detract from it. "To observe the Sabbath day properly is the plain duty of every Latter-day Saint—and that includes the young men and young women and boys and girls," Joseph F. Smith, sixth president of the Church, declared in 1909. "It may seem strange that it should be necessary to repeat this oft-asserted fact. But there appear to be people, and sometimes whole communities, who neglect this duty, and therefore stand in need of this admonition." President Smith elaborated further,

> Men are not resting from their labors when they plow, and plant and haul and dig. They are not resting when they linger around the home all day on Sundays doing odd jobs that they have been too busy to do on other days.
>
> Men are not showing zeal and ardor in their religious faith and duty when they hustle off early Sunday morning on the cars, in teams, in automobiles, to the canyons, the resorts, and to visit friends or places of amusement with their wives and children. They are not paying their devotions in this way to the Most High.[17]

In virtually every general conference in every decade, Church leaders have uttered similar teachings on appropriate Sabbath day activities. Additionally, sermons on the spiritual nature of and blessings associated with the Sabbath can be found, more than can be cited in this chapter. Since the days of Brigham Young there has not been a dearth of reminders—some gentle and others not so much—

of God's commandment to "remember the Sabbath day, to keep it holy" (Exodus 20:8). Clearly, Latter-day Saint observance of the Sabbath was not to the level, both attitudinally and behaviorally, that Church leaders desired. As such, there continued to be emphasis on the Sabbath, both in sermons from the pulpits in every congregation, but also in important changes to Church structure and programs. Several organizational and administrative changes were also made to promote greater Sabbath observance. These included the creation of the Sunday School and moving the regular once-a-month day of fasting and priesthood meetings from weekdays to Sundays.

With the rise of commercialism, including businesses being open on Sundays and competition from entertainment and recreation, including professional sports broadcasts on television, personal and family Sabbath observance and regular church attendance waned in the late twentieth century. The concept of a "weekend" took its toll, not just on Latter-day Saint Sabbath worship, but perhaps on other Christian denominations and Jewish communities. Latter-day Saint leaders sought to address this problem in their faith community in 1980 with the consolidation of all Sunday meetings into a single three-hour block. One of the primary reasons for the change was to "emphasize home-centered Sabbath activities."[18]

While this administrative change of the Sunday meeting schedule, reduction of some weekday meetings, and increased emphasis on "home-centered Sabbath activities" may have initially increased Latter-day Saint church attendance and attention to keeping the Sabbath more holy, over time the desired outcomes arguably fell short of the mark. Undoubtedly, many factors were at play, including the overall secularization of society. The Pew Research Center reported that in the United States between 2007 and 2014, there were marked declines in religious affiliation and in intensity of religious belief and practices. The fastest growing demographic in this study were the "nones"—those who professed no religious affiliation. This was particularly pronounced among younger people, those often characterized as "Millennials."

The Church of Jesus Christ of Latter-day Saints is not immune to this trend, although the Church doesn't publish statistics of those who leave the Church formally or merely stop participating with their local congregation. Yet much anecdotal evidence at the end of the twentieth and into the twenty-first centuries caused one prominent Latter-day Saint Church leader to address the concern that members, particularly younger members, were "leaving in droves." Putting that phrase in context, Elder Marlin Jensen of the Seventy, the Church's third highest leadership body, and Church Historian, later stated that the "attrition has accelerated, in the last five to 10 years, reflecting the greater secularization in society." Jensen observed that "many religions have been suffering similarly" and that although there has been a trend to less religious affiliation and practice, the restored Church has never been more vibrant. "I think we are at a time of challenge," he noted, "but it isn't apocalyptic."[19]

Understandably, leaders of The Church of Jesus Christ of Latter-day Saints looked for ways to promote greater faith and devotion by staying the tide of secularism that had affected so many members, both young and old. A generation earlier, Church president Harold B. Lee had observed, "The Sabbath breaker shows early the signs of his weakening in the faith," which leads to neglecting spiritual duties and a "mind [that] because of spiritual starvation soon begins to have doubts and fears."[20] Just as Brigham Young in the mid-nineteenth century and Harold B. Lee in the mid-twentieth century had warned that failure to keep the Sabbath day holy would cause their faith and the "spirit of their religion" to leak out of members' hearts, modern Latter-day Saint prophets and apostles again sought to "plug the holes." In their minds, the key to returning to greater faith and religiosity, stronger families, and prosperity was to be more faithful in observing the Lord's day.

The primary focus for the training of Church general authorities and officers at the 2015 general conferences of the Church was the Sabbath day. "Of all the organizational or policy changes or doctrinal training that could hasten the work of salvation at this time," said Elder M. Russell Ballard of the Quorum of the Twelve Apostles of the Church of Jesus Christ, speaking on behalf of the senior leadership of the Church, "elevating the spirit and power of the Sabbath day would be most influential in drawing members and families to the Lord Jesus Christ."[21]

This renewed emphasis on the Sabbath as a means of spiritual strength, given in the leadership training meeting at general conference, was delivered to local congregations throughout the world. Videos of the training meetings were shown to local leaders and members; and making the Sabbath a delight, as Isaiah anciently admonished, became the topic for sermons in worship services and conferences, instruction in classes and groups, and discussions among members and families. Six months later additional training was provided to Church leaders and members in the same manner. The focus on keeping the Sabbath holy was sharpened. "In the natural revelatory process the Lord made known His wish that His ancient commandment regarding the Sabbath, or as the scriptures describe it, 'His perpetual covenant with His people,' be brought to the fore," Elder D. Todd Christofferson stated on behalf of the First Presidency and Quorum of the Twelve Apostles.

> We realize that a deeper understanding of the meaning and purposes of the Sabbath day would bring to the Latter-day Saints a more profound faith in God and in His Son Jesus Christ and the Atonement of Christ. This would build strength in the members of the Church far greater than could be achieved by any programmatic means. We saw that observing the Sabbath could lead to full conversion and spiritual resilience in the Saints.[22]

Other important changes in the Church meeting structure and curriculum, coupled with renewed emphasis on Sabbath observance, came in the October 2018 general conference. Reducing the Sunday meeting schedule from the three-hour block established in 1980 to a two-hour block—one hour for a worship service and one hour for instruction—was implemented in 2019. This development, Russell M. Nelson, President of The Church of Jesus Christ of Latter-day Saints, explained, was a direct outgrowth from and an augmentation of "our efforts over these recent years to hallow the Sabbath—to make it a delight and a personal sign to God of our love for Him."[23]

DOCTRINAL FOUNDATION

Latter-day Saints, like other Bible-believing Christians, can trace their understanding of the doctrine of Sabbath to Sinai, where God commanded his people to "remember the Sabbath day, to keep it holy," and to the prophetic teachings found in the Hebrew Bible. While Latter-day Saints observe the Sabbath on a different day and in different ways from Jews, they, nonetheless, view the Sabbath as a holy day designed by God to bless and sanctify his people. Likewise, Latter-day Saints embrace the teachings of Jesus, found in the New Testament, regarding honoring the Sabbath as God intended. "Wherefore the Sabbath was given unto man," Jesus taught, "for a day of rest; and also that man should glorify God" (Joseph Smith Translation Mark 2:26). The Book of Mormon, another canon of scripture for Latter-day Saints, also records that the commandment to remember and keep the Sabbath holy had been taught and was lived by the ancient covenant people in the Americas (see Jarom 1:5; Mosiah 13:16–19; 18:23).

Reiterating the commandments given to Moses, particularly concerning the Sabbath, and the teaching of Jesus in the New Testament, the Prophet Joseph Smith declared to the Latter-day Saints a revelation given to him in August 1831. This becomes, arguably, the most important statement concerning Sabbath-day observance to Latter-day Saints.

> Thou shalt offer a sacrifice unto the Lord thy God in righteousness, even that of a broken heart and a contrite spirit. And that thou mayest more fully keep thyself unspotted from the world, thou shalt go to the house of prayer and offer up thy sacraments upon my holy day; For verily this is a day appointed unto you to rest from your labors, and to pay thy devotions unto the Most High. (Doctrine and Covenants 59:8–10)

Within these verses of canonized scripture lie the doctrine of Sabbath in Latter-day Saint thought and practice. The Latter-day Saint doctrine of Sabbath—a fundamental expectation for Church members—seems to boil down to these two phrases from Joseph Smith's 1831 revelation: "rest from your labors" and "pay thy devotions unto the Most High." All of the teachings and commentaries by Church leaders from Joseph Smith to the present and the many developments—such as changes to Church structure, meeting schedules, and curricular emphases—reflect and build upon those two things. More so than ever in its nearly two hundred years of existence, leaders of The Church of Jesus Christ Latter-day Saints are leading members to the spiritual dimensions of keeping the Sabbath day holy. Current Church president Russell M. Nelson has made teaching the importance of the Sabbath a hallmark of his ministry. "Faith in God engenders a love for the Sabbath," he said. "Faith in the Sabbath engenders a love for God. A sacred Sabbath truly is a delight."[24] Because of his emphasis and the persistent training coming from leaders to rank and file members, Latter-day Saints today appear to better understand, like their devout Jewish and Christian brothers and sisters, that holiness—the ultimate aim of the Sabbath—isn't as much about *behaviors* as it is about *devotion*. So, if those two phrases in the 1831 revelation to Joseph Smith about the purposes for honoring the Sabbath day largely constitute the Latter-day Saint doctrine, what do they mean to members of the Church today?

"Rest from Your Labors"

"And on the seventh day God ended his work which he had made; and he *rested* on the seventh day from all his work which he made. And God blessed the seventh day, and sanctified it: because that in it, he had *rested* from all his work which God created and made (Genesis 2:2–3; emphasis added).

For centuries there have been theological debates regarding what it means that God rested after the Creation and what role rest has in keeping the Sabbath holy. Latter-day Saint theology, like that of many groups within Judaism and Christianity, views Sabbath rest as both physical and spiritual. Clearly, physical (and emotional) rest and rejuvenation are vital, but the rest offered by the Sabbath is spiritual. This higher dimension of Sabbath worship is reflected in the thought and theology of both Christians and Jews. "The word Sabbath properly signifies, not common, but *sacred* or *holy* rest," Thomas Shepard, Cambridge-educated Puritan minister and founder of Harvard University, wrote in 1649.

> The Lord, therefore, enjoins this rest from labor upon this day, not so much for the rest's sake, but because it is a medium, or means that holiness which the Lord requires upon this day; otherwise the Sabbath is a day of idleness, not of holiness; our cattle can rest but a common rest from labor as well as we; and therefore it is man's sin and shame if he improve the day no better than the beasts that perish.[25]

According to Jewish philosophy, when God finished the work of creation, he found that something was missing. The universe would not be complete or good until there was a Sabbath and the *menuha* it brings. Rabbi Heschel explained:

Menuha which we usually render with "rest" means here much more than withdrawal from labor and exertion, more than freedom from toil, strain or activity of any kind. *Menuha* is not a negative concept but something real and intrinsically positive. This must have been the view of the ancient rabbis if they believed that it took a special act of creation [by God] to bring it into being, that the universe would be incomplete without it.

"What was created on the seventh day? *Tranquility, serenity, peace* and *repose.*"

To the biblical mind *menuha* is the same as happiness and stillness, as peace and harmony. . . . It is the state wherein man lies still, wherein the wicked cease from troubling and the weary are at rest. It is the state in which there is no strife and no fighting, no fear and no distrust. The essence of good life is *menuha.*[26]

These Christian and Jewish views of rest resonate with members of the Church of Jesus Christ and can also be seen in current Latter-day Saint teachings and practices. For example, the change in Church meeting schedule from a three-hour block to two hours is not intended merely to give members more time for a Sunday nap and less time in meetings. Rather, Sabbath rest, both the physical and spiritual, is intended to give a portion of God's holiness as man's actions and attitudes are focused more on eternity than on the tyranny of the here and now. Church leaders consistently invite Latter-day Saints to experience the "rest of God" not just "rest." Church President Joseph F. Smith taught that the Sabbath as "a day of rest" is "a change from the ordinary occupations of the week, but it is more than that."

It is a day of worship, *a day in which the spiritual life of man may be enriched.* A day of indolence, a day of physical recuperations is too often a very different thing from the God-ordained day of rest. Physical exhaustion and indolence are incompatible with a spirit of worship. A proper observance of the duties and devotions of the Sabbath day will, by its change and spiritual life, give the best rest that men can enjoy on the Sabbath day.[27]

With this understanding, Latter-day Saints view the Sabbath as a foretaste, even if just a small nibble, of eternal life that God offers to the faithful. In contrast to the profane and mundane activities of other days that wear one down, the Sabbath is to be spiritually satisfying and sanctifying. Sabbath observance can make one stronger, more in tune with God, and better equipped to deal with the challenges of this life because he or she has "tasted" God's rest. Latter-day Saints would agree with Rabbi Abraham Heschel's sentiments. He wrote, "Unless one learns how to relish the taste of Sabbath while still in this world, unless one is initiated in the appreciation of eternal life, one will be unable to enjoy the taste of eternity in the world to come. Sad is the lot of him who arrives inexperienced and when led to heaven has no power to perceive the beauty of the Sabbath."[28]

"Pay thy devotions unto the Most High"

Latter-day Saints are taught that on the Sabbath they are to "pay [their] devotions," but what does that mean? That is an issue that continues to challenge Latter-day Saints. How can one increase the spirit of worship on the Sabbath and protect against a "crowding out" by external interests and responsibilities, some of which may be viewed as important and helpful to others. A common issue reported by Church members is the conflict between meaningful personal and family Sabbath time and serving in formal Church callings that demand much time and emotional energy on Sundays. It is not easy to remember that service in the Church to fellow members is one part of Sabbath worship, but not the only part nor the most important part. It is a delicate balance for many. What then does it mean to "pay our devotions" in the "house of prayer"?

Devotions is defined as any expressions—attitudinal, behavioral, emotional, verbal, etc.—of love and affection, loyalty, gratitude, faithfulness, commitment, adoration, and worship. Devotion is a state of connectedness. In the context of Sabbath observance, as defined in the important revelation to Joseph Smith recorded in section 59 of the Doctrine and Covenants, two important words are used to define how a Latter-day Saint "pays" his or her "devotions unto the Most High." Those words are *oblations* and *sacraments*. They are not synonyms; yet they are related. Each is an essential part of what Latter-day Saints see as the sanctifying power of the Sabbath.

The word *oblation* means "an offering, a gift of gratitude, a token of one's love, an act of worship." A footnote in the study aids at the bottom of the page for Doctrine and Covenants 59:12 in the 1981 edition specifically defines *oblations* as "offerings, whether of time, talents, or means in service of God and fellowman." Thus to Latter-day Saints, the Sabbath is a day to offer time and talents in service to God and others. In other words, giving a talk in worship services, teaching a class to young children, serving as a greeter, participating in class discussion, or any number of other things done each Sunday by Latter-day Saints in their respective congregations may, in fact, be an "offering of oblations." Attending worship services, associating with fellow believers, and fulfilling responsibilities at Church are certainly appropriate Sabbath activities. The question, however, is whether one is truly *giving*—giving to God from one's heart and soul offerings of love, gratitude, and worship. That is a question that can only truly be answered by God and the individual. That is why trying to determine how to keep the Sabbath day holy is so difficult.

There is a closely related word—*obligation*. It has both positive and negative connotations, depending on the context. On the positive side, an *obligation* is "an act or course of action to which a person is morally or legally bound; a duty of commitment." In making covenants, Latter-day Saints become *obligated* to live that covenant. They have chosen that course, and it becomes a duty. Unfortunately, in today's vernacular the words *obligation, obligate,* and *obliged* are most commonly understood to mean doing something "because I have to" out of some external expectation or requirement. Whatever the definition, the application to the Sabbath is apparent. Some keep the Sabbath day holy because they are obligated to do so. Some have progressed to living appropriate Sabbath standards out of some sense of spiritual duty or in obedience to covenants made within the Church. Ultimately, however, true Sabbath observance, as Latter-day Saints would view it, requires attitudes and actions to move from *obligation* to *oblation*—giving a personal offering of love and gratitude to God. This understanding of the Sabbath leads one beyond just giving up certain things on the Sabbath, or sacrificing, to giving ourselves to God, or consecrating ourselves. In this manner, how one lives and loves the Sabbath becomes an individual "sign" to the God of the Sabbath. This thought reflects what President Russell M. Nelson has taught:

> In my much younger years, I studied the work of others who had compiled lists of things to do and things *not* to do on the Sabbath. It wasn't until later that I learned from the scriptures that my conduct and my attitude on the Sabbath constituted a *sign* between me and my Heavenly Father. With that understanding, I no longer need lists of dos and don'ts. When I had to make a decision whether or not an activity was appropriate for the Sabbath, I simply asked myself, "What *sign* do I want to give to God?" That question made my choices about the Sabbath day crystal clear.[29]

The word *sacraments* as used in Doctrine and Covenants 59:12 is generally understood by Latter-day Saints to mean the ordinance of the sacrament of the Lord's Supper (communion). While the ordinance certainly is central to the Latter-day Saint Sabbath day and has been emphasized by Church leaders throughout the Church's history, it is important to note that the foundational revelation regarding worship on the Lord's day used the plural term *sacraments*. It doesn't say "partake of *the* sacrament," but rather "offer up thy sacraments upon my holy day" (Doctrine and Covenants 59:9).

The English word *sacrament* comes from the Latin *sacramentum*, which has at its root *sacro*, meaning "to consecrate or hallow." In this sense, that which is consecrated unto God as a holy offering is a sacrament—a sacred gift of devotion (oblation) which yields greater sanctification and holiness to the giver.

So what do *sacraments* have to do with "keeping the Sabbath day holy?" In Latter-day Saint thought, the answer is simple—everything. A person can rest without sacraments—without giving anything to God, without any activities devoted to religious worship, without any thought of seeking holiness. That is called recreation. Likewise, a person can attend church—even partake of the ordinance of the sacrament of the Lord's supper—without seriously "paying [his or her] devotions unto the Most High." That is called church activity. But making the Sabbath a holy day, a day of delight, as prophets both ancient and modern have urged the people to do, involves more than just rest and church activity. It requires, as one senior Latter-day Saint leader taught, "spiritual renewal and worship" and "regeneration and the strengthening of our spiritual being."[30]

It is this kind of Sabbath experience that yields the blessings of God prophesied and promised by holy men throughout history—the "fulness of the earth" (Doctrine and Covenants 59:16), "the heritage of Jacob thy father" (Isaiah 58:14), and the "glory of the Lord shall be thy rearward. Then shalt thou call, and the Lord shall answer; thou shalt cry, and he shall say, Here I am" (Isaiah 58:8–9). It is this kind of Sabbath experience that Latter-day Saint leaders are today urging with their admonitions and the programmatic and cultural changes within the Church. Will it yield the desired results—greater faith in the world, deeper love for God and others, stronger families, and increased personal spirituality? The old adage is "time will tell." But in reality, time may not tell.

With deep-seated traditions and practices, for which many Latter-day Saints have holy envy, Jews have honored the Sabbath for millennia. But the impact Sabbath has had on them through the centuries cannot be fully measured or understood by the number of candles lit or prayers offered. For Jews and Latter-day Saints alike, the Sabbath's *influence* may be seen in one's activities, but its spiritually transformative *power* is between the individual and God. The Sabbath, as Rabbi Heschel wrote, "becomes a way to find God's presence."[31] In a similar vein, President Nelson promised the Latter-day Saints in October 2018 that if they would seek "conscientiously and carefully to transform their home into a sanctuary of faith" and "diligently work to remodel [their] home into a center of gospel learning, over time [their] Sabbath days will truly be a delight. [Their] children will be excited to learn and live [God's] teachings, and the influence of the adversary in [their] life and [their] home will decrease. Changes in [their] family will be dramatic and sustaining."[32] What greater blessings could one desire? In both Jewish and Latter-day Saint thought, isn't that what the Sabbath is, or at least should be, all about?

NOTES

1.   Hans Gustafson, "Suppressing the Mosquitoes' Coughs: An Introduction to Holy Envy," in *Learning from Other Religious Traditions: Leaving Room for Holy Envy*, ed. Hans Gustafson (New York: Palgrave Macmillan, 2018), 3. See also https://fairmormon.org/archive/publications/breaking-the-rules-critics-of-the-lds-faith; https://bulletin.hds.harvard.edu/articles/winter2007/interview-krister-stendahl.

2.   Quentin L. Cook, "Shipshape and Bristol Fashion: Be Temple Worthy—in Good Times and Bad Times," *Ensign*, November 2015, 41.

3.   This notion of the Sabbath as a queen is rich in Jewish thought. Reference is made to this point in the Talmud; see *Shabbat* 119a. Additionally, one might look to *Lecha Dodi*, a Sabbath hymn from the sixteenth century CE. For a modern liturgical reference to the Sabbath as a queen, see *Mishkan T'filah: A Reform Siddur* (New York: Central Conference of American Rabbis, 2007), 128.

4. Abraham Joshua Heschel, *The Sabbath* (New York: Farrar, Straus and Giroux, 2005), 18.

5. Heschel, *Sabbath*, 10.

6. Journal of Joseph Smith, 20 March 1836; in Dean C. Jessee, Mark Ashurst-McGee, and Richard L. Jensen, eds., *Journals, Volume 1: 1832–1839*, vol. 1 of the Journals series of *The Joseph Smith Papers*, ed. Dean C. Jessee, Ronald K. Esplin, and Richard Lyman Bushman (Salt Lake City: Church Historian's Press, 2008), 198.

7. Journal of Joseph Smith, 29 November 1835; *JSP*, J1:112.

8. Journal of Joseph Smith, 30 November 1834; *JSP*, J1:47.

9. Journal of Joseph Smith, 11 October 1835; *JSP*, J1:71; also William E. McLellin Journal, 12 May 1833, in *The Journals of William E. McLellin*, ed. Jan Shipps and John W. Welch (Provo, UT: BYU Studies, Brigham Young University; Urbana: University of Illinois Press, 1994).

10. For the historical introduction to this section of the Doctrine and Covenants, see Revelation, 7 August 1831 [D&C 59], in Matthew C. Godfrey, Mark Ashurst-McGee, Grant Underwood, Robert J. Woodford, and William G. Hartley, eds., *Documents, Volume 2: July 1831–January 1833*, vol. 2 of the Documents series of *The Joseph Smith Papers*, ed. Dean C. Jessee, Ronald K. Esplin, Richard Lyman Bushman, and Matthew J. Grow (Salt Lake City: Church Historian's Press, 2013), 30–35.

11. William W. Phelps, "Gently Raise the Sacred Strain," *Hymns* (Salt Lake City: The Church of Jesus Christ of Latter-day Saints, 1985), no. 146; see also Bruce A. Van Orden, *We'll Sing and We'll Shout: The Life and Times of W. W. Phelps* (Provo, UT: Religious Studies Center, Brigham Young University, 2018), 44–45; Van Orden writes that Phelps's understanding of Joseph Smith's teaching was that "clearly, the blessings of Zion were contingent in part upon honoring the Sabbath."

12. Paul H. Peterson, "The Mormon Reformation" (PhD diss., Brigham Young University, 1981); John Turner, *Brigham Young: Pioneer Prophet* (Cambridge: Harvard University Press, 2012), 254–64; Gene Sim-

mons, *Mormon Thunder: A Documentary History of Jedediah Morgan Grant* (Urbana: University of Illinois Press, 1982).

13. Brigham Young, in *Journal of Discourses* (London: Latter-day Saints' Book Depot, 1881), 6:195.

14. Brigham Young, in *Journal of Discourses*, 15:83.

15. Brigham Young, in *Journal of Discourses*, 15:83.

16. Brigham Young, in *Journal of Discourses*, 15:82.

17. Joseph F. Smith, *Improvement Era*, 1909–10, 842–43.

18. "Church Consolidates Meeting Schedules," *Ensign*, March 1980; https://churchofjesuschrist.org/ensign/1980/03/news-of-the-church /church-consolidates-meeting-schedules.

19. Stephen Smoot, "Reports of the Death of the Church Are Greatly Exaggerated," January 15, 2013, https://fairmormon.org/blog/2013 /01/15/reports-of-the-death-of-the-church-are-greatly-exagger ated; "Elder Marlin K. Jensen Questions and Answers," Archive .org, August 31, 2015, https://archive.org/details/ElderMarlinJensen QuestionsAndAnswers; Peter Henderson and Kristina Cooke, "Special Report: Mormonism Besieged by the Modern Age," Reuters, January 30, 2012, https://uk.reuters.com/article/uk-mormonchurch /special-report-mormonism-besieged-by-the-modern-age-idUK TRE80T1CP20120130. It should be noted, however, that Church leaders disputed the characterization that there were members "leaving in droves," and official Church statisticians reported that there was not a precipitous drop in activity rates or resignations of Church membership.

20. Harold B. Lee, "Take Time to Be Holy," radio address, April 22, 1945; later published in *Decisions for Successful Living* (Salt Lake City: Deseret Book, 1973), 142–50.

21. M. Russell Ballard, general conference leadership training, April 2015, https://churchofjesuschrist.org/broadcasts/archive/general-confer ence-leadership-training/2015/04; see "Church Leaders Call for Better Observance of Sabbath Day," *Church News*, July 15, 2015,

https://churchofjesuschrist.org/church/news/church-leaders-call-for
-better-observance-of-sabbath-day.

22. D. Todd Christofferson, general conference leadership training, October 2015, https://churchofjesuschrist.org/broadcasts/archive/general
-conference-leadership-training/2015/10.

23. Russell M. Nelson, "Opening Remarks," *Ensign*, November 2018, 8.

24. Russell M. Nelson, "The Sabbath Is a Delight," *Ensign*, May 2015, 132.

25. Thomas Shepard, *Theses Sabbaticae* (1649; repr. Dahlongea, GA: Crown Rights Book, 2002), 254.

26. Heschel, *Sabbath*, 22–23.

27. Joseph F. Smith, "Observing the Sabbath: That Your Joy May Be Full," in *Teachings of the Presidents of the Church: Joseph F. Smith* (Salt Lake City: The Church of Jesus Christ of Latter-day Saints, 2011), 237; emphasis added.

28. Heschel, *Sabbath*, 74.

29. Nelson, "Sabbath Is a Delight," 130; emphasis in the original.

30. James E. Faust, "The Lord's Day," *Ensign*, November 1991, 34.

31. Heschel, *Sabbath*, 13.

32. Russell M. Nelson, "Becoming Exemplary Latter-day Saints," *Ensign*, November 2018, 113; emphasis deleted.

11

JEWISH LITURGY AND THE RELIGIOUS IMAGINATION

TAMAR FRANKIEL

Jewish liturgy is rooted in exile—the dislocation caused by the loss of the Temple in Jerusalem, twice. The first destruction, followed by the Babylonian exile of the sixth century BCE, appears to have led to the creation of certain liturgical practices, particularly the reading of Torah, that were reestablished in Israel with the rebuilding of the Temple and return of a partial self-government as recorded in the books of Nehemiah and Ezra (arguably mid-fifth century BCE). Tradition tells us that the *Anshei Knesset HaGedolah*, or "Men of the Great Assembly" established by Ezra, elaborated some prayers for holy days on the Jewish calendar and certain blessings for food, but the details cannot be verified since the transmission was oral.

The next recognized liturgical developments, this time from a sectarian source, emerge from the Qumran community. After decades of analysis of the Dead Sea Scrolls, most agree that around the time of the Maccabean revolt and establishment of a new status quo in the Jerusalem temple (ca. 150 BCE), a community seceded and created its own practices, probably led by priests but without a temple. The scrolls, presumably hidden in a time of danger, preserved their calendar, their strict purity practices, and their psalms and songs. These provide a suggestive background for understanding an intensely dedicated Jewish group that looked forward to restoration, but we still have no evidence of an enduring devotional community not led by priests.

Indeed, as James Watts has shown, priests and temple were at the center of Jewish life in the postexilic period even more than in the period of kings. Temple leadership was so strong during the postexilic period that one extended family, called by scholars the Oniads, not only managed the temple but ruled the Jewish people from 515 to 150 BCE. Their influence probably extended over the Samaritan temple, and when the Jerusalem temple was taken over by the Hasmoneans, one of their priests established a temple at Leontopolis in Egypt that lasted from 150 BCE to 73 CE. Despite the internecine struggles of different groups of priests at certain periods, there was almost no criticism of the priesthood and temple as institutions until the first century CE.[1] Recognizing the strength of the priestly tradition can help us understand how devastating it was to experience once again the destruction of the Temple—and the enormity of the task of creating a different kind of liturgical life for the Jewish people after 70 CE.

Nevertheless, the sages of the new Sanhedrin in Yavneh/Usha began that task and handed it on to their successors in the second century, then into Mishnaic and Talmudic times.[2] They had to create a liturgy that did not depend on the Temple—and yet, as this paper will argue, the Temple was present in imagination, along with other key elements of Jewish tradition, even though it no longer existed physically. Rabbinic Judaism, the new form of religious practice that emerged after the destruction, frequently drew parallels to ancient sacrifice and Temple practice.[3] Table fellowship, with its incorporation of dietary laws, the saying of blessings, and ritualized symbolism of food and drink, reenacted the celebrations of communion with God that priests and people had enjoyed at the Temple.[4] Beyond that (and usually preceding the meals in the community's daily schedule) were the developing liturgies for Shabbat, holidays, and weekdays, rich with song, chant, and supplication.

We must note one other key point in this development before trying to understand the liturgy itself: historically, written prayer books did not exist. Siddurim with the standard liturgy, very similar to what traditional Jews use today, are known only from the ninth century CE onward. This means that for at least six hundred years the liturgy was mostly learned by oral repetition. Of course, individuals and particularly prayer leaders probably wrote and shared prayers and even created small devotional books. One such Hebrew book, containing psalm verses and supplications, was found at Dunhuang on the Silk Road, left behind sometime between 400 and 1000 CE, probably by some Jewish merchant traveling from Persia to China.[5] But the rarity of such books suggests both their private provenance and the general reliance on oral learning.

There is, however, one exception to that rule—one book of devotional literature that was already written and widely copied, namely the Book of Psalms (Tehillim). The nonrabbinic movement known as the Karaites, which emerged in the late 700s after the Islamic conquests in the Middle East, held that the only acceptable liturgical songs were the psalms.[6] In my view, it's quite likely that the growing strength of the Karaite movement created the pressure that led the rabbis to write down their system of prayers, giving it an authority that could compete with the dissidents' more "fundamentalist" view of liturgy.

We would expect in any case to find psalms in rabbinic liturgy as well. As we will see, an entire section of traditional liturgy is built around a selection of psalms. But they are framed in a rabbinic mode, and that is what we want to understand.

THE LADDER OF PRAYER

Jews at prayer take for granted a basic four-part morning prayer service, with portions of the first two parts regarded as essential, and virtually all of the third and fourth required.[7] On Shabbat and holidays, those latter two sections are expanded with additional celebratory psalms and special prayers. Two other shorter prayer services occur in the afternoon and evening; the afternoon service omits the third part, and the evening is a much-abbreviated version of the morning service.

The two essential parts are historically older parts of a formal service. The oldest (third section) is known as the *Shema and Its Blessings* or *k'riat Shema* (recital of *Shema*, which means "hear") and comprises three biblical paragraphs enclosed within a set of rabbinically composed blessings. The Mishnah (ca. 200 CE) tells us that the recital of Shema was performed by priests in the Chamber of Hewn Stones around the time of morning sacrifices but was separate from the public sacrificial ritual. That ceremony is quite possibly much older, but we don't know precisely when these three paragraphs were selected as the ones to recite or indeed if they were all chosen at the same time. The first lines of the recital were made more famous in later times by the New Testament citing them as one of what Jesus considered the two most fundamental commandments, essentially the basis of Jewish faith (with slight variations from the Hebrew Bible): "Hear O Israel, the Lord our God, the Lord is One: And you shall love the Lord your God with all your heart, with all your soul, with all your mind, and with all your strength" (Mark 12:29–30 New King James Version).

The other required piece, the Amidah (meaning "standing"), was constructed (or, hypothetically, redeveloped from unknown earlier communal prayers) in the aftermath of the first war with Rome as the rabbis struggled to reconstruct Jewish communities, starting with their students and families. The prayer essentially outlines the community's ideal of a redeemed society. In a traditional congregation today (Orthodox or Conservative),[8] each person recites the Amidah, followed by the congregational leader's recitation of the prayer. In Reform and most other services, an alternate ancient order is followed: the first three blessings of the Amidah are recited aloud together, then each person prays the rest of the prayer privately. Using a basic framework filled out with different content depending on whether it is Shabbat, holiday, or weekday, this second core prayer, which constitutes the fourth of the four main sections, was called by the rabbis of the Talmud *ha-Tefillah*, *the* prayer. Most of the content is similar across denominations, although the Reform movement replaced the idea of the resurrection of the dead with more general language of renewal, and eliminated most messianic allusions. With these and other less dramatic literary license, the ideas expressing the Jewish desire for complete redemption of the world have sometimes been adapted to modern belief.

The second section—called *Pesukei d'Zimrah*, or verses of song—became customary before the formal call to prayer that precedes the saying of the Shema liturgy, presumably to inspire and focus the devotion of those gathering for prayer. This section, while composed almost entirely of psalms and other biblical citations, is also book-ended by rabbinically composed blessings. The first section, recited before all of the above, is called Morning Blessings; these were originally said at home to start one's morning devotions, but since the medieval period they have been added to the very beginning of the morning synagogue service to help those who could not or did not say them at home.[9]

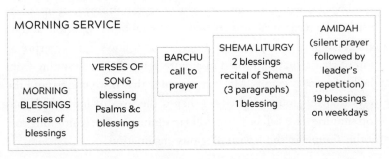

MORNING SERVICE					AMIDAH
MORNING BLESSINGS series of blessings	VERSES OF SONG blessing Psalms &c blessings	BARCHU call to prayer	SHEMA LITURGY 2 blessings recital of Shema (3 paragraphs) 1 blessing		(silent prayer followed by leader's repetition) 19 blessings on weekdays

The following is an outline of the parts of the morning service:

1. Morning Blessings—series of blessings, personal
2. Verses of Song—psalms and songs bookended by two blessings [Call to prayer]
3. Shema and Its Blessings—recital of biblical paragraphs bookended by two blessings at the beginning and one at the end
4. Amidah (standing prayer—silent followed by leader's repetition)—nineteen blessings / requests, communal ("we")

On days when the Torah is read publicly, the ritual reading comes after the above four-part liturgy. Then, on Shabbat, the New Moon, and holidays in traditional congregations, there is another prayer service known as *Musaf* ("additional"), which is primarily another Amidah.

Moreover, these four parts of the service came to be regarded, in some branches of the Jewish mystical tradition, as outlining a path for a spiritual journey.[10] Like the liturgy, mystical traditions existed from the second century onward. We have literature alluding to journeys of spiritual ascent; we know that there were "schools" of mystical thought, including *ma'aseh bereishit*, the work of creation, and *ma'aseh merkavah*, the work of the chariot.[11] In the Middle Ages, the tradition of Ezekiel's chariot as described in chapter 1 of the biblical book of Ezekiel was merged into a "Four Worlds" cosmology that could help shape a devotee's understanding of the four parts of the prayers, as well as the poetry that was composed to embellish them over the centuries.

The above provides an overview of Jewish liturgy in terms of its history, the basic structure created by the rabbinic tradition, and its embellishment by mystical readings. What follows is my interpretation of that structure rooted in a more general understanding from the history of religions. My assumption is that if we understand the ways that religious imagination shapes the lives of individuals and communities, we will be better able to illuminate the continuing role of the Temple in the Jewish religious imagination.

SACRED SPACE IN POIESIS

From very ancient times, people created temples and shrines to provide sacred space for religious practice. Mircea Eliade and many scholars before and after have documented around the globe the centrality
of the sanctified space that connects heaven and earth. Often sacred
space is connected to a concept of sacred time, the archetypal time of
beginnings, and a calendar that brings communities back again and
again to the mystical strength of those beginnings.[12] But, under all
kinds of pressures, old forms eventually die or are destroyed. The
shattering of a society's space/time continuum, architecturally portrayed in temple and calendar, can be devastating to the community.
What can replace the elegant architectural presentation of heavenly
harmony and power? Can it be redescribed in writing? In song? Or
inscribed on the human body itself? The variety of answers to that
question in many cultures can lead us into the depths of religious
history.

One possibility is that the destruction of an external form may
generate a movement inward, an interiorization of the images by
which people have lived and breathed. The religious imagination
sets to work, exercising an inner process with the forms enshrined in
memory and words. Eliade grasped, for example, that ancient yogic
practices were an interiorization of Hindu sacrifice. In Buddhism we
see temples transformed into sand paintings and mandalas as foci of
meditation. In Judaism's late Second Temple and rabbinic period,
the confluence between mystical ideas, the decline of centralized
worship, and a new liturgy in flux for a few centuries led to a Jewish
version of such a process. I would call it the *interiorization of the priesthood* and, with it, the *domestication of the temple.*

We don't usually think of Judaism this way, particularly because
we tend to think of the priesthood as having come under devastating
critique. Priesthood has been stereotyped as an "external" religion,
ritually obsessive; corrupt, invested in power and money; distant from
the people.[13] But that may be anachronistic for second-century Jews.

Such a critique is heard among Jews much later, claiming Judaism is *not* priestly and thus is distinct from Christianity, after that daughter religion had developed its atonement theology and strengthened its own concepts of priesthood. Even today, Jews will often distinguish their beliefs from Christian theologies by negating priesthood: "We don't need an intermediary." But in the early centuries when rabbinic Judaism was developing its liturgy, there was most likely a continuing influence of priest and temple imagery on the communal psyche, even as it sought transformation in light of the new situation. And, as we will see, it had nothing to do with whether or not there was an intermediary.

Another intriguing factor is the presence of Kohanim and Levi'im, descendants of priestly families, among the leading rabbinic figures at the turn of the second century when the core prayer service was being solidified. The first two leaders of the new Sanhedrin after the destruction were not of priestly descent—Rabbi Yohanan ben Zakkai (d. ca. 80) and following him, Rabban Gamliel, who presided over the composition of a new liturgy for the Amidah. Gamliel claimed descent rather from the line of David. But Gamliel married his sister to Eliezer ben Hyrcanus, who was a Kohen. Other leaders include Eleazar ben Azariah, who traced his lineage ten generations to Ezra the Kohen (better known in tradition as "Ezra ha-Sofer," the Scribe), and Joshua ben Hananiah, a prominent Levite, who had sung in the Temple as a boy.

Even before the destruction, the Pharisees appear to have been bringing priestly behavior into the households of Israel—what I would call the domestication of the temple. Examples include washing hands before meals (associated with Pharisees in Luke 11:38), having special meals for the brotherhood followed with blessings (similar practices are also attested at priestly Qumran), encouraging *kiddush* and *havdalah* blessings at home to open and close the Sabbath, which was a priestly temple practice claimed to go back to the postexilic Great Assembly. The home was increasingly regarded as a sanctified place, and women were honored in the home, even though it was primarily the men who learned the rituals for prayer in the community as well as for their families. The later Talmudic statement that a person's table has become like the (temple) altar was an epithet for the gradual domestication of a whole range of priest-like practices embedded in memory as part of the lost temple. This process, including internalizing aspects of the priesthood among laypeople, had begun before the war, before the Temple was lost.

Some scholars have suggested that in the rabbinic religious imagination, there was a tendency to deemphasize Zion and elevate Sinai.[14] Whereas the priests had focused on the cosmic importance of the Temple (exemplified in the Torah by parallels between creation and *mishkan*),[15] the rabbis of the scribal classes (*sofrim*) shifted toward Torah learning and with that, the Exodus and Sinai.[16] This shift would become the foundation of rabbinic Judaism. Nevertheless, I would argue that the priestly tradition remained alive and well in the liturgy—implicitly in its structure, explicitly in many of its themes that were creatively merged with scribal concerns.

To see this, we will examine first the Shema section (the third of the four parts), for it contains the keystone of the Jewish affirmation of faith as it evolved among the rabbis. As Rabbi Reuven Kimelman has argued, we definitely have a Shema liturgy, not simply a biblical recital. It may have been inherited from the Temple; and if so, it was further adapted in the service as we have come to know it. Below is its basic outline. The paragraphs are indented in a "step" formation to indicate that the overall structure is the inverted parallel type called chiasmus, in which I have identified the parts as ABCBA. In the description that follows, it will become clear how these parts are inwardly related to one another.

Shema and Its Blessings
> [Call to communal prayer: Let us bless! with response]
> A$_1$ First blessing: Who Creates Light
>> B$_1$ Second blessing: Eternal Love
>>> C Recital of Shema sections from the Bible—three paragraphs
>> B$_2$ Third blessing, part 1: True and Certain
> A$_2$ Third blessing, part 2: Redemption

After the call to communal prayer, the first act that the community performs is a cosmic celebration of sunrise with a blessing on the Creation of Light (A$_1$). This is probably a direct import from the temple.[17] Prayer at sunrise was a priestly act; sunrise is naturally symbolic of creation and re-creation, but this prayer makes it explicit: *In His goodness He renews every day the work of creation.*

The first blessing continues by referencing Psalm 104 via a quotation, "How abundant are your works, Lord! You made them all in wisdom; the earth is full of your creations." Lurking behind that verse in the psalm is the creation story of Bereishit (Genesis), which is well known to be a priestly composition. Sun and stars, all the lights, are referenced, also reflecting the priestly love of cosmic grandeur (I suspect these people are now reincarnated as NASA astrophysicists). A "sitting Kedushah," angels singing the words of prophetic vision (including the Trisagion), also came to be included. While older liturgy scholars like A. Z. Idelsohn thought this Kedushah was a late addition promoted by some peripheral but activist mystics, it fits with a priestly vision because the vision of God in Isaiah explicitly references the holiness of the Temple.[18]

The second blessing (B$_1$ in the chiasmic form) celebrates God's love, demonstrated in the teaching and learning of Torah. It was probably composed by a poet among the sages not long after the middle of the second century CE. Its opening words in most Sephardic versions are *Ahavat olam*, "eternal love," while in the Ashkenazic morning prayer it begins with *Ahavah rabbah*, "great love." The phrase "eternal love" comes from Jeremiah 31:32. In that chapter Jeremiah also speaks of a "new covenant," wherein, as God says: "I will put my Torah in their insides, I will write it on their hearts" (my translation). This is fundamentally an affirmation of interiorization: the teaching will no longer be outside you, the covenant is inscribed *in* you, thus demanding an effort of religious imagination. In this case, the blessing expresses love in imagery that comes clearly from the scribal tradition: the love of God is compared to the love between teacher and student.

> Our Father, our King,
> for the sake of our fathers who trusted in You,
> and You taught them the laws of life,
> also be gracious to us and teach us.
> Our Father, compassionate Father,
> Ever compassionate, have compassion on us.
> Instill in our hearts to understand and to discern,
> to listen, to learn, and to teach,
> to watch over and do and fulfill
> all the teachings of Your Torah, in love.[19]

Kimelman calls the intense expression of reciprocal love in this prayer "unparalleled."[20] It is a significant innovation over the parent/child or marital imagery familiar in previous centuries from Tanakh (Exodus, Hosea, Song of Songs). Note that this rabbinic imagery is quite different from the priestly imagery of cosmic grandeur in the previous blessing, but placing the more intimate prayer of divine love next to the celebration of cosmic creation suggests that the first (A) is exterior or macrocosm, the second (B) interior or microcosm.

The Shema recital itself (C), beginning "Hear, Israel," opens not with the revelation at Sinai, interestingly, but with Deuteronomy's context of the Israelites on the plains of Moab, when Moses is speaking in his own words, as *Moshe Rabbenu*, "Moses our rabbi," our master.[21] This is interesting since the prior blessing has emphasized the transmission from teacher to student as a paradigm of love. Moses in this passage, as in all of Deuteronomy, is the preacher/teacher presenting the first Oral Torah.

The first two passages from the Bible recited in the Shema emphasize the relation of covenant in the form "you shall do . . . and if you do, I [God] will do . . ." However, the third biblical passage recited here is from Numbers rather than Deuteronomy. It prescribes the wearing of a ritual garment with *tzitzit*, fringes on the corners, as a reminder of the commandments. The first two paragraphs also mentioned symbolic ornaments, *tefillin* (phylacteries) on one's hand and arm, and the *mezuzah* on one's doorposts and gates. Both *tefillin* and *mezuzot* reference the Torah, but because they contain texts inside, they—together with *tzitzit*—are also a domestication of the temple, where the ark contained holy words and the priests wore holy garments. As one of his garments, the high priest wore a special band on his forehead, the same place where on weekdays a person places one box of *tefillin*.

Further, when Jews say the first lines of the Shema, we traditionally cover our eyes with one hand. Usually it is taught that we cover our eyes to avoid distraction ("lest your eyes go astray"). But also, the hand gesture could allude to the priestly headband on which was written, "Holy to the Lord." And was not Moses's face radiant with light so that he had to cover it with a veil? If the recital of Shema evokes Sinai, the giving of Oral Torah, and the priestly service in the temple all together, it is indeed a moment of high drama for the inner life.

As I suggested above, even the body can be inscribed with imaginings of the lost Temple and its priests. The rabbis selected these instructions from the Torah to recite daily, but also followed the instructions, creating memorials—that is, physical items and gestures—that serve as signals to the religious imagination. In this sense, the Shema recital has interiorized the cosmos even further, moving from the abstract idea that God loves us and teaches us to Moses personally teaching us to say them with our mouths, to inscribing words and symbols of the teachings at the entryways to our homes, in ritual clothing and ornaments.

We turn now to the third blessing, which immediately follows the recital of the biblical paragraphs. In our tradition, this blessing has two commonly used names: *Emet v'yatziv*, "True and certain," and *Ge'ulah*, "Redemption." Correlatively, it has two fairly distinct sections, which I have marked as B_2 and A_2. The Mishnah says that an *Emet v'yatziv* was recited in the Temple as a response to saying Shema, and indeed our current third blessing contains a version that would correspond to such a description. It bears all the marks of a priestly composition, with a chanting series in groups of six and seven parallel verses. A partial excerpt:

> *True* and firm
> and established and enduring / and right and faithful /
> and beloved and cherished / and delightful and pleasant /
> and awesome and mighty / and perfect and accepted /
> and good and beautiful
> is this faith to us forever. [7 pairs]

> *True* is the eternal God, our King, Rock of Jacob, Shield of our salvation, throughout all generations

> > He endures / and His name endures / and His throne is established / and His kingship and faithfulness forever endure / and His words are living and enduring, faithful forever / forever and to all time [6]

> > > upon our ancestors and upon us / upon our children and our descendants / upon all the generations of the seed of Israel Your servants / on the first / and on the last, [6]

> > The Word is good and enduring forever.

The affirmation continues with four shorter parts beginning with the word *true*. Clearly, an affirmation of truth is a natural sequel to the recital of Shema: those passages we just recited are eternally true. In the prayer form, B_2 is the students' response to the loving teacher of B_1. The response is emotional ("beloved and cherished, delightful and pleasant") and intellectual ("true and firm"), uniting in the loyalty of faith.

The second part of the third blessing (A_2) is different. The chanting ends, and the words tell a story in poetic form, expanding on the theme of redemption by describing the rescue of the Israelites at the splitting of the sea and quoting the Song of the Sea itself. Remarkably, at the same time, the stanza appears to mirror the first blessing on the Creation of Light (A_1). Where the *Yotzer Or* portrayed angels proclaiming God's grandeur and holiness, here the redeemed *people* are proclaiming God as savior at the Exodus. Here's what the mirroring looks like.

Yotzer Or, Creator of Light:

> To God the Blessed, the holy beings
> offer sweet melodies;
> to the King, the living and enduring God,
> songs they will sing and praises proclaim.

Ge'ulah, Redemption:

> For this, the beloved ones praised and exalted
> God; the cherished ones sang psalms, songs and
> praises, blessings and thanksgiving
> to the King, the living and enduring God.

Yotzer Or, Creator of Light:

> For He alone performs mighty acts
> makes new things
> is master of wars
> sows righteousness
> causes salvation to sprout
> creates healing—
> Lord of wonders,
> awesome in praise.

Ge'ulah, Redemption:

> He humbles the haughty
> raises the lowly
> frees captives
> redeems those in need
> helps the poor
> answers His people. . . .
> Who is like You, resplendent in holiness,
> awesome in praise, doing wonders?

Thus creation, the subject of the first blessing, is mirrored by the redemption of God's people, which is essentially a new creation, at the end of the third blessing. Remarkably, such acts as freeing captives and helping the poor are parallel to creation of fundamental principles like righteousness or powers like healing and salvation.

This completes the structure of the chiasmus. As Rabbi Kimelman has noted, such structures do not posit a narrative movement from beginning to end (creation to revelation to redemption, as one familiar interpretation goes),[22] but rather point to the center—in this case the recital of the Shema.[23] Kimelman sees this center as emphasizing divine sovereignty.[24] I would suggest, as a supplementary understanding, that the central act is covenant renewal in a vast cosmic framework under the sovereignty and love of God.

We can summarize this poetic dynamic as follows: The Creator God who is "holy, holy, holy" in the first blessing is the same God that took the Jewish people under his wing, taught them the fundamental truths—the "laws of life"—and inscribed those teachings on their hearts in the second blessing. Now the final (third) blessing of this section completes the chiasmic circle, as the "beloved ones"—God's people—experience a cosmic event, the Splitting of the Sea, which reenacts creation.[25] Moreover, the redemption at the sea is also an illustration of the covenant of love and as such is a "true and enduring" affirmation of the proclamations of the Shema. This amazing poetic composition unites Exodus-Sinai with Creation-Zion.

Seeing and experiencing the prayer in this way, one enters into a role that is far from ordinary. Heirs of the redeemed people, millennia later, are actualizing the priestly/angelic role in praising God's grandeur, power, and holiness.

PRIEST, PROPHET, AND PRAYER

Now we will briefly discuss the fourth section of daily prayer, the Amidah. We understand historically that Rabban Gamliel and his colleagues wanted to create a prayer that would unite a shattered community, now the second generation since the destruction. As noted above, many descendants of priests were in the extended community that gathered around Yavneh, perhaps even former sectarians from Qumran, as well as sons and grandsons of those who had been killed defending against the Romans (as was Gamliel himself). This group of brilliant and devoted men knew that the priests had once united the people; and so they would again, not with the sacrifices but with a unique and powerful prayer.

Rabbi Jonathan Sacks has pointed out that the dramatic highlight of the Amidah is the communal Kedushah (again containing the Trisagion), everyone standing with feet together, imitating the angels as tradition teaches.[26] The Amidah contains phrases from the atonement literature of Yom Kippur, the holiest day of the year, which recapitulates priestly practice. It continues with prayers for the holy city, for the restoration of sacrifices and for the Davidic (royal/patriarchal) lineage. In contrast to the Shema liturgy, the Amidah does not mention the Exodus from Egypt and only once the word *Torah*—and that occurs not in the prayer for knowledge but rather in the prayer for repentance.

Yet there are scribal themes within the Amidah as well. Its first blessing/request (out of nineteen) alludes to a history of redemption that featured the patriarch Abraham (who is also considered to have received a priestly blessing) but also includes phrases that were favorite tropes of the rabbinic tradition. Its second blessing, a celebration of God's life-giving power, includes the promise of resurrection, a Pharisaic doctrine. Petitions occurring in the weekday prayer service ask God to reestablish rule by the judges "as at first"—judges being *shoftim*, who would have been seen as similar to the rabbis in that their appointment was based on merit in God's eyes rather than dynastic lineages. On the other hand, the petition for protection of all the righteous speaks of the "remnants of the *sofrim* (scribes)," as though there were few of them still around.

The language of most of the Amidah's blessings is rooted in prophetic literature, which may well have been the "meeting place" for priestly and rabbinic traditions. Almost every blessing in the Amidah has a biblical reference standing behind it, from Isaiah, Jeremiah, Ezekiel, or Psalms, a lineage that both priests and sages claimed for themselves.

Ultimately, the rabbis decided that the Amidah could be led by anyone in good standing in the assembly, but the priestly blessing was still the conclusion to the prayers: "May the Lord bless you and keep you, may the Lord cause His face to shine upon you and be gracious to you, may the Lord lift up His face to you and grant you peace." This was the conclusion to every sacrificial service in the Temple, a text that comes down to us from the time of Aaron.

These two most important sections of Jewish liturgy thus reveal the strong hand of rabbinic composition or reworking of older texts, but they still retain many elements of priestly liturgy and priestly concerns. Opening with the prayer for light and closing with the priestly prayer for peace are liturgical moments that enclose the entire two core sections in memories of Temple practice.

CELEBRATION AND VISION

Pesukei d'Zimra, the (second) section of song, evolved over the centuries as a way of preparing for the Shema liturgy. It was probably intended to be sung responsively, the most common style in ancient times before a standard prayer book existed. The prayer leader, modeled on the priest in the Temple, chanted certain phrases, which might be quite varied, while the congregation responded with a familiar line or lines.

Many of the psalms chosen for the verses of Song bring the Temple into clear focus. The section opens with a song of celebration when David brought the ark to Jerusalem. David is highlighted as the poet-king who longed for God's house and sang of it, even though he did not build it. This in-between perspective, holding a vision of the Temple but not yet building it, turns out to be the condition of the Jewish people post-70 CE: the Temple remains part of their world of living thoughts, but is not manifest in reality. The framework here also portrays David as the pray-er, the one in deep relationship to God, who at the central point of this section leads the people in saying, "Happy are they who dwell in Your House, they are ever praising you" (Psalm 84:5).[27] Psalms 145–50 follow, like a processional of all the beings of creation singing on their way to the great cosmic celebration of praise. In case we are distracted, the blessing of acclamation after these psalms makes it clear:

> Blessed is Adonai forever, Amen and Amen. *Blessed is Adonai from Zion, Dweller of Jerusalem—halleluyah!* Blessed be the Lord God of Israel, who alone does wonders, and blessed be the name of His Glory forever, and may His Glory fill the whole earth, Amen and Amen.

In the religious imagination, God is in Zion and Jerusalem, and from there his glory—equivalent to the *Shechinah*, Divine Presence, or divine manifestation—fills the earth. This is a Temple vision.

Prior to this, the first section of Morning Blessings is a private ceremony. Its intent is clearly for the pray-er to express gratitude and prepare for a day of service to God, donning one's spiritual garments with thanks for body, soul, and the guidance of Torah. Are these priestly? They are not blessings of purification, like the cleansing from sin that so occupied the Qumran community; rather, they deliver a strong message that the body and soul God has bestowed on a person are good. On the other hand, the blessings over Torah include a recital of the Priestly Blessing—startlingly, in private. The blessing is presented in the mode of fulfilling the commandment to study, and so is recited as a Torah text. But implicitly, imaginatively, it also points to the radical idea of the ordinary Jew as a priest before God. Here too, we see the rabbinic imagination gently imbuing priestly ideas within the whole people.

Thus, in implicit and sometimes explicit ways, we find in the Jewish daily prayers a liturgy that offers a path to interiorization of the priesthood. Jews become, in imagination, celebrants of cosmic creation and divine holiness like the ancient priests, while also celebrating the love of God generated in the heart through the gift of Torah. This interiorization and transformation has been the principal dynamic of Jewish prayer for as many as eighteen centuries.

One of prayer's primary purposes is to transform individuals into willing vessels of God by renewing the covenant daily and by being infused with continuous reminders of divine process in the world. In particular, we are asked to grasp imaginatively, through the words of *tefillah*, the grandeur of creation and redemption, which is also re-creation. Through that process in the Shema liturgy, one can enter into the covenant.

Then one can speak with God—the "silent speaking" that is the Amidah. There, using the words of prophets—entering into the role of prophet-priest—the petitioner looks toward the redemption of the world, in partnership with God. This prayer asks us to envision the continuous gifts of God to the patriarchs, matriarchs, and ancestors through the centuries, as certain as the rain in the land and the renewal of dew. We do not forget the pain in the world; we plead with God by echoing the words of the prophets who spoke of distress and brokenness. But we also hold the vision of a people guided by fair, just, and devout leaders, centered in the land and city bequeathed from ancient times, where prayer is answered, where health and prosperity and peace are part of the natural course of things—the world as God intended it to be.

Through this prayer the petitioner stands like the priests in service and like the angels in attendance on God. There is respectful bowing at beginning and end of the prayer, but no kneeling or prostration (except on Rosh HaShanah and Yom Kippur), no sense of abject submission. The liturgy grants to all the status of priest at his/her proper work, the cocreator with God, or, in other terms, a channel for divine energy to come into the world. "Make me a sanctuary that I may dwell among you," said God in giving the instructions for the original *mishkan*, the temple-prototype for the wilderness. Now, the imaginal sanctuary created by liturgy, given life through words spoken and sung, is the place of God's presence today in the heart and mind.

NOTES

1. James W. Watts, "Scripturalization and the Aaronide Dynasties," *Journal of Hebrew Scriptures* 13 (2013): 3–4, https://surface.syr.edu/cgi/viewcontent.cgi?article=1076&context=rel.

2. Liturgical development received encyclopedic treatment in the early twentieth century by Ismar Elbogen, *Jewish Liturgy: A Comprehensive History* (German, 1933; Hebrew, rev., 1972; English, Philadelphia: Jewish Publication Society and Jewish Theological Seminary of America, 1993); and a shorter survey by A. Z. Idelsohn, *Jewish Liturgy and Its Development* (New York: Holt, 1932; 1995). These are now dated. Stefan C. Rieff covers much of the same ground while bringing in later insights in his *Judaism and Hebrew Prayer: New Perspectives on Jewish Liturgical History* (Cambridge: Cambridge University Press, 1995). In recent times, however, the scholarship of Rabbi Reuven Kimelman, published in various journals and anthologies, has gone far beyond that of his predecessors and is particularly relevant in the study of the basic framework of liturgy. See his recent publication, *The Rhetoric of Jewish Prayer: A Literary and Historical Commentary on the Prayerbook* (Oxford: Littman Library of Jewish Civilization, 2019). Kimelman's methods and insights have greatly enriched my work.

3. The *locus classicus* for prayer replacing sacrifice is Hosea 14:2 (KJV), "so will we offer the words of our lips instead of calves." An explicit parallel comes from the Talmud (*Brachot* 26b): "R. Yehoshua ben Levi says: The *tefillot* were instituted to correspond to the daily offerings." Other aspects of Jewish practice, including fasting and charity, were also regarded as paths to forgiveness from God, as is most famously illustrated in the High Holy Day liturgy prayer, *Unetaneh Tokef:* "Repentance, prayer, and charity avert the Divine decree." Study of the laws of sacrifice was considered as satisfying the laws of sacrifice: "Rabbi Shmuel bar Nachmani brings from Rabbi Yochanan [ben Zakkai], "These are Torah scholars, who engage in Torah study in every place. God says, "I ascribe merit to them as though they burn and present offerings to My name" (*Menachot* 110a). See also Leon A. Morris, "The Imaginative Power of Sacrifice," *Shema: A Journal of Jewish Ideas* (August 1, 2013), http://shma.com/2013/08/the-imaginative -power-of-sacrifice/.

4. According to the Talmud, this was the interpretation of both Rabbi Yochanan and Rabbi Eleazar: "As long as the Temple stood, the altar atoned for Israel, but now a man's table atones for him" (*Berakhot* 55a).

5. Among other sources to read about the texts in the Dunhuang man-uscript collection among the Mogao Caves, see Jacob Mikanow-ski's article at https://newyorker.com/tech/elements/a-secret-library -digitally-excavated. I was able to see this Hebrew text when the Getty Museum in Los Angeles hosted an exhibit of the cave replicas and a sampling of the objects.

6. For a recent treatment of the Karaite movement, see Y. Yaron and Joe Pessah, *An Introduction to Karaite Judaism: History, Theology, Practice, and Culture* (New York: Qirqisani Center, 2003).

7. Orthodox law does not require women to participate in formal prayer at all because of an exemption from "time-bound" commandments. Women are assumed to be primarily involved in family and house-hold matters, and because of that, an expectation to be present in syn-agogue at a precise time would be onerous to them. Reform Judaism does not consider *halachah* binding, so laws that distinguish men and

women in prayer are not relevant. Conservative Jews officially expect women who become rabbis or cantors to commit to the same requirements as men.

8. While the Conservative movement is considered one of the liberal denominations on social issues, it is liturgically far more conservative. Until its latest revision of the prayer book (2016), it was almost identical to Orthodox prayer books except for changes in blessings relating to men and women and other gender-inclusive language. I have not yet examined it closely, but it is notable that the new *Siddur Lev Shalem* no longer includes a weekday morning service.

9. In a traditional siddur, other prayers besides the series of required blessings are also printed in the first section. These include optional devotional recitals of biblical and rabbinic texts, as well as prayers that probably belonged to different older customs.

10. I have developed this approach at length in my book *Loving Prayer: A Study Guide to Everyday Jewish Prayer* (Santa Fe: Gaon Books, 2017). My resources include, prominently, Rabbi Elie Munk, *World of Prayer*, vol. 1: Daily Prayers (New York: Philip Feldheim, 1953); Aryeh Kaplan, *Inner Space: Introduction to Kabbalah, Meditation, and Prophecy*, ed. Abraham Sutton (Jerusalem: Moznaim Books, 1990); Rabbi Zalman Schachter-Shalomi, *Davening: A Guide to Meaningful Jewish Prayer*, with Joel Segel (Woodstock, VT: Jewish Lights, 2012).

11. Peter Schäfer, *The Origins of Jewish Mysticism* (2009; English, Princeton: Princeton University Press, 2011), has produced an insightful treatment of the textual history leading up to and including the Hekhalot literature of mystical ascents. His valuable introduction is a brilliant analysis of scholarship from Gershom Scholem onward. He identifies in particular a branch of the Hekhalot literature that advocated a *unio liturgica* as the goal of prayer and contemplation. This may be the closest cousin to the framework of the traditional liturgy, if we allow for its being tamed by the rabbinic and Gaonic traditions over the centuries.

12. Mircea Eliade, *The Myth of the Eternal Return: Or, Cosmos and History* (Princeton: Princeton University Press, 1954).

13. In Israel of the second century BCE to the first century CE, there was certainly controversy about the priesthood and complaints about its corruption. But the argument was not about priesthood as such; rather, it was that priestly classes had usurped the rights of royalty; Levi had taken the role designated to Judah. Priests had elided the distinction between priest and king. And this had led priests into collaboration with oppressive external rulers such as the Romans. As to the stereotype of priests being ritually obsessed practitioners of an "external" religion, some scholars have suggested that such critiques came from the scribal classes—progenitors of the Pharisees, which in turn probably gave rise to the Rabbis—who were in intense competition with the priestly and patriarchal classes before and possibly after the destruction. See Tzvee Zahavy, "The Politics of Piety: Social Conflict and the Emergence of Rabbinic Liturgy," accessible online at http://tzvee.com/Home/the-politics-of-piety. However, in the second century, the new Judaism descended from Pharisees apparently reversed course, honoring those of priestly lineage, and gave them precedence in the ritual of reading the Torah. Later Christian polemic declared the temple and its priests and sacrifices inferior to their new rituals, which also became "external" and were managed by a priestly class. We should not accord validity to such stereotypical views of religious practice.

14. The terminology is from biblical theologian Jon Levenson, *Sinai and Zion: An Entry into the Jewish Bible* (New York: Harper & Row, 1985).

15. Nechama Leibowitz, in her commentary on Exodus 25, parashat Trumah, Studies in Shemot (New York: World Zionist Organization, 1978), pointed to the identification of these parallels in the German Bible commentary by Franz Rosenzweig and Martin Buber, *Die Schrift und ihre Verdeutschung* (Berlin: Schocken, 1936), 116–17, 39–42. Online in Hebrew at http://nechama.org.il/pages/167.html.

16. Among the shifts that were emphasized by the champions of Torah study were making the Passover Seder at home a primary ritual of the year, marking every holiday as "a remembrance of the Exodus from Egypt," and harvest festivals like Shavuot and Shemini Atzeret becoming celebrations of the Torah, with Sukkot being a reminder of God's protection in the wilderness years. Without attaching dates to any of these changes, one can easily see the overlay of Torah/Sinai on not simply "nature festivals" but on three priestly pilgrimage festivals and on Shabbat, which was a celebration of Creation.

17. Some scholars argue that the blessing recited before the Shema recital in the Temple was not the blessing for light but a blessing over Torah. Kimelman holds that it was probably a different blessing of acclamation to God. I see no particular reason why we should reject the *Yotzer Or*, in some version similar to the present one, as a candidate. The Mishnah's account of the semiprivate liturgy in a chamber of the Temple is as follows (M. *Tamid* 5:1):

> The appointed one [of the priests] said to [the others]: "Bless one blessing," and they blessed. Then they recited the Ten Commandments, *Shema*, *Vehaya im shamoa*, and *Vayomer* [the three paragraphs of the Shema]. Also they blessed the people with "True and faithful," "Service," and the Priestly Blessing. On Shabbat they added a blessing for the outgoing watch.

18. Marvin Sweeney has noted that the traditional opposition between prophet and priest is overdrawn, as many figures combined the two roles; see his *The Prophetic Literature* (Nashville: Abingdon, 2005), 132–36.

19. The translation of prayers follows Rabbi Jonathan Sacks, in the *Koren Sacks Weekday Siddur*, Ashkenaz (Jerusalem: Koren Publishing, 2014).

20. Reuven Kimelman, "The Shema' Liturgy: From Covenant Ceremony to Coronation," in *Kenishta: Studies in Synagogue Life*, ed. J. Tabory (Ramat Gan, Israel: Bar-Ilan University, 2001), 51n142.

21. According to the Mishnah (*Tamid* 5:1), the recital from Deuteronomy was originally accompanied by the recital of the Ten Commandments from Exodus, but the latter recital stopped sometime in the third century CE. The reason given in the Talmud is misinterpretation by the Christians (Y. *Brachot* 3c; B. *Brachot* 12a).

22. This is clearly articulated in Franz Rosenzweig's *The Star of Redemption* (New York: Holt, Rinehart and Winston, 1971); however, it may have sources in premodern commentators.

23. Rabbi Jonathan Sacks discusses chiasmus on pp. xxiii–xxiv of the introduction to *The Koren Siddur* (Jerusalem: Koren, 2017), his recent translation of the traditional prayer book (Jerusalem: Koren, 2009). I have developed applications of the structure of chiasmus in many places in the weekday morning service in my book *Loving Prayer*. Of relevance to my argument here, Rabbi Dr. Jacob Milgrom points out a similar structure running through the entire book on Leviticus, in which he calls the structure a ring with a latch. See Milgrom, "Introduction: The Structure of Leviticus," in *Leviticus: A Book of Ritual and Ethics*, Continental Commentaries (Minneapolis: Augsburg Fortress, 2004). Leviticus is, of course, a priestly document. However, chiasmus seems to have been widely used in the ancient world, and Jewish texts have no unique claim on it. Nevertheless, the use of chiasmus in the Shema liturgy has been highlighted by Kimelman; he insists that with the Shema blessings, "a linear reading must give way to a chiastic one." See Kimelman, "Shema' Liturgy"; the discussion of chiastic structure begins on page 25.

24. In this context Kimelman states, "The purpose of the prayer is to get the worshiper to construe his/her experience in a manner that will confirm its theological agendum." Kimelman, "Shema' Liturgy," 26. Prayer—at least formal prayer stated in words—is inspirational with an intention that points in a certain theological direction. Decades ago the brilliant anthropologist named Clifford Geertz made a similar statement from a theoretical point of view in his seminal essay

"Religion as a Cultural System," in *Anthropological Approaches to the Study of Religion*, ed. Michael Banton (London: Tavistock, 1966), 1–46:

> For it is in ritual—that is, consecrated behavior—that this conviction that religious conceptions are veridical and that religious directives are sound is somehow generated. It is in some sort of ceremonial form—even if that form be hardly more than the recitation of a myth, the consultation of an oracle, or the decoration of a grave—that the moods and motivations which sacred symbols induce in men and the general conceptions of the order of existence which they formulate for men meet and reinforce one another. In a ritual, the world as lived and the world as imagined, fused under the agency of a single set of symbolic forms, turn out to be the same world.

Originally published in the 1960s, this essay is in his book *The Interpretation of Cultures: Collected Essays* (London: Fontana Press, 1993), 112.

25. Inter alia, David Fohrman, "Creation and Uncreation," *The Exodus You Almost Passed Over* (n.p.: Aleph Beta Press, 2016).

26. Rabbi Jonathan Sacks speaks explicitly of the merging of two traditions: prophetic prayer and priestly sacrificial service. In the Amidah, which is said twice, "The silent Amida recalls the prayers of individuals in the Bible, while the Leader's repetition recalls the sacrifice." *Koren Siddur*, p. xxi. Zahavy, "Politics of Piety," notes that the Amidah contains more priestly themes than does the Shema section of the liturgy. I have shown in my book *Loving Prayer* that the Amidah also follows a chiasmic structure, but it is too lengthy to replicate here.

27. Hebrew Bible translations follow JPS unless modern usage dictates a change.

12

LATTER-DAY SAINT LITURGICAL PRACTICE: THE PSALMS AND THE DAY OF ATONEMENT

SHON D. HOPKIN

A Latter-day Saint or those who have attended Latter-day Saint worship services might read the title of this essay with some confusion. The term *liturgy* applies only in a very general sense to Latter-day Saint worship practices. Latter-day Saint worship services, outside of the singing of hymns and the weekly ordinance known as the sacrament, are purposely devoid of much religious ritual, thus mirroring the "low church," or simple, worship practices of many Protestant traditions. Notwithstanding this reality, Latter-day Saint religious structure and practice—with its hierarchical priesthood organization; with its emphasis on numerous priesthood ordinances such as the blessing of babies, baptism, confirmation, blessings of health, the sacrament (known as communion or the Eucharist in other Christian traditions), and the dedication of graves; and finally with the complexity of religious rituals performed in Latter-day Saint temples—cannot truly be termed low church. Rather, these beliefs and behaviors situate Latter-day Saints, not surprisingly, somewhere on the outside of the typical low church / high church divide that is often used to characterize the quantity of liturgical practices present in the worship patterns of different Christian denominations.

Latter-day Saints do have their own type of liturgical understanding and practice. Those practices build on biblical imagery and texts but also reflect the development of Christianity throughout the centuries, combining Latter-day Saint views of the ancient with modern application to create a unique blend in Latter-day Saint worship. This essay will demonstrate the ways in which Latter-day Saint worship connects with biblical imagery—first with the psalms and second with imagery from the biblical tabernacle and the Day of Atonement. The explanations expressed herein reflect Latter-day Saint reasoning and understanding of biblical images and practices.

USE OF THE PSALMS DURING FIRST AND SECOND TEMPLE WORSHIP[1]

Numerous biblical scholars see the existence and use of many of the psalms as connected to worship in the temple of Solomon or later in the Second Temple.[2] First and Second Chronicles—likely written by a temple Levite around 350 BCE during the time of the Second Temple—connect Israelite music directly to the office of the Levites and a temple setting.[3] First Chronicles 15 depicts David leading a procession in song and dance as the Israelites brought the ark of the covenant, the most central symbol of God's presence, back among the Israelites to reside in the tabernacle. As the Levites made holy sacrifices and entered into the tabernacle, or temple, David delivered a psalm of thanksgiving (see 1 Chronicles 16:4–36) and urged his people to "sing unto [the Lord], sing psalms unto him. . . . Glory ye in his holy name. . . . Seek the Lord and his strength, seek his face continually" (1 Chronicles 16:9–11). In this text, David thus connected music with the temple activity of seeking the face of the Lord as found symbolically at the ark. In 2 Chronicles 5:12–13, similar behaviors at the dedication of Solomon's temple, when the holy presence of God actually entered his temple, are recorded. The text makes clear that the Levites had been sanctified and were dressed in sacred temple robes of white. The Levitical "trumpeters and singers were as one, to make one sound to be heard in praising and thanking the Lord . . . when they lifted up their voice . . . then the house was filled with a cloud, even the house of the Lord" (2 Chronicles 5:13). This passage points to the music and singing itself as the behavior that directly led to the presence of God entering into the temple.

The themes expressed by the psalms connect closely with the purposes of temple worship and animal sacrifice under the Mosaic covenant: forgiveness, prayers of thanksgiving, pleas for aid in trials, holy festivals, the anointing and support of kings, songs to prepare for temple worship, and religious instruction.[4] These themes are also familiar to Latter-day Saints, who know the temple as a place for prayers of thanksgiving and requests for divine help, a place where they can contemplate and celebrate the mercy and might of God over the history of his interactions with mankind, a place of gospel instruction, and a place where they enter into covenants of holiness through priesthood ordinances.

USE OF THE PSALMS IN CHRISTIAN WORSHIP

Christian churches appear to have begun their use of the psalms in their worship services soon after the establishment of Christianity. Paul directed Christians to worship by "speaking to [them]selves in psalms and hymns and spiritual songs, singing and making melody in [their] heart[s] to the Lord" (Ephesians 5:19). Eventually in both the Eastern Orthodox Church and in the Roman Catholic Church, a cycle of psalm singing was designed that would allow all 150 psalms to be repeated every week, such as in the Eastern Orthodox Kathismata[5] or the Roman Catholic Liturgy of Hours or Divine Office.[6] The Eastern Orthodox Church uses psalms in its rites of consecration, ordination, and the Eucharist, and the Roman Catholic Church uses various psalms in rites of baptism, confirmation, Holy Communion, matrimony, funeral services, ordination, and consecration of churches. With their decreased emphasis on liturgy, Protestants often sing psalms in their worship services but do not always connect the psalms directly with specific ordinance or ritual. This Protestant usage of the psalms is mirrored in Latter-day Saint worship as well, as will be shown.

Since the psalms come from Hebrew poetry, which does not demonstrate strict meter, music that adhered faithfully to the text could not be metrical in the modern sense. For this reason, the music of the psalms continued without meter until the sixteenth century. A departure from long-held traditions with relation to the psalms began during the Reformation in connection with the translation of the scriptures into languages understandable to the laity and a growing distaste for the strict liturgical and ritual styles employed by the Roman Catholic Church. The popular, metered, and religious tunes that had previously been used for other hymns were now adopted for the psalms, and eventually tunes that had been used for nonreligious singing were even connected with psalms.[7] Two additional trends were reinforced in this shift. First, although harmonies had already been in use for hundreds of years in singing the psalms, the versification of the psalms allowed for greater creativity and diversity in harmonizing by a lay audience rather than just by the choir, since it made the psalms into recognizable tunes that were often repeated. Second, while dynamics had previously been employed to emphasize the meaning of specific words in the text, the importance of dynamics increased in order to focus on artistically moving music.[8]

Although there was certainly some loss in meaning with these alterations, the memorability of the tunes may have enhanced the congregation's understanding of the overarching sentiment of the psalms and allowed these scriptural prayers to be called to mind more readily in times of personal need. Because the tunes were easy to learn, the congregation was able to participate more readily in the unifying process of worship through singing.[9] With the greater liveliness of some of the tunes, the body was inclined to respond with the heart and mind in an emotional and physical response. In this sense, the tunes helped prepare the congregation for connection with the divine, as in ancient temple worship and early Christian liturgy. Since this style of singing differed from typical forms of speech in regard to meter, rhythm, and rhyme, it enhanced the sense that the singers had entered into sacred time and space and that they were worshipping in orderly forms pleasing to God; the order and organization of a metered hymn mirrored the order and organization found in heaven.

In other words, for these Christians the harmonies bore witness to the natural order that had been restored and made possible to Christians through the power of Jesus's sacrifice. The beautiful harmonies gave the sense that the singers were each contributing in their own ways that, in the composite, became a unified plea or witness of God's love and power. This approach helped the congregation feel they had entered into conversation with angelic choruses who were singing with them in praise of God.[10] The increased use of minor keys that resolved and leading notes that reached completion at the end of the hymn reflected the ritual feeling of a soul in a liminal state moving into a state of aggregation. The dynamics helped raise the soul of the singer into ecstatic or reverent communion with the divine, whichever the setting required. Thus, sacred time was still marked by singing psalms although they were sung in a different form than they had been before.

PSALM USAGE IN LATTER-DAY SAINT WORSHIP SERVICES

Although Latter-day Saints infrequently use unmetered, traditional versions of the psalms sung as special musical numbers during their sacrament meetings, their organized use of the psalms in their weekly worship clearly follows the Protestant pattern of metered, rhymed, and altered versions of the psalms that makes them more accessible to the congregation.[11] Some of these psalmic hymns—such as "We Love Thy House, O God,"[12] "For the Beauty of the Earth,"[13] or "Rejoice, the Lord Is King"[14]—are traditionally used to open or close the weekly sacrament meeting. Other hymns deriving from the psalms—such as "Father in Heaven"[15] or "Precious Savior, Dear Redeemer"[16]—are connected more closely with the sacred ordinance of the sacrament. The purposes of the psalms and of music is to create a sacred time and space and to bring the soul into communion with God. In Latter-day Saint worship services, an opening hymn is always sung, demarcating the movement into sacred time and space, a movement into a holier sphere. The second hymn, usually sung by the congregation prior to the ordinance of sacrament, then signifies an additional movement into an even holier space, a holy of holies in which Latter-day Saints seek to symbolically enter into the presence of God through the sacrament ordinance. The closing hymn demarcates the end of this sacred time and a movement back into more typical patterns of behavior and speech.

When Joseph Smith restored the practice of ancient temple worship, weekly Latter-day Saint worship services retained a feeling similar to Protestant worship, focused on preaching the word, singing, and celebrating the sacrament. More involved ritual ordinances were reserved for the holy precincts of the temple, which left behind lower-church Protestant practices to restore, from a Latter-day Saint perspective, the higher-church practices to their proper place. Although temple practices do not include singing psalms today (except during temple dedications, when music is common), the nature of instruction might be considered as similar to singing in many ways: the call and response used in the temple, the physical engagement of the body in the temple ordinances, and the prescribed, orderly nature of these ritual behaviors all serve to mark the entrance into sacred space and time, with the actions marking the movement through the ritual stages of separation, liminality, and aggregation. Latter-day Saint temple worship mirrors, in some respects, the ancient liturgical purpose of the psalms in ways that are not immediately apparent.

IMAGERY OF THE DAY OF ATONEMENT

The Passover is the Mosaic festival most overtly connected to Christ's passion in the New Testament.[17] According to the three Synoptic Gospels, Christ himself provided the imagery when he used the Passover meal (see Luke 22:15) to celebrate his atoning sacrifice, thereby preparing the way for the later Christian rite of communion or Eucharist, called the sacrament by Latter-day Saints.[18] "While they were eating, Jesus took bread, and when he had given thanks, he broke it and gave it to his disciples, saying, 'Take and eat; this is my body.' Then he took a cup, and when he had given thanks, he gave it to them, saying, 'Drink from it, all of you. This is my blood of the covenant, which is poured out for many for the forgiveness of sins'" (Matthew 26:26–28 New International Version). Paul also presented Christ as the Passover lamb, emphasizing the image of the feast of unleavened bread—the communal meal located outside the boundaries of the temple: "For Christ, our Passover lamb, has been sacrificed. Therefore let us keep the Festival, not with the old bread leavened with malice and wickedness, but with the unleavened bread of sincerity and truth" (1 Corinthians 5:7–8 NIV).

Notwithstanding the central imagery of the Passover sacrifice and meal,[19] they were not the only Mosaic practices that provided foundational symbols for Christianity. The imagery from the Day of Atonement, the most sacred festival of the Jewish year, was prevalent in descriptions of Jesus's redemptive mission as found in the Epistle to the Hebrews and elsewhere.[20] It also supplied symbolic imagery for Christian sacraments such as the communion or Eucharist. In similar ways, Book of Mormon authors relied upon images and themes from the Day of Atonement. Although Latter-day Saints do not observe the Day of Atonement as a holy day or engage in Day of

Atonement practices as found in the biblical text or in modern Jewish practice, Latter-day Saint ordinances also build upon images rooted in the Day of Atonement. Both traditional Christian and Latter-day Saint sacraments take on added meaning when viewed through the light of the high priest's divine ascent into the holy of holies on the Day of Atonement. The festival of Yom Kippur was the "acme of all temple rituals."[21] It continues to exert influence in Christianity today, although that influence is rarely recognized.

Even though the westward journey of the priest—through the doors of the temple into the holy place and to the altar of incense before the veil—was reenacted on a daily basis, only the activities of Yom Kippur completed the imagery of the return into the presence of God, as the high priest was allowed to pass the cherubim or angels stitched upon the veil into the symbolic presence of God displayed by his throne, the mercy seat (Hebrew *kapporet*) in the holy of holies.[22] This high-priestly procession reflects the journey of Israel past the cherubim placed eastward of Eden and back into the presence of God, reversing the effects of the fall of Adam and Eve. Entrance into the presence of God entailed the risk of death if the high priest was not appropriately prepared through proper dress, rituals of washing and anointing, the offering of designated sacrifices, and the tenfold repetition of the name of God[23] (pronounced only by the high priest and only on this most sacred of days).[24] The danger of entering the presence of God explains one of the symbolic purposes of the cherubim: to protect mankind from inappropriate entrance but also to grant entrance when the individual was appropriately prepared and authorized. The Day of Atonement was the only day of the year that allowed the community of Israel as a whole to receive absolution from its sins. The loss of the temple in 70 CE was deeply felt by Jews and presumably had a significant impact on Christians as well.[25] Since the loss of the temple, Jews continue to treat Yom Kippur as the most sacred day of the year. Like some of the Christian practices that will be described in the next section (and as a likely influence on those practices), Jewish worship on Yom Kippur built on temple imagery with significant and necessary modifications. No longer are priests or priestly descendants a significant part of the Yom Kippur liturgy (although the rabbi might be viewed as playing a complementary role). The curtain, or *parochet*, that covers the ark of the biblical scroll is removed during the service, but it is only reminiscent of the veil covering the holy of holies in the ancient temple and is not viewed as its equivalent.

NEW TESTAMENT AND LATER CHRISTIAN USE OF DAY OF ATONEMENT IMAGERY

No New Testament passages develop the connection of the symbolic imagery of the Day of Atonement with Jesus's offering more extensively than the Epistle to the Hebrews (typically dated ca. 60–95 CE). Hebrews 9 outlines the imagery of the tabernacle, in a sense re-creating the journey of the high priest through the tabernacle on the Day of Atonement:

> Now the first covenant had regulations for worship and also an earthly sanctuary. A tabernacle was set up. In its first room were the lampstand and the table with its consecrated bread; this was called the Holy Place. Behind the second curtain was a room called the Most Holy Place, which had the golden altar of incense and the gold-covered ark of the covenant. . . . Above the ark were the cherubim of the Glory, overshadowing the atonement cover. (Greek *hilastērion*, Hebrews 9:1–5 NIV)

The passage goes on to describe that the priests proceeded only to the westernmost side of the holy place, before the veil, and that only the high priest, on one day of the year (the Day of Atonement), proceeded beyond the holy place and into the holy of holies (see 9:6–7). Even the high priest would enter the holiest place only after preparing carefully with the sacrifice of an animal (imagery pointing to the altar of sacrifice) along with gifts of food and drink (pointing to the table of showbread), ceremonial washings (pointing to the laver of water), and other "external regulations" (9:9–10).

Christ, on the other hand, entered into the presence of God by virtue of his own blood (Hebrews 9:12). After reviewing the significance of Jesus's offering, Hebrews uses the imagery of the divine ascent to encourage Christians forward into the presence of God. In the past only the high priest could enter God's presence, and this only as symbolized by the earthly tabernacle. Now all can walk the divine way (see Hebrews 10:20), entering into God's presence in heaven because of Jesus's atoning sacrifice:

> Therefore, brothers and sisters, since we have confidence to enter the Most Holy Place by the blood of Jesus, by a new and living way opened for us through the curtain, that is, his body, and since we have a great priest over the house of God, let us draw near to God with a sincere heart and with the full assurance that faith brings, having our hearts sprinkled to cleanse us from a guilty conscience and having our bodies washed with pure water. (Hebrews 10:19–22)

In these verses, the imagery of the Day of Atonement serves to remind Christians of the importance of faith in the atoning blood of Christ sprinkled upon them and of having their bodies washed with pure water (using the imagery of the laver, probably to suggest Christian baptism).

Historically, Christians did not only use connections with the Day of Atonement in their texts, but they also implemented them in their liturgy. Beginning in the second century, bishops and others who officiated in mass were called "high priests" and "priests," officiating by authority of the "high priesthood."[26] The *hilastērion* (that is, "place of atonement") became the holy of holies in the Greek church, where the emblem of the Divine Liturgy—the blood of the sacrifice—was carried by the Christian "high priest." *Anaphora* is the Greek word in the Septuagint used for the priestly offering of a sacrifice under the Mosaic covenant. This word is used in Eastern Orthodox Christian services as a title for the priestly prayer in which the sacred name of God is spoken through priestly authority and the symbols of bread and wine are consecrated as the body and blood of Christ in the holiest section at the rear of the church. The area is separated by a veil—known as an iconostasis in Orthodox churches—on which are typically found the images of Mary or other saints (mirroring the cherubim on the temple veil). Incense (mirroring the altar of incense) is often lit before this veil or iconostasis and is kept burning during the liturgical celebration. At times the emblems of the Eucharist are placed behind the curtain, veil, or separation and in the holy of holies on the holy table, sometimes referred to as a throne. With its position standing in the holy of holies, this table can appropriately signify the mercy seat over which the Eucharist is prepared and consecrated as Christ's flesh and blood, meaning that God's presence dwells there over the table. After the high priestly prayer, the emblems of the Eucharist are brought out, still covered in a veil or cloth, which is then removed following more prayer, allowing the worshippers to enter symbolically into the presence of God in replication of the divine ascent.[27]

DAY OF ATONEMENT IMAGERY IN LATTER-DAY SAINT SACRED TEXTS: THE BOOK OF MORMON[28]

The Book of Mormon prophet known as Nephi used the imagery of the high priestly ascent into the holy of holies to teach "the doctrine of Christ" (2 Nephi 31:2), a term also found in the King James Version[29] of Hebrews 6:1, where it is connected with faith, repentance, baptism, the laying on of hands (presumably for the gift of the Holy Ghost), judgment, and resurrection. As with Hebrews 8–10, Hebrews 6 encourages the saints to continue in diligence by hope until the end (see Hebrews 6:11, 15), allowing the worshipper to pass beyond the veil into the holy of holies (see Hebrews 6:19), thus following the example of Christ, who passed there first as "a fore-runner" (Hebrews 6:20). Nephi's account is structured to follow a similar trajectory, showing how Christ first set the example in ful-filling the doctrine of Christ as forerunner, then demonstrating how Christ's disciples must follow that example, continuing on from the first principles and ordinances to enter into the presence of God and know him face to face (see 2 Nephi 31:11–12).

The imagery of the divine way or ascent begins outside the tem-ple/tabernacle with the preparatory behavior of repentance, moving by faith to and then past the altar of sacrifice—which Jesus states is the sacrifice of a repentant, "broken heart and a contrite spirit" (3 Nephi 9:20)—then to the ordinance of baptism, symbolized by the laver of water. Baptism by water then leads along the strait path or way (as in Hebrews 10:20). The way or path leads through the narrow gate symbolized by entrance into the temple proper. Here, inside God's house, as a covenant member of the household of God (see Ephesians 2:19), the worshipper can receive the baptism of fire and see by the light of the Holy Ghost, potentially symbolized by the blazing menorah or lampstand inside. As Nephi states it, "Where-fore, do the things which I have told you I have seen that your Lord and your Redeemer should do; for, for this cause have they been shown unto me, that ye might know the gate by which ye should enter. For the gate by which ye should enter is repentance and bap-tism by water; and then cometh a remission of your sins by fire and by the Holy Ghost" (2 Nephi 31:17). Again, repentance (symbolized by the altar of sacrifice) and baptism (symbolized by the laver of water) lead the worshipper through the narrow gate (symbolized by the temple doors) and into the covenant community (symbolized by the temple). Then the disciple receives the Holy Ghost (symbolized by the blazing menorah) and is prepared to move forward.

At that point, standing inside the doors of the temple, the image of cherubim or guardian angels would be visible on the other end of the well-lit room, encouraging the worshipper forward to the veil, the curtain that protected and led into the holy of holies. Nephi teaches that "feasting" on the words of Christ and receiving the Holy Ghost will allow the disciples to move forward on the holy way and learn to "speak with the tongue of angels."

> I suppose that ye ponder somewhat in your hearts concerning that which ye should do after ye have entered in by the way. But, behold, why do ye ponder these things in your hearts? Do ye not remember that I said unto you that after ye had received the Holy Ghost ye could speak with the tongue of angels? And now, how could ye speak with the tongue of angels save it were by the Holy Ghost? Angels speak by the power of the Holy Ghost; wherefore, they speak the words of Christ. Wherefore, I said unto you, feast upon the words of Christ. (2 Nephi 32:1–3)

The image on which Nephi is relying to impel his audience forward, "feasting" on the words of Christ, is that provided in the holy place by the table of showbread, on which stood bread and wine. This bread and wine provided a symbolic, communal feast with God, symbolizing the strengthening power of the word of God (and possibly also symbolizing the importance of the Eucharist or sacrament) to move forward in the name and power of Christ.

The worshipper has now proceeded past the menorah and the table of showbread and stands before the altar of incense at the veil. Although the altar of incense was not used in the description of the divine ascent in Hebrews, the New Testament interprets the altar of incense as a symbol for prayer (see Revelation 8:3 and Luke 1:10). Accordingly, at this point in Nephi's description Nephi states that if the readers cannot understand what he is trying to teach, it is because they "ask not, neither do [they] knock" (2 Nephi 32:4). The key to move forward, speaking with the tongue of angels, is found through praying, asking, or knocking at the veil, which leads to the holy of holies.

The worshipper is left at the veil, seeking to speak the tongue of angels by a reliance on the word of God and the gift of the Holy Ghost. Nephi then states that this is as far as the doctrine of Christ can take them: "Behold, this is the doctrine of Christ, and there will be no more doctrine given" (2 Nephi 32:6). Nephi continues, however, showing how the divine ascent will conclude: "There will be no more doctrine given until after he shall manifest himself unto you in the flesh. And when he shall manifest himself unto you in the flesh, the things which he shall say unto you shall ye observe to do" (2 Nephi 32:6). Nephi has promised that if the worshipper will endure appropriately, it is possible to pass through the veil and enter into the presence of God, seeing him face to face in the flesh.[30] He then indicates how sacred this knowledge is, stating that the Spirit will not allow him to say more. He mourns at the foolishness of mankind, "for they will not search knowledge, nor understand great knowledge, when it is given unto them in plainness, even as plain as word can be" (2 Nephi 32:7). He has taught the reader in language as simple and plain as possible how to enter into the presence of God, but he worries that the message will be lost. He therefore backtracks, reminding the worshipper that the key to understanding is prayer (see 2 Nephi 32:9). Prayer and asking, or knocking, are what will allow the reader to conclude the divine ascent.

Moroni's edited account of the brother of Jared—although he lived centuries before the existence of Moses's tabernacle or the temple of Solomon—demonstrates an abbreviated form of this same divine ascent. He has ascended into a mountain and is praying for divine assistance. His mighty prayer of faith is the key that allows him to enter into God's presence (see Ether 3:1–6). In response to his plea, God pierces the veil resting upon the mind of the brother of Jared (see Moroni's specific use of veil language in Ether 3:6, 19, 20; 4:15; 12:19, 21), and he is allowed to see God's finger as it touches the stones God has prepared. Having seen God's hand, the brother of Jared longs to see more. Taking the first glimpse of God's hand as evidence that God has a visible body and that God will allow him to see his entire body, the brother of Jared boldly pushes through the veil to stand in the presence of God, completing the process of the divine ascent.

LATTER-DAY SAINT ORDINANCES AND
THE DAY OF ATONEMENT

In many respects, Latter-day Saint chapel worship may seem devoid of this divine pattern found in its most central sacred text. This absence may exist primarily because that imagery—the highest of divine ritual patterns provided by the Mosaic covenant, allowed in its fullest expression only on the Day of Atonement—was designed by Joseph Smith as part of modern Latter-day Saint temple practice. From a Latter-day Saint perspective, after the destruction of the temple Christians began to adopt and adapt temple practices into their church religious worship, thus situating practices intended for the temple within the confines of the church building.[31] Since most Christians came to view temples as a fixture of Old Testament practices that provided a foundation for Christian worship, this would not have been considered inappropriate. When the Reformation occurred, Protestants questioned these strange liturgical forms. Not seeing them clearly delineated in the New Testament and thus believing they were not a part of true, biblical worship, they eliminated them from their worship services. As discussed in the section on psalms, Latter-day Saints, who do believe in the importance of temples, maintain simple styles in their church worship that reflect Protestant practice. They have placed high church worship in the temple.

That being said, imagery from the Day of Atonement can be found in all Latter-day Saint ordinances of salvation. First, Day of Atonement imagery is found in the sacrament. In that ordinance, priests stand at the veil to the presence of God, as symbolized by the cloth covering the elements of the sacrament. One kneels at the veil, pronouncing a priestly prayer that clearly states the name of God while the entire congregation also prays for the forgiveness of sins. At times, in a manner similar to the Day of Atonement, the congregation comes fasting to this ordinance. The congregation always comes in mourning, with broken heart and contrite spirit (see 2 Nephi 2:7). After the prayer, the priests gain access to the presence of God through the veil that has been parted. They then deliver the symbols of God's presence to other priesthood holders, who invite the congregation, one by one, symbolically into the presence of God. The bishopric could be seen as having the role of the guardian cherubim, overseeing the process and ensuring that it is done correctly, both through worthiness interviews with individual members and through verifying the correct performance of prayers and procedures during the ordinance. It is highly dangerous to enter into the presence of God. Indeed, both Paul and Jesus stated that whoever eats and drinks unworthily "eateth and drinketh damnation to his soul" (3 Nephi 18:29; see 1 Corinthians 11:29).

Baptism and confirmation in the Latter-day Saint tradition serve as other examples of the divine ascent. The disciple has been interviewed by the bishop, or by a missionary, who acts as an angelic guardian of the path into the presence of God and seeks to help the worshipper enter God's presence appropriately (see Moroni 6:1–6). The individual brings a "broken heart and a contrite spirit" (3 Nephi 9:20), has demonstrated repentance, and has changed clothes, typically dressing all in white. Two figures stand as witnesses at the edge of the baptismal font, guarding the pathway into the presence of God. The priest officiates, declaring his authority and speaking the name of Father, Son, and Holy Ghost while signifying his authority by his upraised arm. He then lowers the disciple backwards into the water, symbolic of death or the fall of Adam and Eve. Immediately after, he pulls the participant upward through the veil of the baptismal waters into a new life as part of God's covenant people "in the household of God." The divine ascent is completed in the ordinance of confirmation as God uses the priesthood holder to reach his hands through the veil, as they are placed on the disciple's head, and as the worshipper is granted the authority and power to always stand in the presence of the Spirit of God, provided she or he maintains the appropriate standards of worthiness. The high level of risk entailed by this new status is signified by the title of the unforgiveable sin, believed by Latter-day Saints to be possible only as a full and overt rejection of God after having entered purposely and knowledgably into his covenant family. To "blaspheme against the Holy Ghost," according to Mark 3:29, is a sin that puts one in danger of eternal damnation.

Latter-day Saint temple practices reveal Day of Atonement imagery most clearly. Entering the temple, the worshipper immediately finds the way forward impeded by two priesthood holders, waiting to check the patron's temple recommend, which was granted earlier in a dual interview process with the Latter-day Saint bishop and then stake president, who stand as guardians, seeking to ascertain full preparation to enter the temple. One of the most sacred ordinances available for Latter-day Saints is known as the endowment. It entails a symbolic journey, mirroring the Latter-day Saint understanding of Adam and Eve's journey out of the Garden of Eden into mortality and back toward the presence of God through making sacred covenants. The ordinance is replete with veil symbolism, angelic guides and guardians, learning to "speak the tongue of angels," and a symbolic movement back into God's presence in what is known as the celestial room. Although not openly discussed by Latter-day Saints, the temple re-creates the ancient biblical concept of the divine ascent in the most overt form found in the religion. As Brigham Young put it, "Your endowment is, to receive all those ordinances in the house of the Lord, which are necessary for you, after you have departed this life, to enable you to walk back to the presence of the Father, passing the angels who stand as sentinels, being enabled to give them the key words."[32]

CONCLUSION

Although Latter-day Saint worship is certainly not known for its liturgical richness, its worship patterns and religious rituals do exhibit biblical features, particularly those mirroring the divine ascent into the presence of God. The use of psalms, both in singing during sacrament worship services and in thematic connection with temple worship, and the application of Day of Atonement imagery demonstrate the desire to connect with the divine by building on the foundations of biblical understandings and practices.

NOTES

1. This section of the chapter is almost entirely drawn from a previously published paper: Shon D. Hopkin and J. Arden Hopkin, "The Psalms Sung: The Power of Music in Ancient Worship," in *Ascending the Mountain of the Lord: Temple, Praise, and Worship in the Old Testament*, ed. David R. Seely, Jeffrey R. Chadwick, and Matthew J. Grey (Salt Lake City: Deseret Book, 2013), 331–50.

2. See, for a few examples, Sigmund Mowinckel, *The Psalms in Israel's Worship*, trans. D. R. Ap-Thomas (Oxford: Basil Blackwell, 1962), 2:29–31; Svend Holm-Nielsen, "The Importance of Late Jewish Psalmody for the Understanding of the Psalmodic Tradition," *Studia Theologica* 14, no. 1 (1960): 1–53; Erhard S. Gerstenberger, *Psalms Part I: With an Introduction to Cultic Poetry* (Grand Rapids, MI: Eerdmans, 1988), 108–13; Claus Westermann, *Praise and Lament in the Psalms* (Edinburgh: T. & T. Clark, 1981), 64–79; Margaret Barker, *Temple Themes in Christian Worship* (London: Bloomsbury T&T Clark, 2008); Laurence Paul Hemming, "With the Voice Together Shall They Sing," *BYU Studies Quarterly* 50, no. 1 (2011): 25–45; Andrew Wilson-Dickson, *The Story*

of *Christian Music: From Gregorian Chant to Black Gospel*, 1st ed. (Oxford: Lion Book, 1992). 20; William Lee Holladay, *The Psalms through Three Thousand Years: Prayerbook of a Cloud of Witnesses* (Minneapolis: Fortress Press, 1993), 17–18.

3. Holm-Nielsen, "Importance of Late Jewish Psalmody," 1–53.

4. Baruch A. Levine, "Leviticus, Book of," in *Anchor Bible Dictionary*, ed. David Noel Freedman (New York: Doubleday, 1992), 4:311–21.

5. John Alexander Lamb, *The Psalms in Christian Worship* (London: Faith Press, 1962), 47–69.

6. Lamb, *Psalms in Christian Worship*, 80–127.

7. Walterus Truron, "The Rhythm of Metrical-Psalm Tunes," *Music and Letters* 9, no. 1 (1928): 29–33. See also Charles P. St-Onge, "Music, Worship and Martin Luther" (working paper, Concordia Theological Seminary, Fort Wayne, Indiana, 2003).

8. Karl Kroeger, "Dynamics in Early American Psalmody," *College Music Symposium* 26 (1986): 100–103.

9. Kroeger, "Dynamics in Early American Psalmody," 105.

10. Kroeger, "Dynamics in Early American Psalmody," 105.

11. The psalms that either have been put to music in the current Latter-day Saint hymnal or are somewhat reflected in the hymns are Psalms 5, 8, 16, 23, 25–33, 36, 37, 43, 47, 48, 55, 62, 68, 69, 73, 82, 84, 86, 87, 90–92, 95, 97–100, 104, 107, 119, 121, 126, 138, 143, and 145–50.

12. William Bullock, "We Love Thy House, O God," *Hymns* (Salt Lake City: The Church of Jesus Christ of Latter-day Saints, 1985), no. 247.

13. Folliott S. Pierpoint, "For the Beauty of the Earth," *Hymns*, no. 92.

14. Charles Wesley, "Rejoice, the Lord Is King!," *Hymns*, no. 66.

15. Angus S. Hibbard, "Father in Heaven," *Hymns*, no. 133.

16. H. R. Palmer, "Precious Savior, Dear Redeemer," *Hymns*, no. 103.

17. "The most distinctive appropriation of a Judaic festival within the church was occasioned by Passover." See Bruce D. Chilton, "Festivals and Holy Days: Jewish," in *Dictionary of New Testament Background*, ed. Craig A. Evans and Stanley R. Porter (Downers Grove, IL: InterVarsity Press, 2000), 376.

18. Matthew 26:1–25; Mark 14:1–24; Luke 22:1–20; John 13:1. For the earliest account of the Last Supper, see Paul's description in 1 Corinthians 11:23–26.

19. The Old Testament Passover provided much of the structuring symbolism for the Christian Eucharist. It was a time when the Lord "passed over" the children of Israel and did not destroy them because of the identifying mark of the blood of the lamb upon their doorposts, just as the identifying mark of the Eucharist identifies Christians. Passover was a time that celebrated the departure of Israel from the world. It was a time when the Israelites removed the leaven from their homes and their lives, both as a symbol of the urgency to depart from their captive state and later as a symbol of removing sin. The lamb without blemish was killed in a joyous festival that celebrated the planting of seeds in the ground, as Jesus's body would be planted in the ground. All of these themes provided an excellent foundation for the rite designed to reconnect Christian disciples with God as they departed from sin and became unified with Christ by partaking of his flesh and blood.

20. Other New Testament authors write about Jesus as the "Lamb of God" (John 1:29), as a "sheep [led] to the slaughter" (Acts 8:32, quoting Isaiah 53:7), and as "a lamb without blemish and without spot" (1 Peter 1:19). These references can connect Jesus either with the daily burnt offering, with the Passover lamb, or with other temple offerings.

21. Daniel Stökl Ben Ezra, *The Impact of Yom Kippur on Early Christianity: The Day of Atonement from Second Temple Judaism to the Fifth Century* (Tübingen, Germany: Mohr Siebeck, 2003), 28.

22. For this understanding, see Exodus 25:21; 1 Samuel 4:4; 2 Samuel 6:2; 2 Kings 19:15; 1 Chronicles 13:6; Psalms 80:1; 99:1; Isaiah 37:16.

23. This is a late tradition recorded in Jerusalem Talmud *Yoma* 3:7 and in the Babylonian Talmud *Yoma* 39:2. The two sources differ as to when the name was pronounced.

24. "The sanctuary purification is a very dangerous chore, so special precautions must be taken. If these were not observed, the officiator would perish (Lev 16:2, 13)." David P. Wright, "Day of Atonement," *Anchor Yale Bible Dictionary*, 2:73. The legend of a rope tied around the waist or ankle of the high priest in order to pull out his body if he dies in the presence of the Lord is not found until medieval times.

25. See Hugh Nibley, "Christian Envy of the Temple," *Jewish Quarterly Review* 50 (1959–60): 97–123, 229–40; reprinted in Nibley, *Mormonism and Early Christianity* (Provo, UT: FARMS; Salt Lake City: Deseret Book, 1987), 391–434.

26. G. W. H. Lampe, ed., *A Patristic Greek Lexicon* (Oxford: Oxford University Press, 1978), 239.

27. Cyprian, Epistle 63, in *Ante-Nicene Fathers: Fathers of the Third Century*, vol. 5, trans. Ernest Wallis (Edinburgh, 1885), 63:14:4.

28. The connection between divine ascent imagery and 2 Nephi 32 in the Book of Mormon is not a traditional, long-standing interpretation of that text. I first proposed it in Shon D. Hopkin, "Representing the Divine Ascent: The Day of Atonement in Christian and Nephite Scripture and Practice," in *The Temple: Ancient and Restored* (Salt Lake City: Eborn Books, 2016), 325–48. This section of the paper is closely connected to that paper.

29. The King James Version is the preferred translation in The Church of Jesus Christ of Latter-day Saints.

30. This, of course, is not the only interpretation of this verse. On another level, Nephi could also be teaching the Nephites that they need to follow their current understanding and the practices of the law of Moses until Christ will appear to them (as recorded in 3 Nephi 11). At that point, they should follow the teachings that he brings. Although this is in one sense the most straightforward understanding of 2 Nephi 32:6, the following verse, in which Nephi mourns that his readers will misunderstand his true intent, seems to indicate that he is communicating another message that could be missed, although it was explained with great clarity.

31. See Nibley, "Christian Envy of the Temple."
32. John Widtsoe, ed., *Discourses of Brigham Young* (Salt Lake City: Deseret Book, 1954), 416.

CULTURE AND POLITICS

PART FOUR

The final section of this book, part four, "Culture and Politics," shows that although Jews and Latter-day Saints often bind themselves to community through religious ties, this is not the only place in which both groups can or should engage with one another. Holli Levitsky, a scholar of literature, explores the cultural representations of Jews in American Jewish literature. In a number of discussions during the dialogue, there were common conclusions about the ways that Jews and Latter-day Saints have been portrayed in film and literature. Levitsky's piece here is an exemplary look at how those portrayals developed and what they mean.

Steven Windmueller adds statistical data to portray and examine Jewish attitudes of Zionism, Israel, and political engagement. His expertise in these areas provides rich data and commentaries on the place of Israel in contemporary Jewish American society. Although largely focused on political activity, Windmueller also provides room for reflection on how communities engage with these important topics in their framing of identity and place in the modern world.

In response to Windmueller's article, Quin Monson and Kelly Duncan provide a reciprocal look at Zionism and attitudes toward Israel among Latter-day Saints and evangelical Christians, providing a careful reflection on differences and similarities between these two communities.

13

A LIMITED HISTORY OF JEWISH AMERICAN LITERATURE

HOLLI G. LEVITSKY

FORMATION OF A CANON

Following World War II, colleges and universities in the United States began to expand their courses of study to meet the needs of new populations of students. Young men of all social and economic classes returning from the war took advantage of the GI Bill to enroll in degree programs they otherwise could not afford. Colleges welcomed veterans, women, and recently arrived European immigrants into the academy with open arms, and newly formed liberal arts curricula grew into rigorous specialized disciplinary programs. In the relatively new departments of English, subdisciplines began to form, expanding the teaching of English literature into the teaching of literature in English. For decades, such departments had been teaching oratory, oral composition, and linguistics, only adding literature to the teaching of English at the very end of the nineteenth century. At this time, English literature was primarily comprised of the writings of Geoffrey Chaucer, John Milton, and William Shakespeare, among others. (These institutionalized classics grew into the canon of Great Literature, universally accepted authors and texts impervious to change until the outbreak of the culture wars that began in the 1980s and that continue to battle within today's English departments.) The study of popular fiction, poetry, and drama and the emergence of subdisciplines (such as global or world literature in English)—as opposed to the literary classics—was a welcome addition to the campus curriculum. In many cases, English departments offered tracks of study in American literature, which was at the time considered popular rather than classic or canonical. Over time, a canon of American literature eventually developed, and many of the sources are still taught today as canonical.[1]

Still, as a newly formed canon, American literature necessarily evolved and shifted. A hard definition of an American national literature was challenged by the successful publication of many new books in the 1950s and 1960s. Many of these writers were Jewish. As their books were read by the American public and discussed by reviewers and critics, the conversations shaped a canon of Jewish American *belles lettres*, and the subdiscipline of Jewish American literature began to form within the study of American literature. (An illustration of the popularity of ethnic American literature as a subject of scholarly study can be seen in the dozens of subdisciplines formed under the umbrella organization of the ALA [American Literature Association],[2] including Jewish American literature, which itself gave birth to the subdiscipline of American Holocaust literature.) With the new wealth of Jewish American authors, texts, and critics, graduate students in English could study Jewish American authors and undertake thesis and dissertation projects in the field. Undergraduates in American literature survey courses might find a few Jewish American writers represented in their American literature anthologies. Decisions about inclusion in these anthologies were generally made by a small body of men who were published scholars or series editors for major academic presses. It's hard to say why some writings made it into anthologies while others did not. Certainly there were more than a few factors to consider at each turn, although this first wave of celebrated Jewish American writing included Jewish writers only, and only as part of a larger disciplinary canon of American literature.

This same era produced powerful literary and cultural critical voices, many of whom were Jewish, but whose erudition was directed primarily at American literature at large. This general focus did not prevent the first critical studies of Jewish writers and thematic works on Judaism during this same era. According to many of these literary critics (including Leslie Fiedler, Lionel Trilling, Irving Howe, and others),[3] in looking backwards, a particular Jewish literary history could be seen to emerge in the twentieth century. In consideration of books written about Jews by Jews, the critics organized their findings into three general categories that correspond to historical eras and thematic exigencies:

1. During the late nineteenth and early twentieth centuries, literary writing by Jews mostly addressed the immigrant experience. Abraham Cahan's *The Rise of David Levinsky*, Henry Roth's *Call It Sleep*, and Anzia Yezierska's *Bread Givers* offer deeply drawn Jewish characters who experience different social and economic worlds. As immigrants, each of these authors struggled to employ English in ways that met the artistic demands of literature and that conveyed the reality of their immigrant experience.

2. The midcentury era—through the 1960s—brought attention to a trio of writers who considered themselves more American and less Jewish: Saul Bellow, Bernard Malamud, and Philip Roth (who died only a few months before this writing in 2018). These writers wrote about the Jew in American life as a (mostly) assimilated figure still experiencing life through the lens of religion and culture but whose Jewishness was at times no more than a single factor of identity.

3. From the 1960s, writers began to address what Freud might call "the return of the repressed" and began to tackle the Holocaust through the imagination. Writing early in that era, Edward Lewis

Wallant's searing novel *The Pawnbroker*, about Holocaust survivor Sol Nazerman, is considered the first American postwar Holocaust novel. As more details about the Jewish catastrophe in Europe surfaced, Jewish American novelists of note—such as Joseph Heller, Cynthia Ozick, and Marge Piercy, among others—tackled the Holocaust both directly and obliquely.[4]

In each historical period, writings by Jews reflected the American context in significant ways, including American views toward Jews and Jewishness. The eras of Jewish life represented in these critical studies map to both synchronic and diachronic trends, which literary scholars continued to follow to the end of the twentieth century and up to the present moment. From the 1980s onward, Jewish American literary output has flourished, producing some of the best writing in English. Literary and cultural critics continue to map this writing, identifying authors and their works that grapple with the ever-larger, modern implications of American Jewishness, Holocaust postmemory, Jewish emigration, and more. Some of the more celebrated of these authors include Michael Chabon, Jonathon Safran Foer, and Nicole Krauss—to name only a few.[5]

If we seek to be inclusive, acknowledging the diversity of Jewish writing in the United States, Jewish literary creativity has existed since the first Jews arrived in New York in 1654 until this very moment. The earliest Jewish immigrants were Sephardic, descended from the many thousands of Jews expelled from Spain and Portugal beginning in 1492. In the eighteenth century, they were joined by Ashkenazi immigrants from London, the British Caribbean, and the Continent.[6] Thus the canon of Jewish American literature includes writers of Yiddish and Hebrew, spoken by Ashkenazi Jews, and those raised in other hybrid-linguistic environments, such as Ladino or Judeo-Arabic.[7] Some wrote only in their national language (i.e., German, Romanian) even if they were not citizens of that land. Jewish American literary activity has equally embraced diverse genres; writers communicated through public and private platforms available for consumption to all who were literate, including, from the earliest years, such forms as petitions, sermons, diaries, public and private letters, prayers, historical dramas, poetry, newspaper columns, editorials, articles, and serialized novels. The common element among the writers might only have been that they were Jewish.

These historical voices suggest that Jewish writing is expansive. It has room for many possibilities, including gentile writers who depict Jewish characters. As we will see, in the earliest days, some of the most positive depictions of Jews came from the pens of gentiles. Yoking together Jewish and non-Jewish representations of the Jewish image provides a multidimensional and multidirectional literary history, one in which the image changes and evolves in contact with American life and culture. The result is a deeper understanding of Judaism in America and the challenges and opportunities faced by its Jewish citizens and immigrants.

DECONSTRUCTING THE CANON

In general accordance with these categorizations, the critical assembly of such material must be synthesized on a level of consistency that operates on both a thematic and a historical level, and there are few better ways to do this than to reassemble the material in newly significant ways, from new perspectives, and through a modern lens. And what better way to guide these new perspectives than by asking questions? Perhaps the most important area of questioning is the meaningfulness of retaining Jewish identity in America (and what that Jewish identity looks like). In essence, how does American literature represent Jewish identity through its cultural transitions in America? Have writings by and about Jews and Jewish life in America helped to preserve it? Can there be a "Jewish American" literary canon without a clear definition of "Jewishness" as it evolves over time?

As I hope to show, Jewishness was once considered an important theme of American literature, particularly in the 1960s; however, postmodern, poststructuralist literary theories, such as deconstruction, called into question such thematic codification, and the general significance of the term began to dwindle in conjunction with a solidified, established meaning. Suddenly, to talk about the Jew in American literature begged the question of "What is a Jew?" and "What is Jewishness?"[8] As identity politics began to insert itself into literary studies, the inevitable question became "What is Jewish literature?" "Must it be written by a Jew?"—the definition of which had already been called into question. "Must it cover a Jewish theme?"—the category of which had also already been called into question. "Or must it have Jewish characters?"—an aspect that had long dominated the study of the Jewish image in literature in general.

My contribution can be divided into a brief, limited historiography of the image and self-image of the American Jew, as reflected in *belles lettres*—a discussion of how, rather than what, Jewish literature within the larger category of American literature is considered today. My discussion of both the shifting image of the Jew in literature by Jews and non-Jews, as well as the more contemporary scholarly understanding of what Jewish literature is, has been informed by the following three studies:

1. Louis Harap's *The Image of the Jew in American Literature: From Early Republic to Mass Immigration*.[9] This book is an in-depth examination of the Jewish image in poetry, drama, and fiction written by Jewish and non-Jewish contributors from the late eighteenth century to around 1900.

2. Sol Liptzin's *The Jew in American Literature*[10] extensively examines the shifting meaning of Jewishness in America.

3. *The New Diaspora: The Changing Landscape of Jewish American Fiction*, edited by Victoria Aarons, Avinoam Patt, and Mark Shechner.[11] This book offers its theme and argument in the epigraph, quoted from Bernard Malamud's short story "Angel Levine": "'A wonderful thing, Fanny,' Manischevitz said. 'Believe me, there are Jews everywhere.'"

Each of these three now classic texts—two written eight years apart, the third forty years later—focuses on a particular era of American literary output by or about Jews while illustrating the existential question at the heart of the Jewish narrative: How do American Jews maintain their identity against the shifting landscape of American history? Each book, in its own time and way, helped popularize and romanticize Jewishness in American literature, validating its status in the canon.

After a lack of representation, the prevalence of Jewishness in literature—at least from a thematic standpoint—culminated in the 1960s, by which time Jewishness had become an important theme of American literature, assisted by the critical studies cited above. The Jew became a cultural staple of resistance, identity, and courage among United States intellectuals and artists. In 1965 Saul Bellow's outstanding bestseller *Herzog* encapsulated this newfound love of the thematic Jew.[12] *Herzog* is centered on the complicated world of a Jewish American childhood. In the many novels by Jewishly educated Bellow, Jewish characters play significant roles, and a Jewish milieu is quite common. In the same year, the non-Jewish writer James A. Michener repeated history with his bestseller *The Source*, a sweeping historical novel that surveys the entire history of the Jewish people from the premonotheistic days through the birth of the modern State of Israel.[13] Both books embody the 1960s' view of the significance and cultural resilience that Jewishness has been envisioned to represent—something that both American and Jewish audiences alike craved at the time.

As Jews assimilated into American life and culture, they were molded more by daily American experiences and, to a lesser degree, by ever-paling, ever-rarer Jewish experiences. Yet when the Holocaust emerged in global consciousness (during the internationally aired Eichmann trial in 1961), it became clear that the Jewish catastrophe disassociated Jewishness from the American experience. The Holocaust raised the existential specter of Jewish existence—

and thus identity—for all Jews, regardless of their level of practice or belief. More even than the meaningfulness of retaining Jewish identity, the Jewish American writers of the 1960s and 1970s were focused on the Jew as "other" in American life.

EARLIER AMERICAN CONNECTIONS TO JEWS

The colonial era solidified the connection between America and the Jews through the specifically Abrahamic language of the Bible. The holy book (which, to them, spelled out God's will) was the supreme authority for the Puritans who colonized New England. Hebrew, along with Latin and Greek, was considered a tremendously important language in religious and higher education and was taught by eminent scholars in the field and at such august institutions as Harvard and Yale, to name only two. Despite the presence of Jews in an ever-increasing number of colonies and despite the Jews' growing affluence and economic importance, they hardly influenced the new world order. It was biblical—not living—Judaism that inspired the creative minds of the era. Contemporary, living Jews were frequent targets of conversion. The early colonialists had a zeal for saving Jews for Christianity, but they were also of the mind that in order to save them, they needed all twelve tribes to accept the religion. To many Puritans, the evidence was irrefutable that the North American Indians were the offspring of the dispersed tribes of Israel.[14]

When the Continental Congress adopted the Declaration of Independence on July 4, 1776, it also approved a resolution appointing Benjamin Franklin, John Adams, and Thomas Jefferson as a committee to prepare a suitable seal for the newly proclaimed United States of America. There was general agreement that biblical symbolism was most appropriate. Franklin suggested that the seal ought to show Moses lifting up his wand, dividing the Red Sea, while Pharaoh was being overwhelmed by its waters. Jefferson proposed that it show the children of Israel in the wilderness, led by a cloud by day and a pillar of fire by night. The Great Seal, which was finally adopted after careful consideration, shows a pyramid representing the thirteen colonies, topped by the all-seeing eye of Jehovah, who is surrounded by a cloud of glory—a symbol of the protecting Divine Presence.

As the new nation debated the shape of the governmental structures, the ancient Hebrew commonwealth continued to serve as a model. Sermons at the time compared the "Republic of the Israelites" with the nascent American states, identifying the Israelite union of twelve tribes as a model for the American union of thirteen states. In their hope for ratification of the newly written American Constitution, the leaders of the commonwealth saw in the Hebrew Torah a complete code of laws—the merits of which founded themselves upon principles of reason, justice, and social virtue. One commonwealth leader wrote, "We cannot but acknowledge that God hath graciously patronized our cause, and taken us under his special care, as he did his ancient covenant people."[15] Under the adopted Constitution, the separation of church and state became a cardinal principle of American democracy, so whatever restrictions Jews suffered from in their respective states were abolished in the course of time; however, Jews continued to be judged by American viewers in light of their biblical past rather than on their collective achievement or contemporary significance, and the lack of almost any artistic representation of any kind proved foundational to perpetuating this one-dimensional perception. Certainly, there were no published creative literary figures among them throughout the colonial and revolutionary eras. Even as subjects for literature, Jewish people and the Jewish identity were generally unnoticed in the American cultural landscape before the nineteenth century.

Interestingly, the first notable image of a Jewish figure came in an 1858 novel by John Richter Jones, a non-Jewish writer who fictionalized the prominent revolutionary patriot Hayim Salomon as pawnbroker Solomon Isaacki. The character appeared multiple times, but the most prominent placement was in *The Quaker Soldier: Or, The British in Philadelphia*. His notability came not just from his heroism but also from his total portrayal differing from the offensive Jewish stereotypes that still emerged in English fiction. He was described as follows:

> The face and forehead were grand, full of intellect and benevolence with a slight seasoning of something like cunning, though not enough to impair the general effect; you could not but wonder what these features were doing on the shoulders of a pawnbroker. . . . In support of the cause of the Revolution none was more ready to sacrifice what men hold more precious; few were more meritorious.[16]

It was in the shop of this pawnbroker that the American patriots met and plotted against the British, and it was he who, at the close of the narrative, led the American rebels to the rescue of the heroine who had been abducted by the British. He is heroic but multidimensional rather than idealized.

Earlier in the same century—in the days of the young republic— there were literary Jews whose work made an impact on the American artistic vocabulary; however, for reasons that stretched varieties of both business purposes and personal values, most of them chose not to include Jewish figures or Jewish subjects in their plays, novels, and poetry. Despite a platform of potential expression, Jewish identity continued to suffer from egregious underrepresentation in light of the false, stereotypical misrepresentations popularized by non-Jewish creators—even with Jewish writers prevalent in the American literary scene. The most plausible explanation seems to be that Jewish writers did not want to present bad Jews and that audiences did not want to see good Jews represented—except biblical ones— despite the fact that readers and theatergoers might have pleasant daily contacts with Jews. American audiences had so long been fed on Shylock, the flint-hearted Jew of Venice; Barabas, the monstrous

Jew of Malta; and other villainous Jews by other English writers that they were not ready to accept Jewish characters that ran counter to the established tradition of the wicked and miserly stage-Jew.

Still, during those early days, with few exceptions, the New Englanders continued to see Jews in the light of biblical prophecy and Talmudic lore. The era's non-Jewish poets did not show keen insight into Jewish American reality but did glorify the Jewish past and revivify half-forgotten legends. They continued the tradition of philo-Semitism,[17] which had been brought to America's shores by their colonial forebears. Philo-Semitism was clearly the effect of see-ing Jews prophetically.

As Jews escaped the pogroms of Eastern Europe to seek refuge in America, Jewish Americans began to see the reality of life for their coreligionists. One of the most talented and influential Jewish lyric poets of the era, Emma Lazarus, was a crucial exception to the trend of Jewish creators excluding Jewish characters and subjects in their work. Lazarus, of course, was the author of the poem "The New Colossus," whose verses are engraved on the pedestal of the Statue of Liberty. While the poem does not directly reference Jews, Lazarus's inspiration came from her experiences in getting to know the refu-gees from the Russian pogroms firsthand. In them she recognized her kinsmen. She spent her life as a Jewish prophetess of sorts, using her poetry to urge Jews in America to, as one critic put it, "reestab-lish themselves as an independent nationality . . . awaken from their assimilationist delusions . . . raise again the banner of the Jew . . . let resound once more the battle anthems that led them to victory over pagans and idolaters and that ennobled them even in defeat."[18] She envisioned the rise and growth of two strong centers of Jewish creativity—Palestine and America. In both lands Jewish faith would flourish, Jewish talent would thrive, and Jewish culture would be in a constant exchange with both Eastern and Western cultures—being a part of both, as well. Her robust, poetic output carried that call to the masses.

With the beginning of mass immigration of Eastern European Jews in the 1880s, the reality of Jewish American life was bound to modify traditional stereotypes, which had been inherited from theological and fictional prototypes rather than reality. The dominant literary prototype was the villainous Jew of the English motherland as he had evolved during the centuries from such early writers as Chaucer, Marlowe, and Shakespeare to later authors like Walter Scott and Charles Dickens. The new immigrants bore no resemblance either to the literary stereotypes of Shylock and Fagin or to the more religious images of Abraham and Moses. Legend and reality were in conflict, so writers and audiences had to be reeducated to accept—as well as portray—the living human beings as real, breathing, Jewish humans, rather than as historical saints or mythical bogeys.

Russian Jews who immigrated from the 1880s until the First World War brought with them a hope for America as the "New Exodus," continuing the biblical reference point—that is, the metaphor of the promised land. In their stories, writers such as Abraham Cahan and Henry Roth recorded their battles for economic survival and their concern that Jews were turning away from traditional rituals of Orthodoxy (some even becoming atheists); instead, they observed, Jews were turning toward socialism, driven by reasons of alternate economic relief and continued hardship. Mary Antin, who titled her 1912 autobiography *The Promised Land*, created a literary sensation for detailing her successful assimilation to American ways and of her happy acceptance into American society.[19] With that said, before her death she turned from atheism back to Judaism. Anzia Yezierska, perhaps the most recognizable and influential of the Jewish immigrant writers of the era—and a talented realist—recorded the disappointment and weariness of the immigrants who anticipated the "golden country" but suffered poverty, cruelty, and obscurity instead.[20]

Between the two world wars, Jewish life increased in complexity and difficulty, even while the environmental forces of assimilation continued to challenge the essence of Jewish identity. At the same time, anti-Semitism—which could formerly be dismissed as mostly a nuisance—began to take on toxic forms as poisonous Nazi or Nazi-like doctrines formed in Europe and America. Jewish writers reacted in a variety of ways; some by reaffirming their Jewishness; others by bursting out with Jewish self-hatred. Rebounding from prejudicial outbursts, some took refuge in Zionism or returned to ancestral traditions. Others joined in the vociferous attacks against Jews by self-deprecation and self-vilification.

The 1930s and 1940s brought the era of the uprooted and the estranged Jewish intellectuals—the children of the Eastern European immigrants who planted themselves firmly in the American soil. Many of them revolted against both Jewish and American realities, taking refuge in hedonism, aestheticism, communism, and psycho-analytic self-dissection. This generation includes the Jewish writer Laura Z. Hobson, whose bestselling novel *Gentleman's Agreement* later that same year (1947) became a very successful Hollywood film.[21] In the story, the central character, a non-Jewish journalist, takes an assignment to write a series of articles on anti-Semitism. During his research, he is shocked to discover the degree of anti-Semitism rampant in a typical American community.

The early Saul Bellow also falls into this era, exhibiting a perpetual backgrounding of Jewishness articulated as the dissolution of the Jewish personality in contemporary America—not its reintegration.[22] Herman Wouk's very popular novels also revealed an estrangement from the nature of Jewishness, but by the end of the 1950s public fashion had shifted, and a more positive approach toward Jewishness was preferred—as evidenced by the huge success of Leon Uris's epic novel *Exodus* about the creation of the modern State of Israel.[23] This changed attitude on the part of readers and writers came about as a result of the rise of Israel in 1948 and its consolidation after the victorious Sinai campaign of 1956.

Jewish acculturation was a dominant trend among European immigrants ever since the founding of the United States. Such integration in American life required some degree of memory loss, even if that loss was of a homeland not their own. Still, because of their religious differentiation from the majority of the American population, Jews were able to preserve certain aspects of their uniqueness longer than other minority groups.

The greatest impact on Jewish writers of the 1950s and 1960s was not the Holocaust, as we might expect. That would be inherited by the second- and third-generation writers of the 1970s and beyond. Rather, what held the greatest core significance to the generation of creators in the '50s and '60s was the establishment of the State of Israel in 1948. For Jewish people everywhere, the creation of Israel proved to be the most profound influence upon the personality and expression of the culture, and such was mirrored in its literary and cultural output.

The culmination of a millennial dream, the new state changed the attitude even of the estranged and uprooted Jews toward their historic heritage and compelled them to rethink their relationship to their fellow Jews. After the success of *Exodus*, there came more novels of Jewish affirmation. The next most influential might have been James Michener's *The Source*. Michener repeatedly affirmed—through the words and deeds of his characters—the desirability both of a Jewish state and of a diaspora as expressions of Jewish destiny. (Leading the story with three archaeologists of different faiths, the novel broke new ground in the representation of interfaith experiences between a Jew, a Muslim, and a Christian.)

A new pattern was emerging in American fiction. Judaism was being painted in such attractive colors that a tradition of many centuries was being reversed. The literary tradition that required the Jew or his beautiful daughter to discover the truth of Christianity yielded to the opposite approach, which had the non-Jew discover the deeper truth of Judaism. The novels and short stories of Bernard

Malamud, Philip Roth, Arthur Miller, Norman Mailer, and Irwin Shaw fit into this pattern.[24] Additionally, the impact of Israel slowed down ultra-assimilationist tendencies, buttressing resistance to the conformist American environment. The questions of Jewish identity grew ever more insistent. What did it mean to be a Jew in America with a reborn Jewish state?

There is a great diversity of Jewish expression in America, thanks to Jewish immigration. Since the turn of the twenty-first century, an increasing number of Jewish writers who reside in North America are not Americans by birth. They arrive from Mexico, Guatemala, South Africa, France, and elsewhere. There is also a great output: Jews are writing and publishing in ever greater numbers, and North America is one of the epicenters of this burgeoning productivity. This new writing is less-defined by hyphenated titles such as Jewish-American, having become more pluralistic—a "modern Jewish literary complex," to quote literary historian Dan Miron, that is "vast, disorderly and somewhat diffuse."[25] It looks ahead to new forms of Jewish self-awareness as much as it looks back for history, sustenance, and collective memory (including the memory of the historically significant great migration of European Jews from 1881 to 1924).

New Jewish writing seems to have more in common with the broad currents of contemporary American fiction, so much of which is the work of émigrés. The new population of Jewish writers appears to mirror a broader movement in American literature: writers come from afar to seek sanctuary in America and find their voices in a country and a language that offers them protection and opportunity. From that point of view, immigrant Jews are less-special cases—that is, they are typical examples of new Americans, putting down roots in an adopted land and a new language. They are part of a larger global movement, and their literature reflects both their commonality with other cultures and their distinctive history. Still, the vast amount of writing by and about Jews is proof enough that the arc has moved from archetype to reality. At any rate, we're still here.

NOTES

1. W. R. Parker, "Where Do English Departments Come From?," *College English* 28, no. 5 (February 1967): 339–51. This 1967 publication provides the best context for understanding the development of the modern English department in its own time, which is the nature of this survey.

2. American Literature Association (n.d.), retrieved from http://americanliteratureassociation.org.

3. Leslie Fiedler, *Fiedler on the Roof: Essays on Literature and Jewish Identity and Love and Death in the American Novel* (Boston: Godine, 1992); Irving Howe, *World of Our Fathers: The Journey of the East European Jews to America and the Life They Found and Made* (New York: New York University Press, 2001); Lionel Trilling, *The Liberal Imagination* (New York: Viking, 1950).

4. Joseph Heller, *Catch-22* (New York: Dell, 1970); Cynthia Ozick, *The Shawl* (New York: Vintage, 1990); Marge Piercy, *Gone to Soldiers* (New York: Simon and Schuster, 2016).

5. Michael Chabon, *The Amazing Adventures of Kavalier and Clay* (New York: Random House, 2012); and *The Yiddish Policemen's Union* (New York: Harper Perennial, 2008); Jonathan Safran Foer, *Everything Is Illuminated* (London: Penguin Books, 2003); Nicole Krauss, *Great House* (New York: W.W. Norton, 2011).

6. Roger Daniels, *Coming to America: A History of Immigration and Ethnicity in American Life* (New York: Harper Perennial, 2002).

7. See Jules Chametzky, John Felstiner, Hilene Flanzbaum, and Kathryn Hellerstein, *Jewish American Literature: A Norton Anthology* (New York: W.W. Norton, 2001), 13.

8. See Morris N. Kertzer, *What Is a Jew?* (New York: Touchstone, 1996).

9. Louis Harap, *The Image of the Jew in American Literature: From Early Republic to Mass Immigration* (Philadelphia: Jewish Publication Society of America, 1974).

10. Sol Liptzin, *The Jew in American Literature* (New York: Bloch, 1966).

11. Victoria Aarons, Avinoam Patt, and Marc Shechner, eds., *The New Diaspora: The Changing Landscape of American Jewish Fiction* (Detroit: Wayne State University Press, 2015).

12. Saul Bellow, *Herzog* (New York: Viking, 1964).

13. James A. Michener, *The Source: A Novel* (New York: Random House, 1965).

14. For example, Manassa ben Israel, *The Hope of Israel*, ed. Gerard Nahon and Henri Mechoulan (Liverpool: Liverpool University Press, 2004).

15. Samuel Langdon, "The Republic of the Israelites an Example to the American States: A Sermon Preached at Concord, N.H., June 5, 1788" (Exeter: Lamson and Ranlet, 1788), 32.

16. J. R. Jones, *The Quaker Soldier: Or, The British in Philadelphia* (Paris: Ulan, 2012), 98.

17. *Lexico* (Oxford University Press, 2019), s.v. "philo-Semiticism," meaning "friendship towards or support of Jews."

18. See https://gutenberg.org/files/3473/3473−h/3473−h.htm.

19. Mary Antin, *The Promised Land* (Boston: Houghton Mifflin, 1912).

20. Anzia Yezierska, *Bread Givers* (New York: Persea, 2003), 9.

21. Laura Z. Hobson, *Gentleman's Agreement* (New York: Simon & Schuster, 1947).

22. Bellow's best-known works include *The Adventures of Augie March* (London: Penguin Classics, 2006); *Henderson the Rain King* (London: Penguin Classics, 2012); *Herzog* (London: Penguin Classics, 2003); *Mr. Sammler's Planet* (London: Penguin Classics, 2004); *Seize the Day* (London: Penguin Classics, 2003); *Humboldt's Gift* (London: Penguin Classics, 2008;) and *Ravelstein* (London: Penguin Classics, 2001).

23. See, for example, Herman Wouk, *This Is My God* (New York: Back Bay Books, 1992); and *Marjorie Morningstar* (New York: Back Bay Books, 1992). See also Leon Uris, *Exodus* (New York: Doubleday, 1958).

24. See, for example, Bernard Malamud, *The Assistant* (New York: FSG Classics, 2007); *The Fixer* (New York: FSG Classics, 2004); and *The Tenants* (New York: FSG Classics, 2003); Phillip Roth, *Goodbye Columbus: And Five Short Stories* (New York: Vintage International,

1994); *Portnoy's Complaint* (New York: Vintage International, 1994); *Irwin Shaw* (Chicago: University of Chicago Press, 2000); and *Short Stories: Five Decades* (Chicago: University of Chicago Press, 2000).

25. Dan Miron, *From Continuity to Contiguity* (Stanford: Stanford University Press, 2010), 276.

14

ZION AND ISRAEL IN JEWISH POLITICAL THOUGHT

STEVEN WINDMUELLER

HISTORICAL AND THEOLOGICAL ROOTS
OF THE JEWISH STORY

Jewish history is constructed around the dual notions of people-hood and the promise of homeland. The covenant between God and the children of Israel would serve as the basis for the historical bond of the Jewish people to their land, and Jews would trace their claim to Israel through a series of covenantal promises made by God to the community. Beginning with Abraham, we are introduced to the idea of holy land: "To your offspring, I assign this land, from the river of Egypt to the great river, the river Euphrates" (Genesis 15:18).[1] Indeed, over the course of their diaspora experience, primarily through their texts, Jews would symbolically revisit this national drama. This was dramatically expressed in Psalm 137, which opens with this powerful motif: "By the rivers of Babylon there we sat down, yea, we wept, when we remembered Zion." Later in that psalm we are reminded,

If I forget thee, O Jerusalem, let my right hand forget her cunning. Let my tongue cling to the roof of my mouth, if I remember thee not; if I set not Jerusalem above my chiefest joy. (Psalm 137:5–6 JPS)

During their two-thousand-year diaspora experience, Jews found meaning and identity in the covenantal promise. Jews came to see themselves as the Chosen People, selected by God to live and rule themselves in their land. Throughout the early centuries of Jewish history, the rabbis constructed these types of mythologies and political messages, all designed to keep "the promise of return and redemption" in the forefront of Jewish belief and practice.

Consequently, the imperative to survive as a people in order to reclaim their political sovereignty shaped Jewish understanding of the centrality of Zion. The Jewish people were stateless longer than any community in history. Political powerlessness defined their condition for much of their exile experience.

The idea of Zion was initially understood as a concept that would only achieve reality if Jews continued to believe and practice their faith. Only later would this theological notion evolve into a Jewish political objective.

The religious motif of return was embedded in all phases of Jewish ritual and prayer, represented most vividly through the final verses of the Passover Haggadah, when one triumphantly proclaims, "Next year in Jerusalem." Indeed, this notion of return, in my view, may not have always been understood as a purely physical transformation as much as a psychological state of being, especially when encountering decades of hate and social rejection.

As a result of being powerless for most of their history, Jews employed the myth of triumphalism through their literature. This mythmaking noted the idyllic character of power and its perfectibility as expressed by God in the scenario of the Garden of Eden or as experienced through Shabbat. Divine election—namely, the Jewish belief in their chosenness—represented a psychological tool designed to offer them comfort and serve as a platform of expectations about the future, especially in periods of exile.

Different Jewish texts must be seen as political roadmaps; for example, the book of Joshua is a political classic as it frames the leadership motif that was required for nation building as well as the principles essential for national unity. Similarly, the book of Esther demonstrated how Jews were able to overcome the politics of hate as symbolized by Haman and move to defend their political interests as symbolized by Esther's willingness to risk her throne for the welfare of her people.

Jewish political tradition has been built on four principles:

- Nation-building (the promise)
- Jewish peoplehood (continuity and covenant)
- Preserving the tradition (guardians of faith and power of memory)
- Making the world whole (*tikkun olam*)

Throughout their history Jews operated under four political conditions: tribal confederacy; nation-state; exile and diaspora; and homeland (the State of Israel). Jews posed two questions throughout their historical journey: "How can we best embrace our tradition and God's covenantal commitment to his people?" "What would it require to bring about a change in our political status?"

The long history of dispersion required the community to creatively adopt its political practices and ideas to deal with their historical realities. The doctrine of *dina de-malkhuta dina* (the law of the land is the law) was introduced in the third century as a means to define how best the community could accommodate to its diaspora political condition. For centuries this principle would permit Jews to govern themselves internally while acknowledging their loyalty to the state. The Kehillah (Jewish communal system) was seen as a Jewish kingdom in miniature. The Jewish people's sustained belief in the coming of the Messiah was an essential ingredient in preserving their faith and strengthening their eternal belief in achieving national renewal. Through their history their rabbis constructed liturgy that reaffirmed the Jewish goal of returning to Zion. Prayer was employed as a political/spiritual tool for their redemption.

I have suggested in my writings that their perfecting the art of self-governance and their promoting communal practice served Jews well during centuries of living without political power and in turn prepared them for modernity. Historian Ruth Wisse referred to this practice as the "politics of complementarity," with which Jews demonstrated their political and economic value to the larger society as a way to protect and advance their social standing.

Across the diaspora Jews developed a system of commerce and a network of intercommunity communications. This web of trans-national connections was essential for sharing ideas and growing their political insights. During these centuries of powerlessness, Jews garnered four political lessons:

- As a minority people, Jews have understood that their power would be limited.
- Realizing that politics is about negotiated outcomes, the Jewish community understood the importance of pursuing coalitions and alliance building and of achieving political consensus.
- Throughout their history Jews have always understood the particular value of political elites or spokespersons to represent the community's interests (*Shtadlanim*).
- Internal Jewish communal politics would often be seen as a barometer of the general political climate.

THE AMERICAN EXPERIENCE

In the American context politics must be seen as part of the Jewish DNA. American exceptionalism suggests the uniqueness of the Jews' American experience. American Jews have embraced politics as part of their Jewish identity and social culture.

The ingredients of American exceptionalism consist of a series of core principles:

- No history of state-sponsored anti-Semitism
- The celebration of voluntarism and communalism
- The multifaith and pluralistic character of the United States
- Constitutional guarantees, including article 6 with its prohibition on "religious tests" for public office along with the First Amendment's affirmation of "freedom of religion, petition and assembly"

Each of America's political traditions contributed to and helped frame Jewish political behavior. Indeed, Jews in America experimented with these political models and ideas. Within American Liberalism, Jews have been central players in refining and promoting the causes of social and economic justice, promoting civil liberties, preserving the separation of church and state, and advancing the collective interests of minorities in this society. Similarly, as part of the neoconservative camp, its intellectual leaders have helped to shape ideas about American democracy, US global interests, and the unique partnership defining Israel's relationship with America.

Jews were seen as political actors within the American story. Over the course of the nation's history, Jews have been committed to and involved with the political process as voters, commentators, candidates, and funders. The depth of their political participation reflects in no small measure their abiding sense that their religious culture and ethnic heritage serve as political roadmaps and in part obligates and inspires them to be participants and actors in the American story. This accounts for the fact that Jews are the most politically engaged religious and ethnic community in this nation, as 85% of eligible Jewish voters participate! Just as the founders of this Republic embraced the idea of America as the "New Zion," such a concept became part of the American Jewish political mindset.

Today Jews can be found in all of the political expressions of American politics, in part reflecting their integration and acceptance into the nation's culture. As part of American Jewish political behavior, two core values are constantly in play with one another: a nationalist perspective—that is, Jewish self-interests—is seen in tension with the universal Jewish imperative of promoting the broader social good.

The presence of a Jewish state for the first time in two thousand years has altered the political status of the Jewish people, giving the community a sense of security and pride, just as it has strengthened and offered new avenues for political engagement and connection. For the first time in centuries, Jews are both political actors within their own nation-state and within diaspora communities across the globe.

MODERNITY AND THE RISE OF ZIONISM

Within the Jewish narrative, the idea of Zion shifted in the nineteenth century from being only a religious concept to emerging as an essential political message. Modernity, with its focus on challenging existing notions on religion, politics, and economics, permitted the introduction of an array of new ideas about nationalism and statehood.

As those new ideas were being introduced, Zionism evolved as the essential political response permitting Jews the opportunity to experience their national aspirations in alignment with other cultures and their goals for nation building. The modern Jewish world of the late nineteenth century viewed the rise of Zionism from two perspectives: Jews who believed that the possibilities of political liberation could only be achieved if a Jewish state were to be established directed their energies toward promoting this opportunity. Others saw their future threatened by the rise of Zionism, their new status as citizens of Western democratic nations would, in their mind, be compromised by the charge of dual loyalty, creating in turn new forms of anti-Jewish expression.

Indeed, for some within the Orthodox Jewish world, the idea of human intervention leading to the establishment of a Jewish state was rejected on the basis that only God could provide for the liberation of his people.[2]

UNPACKING THE ZIONIST NARRATIVE

The Zionist experiment in state building remains a relatively new phenomenon. In the course of the past 150 years, Jews were exposed for the first time in two thousand years to the possibilities of being a sovereign nation.

Yet, even with the emergence of Zionism, Jews continued to disagree as to what the Jewish state's character and content might represent. From the outset, some on the political right concluded that two peoples on one land was a prescription for Jewish destruction, lest the Zionist enterprise immediately reject the countervailing claims of the Arabs. Others envisioned different forms of governance, including various modalities of socialism, while still other Jewish religious activists called for a theocracy, where Jewish law and tradition defined the character and content of this new nation.

Prior to its formation, and most certainly since its inception, the Jewish state faced a series of challenging questions unique to its very existence and identity:

- Was the state's very creation brought about by the Western world's guilt over the Holocaust?
- In light of Arab opposition, does Israel have a right to exist?
- What ought to constitute the definition and territorial composition of the Jewish state?
- How ought Israel to define itself in both Jewish and democratic terms?
- Will the historic vision of a two-state solution give way to a single-state proposal, and what might that new political construct mean?

These questions were being posed not just by Israel's enemies but also increasingly by the larger international community. Many of these same questions were the subject matter for the Jewish community itself as it attempted to define the meaning and substance of the Jewish national experience.

Throughout Israel's seventy years of existence, various political perspectives evolved regarding how Israel would be seen by its enemies and its diaspora and how it would define all its citizens.

Today, the battle over the character and composition of the Jewish state has evoked deep fissures both outside the Jewish homeland and within its borders. An overriding question remains: Ought Israel to be a Jewish and democratic society? Or is it more important to protect the Jewish character of the nation, possibly at the expense of its democratic values?

A report from Pew Research Center revealed that 4 in 10 Jews believe that Israel was given by God to the Jewish people, but this concept is more readily adopted by Orthodox Jews—8 in 10 from this community hold to this belief. Overall, 40% of all American Jews hold to this notion, along with some 84% of Orthodox Jews and 35% of Reform Jews (see fig. 1). Among evangelical Christians 82% support this belief (see fig. 2).

As has been noted in these conversations, the idea of Zion plays an important role for both our communities. And indeed, the early trappings of Christian Zionist support for a Jewish return to sovereignty in the Holy Land represented a significant presence in much of eighteenth- and nineteenth-century American political discourse around the Middle East.

In more contemporary terms, American Jewish political behavior is deeply tied to the modern State of Israel. How Jews view particular political candidates, party platform statements, and actions by the United States in reference to the Middle East and the Jewish state has particular merit for a portion of the Jewish electorate. Indeed, a significant cadre of American Jewish voters places the Israel-US relationship as the centerpiece of its political identity. For other

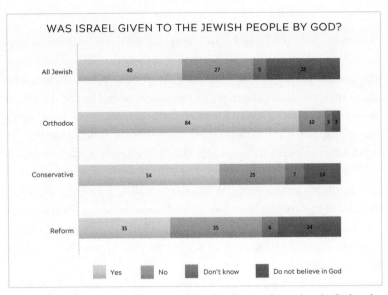

Figure 1. Percentages of American Jews believing that Israel was given by God to the Jewish people.

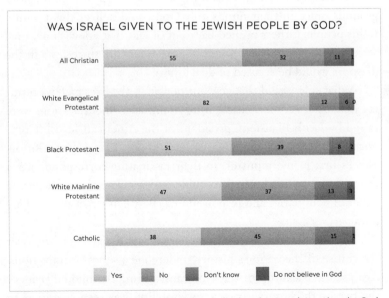

Figure 2. Percentages of American Christians believing that Israel was given by God to the Jewish people.

American Jews the "Israel card" competes with their other top economic, social, and political priorities. This assessment is drawn from the annual survey of one thousand American Jewish leaders who share their political priorities in a survey sponsored by the American Jewish Committee (AJC). Employing this sample study, Israel ranks among the five top political priorities of these AJC Jewish elites.[3] In 2018 Israel celebrated the seventieth anniversary of the Jewish state's rebirth. Several generations of American Jews have participated in the unfolding of this story. While the founding generations both in Israel and in America have now passed from the scene, their imprint on the participation in this rebirth, with all its challenges and uncertainties, is rapidly becoming an important part of Jewish mythology and literature.

Indeed, we need to remind ourselves of how intensely divided the Jewish community was in the 1930s and 1940s over organizing this major political initiative. Notably, the idea of a national Jewish homeland did not resonate with all Jews, sometimes on religious grounds, since in their minds only God could deliver this promise to his people. Others pushed back out of fear that a Jewish national state would evoke a new round of anti-Semitism, since Jews in the diaspora would be accused of dual loyalty.

What role would this new entity play in the lives of Jews residing in diaspora communities? In 1950 this and other questions were raised by Jacob Blaustein, president of the American Jewish Committee, through an exchange of letters with David Ben-Gurion, Israel's first prime minister. In their fascinating correspondence, a framework was established to guide and regulate these uncharted issues of boundaries and responsibilities between Israel and its diaspora partners.

Israel's relationship with its Jewish world partners has, over the course of the nation's history, undergone a series of transitions. Against the backdrop of the Holocaust during the middle years of the twentieth century, Israel's "survivability" was seen as critical to the welfare of the Jewish enterprise. "One people, one destiny" was the dominant motif during the first twenty years of statehood; during that era, Israel indeed enjoyed a broad degree of diaspora support.

Sustainability was the defining element for the next quarter of a century. Here, the nature of the Jewish partnership, symbolized by the UJA (United Jewish Appeal) campaign appeal of the time, "We Are One," rested on garnering and maintaining political, economic, and military support vital to Israel's standing. Over those twenty-five years, Israel moved away from themes that reflected its earlier vulnerable position to one that might be seen as symbolic or even as an exemplar of political and social ingenuity. The Jewish state has emerged as a technologically accomplished nation state with a sophisticated economy and an advanced military. In this third phase Israel emerged from its dependent role to become the dominant player in global Jewish matters, but this moment in time also represented a fundamental disruption in Israel's historic partnership with its diaspora as a widening divide created distance between it and some of its former partners.

On a host of policy matters today, one can find deep divisions between the liberal-oriented attitudes of a majority of American Jews, and the center-right views of the government in Jerusalem who differ over such policy questions as settlements and human rights. More particularly, some Jewish Americans are uncomfortable with recent Israeli initiatives to remove African asylum seekers and proposals that seek to curb the free speech rights of Boycott, Divestment and Sanctions (BDS) supporters or with legislation denying individuals associated with specific anti-Israel movements admission into the Jewish state. Just as American Jewish liberals defended the Obama administration's record on Israel, supporters of Donald Trump embrace his policies in connection with the Jewish state, creating in the wake of these disagreements a significant gap between Israel's historic partners.

Of American Jews, 61% support a two-state solution. By comparison some 50% of the general American public reflects this position. Only 42% of evangelicals, however, accept this option.

Defenders of Israel question whether diaspora communities should have the right to publicly critique Israel over its policies and actions. Ought that privilege be left to the citizens of the Jewish nation? Responders from the diaspora push back, challenging that assumption and noting that Israel was created as the collective expression of the Jewish people, and as such all Jews not only have the right to express their views but have an obligation to assert their ideas.

Beyond these internecine battles, the question of how the international community ought to engage Iran or the issue of what constitutes anti-Semitic behavior in connection with dissent pertaining to Israel reminds us of other elements that today define these conversations.

In place of creative dialogue, one finds only disagreement and discord. Some arguments by American Jewish critics are framed in moral terms, suggesting that Israel ought to be held to a higher standard. In their minds Israel is failing to live up to the Jewish values that have informed and shaped the state's Zionist heritage. Jewish Americans who express their disappointment or despair over Israel's move to the political right have lost their trust in the state. Israel's political establishment is seen as either being politically corrupt or operating around a set of deeply flawed assumptions, thus widening the divide, as demonstrated by the most recent population studies.[4]

The declining levels of Jewish engagement with Israel, especially on the part of younger Jews, present another challenge both to Israeli authorities and to American Jewish leaders. Younger, liberal American Jews seem further removed from any involvement or connection to the State of Israel. This generational shift needs to be placed into some context—one sees greater Jewish connectivity to Israel on the part of Millennial Jews and Generation Z participants who have enjoyed more exposure to Jewish studies and Zionist education than those with more limited access or learning.

The numbers of Jews who have actually visited, studied, or lived for a short period of time in Israel are impressive. In part these results may be tied to the Birthright Israel heritage trips to Israel offered to Jews eighteen to twenty-six years of age and an array of other missions and offerings available to American Jewish audiences.

AGE AS A FACTOR IN SHAPING ATTITUDES TOWARD ISRAEL

In a 2013 examination of pro-Israel sentiment by age, the data confirm that a significantly higher percentage of older American Jews embrace Israel:

- 79% of Jews 65 years of age and older expressed "attachment" to Israel
- 74% of Jews 50–64 years of age expressed "attachment" to Israel
- 61% of Jews 30–49 years of age expressed "attachment" to Israel
- 60% of Jews 18–29 years of age expressed "attachment" to Israel

Of Jews over 65 years of age, 38% were "very attached to Israel," while only 25% of Jews ages 18 to 29 years held such a position—30% of all American Jews hold a strong attachment. Among Orthodox Jews, 61% have a very high level of attachment; in contrast, only 16% of secular or nondenominational Jews do.[5] In surveys completed by the Brand Israel Group, Jewish college students dropped 27 percentage points in their support of Israel from 2010 (84%) to 2016 (57%).[6]

As these debates unfold, the opponents of Israel's politics are dismissed as misguided or worse, undermining the Jewish state by their betrayal to defend and protect this historic experiment in nation building. Each side offers descriptions of the other, seeking to minimize the political standing of their opponents. Terms such as naive, foolish, destructive, and disingenuous are introduced to define the other side.

Indeed, both Israelis and American Jews have their respective visions or images of the Jewish state. Some of these fixed notions are reflected by *romantic perceptions* of an earlier image of the state's Zionist origins. Others might be described as *political realists*, as they focus on the multiple military and security threats that have defined the state's history and that remain its core challenges. Possibly, a third constituency could be defined as *bound by history*, for whom specific events, such as the Oslo Accords and its promise of peace, resonate as pivotal moments in Israel's diplomatic journey; in this cohort particular personalities or events have ultimately defined their vision of how the state ought to act.

With its enthusiastic endorsement of Donald Trump, Israel might symbolically serve as an ideal "red state" base for this president; contrastingly, many American Jews might metaphorically represent a "blue state" constituency, with their overriding opposition to the White House and their current discomfort with Israeli policies.

A February 2017 Gallup Poll noted a 71% level of support for Israel among Americans. Covering an eight-year period, Israel had on average over 60% support from American audiences.[7] As identified in figure 3, pro-Israel support among Americans varies by political party affiliation.

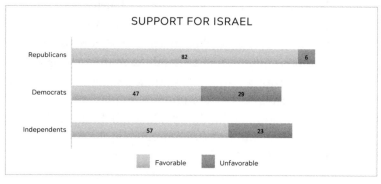

Figure 3. Pro-Israel support among Americans by party affiliation.

An additional study found 76% of Republicans "very attached" to Israel, compared to only 43% of Democrats.[8]

Eighty-four Gallup Polls, dating back to 1967, indicate that Israel has on average the support of 47% of Americans, compared to 12%

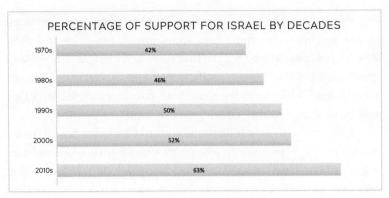

PERCENTAGE OF SUPPORT FOR ISRAEL BY DECADES

1970s	42%
1980s	46%
1990s	50%
2000s	52%
2010s	63%

Figure 4. Average level of support for Israel by decade.

of Americans who support the Palestinians. Of the 150 total polls covering this subject matter, Israel has a 48% to 11% advantage for the Palestinian cause. The average level of support for Israel has been increasing each decade (see fig. 4).[9]

Among non-Gallup polls, there were some thirty-three other studies conducted over the past eight years. These studies identified on average some 55% of Americans as "pro-Israel," with 12% being identified as "pro-Palestinian." This translates to a 4 to 1 advantage for Israel.[10]

Regarding US support for Israel, a 2015 poll reflected that 54% of Jewish Americans and 41% of Americans in general felt that US support was about right (see fig. 5).

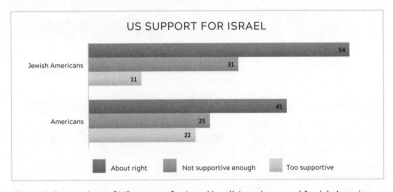

US SUPPORT FOR ISRAEL

Jewish Americans: 54, 31, 11
Americans: 41, 25, 22

About right   Not supportive enough   Too supportive

Figure 5. Comparison of US support for Israel by all Americans and Jewish Americans.

With the issue of intersectionality, American Jews are often forced to choose between their social justice priorities and their Zionist passions. Maybe for the first time in American history Jews are engaging with allies on specific issues over which they find common ground while knowing that these friends espouse views that may be perceived as anti-Israel.[11]

Among Jewish denominational groups, Orthodox Jews demonstrate the highest proportion of support with more than 60% indicating a "very attached" position and another 30% holding a "somewhat attached" outlook. Only 5% of American Jewish Orthodox members are "not at all attached."

The results show that 61% of Orthodox Jews and 47% of American Conservative Jews are seen as "very attached to Israel" in contrast to Reform Jews, of whom only 24% share such a view. Among secular or unaffiliated Jews, the support level drops to 16% (see fig. 6).

Political tensions are also prevalent within Israel itself, as evidenced by a host of domestic policy conflicts. These internal disagreements among Israeli citizens resemble a geopolitical war between "the

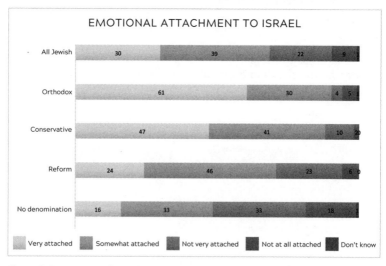

Figure 6. Percentage of American Jews with emotional attachment to Israel.

state of Tel Aviv" with its secular, liberal orientation and "the state of Jerusalem" with its traditional religious and politically conservative perspective.

While many American Jews are experiencing great discomfort about their own nation's current political theatre, Israelis on the political left are expressing concerns about the status of their democracy as scandal and corruption appear to be on the rise. Even while the issues that animate these communities' angst appear to be vastly different, there exists an impasse, even a state of gridlock common to these two political systems. Both nations seem unable to rely on politicians or institutional elites to change the status quo.

AMERICA AND THE IDEA OF ZION:
AN ADDITIONAL REFLECTION

Stepping back, it is important at this point to understand the unique and historical connection of the United States to the notion of Jewish statehood. The theme of Zion was a significant and ongoing motif associated with the birth and evolution of the United States. The American patriots sought to employ the themes of liberation and freedom as expressed in the Exodus story to the nation's revolution. The idea of Zion resonated with American presidents and was employed in different ways to identify America as the new Zion. This natural affinity to the concept of Zion played an important role in binding the United States to the founding and sustaining of the modern State of Israel.

Even within the American political system there was a debate over which political party would be more supportive of Israel. Despite the fact that Israel was viewed for decades as a bipartisan cause, in more recent times there has been an effort by each political party to prove its unique connection to the Jewish state, thereby warranting American Jewish support.

Five themes have dominated this intensive competition:

- Defending Israel in the international arena, more specifically at the United Nations
- Containing Iran while assessing the effectiveness of the Iran Nuclear Accord
- Providing the Jewish state with the necessary military resources to deter its enemies and jointly developing new weapons systems with Israel
- Partnering with Israel in the exchange of military intelligence and technological data while promoting trade and economic development opportunities
- Responding to efforts to undermine Israel through the BDS movement and other efforts to isolate the Jewish state on the global stage

ISRAEL AND ITS PARTNERSHIPS WITH WORLD JEWRY

As the Jewish state has evolved, its partnership with its diaspora communities has changed over time. Three stages seem to define the primary periods of Israel's evolution as a nation-state:

- Promoting the establishment of a Jewish state and marshaling the resources to protect and defend the state (1948–1967)
- Taking pride in its accomplishments while seeking to defend its right to exist (1967–1982) and expanding its inclusion of Jews to those from the former Soviet Union and elsewhere
- Debating the state's definition of its religious character, geopolitical orientation, and civil liberties commitments (1982–2020)

Over more than seventy years of statehood, the diaspora connection with Israel has changed significantly. Once based on a model of partnership, in which the diaspora was seen as essential to the building of the Jewish enterprise, that orientation has radically been transferred from the notion of partnership to the idea of partisanship as diaspora supporters are now expected to embrace the posture and actions of the Jewish state. The changing diaspora landscape, most especially within North America, has altered both the conversation and relationship with Israel.

INTERNAL STATE POLITICS

In more recent years the debate within Israel has shifted. This transition occurred in light of the changing dimensions of Israeli politics and the new demographic realities present both within Israel and within the Palestinian community. The one-state proposal involving several different scenarios has surfaced. One view, promoted by some within the political left in Israel and their Arab counterparts, calls upon both Arabs and Jews to participate in building a binational society. The other, sponsored by an element within Israel's right wing, calls for the relocation of Palestinians to Jordan or to other countries within the Arab world as a means of creating an authentic Jewish nation. Still others, frustrated by the absence of any assurances from the Palestinians, are proposing a one-state option with an array of political arrangements designed to guarantee a Jewish majority.

As Israel operates a parliamentary system of government, its politics are shaped by coalitional arrangements that at any given time can and do reshape the cultural and social landscape of that nation. In recent elections a center-right coalition was successful in forming government majorities and in turn, in moving the country to a more hardline position on an array of domestic and foreign matters.

Increasingly unsettled by recent actions of the Israeli government, the Jewish center-left in the United States has expressed more openly its displeasure with the current government's positions on such matters as settlements, Palestinian rights, questions surrounding political dissent, and the religious status of non-Orthodox Jews.

In 2015 nearly half (48%) of American Jews supported the Iran nuclear deal, while 28% opposed the deal and 25% had formed no opinion.[12] In more recent times the Netanyahu government has alienated Jewish Democrats with the prime minister's overt actions to undercut President Obama over Israel's resistance to the Joint Comprehensive Plan of Action (JCPOA), or Iran nuclear deal, and by its less-than-subtle support during the 2016 campaign for a Trump victory.

President Obama enjoyed a 65% approval rating among Reform Jews in connection with his handling of US-Israel relations. By contrast, only 36% of Orthodox Jews and 26% of evangelical Christians held such a view.

In light of the support the Trump administration is generating toward Israel, one might expect to see further initiatives designed to contain Iran's ability to operate in the region—one of Israel's primary concerns—and to halt its military (nuclear) procurement plans, permitting Israel to grow its settlements and containing the ability of Islamic terrorist/fundamentalist groups to secure greater access within the Arab world, especially with Israel's growing set of Arab partners within the region.

MANAGING THE JEWISH POLITICAL DIVIDE OVER ISRAEL

American Jews are engaged today in an intense debate over their future relationship with the Jewish State. A recent report in *Foreign Policy* magazine noted the relative discrepancy between Israeli views on settlements and the reactions of American Jewry:[13]

- 42% of Israelis support settlements because they enhance security
- 44% of American Jews oppose settlements
- 38% of American Jews question Israel's efforts in seeking peace with the Palestinians
- 61% of American Jews support an independent Palestinian state (2013)
- 40% of Israelis believe in an independent Palestinian state

Many American Jews believe that settlements hurt Israel's security situation (44%), while some (17%) think that settlements enhance
the security of the Jewish state. Half (50%) of Reform and secular
Jews believe that the policy of settlements is problematic to peace,
while only 34% of Orthodox Jews hold this viewpoint.[14]

As I have written elsewhere, many questions pertaining to Israeli
politics remain.[15]

1. Does the liberal Jewish mainstream share any common political ground with its more politically conservative coreligionists?
How might we find ways to open such conversations, especially in
diaspora-Israel relations?

2. The political divide around Israel is a central element in the
battle over the Jewish future. What should the relationship of American Jews with the Jewish state be? Today, various divergent political perspectives define the American Jewish landscape. American
Jewish political conservatives are embracing closer ties between the
Trump administration and Israel's political establishment as they
seek to advance Israel's security. Liberal Jews are seeking to push back
against the expansion of settlements, while promoting a Palestinian-
Jewish dialogue and advancing a human rights agenda. This is a way
to ensure Israel's long-term security. Are there any common threads
here for a shared discussion?

3. Who is permitted to critique Israel? The political right would
argue that the prerogative of criticism belongs only to the citizens
of the Jewish state; its counterpart, the Jewish progressive community, has argued that Jews across the world are partners in the task
of building and defending the State of Israel and as such ought to
be able to participate in a conversation concerning the nature and
character of the Jewish political enterprise.

4. How do we negotiate the Jewish religious divide? One of the
core issues to this division is centered on Jerusalem and the question
of the Kotel (Western Wall). Will Jews find a way to negotiate shared
accommodations in response to their different religious inclinations?

5. Finally, what does it mean to be Jewish in a twenty-first-century environment in which the scourge of anti-Semitism, racism, and ethnic hatred has reemerged? In light of this uptake in political anti-Semitism, will Jews find common ground in order to unite in this battle? We are reminded that the enemies of the Jewish people do not distinguish between the political factions that exist today within the community. Indeed, the rise of the BDS movement represents a new challenge to mainstream American Jewish interests.

Is this the first time in Jewish history that our community seems fractured? No! In fact, the pathways of Jewish history would suggest that Jews have constantly been in contention with one another. Some have argued that this has been an asset, as contentious debate and controversy have stimulated creative responses, great literature, and thoughtful commentaries. Others have viewed these divisions with grave concern, judging our historic infighting as being destructive to our people's well-being over the centuries.

DEMOGRAPHY AND POLITICS

Beyond the level of Jewish engagement, the present political landscape represents some significant new challenges to building the case for Israel with American audiences:

- The rise of Israel's critics, even among younger Jewish Americans, has seen an array of new political expressions challenging the status quo and embracing the BDS campaign.
- Support for Israel within the Democratic Party is weakening.
- The changing demographics within America result in various minority communities increasingly identifying with the case for the Palestinians. This sentiment is in part linked with the intersectionality movement, in which shared victimization aligns aggrieved parties without regard for geography or historical circumstance.

All this suggests that certain generational shifts within this nation have the capacity to potentially challenge how Israel will be seen and embraced by American audiences in the future.

NOTES

1. W. Gunther Plaut, *The Torah: A Modern Commentary*, rev. ed. (New York: Union of American Hebrew Congregations, 1981), 110.

2. See David Biale, *Power and Powerlessness in Jewish History* (New York: Schocken Books, 1986), especially chap. 2, "The Political Theory of the Diaspora."

3. The 2007 American Jewish Committee survey shows "support for Israel" ranking about fifth (tied with several other items) among the "most important" issues in electing a president, https://jewishvirtual library.org/attitudes-of-american-jews-september-2012-2.

4. Steven Windmueller, "Squabbling Siblings: The Israel/Diaspora Divide," eJewish Philanthropy, March 4, 2018, https://ejewishphilan thropy.com/squabbling-siblings-the-israel-diaspora-divide/.

5. Pew Research Center, "A Portrait of Jewish Americans," October 1, 2013, p. 82, https://pewforum.org/2013/10/01/jewish-american-beliefs -attitudes-culture-survey/ (select Complete Report PDF).

6. See Amanda Borschel-Dan, "'Devasting' Survey Shows Huge Loss of Israel Support among Jewish College Students," June 21, 2017, https://timesofisrael.com/devastating-survey-shows-huge-loss-of -israel-support-among-jewish-college-students/.

7. Lydia Saad, "Israel Maintains Positive Image in U.S.," February 15, 2017, https://news.gallup.com/poll/203954/israel-maintains-positive -image.aspx.

8. Lydia Saad, "Americans, but Not Liberal Democrats, Mostly Pro-Israel," March 6, 2019, https://news.gallup.com/poll/247376/ameri cans-not-liberal-democrats-mostly-pro-israel.aspx.

9. Mitchell G. Bard, "American Attitudes toward Israel," *Huffington Post*, April 25, 2013, https://huffpost.com/entry/american-attitudes -toward_1_b_3154507.

10. Bard, "American Attitudes toward Israel."
11. Steven Windmueller, "Deeply Divided Jews Desperately Need to Find Common Ground," *Jewish Journal*, February 6, 2019, https://jewishjournal.com/analysis/293410/deeply-divided-jews-desperately-need-to-find-common-ground/
12. Scott Clement, "Jewish Americans Support the Iran Nuclear Deal," *Washington Post*, July 27, 2015, https://washingtonpost.com/news/the-fix/wp/2015/07/27/jewish-americans-support-the-iran-nuclear-deal/.
13. Bruce Stokes, "Are American Jews Turning Away from Israel?," *Foreign Policy*, March 10, 2016.
14. "Comparisons between Jews in Israel and the U.S.," Pew Research Center, March 8, 2016, https://pewforum.org/2016/03/08/comparisons-between-jews-in-israel-and-the-u-s/.
15. Steven Windmueller, "Angry Jews and Their Political Wars," eJewish Philanthropy, December 15, 2015, http://ejewishphilanthropy.com/angry-jews-and-their-political-wars/.

15

PASSIVE ZIONISM VERSUS CHRISTIAN ZIONISM: LATTER-DAY SAINT AND EVANGELICAL PROTESTANT ATTITUDES ABOUT ISRAEL

J. QUIN MONSON AND KELLY N. DUNCAN

The State of Israel has received significant American support—financial and otherwise—since its establishment in 1948. For example, during the seventy years between 1948 and 2018, the United States has supplied Israel with over $134.7 billion in military, economic, and missile defense aid—making Israel the "largest cumulative recipient of U.S. foreign assistance since World War II."[1] Israel is also viewed favorably by most Americans, especially when compared to how citizens of other countries around the world view Israel. A 2014 BBC poll estimated that 52% of US respondents held "mainly positive" views of Israel, putting the US second only to Ghana in positive views of Israel.[2] In Pew and Gallup polling over many years that asks about "the dispute between Israel and the Palestinians," the percentage of Americans sympathizing with Israel is generally in the mid-40s while support for the Palestinians is typically less than half that level; and a 2018 Gallup poll had Israel's image among Americans at its highest level since 1991.[3]

Americans' religious affiliations have long been known to be related to American attitudes about Israel.[4] In this chapter, we look specifically at attitudes toward Israel among members of The Church of Jesus Christ of Latter-day Saints compared to evangelical Protestants. But first we will review the relationship between religious traditions and support for Israel to put our focus on the views of evangelicals and Latter-day Saints toward Israel in proper context. We find, like many others, that American Jews are the most supportive of Israel, followed closely by evangelical Protestants and then by Latter-day Saints. Our focus then turns to a comparison of the consistently positive attitudes toward Israel of both evangelical Protestants and Latter-day Saints to demonstrate that the underlying motivation behind each group's support differs. While there is an extensive literature on Christian Zionism and its development in Protestant denominations as well as some empirical work examining attitudes toward Israel and religiosity among evangelical Protestants, comparable work does not exist for Latter-day Saints. Our chapter is the first to discuss the concept of Christian Zionism in any significant detail in connection with Latter-day Saints and to present an empirical assessment of attitudes about Israel among Latter-day Saints. Our findings with regard to evangelicals are not new or surprising, but our main contribution is to present clear expectations and empirical evidence for the very positive views toward the State of Israel expressed by Latter-day Saints.

For many evangelical Protestants, support of Israel is rooted in Christian Zionism, or religious beliefs related to biblical ideas of the end time and the return of Jesus that are usually linked explicitly to the modern State of Israel. Among at least some prominent evangelical leaders, Christian Zionism translates to an interest in the success of the State of Israel on the international stage and in turn to explicit support by those leaders for Israel in US foreign policy. Latter-day Saints, on the other hand, while having some similar end-time beliefs as evangelicals, are not proponents of Christian Zionism. The biggest difference is that Latter-day Saints do very little to link their end-time beliefs to the modern political State of Israel. Instead, references to Israel are theological references to the biblical Jewish people or other more general theological teachings. Thus Latter-day Saints, while sharing some theological ideas about the end time with evangelicals, differ in theology by not experiencing the explicit Christian Zionism present in many evangelical denominations.

We provide support for these differences using data from the Pew Research Center that examine public opinion on a standard question about whether one has more sympathy for Israel or the Palestinians. We find evidence for strong effects of religiosity on attitudes about Israel among evangelicals, providing support for the presence of Christian Zionism. The evidence among Latter-day Saints is more nuanced and suggests that while religiosity affects Latter-day Saint views on Israel, an even stronger effect for pro-Israel attitudes occurs because Latter-day Saints overwhelmingly identify as Republicans. In other words, for evangelicals, support for Israel stems from a Christian Zionist theology that is reinforced by partisan signals. For Latter-day Saints, the reverse appears more likely; support for Israel stems more from overwhelming Republican party identification (and the strong partisan support among Republicans that has emerged for Israel in recent years) together with a theology that is generally friendly toward, but not explicitly supportive, of the political State of Israel.

LATTER-DAY SAINTS AND EVANGELICALS: POLITICALLY SIMILAR BUT DIFFERENT

To understand the differences between Latter-day Saints and evangelical Protestants in terms of their attitudes about the State of Israel, it is helpful to understand the similarities and differences on other political issues. At first glance one would expect Latter-day Saints and evangelicals to be quite similar in political outlook, including views about Israel. For example, both groups are consistently among the most Republican in their voting behavior. In terms of partisan identification, Latter-day Saints are the most Republican religious group, followed by evangelicals.[5] However, when comparing political views between Latter-day Saints and evangelicals, "the specifics of Mormons' beliefs align with the teachings and policies of the LDS Church, even when they diverge from the positions taken by other politically conservative groups."[6]

For example, both Latter-day Saints and evangelical Protestants are generally pro-life and pro-traditional marriage, but if survey questions are asked with the right nuance, the positions of each group become distinct with Latter-day Saints answering in ways more consistent with their Church's doctrine or official policy. On the question of abortion (using General Social Survey data), Latter-day Saints favor access to abortion when it involves the mother's health (over 90%) or rape (nearly 80%) at rates comparable to the general population and somewhat higher than what is favored by evangelicals (and Catholics). In turn, the proportion of Latter-day Saints favoring abortion is much lower than the general population and evangelicals and Catholics when it involves a family with lower income that can't afford another child, or a family who doesn't want more children, or for any other reason. In short, Latter-day Saint responses to this particular set of questions on abortion are in the same conservative and pro-life direction as both evangelicals and Catholics, but they are also distinctive in a way that is more lenient in some areas and more conservative in others that more closely follow official Church policy.[7]

This politically conservative but different characterization is also true of political issues related to marriage and immigration and would likely appear on other political issues on which Latter-day Saint teachings or policy are distinctive. Thus we expect something similar to occur when it comes to the idea of Christian Zionism and attitudes about the State of Israel. The difference, when it comes to the State of Israel, is that Latter-day Saint teachings and official policy are ambiguous or even supportive of both sides, while for at least some evangelicals, a very clear connection is made between theology and the State of Israel. Christian Zionism, while difficult to define precisely, is a belief that derives from broader theological teachings like premillennialism and dispensationalism—both of which are dominant eschatological views for many evangelical Protestants.[8] Evangelical Protestants have a distinctive understanding of how and when the end of the world will take place, a period often referred to as the "end times."[9] This view of premillennial dispensationalism is often based on literal biblical interpretations that predict a specific series of etiological events, many of which are centered on the Jewish people and the land of Israel.[10] Up to this point, both Latter-day Saints and evangelicals exhibit quite similar beliefs. The difference is that Christian Zionism for evangelicals takes the next step and connects those end-time beliefs to the modern State of Israel and contemporary politics in a way that is rarely the case for Latter-day Saints. Broadly speaking, Christian Zionism describes "supporters of a Jewish state in some portion of the biblical promised land who draw their main inspiration from Christian beliefs, doctrines, or texts."[11] For our purposes, the key component to this definition is that it involves political support for the State of Israel.

Christian Zionists believe that the Jewish people are the true heirs of the land that is now the State of Israel and that the United States has "a special role and mission in God's plans for humanity, that of a modern Cyrus, assigned the task of restoring the Jews to Zion and thus helping to advance the messianic timetable."[12] In other words, many Christian Zionists believe that Jesus Christ's second coming directly relies on the advent of an official State of Israel.[13] Many cite Genesis 12:3 in the Bible as the basis for this view.[14] According to one scholar, "This verse is by far the most prominent reason that evangelicals cite for their backing of the state of Israel. Every evangelical Zionist I spoke with, leaders and laity alike, [. . .] alluded to this promise of blessing for those who bless Israel."[15] Biblical literalism strongly influences Christian Zionist views in the sense that "to this day, biblical prophecies concerning the restoration of Israel to its ancestral land under the leadership of a Messiah descending from the House of David are accepted literally by many evangelical leaders and laypeople."[16]

While pro-Israel attitudes among evangelicals are rooted in a literal interpretation of scripture, they are also sustained with encouragement from religious leaders and groups. Prominent evangelical leaders who espouse Christian Zionist views that consider America to have a role and mission to act as an advocate for the State of Israel and the Jewish people include Billy Graham, Jerry Falwell, Pat Robertson, Richard Land, Paul Weyrich, and John Hagee.[17] The advocacy even extends into evangelical literature through the work of Hal Lindsey, whose popular Left Behind series has sold nearly 80 million copies and includes references consistent with a Christian Zionist viewpoint.[18]

There is not an extensive literature on Zionism and Latter-day Saints in the same way that there is for evangelicals. As a consequence, we have built on the limited references by doing our own search of official Latter-day Saint sources. We find that in contrast with the Christian Zionism of many evangelicals, Latter-day Saints interpret many of the Bible's references to Israel as broadly referring to the "house of Israel"[19] and consider those who make a covenant with God by keeping God's commandments as a member of the house of Israel.[20] As a result, the Church's efforts in the "gathering of Israel" are carried out through its widespread proselytizing efforts and not through Zionist movements for the Jewish people to reestablish a homeland in Israel or other political support for contemporary Israeli government policies.[21] To be clear, there's no clear opposition to the State of Israel either. However, when rare connections to the State of Israel have been made, they are usually in the form of observations that provide an overview of current events related to the establishment of the State of Israel that stop short of favoring or advocating for a particular outcome or policy.

In addition to the biblical passages referencing Israel that are also used by evangelicals, numerous scriptural passages unique to Latter-day Saint scripture make references to Israel in a way that could be connected to the modern State of Israel. For example, the tenth article of faith begins, "We believe in the literal gathering of Israel . . . ," and several references are made in the Book of Mormon to Jews and their "restoration to the lands of their inheritance" or similar language.[22] But Church leadership or discussion in official Church materials rarely, if ever, connects these references to the modern State of Israel or the conflict occurring there. Latter-day Saint references to Israel could be best characterized as "pro-Jewish" rather than "pro-Israel" because they are mostly devoid of content that can be easily linked to a modern political context. In the words of one scholar, although Latter-day Saints "believe in the eventual descent of Jesus to earth, their hope in that respect lacks the intensity and sense of imminence that characterizes the premillennialist conviction."[23]

In our review and search of official Latter-day Saint websites (including official reports of Church conferences and other meetings) and other materials, explicit references to the modern political State of Israel are extremely rare. The rare mentions that are more explicitly political are typically in "uncorrelated" sources in the sense that they occur in the first part of the twentieth century, earlier in Church history, or in a less-than-official source. In the Latter-day Saint lexicon, the "correlation" movement within the Church organization officially began in the 1960s and continues to this day. It is an effort to streamline and standardize Church curriculum that has also been extended to provide some standardization of doctrinal teaching in official Church publications, including reports of Church conferences.[24] With the existence of official correlation efforts of Church leadership, the lack of any political advocacy for Israel and even the rarity of explicit mentions of the State of Israel in official Church communications are apparently deliberate.

AMERICAN PARTIES AND ISRAEL: THE EVOLUTION FROM BIPARTISAN TO PARTISAN ISSUE

Aside from religious beliefs and the influence of religious leaders, an important source of influence on attitudes about Israel is American political leaders and parties. Since its independence, Israel has been the recipient of longstanding and bipartisan support from the American political leaders.[25] In Congress, support for Israel was an "easy and uncontroversial posture to take" for congressional leaders, and both major party platforms have taken pro-Israel positions starting in 1944.[26] This partisan unity on Israel began to crack in the 1990s, when modest partisan differences in attitudes about Israel began to emerge, a shift that continued through the election of George W. Bush. This divide was encouraged by the simultaneous polarization of political parties on other issues.[27] An analysis of congressional policy making between 1997 and 2001 reveals that as the US House engaged more directly on policy related to Israel, the pro-Israel consensus within the US Congress began to show signs of change with Democrats, liberals, and African-Americans becoming more likely to be sympathetic with the Palestinians as victims of oppression.[28]

An increasing number of Republican candidates refer to Israel in their campaign speeches and debates,[29] while Democratic candidates mention Israel less frequently and address the Israeli-Palestinian conflict with nuanced diagnoses and proposed solutions.[30] Amnon Cavari suggests that "the change in partisan attitudes is explained by both the realignment of religious cleavages with a clear policy agenda, and the polarization of American elites which affects attitudes of partisan identifiers beyond their ideological-religious commitments."[31] In other words, partisan change in attitudes on Israel has occurred both because evangelicals have aligned more with the

Republican Party over time and because Republican and Democratic leaders in Washington have become increasingly divided on the issue.

DATA AND METHODOLOGY

To obtain a sufficient number of Latter-day Saint survey respondents for analysis, we appended data from nineteen separate Pew Research Center surveys spanning the 14-year period between June 2003 and January 2017 that asked the following question: "*In the dispute between Israel and the Palestinians, which side do you sympathize with more, Israel or the Palestinians?*" In addition to having enough respondents from smaller religious traditions, we also used the time period between 2003 and 2017 to avoid too much proximity to any changes in public opinion immediately following the events of 9/11 as well as after the inauguration and during the first months of the Trump administration.[32] Given President Trump's ongoing involvement with Israel and its neighbors, including data points from his presidency is premature. After some basic descriptive information on the data, we first examine the relationships between our main dependent variable using simple bivariate statistics, eventually moving to a series of multinomial logit models to account for our dependent variable's multiple category nature.

The surveys in our aggregated data also included questions measuring each respondent's religious affiliation, born-again or evangelical Christian identity, partisan identity, and other demographics.[33] Overall, Pew surveys use a range of religious affiliation questions. For surveys with a primary focus on religion (such as the Religious Landscape surveys), Pew uses a full battery of questions that allow respondents to be identified by specific denominations and then classified by broad religious tradition, an approach commonly used in political science and sociology research that allows a clear distinction between white evangelical and mainline Protestants.[34] Pew political surveys do not include a full affiliation battery of questions, but instead include a single affiliation question followed by a question for Christian respondents about whether they self-identify as a born-again or evangelical Christian.[35] We have no choice but to rely on the born-again question to differentiate between evangelical and mainline Protestants. This follows the recommendation of Ryan Burge and Andrew Lewis,[36] who find no statistical difference between this approach and the more detailed approach that uses specific denominations.[37]

RESULTS

Figure 1 presents a distribution of the aggregated data over the entire series of the Israel/Palestinians question for all respondents and also separately by religious tradition. Support for Israel among all Americans over the entire series falls just short of one of every two respondents, and support for the Palestinians averages just under one in every six. Across all nineteen surveys, support for Israel hovers in the mid-to-high 40 percentage range for most of the series, ranging from a high of 55% in March 2013 to a low of 37% in July 2005. In addition to choosing between Israel and the Palestinians, sizable proportions of respondents volunteered answers of "both," "neither," and "don't know." A detailed table of all of the surveys used, along with samples sizes and distribution on this key question, is included in the table at the end of this chapter.

Figure 1 also provides a breakdown of the Israel/Palestinian question for several religious traditions. Among religious groups, American Jews are, not surprisingly, the most likely to sympathize more with Israel than the Palestinians at 85%. Notably, evangelical Protestants are more sympathetic toward Israel than any other Christian religious group at 68%. This is consistent with a host of previous work.[38] Latter-day Saints follow closely in third with 61% expressing support for Israel—not quite as strong as support among evangelicals, but closer to them than the much lower support for

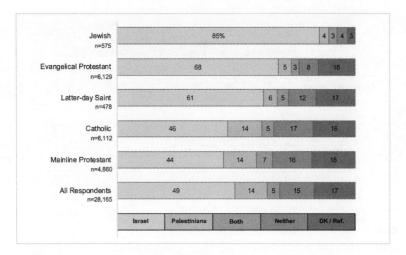

Figure 1. American attitudes toward the dispute between Israel and the Palestinians by religious tradition. Source: Aggregated Pew Research Center Surveys, 2003-2017, n=28,165; may not sum to 100% because of rounding.

Israel expressed by Catholics and mainline Protestants. At first glance, Latter-day Saints and evangelical Protestants appear to be quite similar in their attitudes about Israel.

Figure 2 presents a breakdown of attitudes about Israel by level of church attendance within each religious tradition. For both evangelical Protestants and Latter-day Saints, substantial differences emerge by religiosity. However, church attendance appears to be a somewhat stronger overall predictor of support for Israel among evangelicals. For example, 54% of evangelicals who seldom or never attend church express sympathy for Israel. This support among evangelical non-attenders is higher than the percent of Catholics or mainline Protestants sympathetic to Israel who attend church weekly. Among evangelicals who attend weekly or more, 72% favor Israel, which is roughly comparable to the proportion of nonattending Jews sympathetic to Israel. For Latter-day Saint weekly attenders, sympathy toward Israel is quite strong at 64%, but it is consistently lower than the comparable

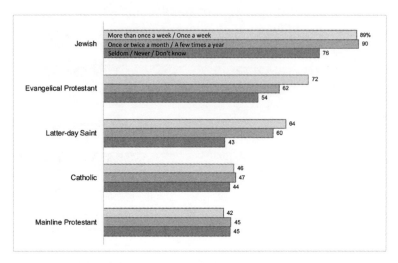

Figure 2. Percentage favoring Israel within major religious traditions by church attendance. Source: Aggregated Pew Research Center Surveys, 2003-2017.

church-attending group among evangelicals, especially among those who attend seldom or never. Interestingly, support for Israel among Latter-day Saints attending seldom or never most closely resembles support for Israel among Catholics and mainline Protestants at any attendance level (where church attendance doesn't appear related to support for Israel).

Figure 3 presents the distribution of attitudes about Israel by partisan identification (with partisan "leaners" coded as partisans) within each religious tradition. The patterns are very similar to those for church attendance. Support for Israel is uniformly high by partisan category for Jewish respondents, with all partisan groups above 80% in support of Israel. Evangelical Republicans are the next most supportive group at 76%, with Latter-day Saint Republicans not far behind at 71%. Catholic Republicans and mainline Protestant Republicans show similar levels of support for Israel at 60 and 58%, respectively. A majority of evangelical Democrats (53%) also support

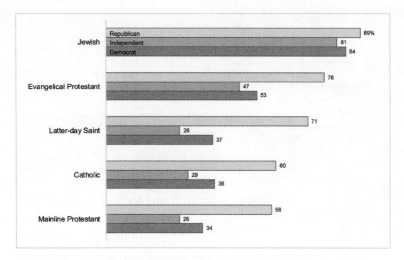

Figure 3. Percentage favoring Israel within major religious traditions by party identification. Source: Aggregated Pew Research Center Surveys, 200--2017; partisan
"leaners" are coded as partisans.

Israel, but support for Israel falls below a majority for Latter-day
Saint Democrats (37%), Catholic Democrats (38%), and mainline
Protestant Democrats (34%). Among pure independents, the support for Israel is the lowest of any partisan category. This is likely not
because these respondents favor the Palestinians, but rather because
larger proportions of pure independents volunteer answers of "neither" or "don't know" (not shown in the figure), perhaps reflecting a
lack of interest or engagement on the issue.

The effects of church attendance and partisan identification on
attitudes about Israel are easier to see and compare between religious
traditions in figure 4, in which the differences between Republicans
versus Democrats as well as weekly church attenders versus nonweekly
attenders from figures 2 and 3 are displayed together. Overall, the
results highlight the partisan differences in support for Israel among
all the religious traditions shown, differences that always exceed the
differences that exist by church attendance. The difference between

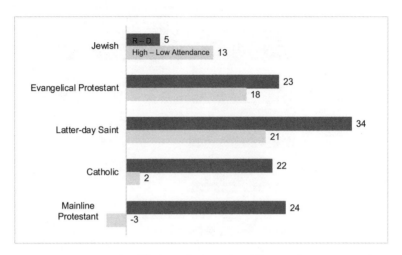

Figure 4. Percentage point differences between Republicans and Democrats and between highest and lowest church attenders by religious tradition. Source: Aggregated Pew Research Center Surveys, 2003-2017. Note: "R - D" is calculated using the Republican minus Democratic percentage point difference from figure 3, and "High - Low" is calculated using the highest church attendance (weekly or more) minus the lowest church attendance (seldom/never) percentage point difference from figure 2.

Republican and Democrat evangelicals in the percentage favoring Israel (23 percentage points), for example, is roughly the same as the difference between Republican and Democrat mainline Protestants (24 percentage points) and Catholics (22 percentage points). More importantly, among evangelicals the difference between Republicans and Democrats in their support for Israel is roughly comparable to the difference between high and low church attenders—both differences are near 20 percentage points with a gap between attendance and partisanship differences of only 5 points.

The data tell a different story for Latter-day Saints. Most importantly, the partisanship gap between Republicans and Democrats is a whopping 34 percentage points, more than 10 points above the 23-point partisan gap among evangelicals. The gap between weekly and nonweekly church attenders among Latter-day Saints (21 percentage points) is comparable to the attendance gap among evangelicals (18 points). Finally, for Latter-day Saints the difference between the partisanship gap (34 points) and attendance gap (21 points) is 13, well above the modest 5-point difference for the evangelical partisan gap (23) and attendance gap (18). The evidence presented so far suggests that both partisan identification and religiosity influence attitudes about the State of Israel for Latter-day Saints and evangelical Protestants but that the influence of each varies considerably by religious tradition.

More sophisticated and complicated multinomial regression analyses (not shown) produce results that essentially reflect the differences discussed above.[39] We estimated a multinomial logistic regression model of support for Israel where support for the Palestinians is the baseline comparison group. In an initial model each religious tradition produces positive and statistically significant effects in the pro-Israel direction, with effect size differences that roughly correspond to the data by religious tradition in figure 1. The strongest impact occurs for the Jewish tradition followed by evangelical Protestants and Latter-day Saints, with other traditions trailing further behind. When an interaction between church attendance and religious tradition is added to the model, it is positive and statistically significant for evangelicals ($p<0.05$) and marginally significant ($p<0.1$) for Latter-day Saints. With this interaction for religiosity in the model, the main effect of religious tradition for evangelicals (or the effect of identifying as an evangelical but not attending church) remains positive and statistically significant, suggesting that something important is being transmitted about Israel within the evangelical tradition, even for those not regularly in the pews on Sunday. For Latter-day Saints, on the other hand, the main effect is effectively zero, suggesting that whatever pro-Israel attitudes are being produced among Latter-day Saints are evident only among the most devout. When variables for partisan identification are added to the model as separate variables for Democrats and Republicans, both are statistically significant predictors of attitudes toward Israel, but in opposite directions, with Republicans more likely to favor Israel and Democrats more likely to favor Palestinians. Most importantly, the religious tradition variables are mostly unchanged with the notable exception of Latter-day Saints, for whom the once marginally significant interaction between affiliation and church attendance completely disappears. On the other hand, for evangelical Protestants, the interaction between religiosity and affiliation remains statistically significant, even when controlling for partisanship. In other words, with party identification in the model, religious affiliation, church attendance, and the interaction between the two are all nonfactors for predicting Latter-day Saint attitudes about Israel, but they remain important and significant predictors of evangelical Protestant attitudes. The results from the statistical model essentially mimic the results presented in figure 4.

CONCLUSION

The results presented here suggest a much clearer connection between religious affiliation and religiosity and support for Israel among evangelicals than exists for Latter-day Saints. The data show a consistently strong relationship between evangelical affiliation and support for Israel as well as a consistently strong relationship among evangelicals between affiliation and religiosity that is roughly the same as the effect of political partisanship. For Latter-day Saints, the relationship between religiosity and attitudes toward Israel is much smaller than the relationship for partisanship, and when examined with more sophisticated statistical models, any statistical relationship between affiliation or religiosity among Latter-day Saints disappears completely when controls for partisanship are introduced.

This returns us to where we began. For many evangelical Protestants, support of Israel is rooted in theological teachings connected to Christian Zionism, or religious beliefs related to biblical ideas of the end time and the return of Jesus that are often explicitly linked to political support for the modern State of Israel. Christian Zionism translates to an interest among some prominent evangelical leaders in the success of the State of Israel on the international stage and in turn to explicit support by those leaders for Israel in US foreign policy and in other ways. This overt connection made among Christian Zionists within the evangelical tradition manifests itself in our analysis most clearly through the significant relationship between affiliation and church attendance for evangelicals on attitudes toward Israel.

On the other hand, Latter-day Saints, while displaying some similar end-time beliefs as evangelicals, do not experience the same kind of clear Christian Zionism from Church leaders or official publications, and there is little, if any, overt theological foundation that we could identify as explicitly supportive of the modern State of Israel. Modern Latter-day Saint leaders do almost nothing to link their beliefs directly to the modern political State of Israel. Instead, references to Israel are theological references to the biblical Jewish people or other more general theological teachings. Thus Latter-day Saints, while sharing some theological ideas about the end time with evangelicals, differ in theology by not experiencing the direct Christian Zionism present in many evangelical denominations.

Thus for Latter-day Saints, it should not be surprising that a much larger share of the difference in attitudes about Israel is explained by partisanship. This suggests that the source of attitudes about Israel among Latter-day Saints is rooted more directly in partisan influence than in anything emanating directly from the Church or its leaders. In short, the pro-Israel attitudes of Latter-day Saints as a group are more strongly tied to their overwhelming Republican partisan affiliation. While many evangelical Protestants hear sermons and see information from their leaders that make clear connections between the modern State of Israel and biblical beliefs, for Latter-day Saints who may identify some of these same connections, they are virtually never made in official Church publications or by Church leaders, especially since the founding of the State of Israel

TABLE. AGGREGATED PEW SURVEYS BY DATE

Question: "In the dispute between Israel and the Palestinians, which side do you sympathize with more, Israel or the Palestinians?" Respondents could also volunteer answers of "both," "neither," and "don't know."

Survey	Dates	Percentage Responding					Sample Sizes		
		Israel	Pales-tinians	Both	Nei-ther	DK/Ref	Total n	LDS n	Jewish n
1	Jan 4–9, 2017	51	19	5	13	12	1502	19	35
2	Apr 12–19, 2016	54	19	3	13	10	2008	47	47
3	Jul 8–14, 2014	51	14	3	15	18	1805	37	42
4	Apr 23–27, 2014	53	11	3	16	17	1501	33	35
5	Mar 4–18, 2013	55	14	3	12	16	1002	18	16
6	Mar 13–17, 2013	49	12	3	12	24	749	17	16
7	Dec 5–9, 2012	50	10	4	13	23	1503	32	25
8	May 25–30, 2011	48	11	4	15	21	1509	24	25
9	Apr 21–26, 2010	49	16	4	12	19	1546	27	34
10	Oct 28–Nov 8, 2009	51	12	4	14	19	2000	32	39
11	Jan 7–11, 2009	49	11	5	15	20	1503	24	23
12	Apr 23–May 6, 2007	49	11	5	17	18	1018	17	25
13	Aug 9–13, 2006	52	11	5	15	17	1506	28	34
14	Jul 6–19, 2006	44	9	5	20	22	996	16	17
15	Oct 12–24, 2005	43	17	5	16	19	2006	28	49
16	Jul 7–17, 2005	37	12	5	19	27	1000	11	12
17	Jul 8–18, 2004	40	13	7	18	22	2009	35	45
18	Feb 24–29, 2004	46	12	8	15	19	1000	8	16
19	Jun 24–Jul 8, 2003	41	13	8	18	20	2002	25	40
Grand Total							28,165	478	575

in 1948. Latter-day Saints might be best called "Passive Zionists" for their strong support for Israel absent any significant overt institutional or leadership advocacy. Perhaps another way to explain the pro-Israel attitudes of Latter-day Saints is through a passive religious influence indirectly from evangelicals via the Republican Party. Given the partisan polarization of attitudes about Israel that has emerged during the last twenty years or so (coinciding with increased affiliation with and influence within the Republican Party by evangelicals), the real possibility exists that Latter-day Saints have been indirectly affected by Christian Zionism through the influence of evangelical Christian Zionists on the increasingly strong pro-Israel positioning of the Republican Party. As Passive Zionists, Latter-day Saints are overwhelmingly pro-Israel because they are overwhelmingly Republican.

NOTES

1. Jeremy M. Sharp, "U.S. Foreign Aid to Israel" (Washington, DC: Congressional Research Service, April 10, 2018), 1, https://fas.org/sgp/crs/mideast/RL33222.pdf; Roby Nathanson and Ron Mandelbaum, "Aid and Trade: Economic Relations between the United States and Israel, 1948–2010," in *Israel and the United States: Six Decades of US-Israel Relations*, ed. Robert O. Freedman (Boulder, CO: Westview Press, 2012), 124–42.

2. BBC World Service Poll, "Negative Views of Russia on the Rise: Global Poll" (British Broadcasting Corporation World News, June 3, 2014), https://globescan.com/wp-content/uploads/2014/06/2014_country_rating_poll_bbc_globescan.pdf.

3. Pew Research Center, "Republicans and Democrats Grow Even Further Apart in Views of Israel, Palestinians" (Washington, DC: Pew Research Center, January 23, 2018), http://people-press.org/wp-content/uploads/sites/4/2018/01/1-23-18-Middle-East-release.pdf; Lydia Saad, "Americans Remain Staunchly in Israel's Corner"

(Washington, DC: Gallup, March 13, 2018), https://news.gallup.com /poll/229199/americans-remain-staunchly-israel-corner.aspx.

4. James L. Guth et al., "Religion and Foreign Policy Attitudes: The Case of Christian Zionism," in *Religion and the Culture Wars: Dispatches from the Front* (Lanham, MD: Rowman & Littlefield, 1996), 330–60.

5. David E. Campbell, John C. Green, and J. Quin Monson, *Seeking the Promised Land: Mormons and American Politics* (Cambridge: Cambridge University Press, 2014), 79.

6. Campbell, Green, and Monson, *Seeking the Promised Land,* 116.

7. Campbell, Green, and Monson, *Seeking the Promised Land,* 116–27.

8. Samuel Goldman, *God's Country: Christian Zionism in America* (Philadelphia: University of Pennsylvania Press, 2018), 5.

9. Samuel Goldman and Jeanne Halgren Kilde, "How Did Left Behind's Particular Vision of the End Times Develop? A Historical Look at Millenarian Thought," in *Rapture, Revelation, and the End Times: Exploring the Left Behind Series*, ed. Jeanne Halgren Kilde and Bruce David Forbes (New York, NY: Palgrave Macmillan, 2004), 33–70.

10. Goldman and Kilde, "Left Behind's Particular Vision of the End Times"; Yaakov Ariel, "The One and the Many: Unity and Diversity in Protestant Attitudes toward the Jews," in *The Protestant-Jewish Conundrum*, vol. 24, Studies in Contemporary Jewry (Oxford: Oxford University Press, 2010), 15–45. In short, the premillennial dispensationalism part of Christian Zionism says that that the end time commences with (and is contingent on) the Jewish people's return to Israel. Once they have returned and reestablished Zion in Israel, Jesus will return to the earth (specifically in Jerusalem) and all believers in Christ will be lifted up in the rapture. After the rapture, a period of tribulation will take place, followed by a millennium, or one thousand years of peace. The Millennium will end in a final uprising of Satan; Jesus Christ and his followers will come out victorious and then eternal life will be established.

11. Goldman, *God's Country*, 4; Stephen Spector, *Evangelicals and Israel: The Story of American Christian Zionism* (New York, NY: Oxford University Press, 2009).

12. Yaakov Ariel, "How Are Jews and Israel Portrayed in the Left Behind Series?," in *Rapture, Revelation, and the End Times*, 137, https://doi.org/10 .1007/978-n1-4039-8021-2_6.2004

13. Eric Gormly, "Evangelical Solidarity with the Jews: A Veiled Agenda? A Qualitative Content Analysis of Pat Robertson's 700 Club Program," *Review of Religious Research* 46, no. 3 (March 2005): 255–68.

14. "I will bless those who bless you, and whoever curses you I will curse; and all peoples on earth will be blessed through you" (Genesis 12:3 New International Version).

15. Spector, *Evangelicals and Israel*, 23.

16. Ariel, "One and the Many," 23.

17. Ariel, "One and the Many," 22; Spector, *Evangelicals and Israel*.

18. Kilde and Forbes, *Rapture, Revelation, and the End Times*; Ariel, "How Are Jews and Israel Portrayed?"

19. In the Bible, for example, see Jeremiah 3:14–18; for similar language in Latter-day Saint scripture, see Jacob 5 in the Book of Mormon and Abraham 2:8–11 in the Pearl of Great Price.

20. Russell M. Nelson, "The Gathering of Scattered Israel," *Ensign*, November 2006.

21. In similar fashion, according to the Bible Dictionary in the Latter-day Saint edition of the King James Version of the Bible, the term *Zion* can refer to a wide range of places and concepts, including Jerusalem; the "New Jerusalem" in Jackson County, Missouri; the various gathering places of the early Church members and pioneers (including Ohio, Missouri, Illinois, and eventually Utah); the American continents; and the metaphorical unity of the "pure in heart."

22. In the Book of Mormon see, for example, 3 Nephi 20:29–33; 29:1–4, 8–9; Mormon 5:12–14.

23. Yaakov Ariel, *On Behalf of Israel: American Fundamentalist Attitudes toward Jews, Judaism, and Zionism, 1865–1945* (Brooklyn, NY: Carlson, 1991), 8.

24. Gregory A. Prince and Wm. Robert Wright, *David O. McKay and the Rise of Modern Mormonism* (Salt Lake City: University of Utah Press, 2005), chap. 7.

25. Amnon Cavari and Guy Freedman, "From Bipartisan Agreement to Electoral Contest: Israel in US Elections," in *The 2016 Presidential Election: The Making of a Political Earthquake* (Lanham, MD: Lexington Books, 2017), 77–96.

26. Marvin C. Feuerwerger, *Congress and Israel: Foreign Aid Decision-Making in the House of Representatives 1969–1976* (Westport, CT: Greenwood Press, 1979), 76.

27. Amnon Cavari, "Religious Beliefs, Elite Polarization, and Public Opinion on Foreign Policy: The Partisan Gap in American Public Opinion toward Israel," *International Journal of Public Opinion Research* 25, no. 1 (2013): 1–22.

28. Elizabeth A. Oldmixon, Beth Rosenson, and Kenneth D. Wald, "Conflict over Israel: The Role of Religion, Race, Party and Ideology in the U.S. House of Representatives, 1997–2002," *Terrorism and Political Violence* 17, no. 3 (2005): 407–26.

29. Cavari and Freedman, "From Bipartisan Agreement to Electoral Contest."

30. Amnon Cavari and Guy Freedman, "Partisan Cues and Opinion Formation on Foreign Policy," *American Politics Research* 47, no 1 (2019): 29–57.

31. Cavari, "Religious Beliefs, Elite Polarization, and Public Opinion," 18.

32. We planned to have a 15-year time-series that began in 2002, but neither of the reports from that year had the necessary religious measurements we were looking for. We excluded the data from May 2006 because there was no measurement for whether Christian respondents identified as born-again. We also excluded the data from September 2011 because there were no measures of religious affiliation.

33. The aggregated data include variables measuring Israel sympathy, religious tradition, whether Christian respondents identified as born-again, church attendance, party identification, and political ideology.

34. Lyman A. Kellstedt et al., "Grasping the Essentials: The Social Embodiment of Religion and Political Behavior," in *Religion and the Culture Wars*, 174–92; Brian Steensland et al., "The Measure of American

Religion: Toward Improving the State of the Art," *Social Forces* 79, no. 1 (2000): 291–318.

35. Pew's religious affiliation question: "What is your present religion, if any? Are you Protestant, Roman Catholic, Mormon, Orthodox such as Greek or Russian Orthodox, Jewish, Muslim, Buddhist, Hindu, atheist, agnostic, something else, or nothing in particular?" Those who fit into the Protestant, Catholic, Mormon, or Orthodox categories or who self-identify as Christian are asked, "Would you describe yourself as a 'born again' or evangelical Christian, or not?"

36. Ryan P. Burge and Andrew R. Lewis, "Measuring Evangelicals: Practical Considerations for Social Scientists," *Politics and Religion* 11 (2018): 749–59.

37. We also used the race question to define a Black Protestant group. This means that even though we don't limit our evangelical and mainline Protestant categories by race, they are overwhelmingly white.

38. For example, Guth et al., "Religion and Foreign Policy Attitudes."

39. For a full presentation and discussion of the regression results, see J. Quin Monson and Kelly N. Duncan, "Passive Zionism vs. Christian Zionism: Latter-Day Saint and Evangelical Protestant Attitudes about Israel" (paper presented at Midwest Political Science Association annual meeting, Chicago, IL, 2019).

What Jews Can Learn from Latter-day Saints: Insights from The Church of Jesus Christ of Latter-day Saints

STEVEN WINDMUELLER AND MARK S. DIAMOND

Passover in July? Not for Jews, but for millions of others who celebrate a holiday replete with narratives of religious persecution, exodus, a perilous journey in the wilderness, and eventual redemption in the promised land. July 24 is Pioneer Day, a major holiday for members of The Church of Jesus Christ of Latter-day Saints, better known colloquially as "Mormons."[1] A state holiday in Utah, Pioneer Day commemorates the first group of Church pioneers led by Brigham Young who arrived in the Salt Lake Valley in 1847.[2]

Both Jews and Latter-day Saints have core narratives of persecution, exodus, and redemption in their respective historical experiences. The harsh servitude of the Israelites in Egypt, their liberation from bondage, and their eventual redemption in the promised land of Israel figure prominently in Jewish tradition. Latter-day Saint pioneers endured severe persecution in New York, Ohio, Illinois, and Missouri before journeying across the country to establish their religious center in Utah. Bronze replicas of the Saints' wagon trains recall their forced exodus from the Midwest and their eventual settlement in the Salt Lake Valley of Utah.

Key features of the Church of Jesus Christ have parallels in Jewish life and thought since Church leaders patterned Latter-day Saint doctrines and rituals in part on the rites of ancient Judaism. Latter-day Saint theology borrows freely from biblical symbolism of Zion and the lost tribes and holds, "We believe in the literal gathering of Israel and in the restoration of the Ten Tribes; that Zion (the New Jerusalem) will be built upon the upon the American continent."[3]

Latter-day Saints view Salt Lake City as the ideological and religious center of their faith. For many members of the Church, Salt Lake City is the new Zion, and America is the new Israel. More than two million Latter-day Saints live in Utah, 60% of the state's population. California's Latter-day Saint population is more than 700,000, while Arizona and Idaho each have Latter-day Saint populations greater than 400,000 living in close proximity to temples and other Church institutions.[4]

Today, The Church of Jesus Christ of Latter-day Saints claims more than 16 million followers across the globe,[5] higher than the estimated Jewish worldwide population of between 13.5 and 14 million. The worldwide Jewish population is growing at a modest pace,[6] with a more robust increase in the United States.[7] In contrast, the Church of Jesus Christ is growing much faster, thanks to high birth rates among Latter-day Saint families and to active proselytizing carried out by missionaries around the world. The Church is experiencing significant growth, especially in the United States (with an estimated population of 6.6 million Latter-day Saints), Mexico, Brazil, Peru, and the Philippines.[8]

Religious communities have a particularly difficult time admitting that they might be able to learn from another faith tradition. Certainly, in the case of the Latter-day Saints, who are seen as an "upstart" faith community celebrating a mere 190 years, what might Judaism as the oldest among Western religions extract from The Church of Jesus Christ of Latter-day Saints? In fact, there may well be a number of instructive organizational and cultural insights based on our own research and experiences with the Church in California, Arizona, and Utah.

DECISION-MAKING

One of the compelling reasons for the Church's success is its stream-lined system of governance. The leadership cohort of the Latter-day Saint community sets core policy, yet the local wards[9] retain the daily operational decisions. This bifurcated system of organizing main-tains both a coherent order for the Church while still providing an individualized mechanism for grass-roots management. Latter-day Saints base their operational structure on the New Testament. The First Presidency and the Quorum of the Twelve Apostles are the highest-ranking bodies; they are responsible for making decisions for the entire Church. Members of the Church regard the apostles as "special witnesses" of Jesus Christ.[10] A leadership cohort of seventy men, referred to as the Seventies, assist the Twelve Apostles. Around the world today, situated in various key locations, are some eight Quorums of the Seventy, fulfilling key administrative responsibilities for the Church.[11]

Latter-day Saint theology is predicated upon the doctrine of continuous or continuing revelation, manifested in a lay hierarchy of prophets, presidents, bishops, and priests. While the Church of Jesus Christ today is far more centralized than Judaism, continuing revelation allows the Church to evolve on matters of faith and ritual in much the same manner that Judaism evolves through the respec-tive halachic processes of Jewish religious movements. To cite one example, the Church prohibited black people from being ordained to the priesthood for more than a century. This ban was overturned in a 1978 declaration by the First Presidency, which announced that Jesus Christ "by revelation has confirmed that the long-promised day has come when every faithful, worthy man in the Church may receive the holy priesthood."[12] This revelation opened the door for men of

African ancestry to serve in priesthood or ecclesiastical responsibilities and furthered the worldwide expansion of the Church of Jesus Christ in subsequent decades.

On the local level, Latter-day Saint bishops retain much of the power in the local community or ward. In turn, a group of wards forms a stake, and the leader of a stake is identified as a president. The term *stake* is taken from the Old Testament's tent imagery and describes the church as being held up by supporting stakes.[13] These functions are rotated among the members, with bishops typically serving for about five years and stake presidents for up to nine or ten years. While the Latter-day Saint community has instituted a more hierarchical system of governance and a decision-making model inspired in part from biblical tradition, the Jewish communal model of federations, synagogue denominations, and national agencies is derived from the federalist system of American democracy with its focus on separation of powers. The Jewish communal system was constructed on a competitive model, and as such one finds institutional competition driving decision-making. In many ways a more collaborative framework of community engagement would serve American Jews well. The Jewish organizational system, unlike the Latter-day Saint model, is driven from the bottom up, as most institutions are established at the communal level, forming linkages and alliances with partner groups across the country. The key principle underlying these loosely aligned sets of organizations is that American Jews understand multiple ways to practice their Judaism.

SELF-RELIANCE AS A RELIGIOUS VALUE

Latter-day Saints give particular attention to the notion of "self-reliance," and in turn, this value is expressed through the Church's focus on generating an array of food and social services designed to serve those in need. The Church of Jesus Christ generally avoids engaging governmental agencies, preferring instead to create their own integrated networks of production, delivery, and distribution of services and products. A specific emphasis on family preparedness with food storage systems and financial management arrangements represents a primary focus of the Latter-day Saint community. It is possible, for example, to obtain many of these products through the more than one hundred Home Storage Centers operated by the Church.[14]

In a similar vein, the focus on Jewish self-reliance was generated in 1654 on the occasion of the arrival of the first Jewish settlers to New Amsterdam.[15] The Dutch West India Company instructed the governor of the colony, Peter Stuyvesant, to permit the arriving community of twenty-three Jews to remain, subject to their "caring for their own." This principle of providing for the needs of the community remained intact until the Great Depression of the 1930s.

While American Jews remain committed to supporting their communal needs, the partnerships between government and the religious sector have dramatically grown over the past eight decades. This has resulted in significant social service, educational, and cultural relationships between Jewish agencies and the public sector.

In more recent years, Jewish communal and religious institutions have adopted different models of practice, into which centralized decision-making and other operational forms of governance have been introduced.

RELIGIOUS STANDARDS/CULTURAL NORMS

The Church has established a very structured set of expectations for its followers, as represented by specific behaviors, family and personal practices, and defined cultural and social norms. Where liberal Judaism and other progressive religious traditions have reduced their set of ritual demands on adherents, Latter-day Saints have maintained their level of religious rules and social expectations similar to traditional Jews and other Orthodox faith communities. One might argue that the value of a religious experience and the importance of a faith community are directly aligned to the personal obligations and investment of time and resources that one gives over to such an enterprise.

GENERAL CONFERENCE AS A TEACHING AND POLICY RESOURCE

Members of The Church of Jesus Christ of Latter-day Saints gather twice a year in Salt Lake City or via satellite for what is known as general conference. Five sessions are held in which Church members receive instruction. These sessions are broadcast worldwide in multiple languages. The Church uses these semiannual opportunities as well to handle Church leadership and policy matters. The impact of convening decision-makers along with Church members offers Latter-day Saints leaders an ongoing opportunity to maintain connections with its membership base, regularly manage the issues of importance to the religious community, and regularly share teachings and policies.[16]

While each of the respective movements within Judaism holds conventions and conferences, these attract interested participants but are not designed on a regular basis to set forth policies. The consistency and centrality of general conference places its importance at the center of the Church's activities. The centrality of Church decision-making and collective action must be seen in sharp contrast to the generally decentralized practices found among many of the denominations within Judaism.

TEMPLES AND COVENANTS

Members of the Church of Jesus Christ revere the Old Testament, the New Testament, the Book of Mormon, the Doctrine and Covenants, and the Pearl of Great Price as sacred scripture, the word of God. Harking back to Israelite worship, Latter-day Saint temples are considered houses of the Lord and figure prominently in Latter-day Saint religious thought and practice. With the destruction of the Jerusalem temple in 70 CE, Jewish religious life transitioned from a sacrificial system to synagogue-based rites of prayer and learning. Latter-day Saints, on the other hand, incorporate temple rites as integral components of their faith and practice.[17]

As of 2019, the Church has dedicated 166 temples around the world. Over the next several years that number will increase to 217.[18] A central feature of each temple is the baptismal font, which rests on twelve oxen representing the twelve tribes of Israel. This imagery is drawn directly from biblical descriptions of Solomon's temple: "[The tank] stood upon twelve oxen: three facing north, three facing west, three facing south and three facing east, with the tank resting on top of them; their haunches were all turned inward" (1 Kings 7:25).[19]

Latter-day Saint doctrine places special emphasis on their members making covenants with God in their temples. Church members speak of themselves as "covenant people" both collectively and individually and view their covenants as modern-day equivalents of biblical covenants. This authoritative covenant theology is the foundation of several notable Latter-day Saint practices, including tithing, volunteerism and mission service, and focus on families.

TITHING AS A COMMUNAL STANDARD

While Jewish tradition references the act of tithing, the Latter-day Saint community operates on this principle. Tithing in Israelite society was mandated to support the landless Levites:

> And to the Levites I hereby give all the tithes in Israel as their share in return for the service that they perform, the services of the Tent of Meeting. . . . But they shall have no territorial share among the Israelites; for it is the tithes set aside by the Israelites

as a gift to the Lord that I give to the Levites as their share. (Numbers 18:21, 23–24)

The overriding biblical obligation of *tzedakah* (charity or righteous conduct) is found in the book of Deuteronomy with its reference to being generous on behalf of those in need:

> If, however, there is a needy person among you, one of your kins-men in any of your settlements in the land that the Lord your God is giving you, do not harden your heart and shut your hand against your needy kinsman. Rather, you must open your hand and lend him sufficient for whatever he needs. (Deuteronomy 15:7–8)[20]

Similar expectations were introduced in the New Testament.[21] In turn, Latter-day Saints have framed this standard of giving as the basis for their ongoing support for the maintenance of the Church: "Our people are expected to pay 10 percent of their income to move forward the work of the Church. . . . Tithing is not so much a mat-ter of dollars as it is a matter of faith. It becomes a privilege and an opportunity, not a burden."[22]

As Jews today debate their current system of congregational dues and charitable giving models, what might be the impact on Jewish life if our institutions were to adopt this biblically inspired framework of taxation? In recent times, Jewish synagogues and organizations are experimenting with different financing schemes as a way to engage new members while retaining existing supporters.

VOLUNTEERISM AND MISSION SERVICE

Latter-day Saint commitment to service represents a powerful motif within their religious culture. This theme is present throughout the Church, as everyone is expected to volunteer on behalf of the community. More directly, full-time mission service today involves some 65,000 young adults, senior adults, and married couples.[23] This commitment creates for the Church a reservoir of volunteers and missionaries who can be found in all corners of the world. In turn, each family must generate the financial resources necessary to sustain their missionaries over their tenure of service.[24]

Imagine if young Jews were willing to set aside their college admission for two years to be servants of the Jewish people, offering their time and talents both within the Jewish world and beyond? "Taglit/Birthright Israel" is an acclaimed project that has brought over 500,000 young Jews on free ten-day trips to Israel since its inception in 1999.[25] Why not turn the success of Birthright Israel into a mission-type experience, in which young Jews move beyond the excitement and value of a Birthright experience and are then challenged to serve the Jewish people and humankind!

Beyond the mission obligation of young Church members, each Latter-day Saint is encouraged to perform some level of service. One can find volunteers in all aspects of Church programming; these encompass serving as teachers and administrators in local congregations, performing in the Tabernacle Choir at Temple Square, maintaining Latter-day Saint facilities and libraries, promoting outreach to other faith traditions, and operating the community's vast social and food services.

A tour of the Church's Welfare Square in Salt Lake City demonstrates the extensive, integrated network of food production and distribution, including canneries, bakeries, food processing plants, transportation services, and bishops' storehouses. For example, in 2014 Church Humanitarian Services delivered wheelchairs to 57,800 people in 48 countries.[26] With its covenantal ethic and high standard of personal volunteerism, the Church is able to provide extensive social welfare and relief services with minimal overhead costs.

APPENDIX 1

FOCUS ON THE FAMILY

The Church's central organizing framework is the family. This can best be understood by the importance given to family time, as represented by the Church's commitment to making Monday evenings a family-focused experience devoted to prayer, study of scripture, family sharing, games, and other fun activities. To some degree, the framework of Shabbat has been adopted and directed to giving particular attention to an evening of shared time together. In recent years, Latter-day Saint leaders have launched a campaign to revitalize family observance and appreciation of Sunday Sabbaths, including more time for families to celebrate the Sabbath at home in addition to the two-hour Sunday meetings attended by Latter-day Saints of all ages.[27] How might the Jewish community refocus some of its attention to heightening the place and role of family in homes, synagogues, and other settings?

LIFELONG LEARNING AS A CORE VALUE

Latter-day Saints turn everyone into a teacher or sermonizer, and by empowering their constituencies they place expectations on the community to be learners as well as teachers. It is not unusual, therefore, to find young children delivering talks or for teens to be teaching their peers and others.[28] This focus on continuous study, which can also be found in Jewish principles of practice, aligns their members to the body of faith.

One of the particularly creative aspects associated with the Latter-day Saint focus on learning is the discipline of study (as early as 6:00 a.m.) in which young people begin their weekday schedule with scriptural and religious instruction in seminary classes each morning before heading to their secular educational classes.[29] These unique educational models ought to be explored by our community as a possible way to strengthen Jewish learning opportunities.

One can identify Brigham Young University (BYU) as the ideological and intellectual center of the Church. Yet beyond its ideological role, BYU also represents the central institution for the academic preparation and training of the Church's future leadership. What might it mean for any number of Jewish academic centers, such as Brandeis University or the various seminaries under the community's auspices, to serve in a similar role in helping to shape the cultural and intellectual thinking of American Judaism?

GENEALOGY AS A CULTURAL RESOURCE

Similarly, Latter-day Saint commitment to generational connections has produced a particular emphasis not only on celebrating and studying one's family origins but also on promoting and celebrating the family unit. The Church holds to the following doctrine:

> We believe that marriage and family ties can continue beyond the grave—that marriages performed by those who have proper authority in His temples will continue to be valid in the world to come. Our marriage ceremonies eliminate the words "till death do us part" and instead say, "for time and all eternity."[30]

The Church's vast genealogical resources remind us of the interest that many Jews have in uncovering their family histories.[31] For the Church, this collection has theological implications; for Jews, this focus is driven in part by the continuity of the Jewish experience and family narratives. How might the Jewish community identify ways to employ genealogy as a valuable educational tool in expanding how we embrace and understand our history and, in particular, unpack the contributions made by earlier generations?

DEBUNKING MYTHS AND FIGHTING PREJUDICE

As members of minority faiths, both Jews and Latter-day Saints are frequently misunderstood by others. Since Latter-day Saint temples are closed to the public after they are dedicated, myths have arisen about the rituals that take place inside. Of late, Church leaders have been more forthright in sharing details about their beliefs and practices to counter negative stereotypes about Latter-day Saints.[32] These efforts have special resonance for the Jewish community with its plethora of organizations, institutions, and campaigns dedicated to countering anti-Semitism.

It is instructive how the Church of Jesus Christ responded to the popular musical *The Book of Mormon*. Latter-day Saint leaders placed ads in *The Book of Mormon* playbills across the country, with messages such as "You've seen the play . . . now read the book" and "The book is always better." It is difficult to imagine a similarly restrained Jewish communal response to a *Book of Tanakh* (Hebrew Bible) that depicted Judaism in such a negative light. Indeed, one can easily picture Jewish leaders organizing noisy public protests, writing strident op-eds in print media, and posting forceful critiques on Facebook and Twitter in a campaign to censure such an anti-Semitic production. Are there lessons to be learned from Church officials who refrain from a "shri gevalt" (loosely, "scream bloody murder") approach to manifestations of such hostility and prejudice?

JEWISH AND LATTER-DAY SAINT "RED BUTTONS"

All religious communities have suffered in one way or another from misunderstandings or religious slander and defamation. All religious communities have suffered persecution at some time in their history at the hands of outsiders. All religious communities have certain "red buttons" that when pressed by outsiders, can end the dialogue. This is not to say that any subject is necessarily taboo. It is only that certain subjects are sensitive and must be handled with care.[33]

This brief survey of parallels between Latter-day Saints and Jewish life and practice would be incomplete without mention of some of the key divergences and contentious issues between the respective faiths and faith communities. Latter-day Saint views of the role of women in Church rituals parallel Orthodox Jewish parameters on gender distinctions but differ markedly from egalitarian norms in Conservative, Reconstructionist, and Reform Jewish institutions and organizations. The Church's positions on marriage equality and LGBT issues, demonstrated in its financial and political support of California Proposition 8 and similar measures, are at odds with the views of most non-Orthodox Jews.

Latter-day Saint proselytizing offends many in the Jewish community and was at the center of the controversy surrounding the opening of the Mt. Scopus campus of Brigham Young University, the Jerusalem Center for Near Eastern Studies. After nearly a decade of protests, Church leaders gave written guarantees that the campus would not be used for missionary work. Thereafter the Israeli cabinet granted BYU a forty-nine-year renewable land lease in 1988. BYU faculty and students have remained faithful to the agreement to refrain from proselytizing activities, while missionaries continue their work in other countries around the world.

Posthumous baptism of Holocaust victims and other Jews is a particularly sensitive issue in interfaith relations between the Latter-day Saint and Jewish communities. Jewish religious and communal leaders reacted strongly to reports of zealous Latter-day Saints performing proxy baptismal rites for Anne Frank, Albert Einstein, Daniel Pearl, and the parents of Nazi hunter Simon Wiesenthal, among others. Despite the Church's commitment to end the practice, the issue of proxy baptisms remains a flashpoint in Latter-day-Saint–Jewish relations.

CONCLUDING REFLECTIONS

Can one imagine a Jewish communal system based on all or some of the organizing principles extracted from the Latter-day Saint experience? Can one imagine a Jewish world marked by tithing, covenants of volunteerism, centralized decision-making, and renewed focus on family life? Since The Church of Jesus Christ of Latter-day Saints is one of the world's fastest-growing religious traditions, it would seem logical for Jews to further study their practices. The Church's effort to regularly revisit its core mission, policies, and operating principles permits them to rethink how best to transmit messages of the Latter-day Saint community. We would do well to live and learn by Ben Zoma's adage in *Pirkei Avot* ("Teachings of the Sages," a tractate of the Mishnah): "Who is wise? One who learns from all persons, as it is written, 'From all my teachers have I gained understanding' (Psalm 119:99)."[34]

NOTES

This essay is an edited and expanded version of an article that was first published in eJewish Philanthropy, July 6, 2015. This essay is included here as an appendix to the volume because of its importance in the history of the project—it served as a first step toward the dialogue's founding.

1. Though this essay was originally published using the terms *Mormons* and *Mormonism*, we have tried to conform to the current style request of The Church of Jesus Christ of Latter-day Saints to refrain from using those terms.
2. "Utah State Holiday—Pioneer Day," Utah State Library, Utah's Online Library, http://onlinelibrary.utah.gov/research/utah_symbols/holiday.html.
3. "The Articles of Faith," The Church of Jesus Christ of Latter-day Saints, https://churchofjesuschrist.org/study/scriptures/pgp/a-of-f/1.10.

While it is true that the rich biblical symbolism is somewhat lost in the Latter-day Saint notion of "Zion," the importance of the biblical theme should not be downplayed. For Latter-day Saints, the physical place of Zion is matched with and not disconnected from their temple theology. While within the modern Church of Jesus Christ Zion is understood as a longing for the qualities or characteristics of a people who are communally invested in the work of God, including social and economic forms of equality and righteous living, it is never disconnected from physical space, either a geographic framing (Missouri) or the physical space of temples.

4. "Mormon Population by State," WorldAtlas, http://worldatlas.com /articles/mormon-population-by-state.html.

5. Worldwide Statistics," http://newsroom.churchofjesuschrist.org/facts -and-statistics.

6. "The Future of World Religions: Population Growth Projections, 2010–2050, Jews," Pew Research Center, https://pewforum.org/2015 /04/02/jews/.

7. "U.S. Jewry 2010: Estimates of the Size and Characteristics of the Population," Maurice & Marilyn Cohen Center for Modern Jewish Studies, Brandeis University, https://brandeis.edu/cmjs/noteworthy /pop.estimates.html.

8. "LDS Church Growth," April 22, 2017, http://ldschurchgrowth.blog spot.com/2017/04/percent-lds-by-country.html.

9. Wards are local congregations that are typically comprised of 300– 350 members who live within a given geographic area.

10. Doctrines and Covenants 107:23: "The twelve traveling councilors are called to be the Twelve Apostles, or special witnesses of the name of Christ in all the world—thus differing from other officers in the church in the duties of their calling."

11. "Organizational Structure of the Church," http://newsroom.church ofjesuschrist.org/topic/organizational-structure-of-the-church.

12. Doctrine and Covenants, "Official Declaration 2."

13. Isaiah 54:2: "Enlarge the size of your tent, extend the size of your dwelling; lengthen the ropes, and drive the stakes firm." See also Isaiah 33:20.

14. "Provident Living: Self-Reliance and Welfare Resources," http://providentliving.churchofjesuschrist.org.

15. See http://jewishvirtuallibrary.org/new-amsterdam-s-jewish-crusader.

16. "General Conference," http://newsroom.churchofjesuschrist.org/article/general-conference.

17. "Mormon Temple Ritual," http://mormonbeliefs.org/mormon_temples/mormon-temple-ritual/. Latter-day Saints do not offer animal sacrifice in their temples, unlike practices in ancient Israel.

18. See http://churchofjesuschrist.org/temples.

19. Unless noted otherwise, translations of biblical verses are from Tanakh—The Holy Scriptures, The New JPS Translation according to the Traditional Hebrew Text (Philadelphia: Jewish Publication Society, 1988).

20. See Leviticus 27:30–33; Numbers 18:21–24; Deuteronomy 14:22–29; and Malachi 3:8.

21. See, for example, Matthew 23:23; Luke 21:1–4; and 2 Corinthians 9:6–10.

22. Gordon B. Hinckley, "Messages of Inspiration from President Hinckley," Deseret News, Church News, December 6, 1997, http://thechurchnews.com/archives/1997-12-06/messages-of-inspiration-from-president-hinckley-106-128909, citing Religion Newswriters Association, Albuquerque, NM, September 14, 1997.

23. "Number of Missionaries Serving from The Church of Jesus Christ of Latter-day Saints," https://mormonmissionprep.com/news/number-of-mormon-missionaries.

24. "Preparing to Serve," https://churchofjesuschrist.org/callings/missionary/faqs.

25. "Our Achievements," Taglit/Birthright Israel, which reports that over 750,000 participants have taken part in Birthright, nearly 100,000 of which are Israelis, http://birthrightisrael.com/about_us_inner/52?scroll=art_3.

26. "Humanitarian Services: Wheelchairs," 2015 visual display in Church-owned Humanitarian Services Center, Salt Lake City.

27. It is noteworthy that members of the Quorum of Twelve and other Church elders have examined traditional Jewish Shabbat practices for potential lessons to be applied to the Latter-day Saint community. While this essay focuses on the question of what Jews can learn from Latter-day Saints, Church leaders believe they have something to learn from Jews regarding Shabbat observance.

28. "Young Men," https://mormonyouth.org/mormon_church/young _men.

29. "Seminary," https://newsroom.churchofjesuschrist.org/topic/seminary.

30. L. Tom Perry, "Why Marriage and Family Matter—Everywhere in the World," Ensign, May 2015, https://churchofjesuschrist.org/study /general-conference/2015/04/why-marriage-and-family-matter -everywhere-in-the-world.

31. The website of the International Association of Jewish Genealogical Societies lists eighty-three member societies in New York, California, Florida, Illinois, Ohio, and numerous other states and foreign countries. https://iajgs.org/membership/member-societies/.

32. See, for example, "Two Apostles Visit Editorial Boards to Address Misconceptions," November 6, 2007, https://newsroom.churchof jesuschrist.org/article/two-apostles-visit-editorial-boards-to-address -misconceptions; and "Meet the Mormons Director," October 20, 2014, an interview with Blair Treu about his 2014 feature-length film "Meet the Mormons," https://churchofjesuschrist.org/inspiration /latter-day-saints-channel/blog/post/meet-the-mormons-director.

33. Reuven Firestone, "Jewish 'Red Buttons,'" in Leonard Swidler, Khalid Duran, and Reuven Firestone, *Trialogue: Jews, Christians, and Muslims in Dialogue* (New London, CT: Twenty-Third Publications, 2007), 89.

34. Pirkei Avot 4:1, in *Siddur Sim Shalom* (New York: The Rabbinical Assembly, 1989).

INTERFAITH DIALOGUES, PRESENTATIONS, AND OTHER PROGRAMS, 2016–2018

FIRST DIALOGUE SERIES, MARCH 2016, PROVO, UTAH

ACADEMIC DIALOGUES

Mark Diamond. "What Jews Can Learn from Mormons."[1] Paper presented at BYU, Wednesday, March 30, 2016. Andrew Reed, respondent.

Shon Hopkin. "Ancient Foundations of a Modern Tradition: Latter-day Saints and the Bible." Paper presented at BYU, Thursday, March 31, 2016. Tamar Frankiel, respondent.

Steven Windmueller. "Reflections on Interreligious Dialogue." Paper presented at BYU, Thursday, March 31, 2016. Brent Top, respondent.

PUBLIC DIALOGUE

Richard Holzapfel, moderator. "Building Bridges of Understanding: Jews and Mormons in Conversation." Panel presentation at BYU, Thursday, March 31, 2016. Mark Diamond and Shon Hopkin, presenters. All members in the dialogue series, Q&A panel participants.

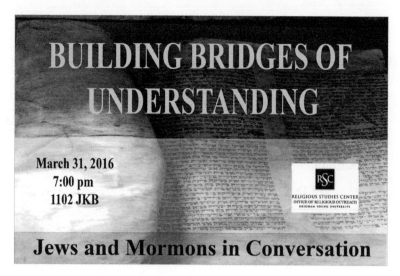

Poster for the First Dialogue Series.

SECOND DIALOGUE SERIES, DECEMBER 2016, LOS ANGELES, CALIFORNIA

ACADEMIC DIALOGUES

Marvin Sweeney and Jacob Rennaker. Covenants in the Jewish and LDS Traditions.[2] Papers presented at AJRCA, Friday, December 9, 2016.

Holli Levitsky and Barbara Morgan Gardner. Images of Mormons and Jews in American Literature. Papers presented at AJRCA, Friday, December 9, 2016.

Tamar Frankiel and Shon Hopkin. Liturgical Development in the Latter-day Saint and Jewish Traditions. Papers presented at AJRCA, Sunday, December 11, 2016.

PUBLIC DIALOGUES AND PRESENTATIONS

Steven Windmueller and Fred Woods. Political Trends in the Mormon and Jewish Communities. Public discussion held at Temple Ramat Zion, Northridge, CA, Friday, December 9, 2016.

End of first day at AJRCA, December 9, 2016. Left to right: Richard Holzapfel, Fred Woods, Ilana Schwartzman, Andrew Reed, Barbara Morgan Gardner, Mark Diamond, Shon Hopkin, Tamar Frankiel, Steven Windmueller, Holli Levitsky, Jacob Rennaker, and Joshua Garroway.

Shon Hopkin and Barbara Morgan Gardner. Questions You've Always Wanted to Ask about the Mormon Church. Presentation and Q&A held at Adat Ari El, Valley Village, CA, Saturday, December 10, 2016.

Richard Holzapfel. Shabbat Torah Sermon on Genesis 28:10–32:3: Torah sermon presented at Leo Baeck Temple, Los Angeles, Saturday, December 10, 2016.

Richard Holzapfel and Ilana Schwartzman. Questions You've Always Wanted to Ask about the Mormon Church. Presentation and Q&A held at Leo Baeck Temple, Los Angeles, Saturday, December 10, 2016.

David Kaufman and Andrew Reed. Images of Jews and Mormons in Hollywood. Papers presented at AJRCA, Sunday, December 11, 2016.

Mark Diamond, Andrew Reed, Shon Hopkin, Larry Eastland (Widtsoe Foundation, USC), Elder Gary Wilde (Church Area Seventy). Sunday Fireside: The LDS–Jewish Academic

Dialogue Project. Presented at Santa Monica Stake Center, Los Angeles, Sunday, December 11, 2016. Mark Diamond, Tamar Frankiel, Steven Windmueller, Shon Hopkin, Andrew Reed, Barbara Morgan Gardner, Jacob Rennaker, roundtable participants.

JOINT CULTURAL AND WORSHIP EXPERIENCES

Shabbat dinner, hosted by Lois and Mark Diamond, Encino, CA, Friday, December 9, 2016.

Shabbat evening service at Temple Ramat Zion, Northridge, CA, Friday, December 9, 2016.

Shabbat morning service and *kiddush* luncheon at Adat Ari El, Valley Village, CA, Saturday, December 10, 2016.

Shabbat morning service at Leo Baeck Temple, Los Angeles, Saturday, December 10, 2016.

Private tour of Skirball Cultural Center, Los Angeles, Saturday, December 10, 2016.

Musical program "Songs of Light" with AJRCA cantorial students held at AJRCA, Los Angeles, Sunday, December 11, 2016.

THIRD DIALOGUE SERIES, MARCH 2017, SALT LAKE CITY, OREM, AND PROVO, UTAH

ACADEMIC DIALOGUES

Mark Diamond and Brent Top. The Sabbath in LDS and Jewish Practice. Papers presented at BYU Salt Lake Center, Friday, March 17, 2017.

Joshua Garroway and Thomas Wayment. Jewish and LDS Views of Paul. Papers presented at BYU Salt Lake Center, Saturday, March 18, 2017.

Closing session at BYU, March 19, 2017. Israel, Zion, and the Holy Land. Left to right: Andrew Reed, Joshua Garroway, Mark Diamond, Brent Top, Holli Levitsky, Tamar Frankiel, Steven Windmueller, Shon Hopkin, Thomas Wayment, Quin Monson, Barbara Morgan Gardner, and Jacob Rennaker.

Steven Windmueller and Quin Monson. Israel, Zion, and the Holy Land—Communal Perspectives. Papers presented at BYU, Sunday, March 19, 2017.

PUBLIC PRESENTATIONS

Holli Levitsky. "Summer Haven: The Catskills, the Holocaust, and the Literary Imagination." Congregation Kol Ami, Salt Lake City, Saturday, March 18, 2017.

Mark Diamond. Sacrament meeting talk, "Shabbat in Jewish Life and Thought." Orem 2nd Ward sacrament meeting, Orem Stake Center, Sunday, March 19, 2017.

Mark Diamond and Tamar Frankiel. "Understanding Judaism." Andrew Reed's classes on world religions, BYU, March 20, 2017.

JOINT LEARNING AND WORSHIP EXPERIENCES

Shabbat services, Congregation Kol Ami, Salt Lake City, Friday and
Saturday, March 17–18, 2017.
Tour of Temple Square and Latter-day Saint Conference Center,
Salt Lake City, Saturday, March 18, 2017.
Latter-day Saint Sunday services (three-hour meeting schedule),
Orem, UT, Sunday, March 19, 2017.
"Mormon" Sunday dinner, hosted by Wendy and Brent Top, Pleas-
ant Grove, UT, Sunday, March 19, 2017.

FOURTH DIALOGUE SERIES, NOVEMBER 3, 2017, WEBCAST DIALOGUE, BRIGHAM YOUNG UNIVERSITY AND LOYOLA MARYMOUNT UNIVERSITY

ACADEMIC DIALOGUES: SESSION 1

Mark Diamond and Andrew Reed. Core Documents of Jewish-
Christian Interfaith Engagement. Topics discussed: Jews,
Latter-day Saints, and evangelizing; covenant; supercessionism.
Both sides of the dialogue team recognized that there is much
room for discussion in this area.

Readings

Nostra Aetate (1965 Roman Catholic statement on the relation of the
church to non-Christian religions).
Dabru Emet (2000 Jewish statement on Christians and Christianity).
"The Willowbank Declaration" (1989 evangelical Christian declaration on the Christian gospel and the Jewish people; this
is more theologically exclusive in nature than the following
reading).

"A Sacred Obligation" (2002 Catholic and Protestant declaration on Christian-Jewish relations).

"God's Love for Mankind" (1978 Church statement on other religions and religious leaders).

"No Religion Is an Island" (1965 lecture by Abraham Heschel at the Union Theological Seminary, published in 1966).

ACADEMIC DIALOGUES: SESSION 2

Janiece Johnson. "Mormon Female Writings." The planned discussion leader on the Jewish side was unable to continue because of other pressing obligations.

Readings

Lucy Mack Smith. *History of Joseph Smith by his Mother*, chap. 18. (This memoir is likely the most-read woman's book among Latter-day Saints.)

Eliza R. Snow. *The Complete Poetry*, poems 97, 152, 156, 263, 413. (Eliza R. Snow was an early Latter-day Saint convert who became a plural wife of Joseph Smith and Brigham Young. She also led the Church's Relief Society for 21 years.)

Virginia Sorensen. *A Little Lower Than the Angels*, chap. 15, fictionalizing a piece of Eliza R. Snow's life. (A recent Brigham Young University graduate in 1942, Sorensen was overwhelmed by the positive attention to her novel about polygamy.)

Stephanie Meyer. *Twilight*, chap. 3. (Meyer, also a BYU graduate, published the first volume of the *Twilight* series in 2005 and has since sold over 100 million copies of the series.)

Stephanie Nielson, "Nie Nie Dialogues" (Mormon Mommy Blog), August 2008, http://nieniedialogues.com/2008/08/; and January 2017, http://nieniedialogues.com/2017/01/. (Nielson is perhaps the most successful Mormon Mommy Blogger. The two selections look at her writing just prior to a tragic accident and then nine years later.)

Laurel Thatcher Ulrich. *Well-Behaved Women Seldom Make History* (2008), introduction, xiii–xxxiv. (Pulitzer Prize–winner Ulrich coined the popular phrase here used as the title for this book. Pages xxvii–xxxi focus on her own experiences that led to that observation.)

ACADEMIC DIALOGUES: SESSION 3

Tamar Frankiel and Barbara Morgan Gardner. Women and Lived Religion in Jewish and Mormon Culture.

Main Jewish readings

Rochelle Furstenberg. "The Flourishing of Higher Jewish Learning for Women." Jerusalem Center for Public Affairs, May 2000 (Letter #429). (http://jcpa.org/jl/jl429.htm).
Susan Handelman. "Feminism and Orthodoxy," http://chabad.org /theJewishWoman/article_cdo/aid/371261/jewish/Feminism -and-Orthodoxy.htm.
Tamar Frankiel. Excerpt from *The Voice of Sarah* (1990). (This piece demonstrates female aspects of the Jewish liturgical calendar.)

Optional Jewish readings

Reflections/advice on a specific women's practice, of the kind that a woman herself might access online (in this case female observance of Rosh Chodesh):
https://reformjudaism.org/practice/ask-rabbi/why-rosh-chodesh -special-women (Reform)
http://hirhurim.blogspot.com/2009/02/women-rosh-chodesh.html (Orthodox)
http://wlcj.org/resources/resources-for-members-and-friend /guidelines-for-rosh-chodesh-groups/ (Conservative)
https://ritualwell.org/rosh-hodesh (Reconstructionist)

Current controversies: Women of the Wall
http://womenofthewall.org.il/mission/
http://womenofthewall.org.il/rosh-hodesh/

Women's ordination (*s'michah*):
http://forward.com/news/national/383736/are-the-orthodox
   -facing-a-schism-over-female-rabbis/
http://jewishweek.timesofisrael.com/sneak-peek-an-analysis-of
   -the-ban-on-women-rabbis/
Orthodox Union's ruling on women's ordination: https://tinyurl
   .com/zcmpg8z

Latter-day Saint readings

These readings all approach similar issues of a woman's place or role in the religious life of The Church of Jesus Christ of Latter-day Saints but do so from varying perspectives—the first from a prominent male Church leader, the second from a well-known female leader, the third from a female voice looking for ways to broaden the impact of women in the Church without overstepping current institutional boundaries of not ordaining women to priesthood office, and the fourth from a well-known Latter-day Saint feminist who advocates greater roles in Church leadership for women, even if it requires changing the current Latter-day Saint practice of not ordaining women to priesthood office:

M. Russell Ballard (apostle). "Women of Dedication, Faith, Determination and Action." BYU Women's Conference, Friday, May 1, 2015, https://womensconference.byu.edu/sites/womens conference.ce.byu.edu/files/elder_m_russell_ballard_0.pdf.
Sheri Dew. *Women and the Priesthood: What One Mormon Woman Believes*, introductory chapter. Salt Lake City: Deseret Book, 2013.
Neylan McBaine. *Women at Church: Magnifying LDS Women's Local Impact*, introductory chapter. Salt Lake City: Greg Kofford Books, 2014.
Joanna Brooks. *Mormon Feminism: Essential Writings*, introductory chapter. New York: Oxford University Press, 2016.

Jewish-Latter-day Saint dialogue group posing outside of Sacred Heart Chapel on Loyola Marymount University Campus, March 15, 2018. Left to right: Jared Ludlow, Steven Windmueller, Andrew Reed, Barbara Morgan Gardner, Joshua Garroway, Brent Top, Mark Diamond, Wendy Top, Quin Monson, and Shon Hopkin.

FIFTH DIALOGUE SERIES, MARCH 2018, LOYOLA MARY-MOUNT UNIVERSITY, LOS ANGELES, CALIFORNIA

ACADEMIC DIALOGUES

Jared Ludlow, Andrew Reed, and Shon Hopkin. "LDS Views of Supersessionism." Papers presented at LMU, Thursday, March 15, 2018. Joshua Garroway, respondent.

Steven Windmueller and Quin Monson. LDS and Jewish Perspectives on Israel. Loyola Marymount University, Friday, March 16, 2018.

Fifth dialogue series, LDS Views of Supersessionism. Pictured from top left proceeding clockwise: Barbara Morgan Gardner, Joshua Garroway, Jared Ludlow, Andrew Reed, Robert Hurteau, Steven Windmueller, Holli Levitsky, Quin Monson. Loyola Marymount University, March 15, 2018. Photo courtesy of Mark Diamond.

Tamar Frankiel and Barbara Morgan Gardner. Living a Dichotomy: Secular and Religious Experiences of Jewish and Mormon Women. Loyola Marymount University, Friday, March 16, 2018. Kristine Garroway, respondent.

JOINT CULTURAL AND RELIGIOUS EXPERIENCE

Tour of Loyola Marymount campus, focusing on interfaith highlights of the university, Thursday, March 15, 2018.
Shabbat dinner, hosted by Michelle and Steven Windmueller, Sherman Oaks, CA, Friday, March 16, 2018.

NOTE

1. Although the title "Mormon" and the abbreviation "LDS" do not fit the current style guide provided by The Church of Jesus Christ of Latter-day Saints, those words are maintained in this appendix when found in the titles of papers and presentations that were given before the change. See "Style Guide—The Name of the Church," https://newsroom.churchofjesuschrist.org/style-guide.

CONTRIBUTORS

MARK S. DIAMOND is a Senior Lecturer in Jewish Studies at Loyola Marymount University and Professor of Practical Rabbinics at the Academy for Jewish Religion California.

KELLY N. DUNCAN graduated in 2019 with a BA in political science from Brigham Young University.

TAMAR FRANKIEL is a retired Professor of Comparative Religion and former President and Provost at the Academy for Jewish Religion California.

JOSHUA D. GARROWAY is the Sol and Arlene Bronstein Professor of Judaeo-Christian Studies and Professor of Early Christianity and Second Commonwealth at Hebrew Union College—Jewish Institute of Religion, Los Angeles.

CONTRIBUTORS

KRISTINE GARROWAY is the Visiting Assistant Professor of Hebrew Bible at Hebrew Union College—Jewish Institute of Religion, Los Angeles.

SHON D. HOPKIN is an Associate Professor of Ancient Scripture at Brigham Young University.

HOLLI LEVITSKY is a Professor of English and Director of Jewish Studies at Loyola Marymount University.

JARED W. LUDLOW is a Professor of Ancient Scripture at Brigham Young University.

J. QUIN MONSON is an Associate Professor of Political Science at Brigham Young University.

ANDREW C. REED is an Assistant Professor of Church History and Doctrine at Brigham Young University.

THALIA RODIS is a CCAR Press Rabbinic Intern.

BRENT L. TOP is the Richard L. Evans Chair of Religious Understanding and Professor of Church History and Doctrine at Brigham Young University.

THOMAS A. WAYMENT is a Professor of Classics at Brigham Young University.

STEVEN WINDMUELLER is the Rabbi Alfred Gottschalk Emeritus Professor of Jewish Communal Service and former Dean of Hebrew Union College—Jewish Institute of Religion, Los Angeles.

DISCUSSION GUIDE

A companion discussion guide to *Understanding Covenants and Communities* is available to support rabbis and Jewish educators in teaching their communities about Latter-day Saints. This guide promotes interfaith dialogue and highlights shared values and histories as well as the diverse beliefs and practices of the Jewish and Latter-day Saint communities. Interested readers are encouraged to download the discussion guide to this book at covenants.ccarpress.org.

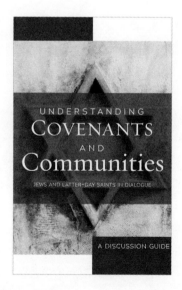

INDEX